Enactments

EDITED BY

RICHARD SCHECHNER

To perform is to imagine, represent, live and enact present circumstances, past events and future possibilities. Performance takes place across a very broad range of venues from city streets to the countryside, in theatres and in offices, on battlefields and in hospital operating rooms. The genres of performance are many, from the arts to the myriad performances of everyday life, from courtrooms to legislative chambers, from theatres to wars to circuses.

ENACTMENTS encompasses performance in as many of its aspects and realities as there are authors able to write about them.

ENACTMENTS includes active scholarship, readable thought and engaged analysis across the broad spectrum of performance studies.

THE UNKNOWN THEATRE OF JERZY GROTOWSKI

Performances in the Theatre
of 13 Rows, 1959–1964

Dariusz Kosiński
with Wanda Świątkowska

TRANSLATED BY MAREK KAZMIERSKI

LONDON NEW YORK CALCUTTA

Seagull Books, 2025

Introduction, Chapters 1–8 and Conclusion © Dariusz Kosiński
Chapter 9 © Wanda Świątkowska
English translation © Marek Kazmierski

First published by Seagull Books, 2025

ISBN 978 0 85742 995 7

British Library Cataloguing-in-Publication Data
A catalogue record for this book is available from the British Library

Typeset by Seagull Books, Calcutta, India
Printed and bound in the USA by Integrated Books International

In memory of Zbigniew Osiński

CONTENTS

Introduction   **1**

CHAPTER ONE
Innocent Wizards
Orpheus after Jean Cocteau   **9**

CHAPTER TWO
Alpha, Omega and That Which Is In-Between
Cain after George Gordon Byron   **39**

CHAPTER THREE
Farce-Mystery, or There Can Be No Other Socialism
Mystery-Bouffe after Vladimir Mayakovsky   **81**

CHAPTER FOUR
Indian Erotica
Shakuntala after Kālidāsa   **114**

CHAPTER FIVE
A Mystery 'in-yar-face'
Forefathers' Eve after Adam Mickiewicz   **161**

CHAPTER SIX
Polishness as Madness
Kordian after Juliusz Słowacki   **213**

CHAPTER SEVEN

Our Acropolis

Acropolis after Stanisław Wyspiański   **286**

CHAPTER EIGHT

'To heaven? You blaspheme in vain'

The Tragical History of Doctor Faustus
after Christopher Marlowe   **345**

CHAPTER NINE

Jerzy Grotowski's Hamlets

Hamlet Study Based on Texts
by William Shakespeare and Stanisław Wyspiański   **391**

Conclusion   **441**

Works Cited   **450**

Index   **462**

Introduction

The present volume—as indicated by its subtitle—is an attempt to reconstruct and reinterpret the performances directed by Jerzy Grotowski at the Theatre of 13 Rows in Opole—renamed in 1962 as the Laboratory Theatre of 13 Rows, and later known worldwide as the Polish Laboratory Theatre. In the chapters that follow, I describe and discuss select performances from the Theatre of 13 Rows in Opole—from *Orpheus*, a work based on a play by Jean Cocteau (1961[1926]), to *The Tragical History of Doctor Faustus*, based on Christopher Marlowe's tragedy (1962[1604]). The last chapter is written by my colleague, Wanda Świątkowska, and devoted to *Hamlet Study*, a 13 Rows production based on texts by William Shakespeare and Stanisław Wyspiański.

Zbigniew Osiński (1986) and other researchers, mainly from Poland, have covered productions from this period. Agnieszka Wójtowicz stands out in particular, having written an entire book devoted to the performances created by Grotowski in Opole from *Orpheus* to *Hamlet Study* (Wójtowicz 2004). In her monograph, Wójtowicz presented a lot of new information she gathered during archival research and interviews with former members and collaborators of the company—actors, stage designers, administrative staff and cultural activists. In at least several cases she substantially increases our store of knowledge about these performances and brings them out of obscurity and back into the limelight (as in the case of *Hamlet Study*). What Wójtowicz's study lacks is a contextualized and deeper analysis and interpretation of the materials she gathered. One also finds important sources missing from her research. In this volume we aim to provide a comprehensive study of Opole performances both in terms of description and critical interpretation. We

2 · DARIUSZ KOSIŃSKI

want to show how rich and important these early performances were, and still are. Far from treating them as merely 'early stages' of Grotowski's theatre, our ambition is to advance serious consideration of these performances by an international body of English readers and researchers.

This goal seems especially important because outside of Poland, Opole performances remain mostly unknown, while the key works on Grotowski's theatre—such as his own famous book *Towards a Poor Theatre* (1968a), *The Grotowski Sourcebook* edited by Richard Schechner and Lisa Wolford Wylam (1997), and *The Theatre of Grotowski* by Jennifer Kumiega (1985)—either totally miss these Opole works, or survey them with little more than general references.[1] Thus the primary objective of our book is to raise awareness about these performances, and to allow them to be rediscovered anew by audiences who are interested in Grotowski's theatre—including those who do not have access to relatively obscure and hard-to-find sources, and those who do not know the most basic facts about his theatre from his years in Opole.

There are some obvious reasons why international reception and research usually focus on the three final theatre productions by Grotowski: *The Constant Prince* (1965), the fifth version of *Acropolis* (1965), and *Apocalypsis cum figuris* (1968–69). These performances were shown around the world and are the only ones available in complete film versions—albeit hard to come by and often in imperfect condition. The majority of materials covering his previous works are not available to researchers and readers who do not know Polish. They remain hidden, unknown, and forgotten partly also due to decisions made by Grotowski himself.[2]

---

1 A key exception in this context is *Acropolis* after Wyspiański. And yet—as I am trying to prove—international research on this performance covers solely the later version from 1965, known from international tours and the film. The first, quite different versions from 1962 are also generally unknown. See more on this subject in the chapter on *Acropolis*.

2 After reaching the peak of his theatre career in the late 1960s and then stopping work on theatre performances, Grotowski decided to hide the traces of his experimental Opole years. Probably in the late 1970s, he ordered to be thrown away most of the archive brought to Wrocław from Opole. That is why many documents are lost. Also in his narration and in the narration of the most faithful, orthodox historian of his theatre—Zbigniew Osiński—the early performances were hidden, poorly described, and interpreted only as stages of the road leading

INTRODUCTION · 3

Even in Poland, Grotowski's early works were in one way or another undervalued and neglected. This is especially true of performances created before *Forefathers' Eve* (*Dziady*) (1961). When they did receive attention, earlier performances were described from a historical perspective that elevated Grotowski's later output as far more important. Members of the Laboratory Theatre company supported this tendency by helping conceal these 'unripened fruits', sidelining them as imperfect attempts or early sketches to be developed in the more mature works which, as would be expected, have received far more attention. But because these matured works are now so well known, we can change our perspective and take a closer look at the 'juvenilia' not as first steps 'towards a poor theatre' (or anywhere else), but as independent, standalone performances and theatre events.

Thus one of the key aims of this book is to rescue the early performances by Grotowski and his Theatre of 13 Rows from an 'evolutionary' narrative, giving them consideration as autonomous works of art. In them we see Grotowski as a director and dramaturg who is experimenting on a spectrum that is much broader than the range with which he is most often associated. The restoration of these early performances constitutes an intervention into the dominant discourse on Grotowski as the creator of the poor theatre, a 'guru' of ritualistic performances, a 'sorcerer and hermit'. This journey to 1960s Opole reveals a young director only just starting out but already filled with confidence, someone who is convinced that he knows what he wants though not yet all that certain how to achieve it. This younger Grotowski was totally eclipsed by his later 'personae'. Grotowski makes up for a lot of shortcomings through the gait and confidence with which he imbued his statements. He is a fierce polemicist and as an artist he is filled with passion for his manifestos. He may be more convincing in his spoken and public proclamations than in his productions. From the very outset, he managed

---

to the most important discoveries and works. The reasons for this are multiple and different, requiring still more research and discussion. My opinion is that Grotowski wanted his public to follow him in what he considered the most important line of his art and research. So from the perspective of later achievements, he himself treated his early attempts as unimportant.

his own image and ably courted attention for his work in ways that were very advanced for 1960s Poland—using provocative disputes and attacks. He was at times uncouth and mean, though also perfidious and funny. He is closer to the pre-war theatre avant-garde, especially to Stanisław Ignacy Witkiewicz and Witold Gombrowicz, or where stage practice is concerned, to Vsevolod Meyerhold as opposed to Konstantin Stanislavsky or Antonin Artaud (not to mention Gurdjieff). Grotowski had not yet donned his trademark sunglasses and black suit, nor his hippie shirts or poncho. It is still easy to recognize him as a product of his generation, the 'Beautiful Twentysomethings'.[3] Having experienced the horrors of war early on in their lives, they engaged in the creation of the 'new world' of Communism with youthful enthusiasm only to experience dissatisfaction with the Communist power in place, and turn entirely against its creators. Grotowski returned to the theatre in 1957 after a few months of intense involvement in politics via an anti-Stalinist revolutionary youth movement. At that time, he declared that his theatre would be engaged in contemporary issues. And so his theatre came to express this engagement, at times openly as in the case of *Mystery-Bouffe* (1960), though it more often appeared in veiled and indirect ways. In the case of the performances covered in this volume, the connections between Grotowski's theatre and his contemporaneous reality are particularly vivid. A principal aim of this book is to put Grotowski's early works into their original social and political context—usually unknown to international audiences.

Another important aspect of research presented in this volume is the possibility of filling in certain gaps in common knowledge about Grotowski's early performances. Unlike our discursive predecessors we had enough time to gather and carefully assess all of the substantial and diverse source materials including scripts, reactions, and comments left

---

3 The *Piękni dwudziestoletni* (Beautiful twentysomethings; 1966) is the title of a popular autobiography by Marek Hłasko that was later adopted as a name for an entire generation of people born around 1930. Children during the Second World War, this generation grew up during Stalinism and at the time of its fall (around 1954–56). They became the leaders of political, cultural and social transformations. Later, many of them—like Hłasko himself—turned into disappointed rebels and bitter outsiders.

behind by artists, reviews and overlooked reports. This information allows us to present Opole performances in greater detail. As a result of the passage of time and gaps in documentary archives the record is not complete. However, we do feel a proud conviction that we have managed to make a large number of discoveries—some perhaps small yet important in relation to the matter at hand. These discoveries keep forcing us to correct previously agreed-upon facts and interpretations, especially those notions circulating around the globe that are based on unverified sources and that lack important context. We want to clarify and correct the record regarding Grotowski's early work by contextualizing it in terms of historical facts and his cultural background.

At the same time we want to present and inspire new ways of interpreting the theatre of Grotowski, to reveal important themes in his work that have not yet been analysed, for example, the power of sexual desire and the possibilities of political activity. Dominant and accepted interpretations of Grotowski's work—initiated by him as well as his collaborators—resulted in obvious themes becoming invisible. Several strong narratives dominate research on Grotowski, and beyond these reports many interested readers lack access to basic materials such as a complete edition of Grotowski's texts published only in Polish and Italian thus far. This reality has led research into his work to diminish while the man himself becomes even more of a mystery. Our intention is to change this state of affairs.

We are aware that many themes, phenomena and contexts covered in this book are unknown to readers who are not Polish. We have attempted to offer up information and pointers in the body of the narrative as well as in footnotes. However, we have kept these to an absolute minimum. With the exception of certain basics, we do not feel obliged to pass on a complete set of data covering all the elements of Polish culture and history to which we will refer. After all, thanks to technological development, most of this additional data can now be sourced online.[4]

---

4 Anyone interested can quickly find all the necessary additional information in the English-language online database grotowski.net/en, especially in its 'Encyclopaedia' section, founded

Considering all the differences that emerge out of the diversity of early Grotowski performances, the chapters of this book maintain a relatively steady structure. In each chapter we present and analyse an Opole performance. First, we discuss the genesis and context of the production under consideration, and then we look into the textual archive in order to show the dramaturgical work undertaken by Grotowski. The bulk of each chapter is devoted to reconstructing each performance starting with a description of the space, scenography and costumes, and continuing with descriptions and interpretations of individual scenes. Having made such reconstructions, we try to interpret the performance as a whole by referencing texts written by Grotowski and Ludwik Flaszen[5]—along with some other important interjections sometimes not directly connected with theatre. This is especially true of the ideas of Giorgio Agamben and Alain Badiou—which I use to interpret the general idea of Grotowski's theatre. The conclusions I draw from the research and use to fill gaps in the historical narrative present a specific model of Grotowski's theatre. I detail and summarize the elements of this model in the book's Conclusion.

We should stress that this volume—which has been created for English-language readers—is the result of combining three books previously published in Polish into one English volume with lots of cuts, edits, rewrites, etc. Dariusz Kosiński wrote two of these books (2015, 2018), Wanda Świątkowska wrote the third (2016). Kosiński previously published in Polish the chapter on *The Tragical History of Doctor Faustus* as an article (2016). All these publications were the results of the research project: 'Jerzy Grotowski: Performances 1957–1964', financed by the

---

and managed by the Grotowski Institute in Wrocław. Broader contexts can be explored on numerous English-language websites devoted to Polish culture and history, especially on culture.pl/en.

5 Ludwik Flaszen (1930–2020) was an important Polish literary and theatre critic who in 1959 joined Grotowski as the literary advisor of his theatre company. He was one of the most important of Grotowski's collaborators, especially during the phase of theatre productions (till 1970). He wrote a series of crucial commentaries to all the performances by the Theatre of 13 Rows and the Laboratory Theatre. In the 1970s he was developing his own workshops on word and literature in theatre. His commentaries on the performances and important essays on Grotowski were published in English in Flaszen 2010. For more information, visit https://rebrand.ly/nzrqf8o.

Polish Ministry of Education and Higher Learning (grant number N N105 417340). Of course, creating one volume out of the three forced us to make some substantial abbreviations. We decided to cut many detailed analyses both of the performances and of different Polish contexts. But we did all we could to preserve the general line of argument and the most important parts of the analyses and interpretations from the Polish books.

The translation of the book from Polish was financed by the Faculty of Polish Studies of the Jagiellonian University in Krakow, our home institution. We are very grateful for this generous support. We also wish to thank Richard Schechner without whose enthusiasm for the English version of our books this volume would have never come to fruition; we were also honoured by the efforts Schechner took to do the final edition of the text.

A special word of gratitude needs to be addressed towards Aaron Ellis who did tremendous work as the copyeditor of the basic translation from Polish. Thanks to his engaged and attentive reading the book was saved from many mistakes and possible misunderstandings.

The book includes a lot of citations from Polish texts previously not translated into English. We did everything to make these translations as clear and precise as we can. But especially with regards to the texts by Grotowski we need to underline that these are not final English translations authorized by the heirs of the artist. As a former member of an international team of editors who prepared the Polish volume of Jerzy Grotowski's *Collected Texts*, I am fully aware how much labour it takes to discuss and work out official translations of Grotowski's texts and statements. I do hope that soon the critical and authorized English edition of all of them will be published. Until that happens, the fragments translated for this volume are just working propositions. Of course where it is possible to use existing, published English translations—as in the case of texts from *Towards a Poor Theatre*—we use them.

The international and Polish communities responsible for analysing and researching Grotowski's theatre came to a crossroads and diverged some decades ago. This was due to a number of factors—including international researchers' lack of fluency in Polish and a relative lack of effort among Polish researchers to share their work with the international community. There are plenty more reasons for this split—for example, the methods that Grotowski used to manage his own image, the ways his story was told and his work commented on. This is not the time or place to address these issues. We conclude this introduction by expressing the hope that our book will contribute to the healing of this rift. This may be too bold an ambition, but we would be happy if this publication led to new forms of research into the fascinating art and thought of Jerzy Grotowski that no longer divide Poland from the rest of the world.

CHAPTER ONE

Innocent Wizards
Orpheus after Jean Cocteau

Prologue: Orpheus in the Hell of Comrade Pharaoh

Orpheus, a performance based on Jean Cocteau's *Orfée*,[1] opened the Theatre of 13 Rows led by Jerzy Grotowski and Ludwik Flaszen. In June 1959, they met with invited actors, and in August, Grotowski worked on the script. Rehearsals started on 15 September, and the premiere took place some three weeks later on 8 October 1959.

It is of course possible to assume that Grotowski decided to stage the relatively simple drama by Cocteau—which seems like a traditional, well-made play compared to the texts Grotowski later staged—because he was short on time. And yet, it is worth asking whether Grotowski might have chosen *Orphée* for more important reasons than simply being in a rush. Maybe in the modernization and restaging of the myth by Cocteau there was something with which Grotowski wanted to contend? The existence of a previously unknown text written by Grotowski a few years before he moved to Opole titled *Orfeusz* suggests an affirmative answer to this question. It is a short theatre piece created in the context of Grotowski's collaboration with the Experimental Student Theatre in Krakow, in the second half of 1956.[2] It represents an important

---

1 Carl Widman's English translation of Cocteau's drama calls the hero and the work 'Orphée', following the French. To avoid any misunderstandings, I am using the English 'Orpheus' as the title of the performance and the name of its hero. I use 'Orphée' only when referring to Cocteau's drama.

2 The Experimental Student Theatre was established in Cracow in July 1956. Grotowski worked with it from then until December 1956, when the company was disbanded because it did not premiere any production. See Zbigniew Osiński (1998: 62–64).

trace of the interest Grotowski had in the story of Orpheus, and simultaneously presents a treatment of the eponymous character who probably could not have been included in the Opole version due to censorship concerns.

In his Kraków play, Grotowski transforms the myth of Orpheus—who after the death of his beloved Eurydice, journeyed down to Hades to bring her back to the present day, making it into a political story. Though the main characters retain their original names, the action takes place in a Polish town mirroring the political climate in the 1950s—a time when the Stalinist system of permanent vigilance and control was in full force. The text represents a vivid and singularly critical portrait of a society that is equally oppressed by a totalitarian system and its own indifference.

Grotowski's Krakow *Orfeusz* is set in a state ruled ruthlessly by 'comrade Pharaoh'. The slim plot of the drama begins when two Robot emissaries of the ruler—named simply Robot 1 and 2 in the script—arrest the pregnant wife of the poet Orpheus right before his eyes. Fearing for himself, the poet does not come to Eurydice's aid. Then without success he desperately seeks the help of others in finding his lost love. When Orpheus asks for help the Polish romantic hero Kordian runs away, Shakespeare's Romeo and Juliet are only interested in each other, and Hansel and Gretel—taught by a Witch to repeat propagandistic phrases—repeatedly chant along with Orpheus the phrase, 'Give me back my Eurydice!' Finally, Orpheus himself descends into 'hell'—a labyrinth of bureaucratic nightmares established by the totalitarian regime. He meets several officials on his journey.[3] Finally, Orpheus meets 'comrade Pharaoh' himself only to learn that this is not a man but an electronic Apparatus to which the two Robots are connected. The Apparatus buzzes menacingly and transmits a scene in which Eurydice is being interrogated by the secret police. They demand she make false confessions implicating Orpheus. Eurydice refuses and throws herself out of an open window.

---

3 Grotowski's stage directions indicate that this is always the same person 'wearing different emblems'.

Despairing, Orpheus becomes indifferent and accompanies two wandering Singers who have decided that Eurydice's death is a good subject for a ballad. The last scene in the manuscript shows the romantic hero Kordian to be the only one shocked by Eurydice's death. The short play ends with an image of Kordian's hands 'dancing' on the bars which, according to the final note in Grotowski's script, was meant to separate the stage from the audience throughout the performance.

The play as written by Grotowski was never staged—mainly due to internal organizational problems within the company. But even if it had been rehearsed, we surmise that state censors would not have allowed it to be performed in public. It was a literally anti-Communist text with a strong political image of Eurydice and Orpheus as victims of an inhuman system ruled by the Apparatus, which was the name commonly used to refer to the Communist Party bureaucracy. The Opole version of the story of Eurydice and Orpheus—though still based on Cocteau's drama—had a different character and a different set of themes. And concealed beneath a modernist and French veneer, the political *Orfeusz* from Krakow was also somehow present in it.

An Infected Room

Cocteau left detailed instructions for the arrangement of the set for his *Orphée*:

> A room in Orphée's villa. It is a strange room, rather like a room of a conjurer. In spite of the April-blue sky and the clear light, one suspects that it is surrounded by mysterious forces. Even familiar objects have a suspicious air.
>
> First of all, in a box in the form of a niche, well in the center, there lives a white horse, whose legs are very much like those of a man. On the right of the horse is another little niche in which an empty pedestal stands framed by a laurel. On the extreme right a door which opens to the garden; when the door is open the leaf hides the pedestal. On the left of the horse an earthenware wash basin. On the extreme left a French window,

pushed half-outwards—it looks on a terrace which surrounds the villa.

In the foreground in the right wall is a very large mirror; in a background a bookcase. In the middle of the left wall a door opening into Eurydice's room. A sloping ceiling closes in the room like a box.

The room is furnished with two tables and three white chairs. On the right a writing table and one of the chairs.

On the left of the stage, the second table which is covered with a cloth reaching the floor, and thereon fruits, plates, a decanter, and glasses like the cardboard items objects of jugglers. One chair stands squarely behind the table, and one nearby to the left.

[...]

Apart from the sky-blue skies and the pad of dark red velvet curtain that borders the top of the little door of the box dissimulating the middle of the horse's body—there is no color.

The scenery should recall the same airplanes and ships of certain photographers.

After all, there is that same harmony, made of harsh simplicity, between the setting, characters, and events as between model and painted canvas in the plain *camaieu* style of card portraits. (Cocteau 1961[1926]: 4)

This set of instructions is detailed as descriptions in naturalistic dramas. However, Cocteau explained its precision in a completely different way, insisting that it is not possible to change the number of chairs and placement of doors because 'this is a practical set, in which the smallest detail plays its part like the apparatus in an acrobatic number' (Cocteau 1961[1926]: 4).

Grotowski and set designer Jerzy Jeleński could not realize all these instructions on the small stage of the Theatre of 13 Rows. However, they did manage to preserve something of the greatest importance—its uneven character, built upon the tension between 'real life resemblance' and evidently cheap items procured at village fairs. They achieved this tension by referencing different experiences and conditions more suited to the play's Polish creators and audiences. As a result, Grotowski and Jeleński managed to translate Cocteau's rules into their own theatrical space—somehow mocking, and simultaneously changing his design in numerous ways.

First and foremost, the stage was set up in a way that left a very narrow, limited space for dramatic action. The way they constructed the scenography within the dimensions and shape of the small performance space pushed the actors almost onto the audience. In other ways, they followed Cocteau's instructions very closely—especially his specification that the set should look like a cheap and tasteless photography studio decoration. Grotowski and Jeleński took things much further in this direction. They built the walls of Orpheus' room out of freestanding screens painted in vertical stripes of white and grey—if my reading of two somewhat faded colour photographs from the Grotowski Institute Archive (henceforth GIA) is correct. This circus-like, bazaar-inspired set design was enhanced by surprising elements such as a Greek column. Peering over the top of the column—as if growing out of it—a Horse surveys the performance. The Horse is animated after the first act as a key character in the play. To add to the set's overall oddball effect, the 13 Rows fabricated a drum, decorated it with white and red triangles and tethered it to the column. Another novel element included in the set was a small carpet lying at random on the right side of the stage—like the carpets used by street magicians and fakirs. As I will show later, the actors' costumes also inspired associations with fairground and folk performances, with circus and cabaret.

In Orpheus' room there were also elements that had nothing to do with the poet's villa or the circus. These elements did not have any 'realistic' right to be there, and this caused consternation among critics. Henryk Vogler was irritated by 'a smashed violin hanging from the ceiling' (1959: 9), which is clearly visible in the photos from the performance. The critic failed to notice a relevant addition to the violin in the form of a large fiddlestick—belonging rather to a cello than a violin—suspended

14 · DARIUSZ KOSIŃSKI

haphazardly on the back wall facing the audience. No critics reported another surprising element of the set—two tall, black candlesticks set up along the back wall. Placed on either side of a triangular niche, the candlesticks provide sharp contrast to the light-coloured set. What is more, only one of those candlesticks—the one on the audience's right—has a candle on it. And this is a special 'blessed candle', which in Poland people place during funeral masses next to the coffins of those who are about to be buried. The addition of these candlesticks to the light, fairground motif of Orpheus' room presents clear dissonance by adding funereal, *thanatic* undertones.

All these odd objects along with relatively micro-proportioned furniture filled the interior, and indicated that—as Cocteau wanted it to be—this was to be 'an ordinary room infected with some sort of mysterious disease leading to "cracking and collapse"' (Grotowski 2012: 162). This is the impression given by the cracked, dirty and crooked walls we see in Orpheus' home. Incredible shadows are cast upon the pale walls by some of the objects placed on stage and hanging over it (the violin!). They constructed the ceiling from uneven, misaligned wooden planks that contrasted with the interior below. The overall impression in *Orpheus* is that of a jolly, fairground stage set that was dumped after years of use, and that now furnishes the apartment of some impoverished inheritors of the avant-garde of the past.

Horse and Carrot

The performance opened when actor Adam Kurczyna appeared on the shallow, low stage of the Theatre of 13 Rows, and uttered a prologue written by Grotowski. I was not successful in finding a full copy of the *Orpheus* script, but Bogdan Danowicz (1959: 7) published this prologue in his review of the performance—

LADIES AND GENTLEMEN!

SIMPLE COMMERCIAL HONESTY FORCES US TO WARN YOU THAT NOTHING HERE HAS ANYTHING TO DO WITH 'MODERNITY'. IT IS POSSIBLE THAT JEAN COCTEAU'S TEXT WAS ONCE UPON A TIME MODERN.

> THIS WAS IN A BYGONE ERA BEFORE THE GREAT WAR. TODAY HOWEVER
> THERE IS ONLY AN IDYLL LEFT, A GENTLE IDYLL OF OUR SENTIMENTAL
> FATHERS. HENCE THE TEXT BY COCTEAU (BEAUTIFUL, THOUGH OUT-
> DATED) SEEMED TO US A USEFUL PRETEXT (LIKE A PARABLE, LIKE A
> BALLAD) TO EXPRESS OURSELVES, TO EXPRESS A LONGING IN OUR
> OWN NAMES, TO SNEER ON OUR OWN ACCOUNT, TO SEARCH FOR A
> SENSE.

The idea of preceding the show with a prologue delivered directly to the audience did not come from Grotowski—Cocteau himself opened his drama with a similar presentation. But Grotowski completely changed its meaning and content. The Theatre of 13 Rows used Adam Kurczyna to declare the generational character of theatrical message in the Opole *Orpheus*'—formulated by people who were separated from the illusions and refined avant-garde notions of their 'sentimental fathers' by the experience of the Second World War. In the eyes of these young people, the 'wild experiments' of the pre-war era looked like child's play—and thus they could only refer to this lineage in the right context and use it for specific ends. They therefore 'honestly' warned their audiences that they were not going to stage Cocteau as a 'renowned modern artist' because they did not see him as such, and that instead they would use his text in order to express themselves—their own longing (for what?), their own sneer (at what?) and their own search for their unique sense of meaning.

The contemporaneity of the Opole performance and the context surrounding it were also expressed by the costumes worn by Orpheus and Eurydice. Exactly as Cocteau suggested, they wore 'costumes in fashion at the time of the performance', but contrary to the author's further instruction, the main heroes were certainly not wearing 'very inconspicuous country clothes' (Cocteau 1961[1926]: 3). Orpheus (Adam Kurczyna) wore light, almost white trousers, a red rollneck top and a black jacket that was customized with embroidery and light-grey, rectangular patches—one on a lower pocket and another much larger one on his breast. Taken on the whole, the costume had the appearance of a ruined garment—Vogler mentions 'Orpheus' ripped-up coat'—and yet it fit right in with the other circus and fairground elements, reminiscent of the patchwork costumes worn by clowns.

Eurydice wore a tight-fitting, strappy blouse and close-fitting, knee-length pants. The costume accentuated the slender figure of Barbara Barska who played the role. The dark colours of her clothes appeared in contrast to the red colour of her soft, flat shoes, her heavily made-up lips and the ribbons that tied two small pigtails that stuck straight out 'as stiffly as if they were wired' (Vogler 1959: 5). Danowicz associated this with the fashion adopted by female visual artists of the time (1959: 7).

In line with Cocteau's text, the first scene showed Orpheus absorbed—listening to the Horse tap out a spiritualistic alphabet. The Horse stood stage left, its large, grey head growing out of the top of a massive Doric column—something akin to melancholic heads from the paintings of Marc Chagall. According to the show programme, the Horse was 'played' by Stanisław Szreniawski. The actor stayed entirely hidden by the column for most of the play. The only part of his body seen by the audience was his arm, which he extended to beat out the letters of the spiritualistic alphabet on the drum suspended from the column.

In describing this creature, Flaszen used the term 'Horse of the Absurd', and when asked directly about what the Horse represented, Grotowski answered, 'The horse is Jean Cocteau *à rebours* [backwards], the Beelzebub of bad poetry and false ideology, a provocateur of Orpheus' spectacular, melodramatic death' (Danowicz 1959: 7). Both descriptions clearly show that in the case of the Horse, a certain shift was made between Cocteau's text and the Opole performance. The latter entered into a polemical discourse with the former. Grotowski took a critical perspective towards Cocteau as an artist who represented a simplified version of existentialism—a fashion during the 1950s and 60s that was incredibly popular in Poland's intellectual circles. The young director challenged this intellectual trend in his two earlier works based on the play *Rodzina pechowców* [The family of the unlucky ones] by Jerzy Krzysztoń,[4] and also dealt with the play in his texts written in the late

---

4 *Bogowie deszczu* [The gods of the rain], the Old Theatre in Cracow, 4 July 1958, and *Pechowcy* [The unlucky ones], Theatre of 13 Rows, Opole, 8 November 1958.

1950s (see Grotowski 2012: 109–13). Grotowski reimagined Cocteau's Horse in a way that completely aligned with Grotowski's cultural diagnosis of Polish society. The Horse helps underscore connections between the play—which ushered in a new era at the Theatre of 13 Rows—and contemporary issues its creators knew all too well.

A photograph by Leonard Olejnik shows the first scene of the Opole performance (inventory numbers 28–30). In the centre of the photograph is Orpheus at a table—half sitting and half kneeling—turned completely towards the Horse at the audience's back-left corner of the stage. The Horse taps out another letter of the cosmic alphabet. Eurydice is seated on the floor behind Orpheus, and to the audience's right. Her pose is composed so that the lines of her body are pointing further to the right of the audience. Her pose is in direct opposition to Orpheus's tense body directed at the Horse. She seems indifferent, and very much distant from that which fascinates and attracts her husband.

The booklet distributed to attendees at the performance featured actors' lines in captions beneath the photographs: 'HORSE (tapping). ORPHEUS: "D . . . , d . . . Horse, say more . . ." EURYDICE: "What patience!" ' These are the lines spoken at the very beginning of the first scene of Cocteau's drama, albeit somewhat shortened (Grotowski 1956). The endpoint is the same as in Cocteau's version—marital crisis caused by Orpheus's overwhelming fascination with the Horse.

This dissonance is clearly stressed by the second photograph included in the booklet. Here, Orpheus is seen standing by the Horse's column holding the animal by its outstretched hand with an almost caressing gesture. Eurydice—evidently displeased—stands erect by the table with her gaze turned towards her husband and the Horse. The caption reads 'ORPHEUS: "I do hope I will one day cast magic spells upon predatory animals." EURYDICE: "You love the Horse, while I come second" ' (Grotowski 1956).

It is of course possible to see in these examples banal scenes from a marriage in crisis, but a slight shift in perception is enough to see these scenes as presenting a very different type of theatre. 'You love the Horse, while I come second' is a grotesque statement, and is almost vulgar in the way it is formulated. It may be seen as a diagnosis of the situation a woman finds herself in when realizing she is in a relationship with a man who is hiding his homosexuality.

There is no firm evidence to confirm that Grotowski tried to take up this theme openly in his version of *Orpheus*. It is not possible to learn anything about this from critics' reviews.[5] I only have suspicions that arise from the conviction that the theme of sexuality was always very much present in Grotowski's work—present but depicted in an obscure way that perhaps only today we are able to see with the help of feminist, gender and psychoanalytical methodologies. The most important texts written on this subject by Grzegorz Niziołek (2011) and Agata Adamiecka-Sitek (2012) refer to the theme of sexuality in Grotowski's later works—*Acropolis*, *The Constant Prince* and *Apocalypsis cum figuris*. However, these sexual themes and motifs were most vividly present in his earlier works, those discussed in this book. Transposed in this way, the Horse becomes an almost singularly, and yet paradoxically, hidden symbol of homosexual longing that destroys the bond between Eurydice and Orpheus.

The next sequence in the conversation between the couple is a typical form of exposition. We get information about a poem whispered by the Horse and sent to a competition, and also about Eurydice's broken union with the bacchantes. In this scene, the ideological conflict is also drawn out more clearly. To achieve this effect, Grotowski and his company used . . . a plate of carrots! At the beginning of the play we find Eurydice grating carrots—an act that was transformed by a simple idea into having effective consequences. Here we have the poet's beautiful and attractive 'muse', dressed in clothes which were not at all designed to be worn for housewife duties, carrying out a trivial task with concrete physical actions. Barska grated a real carrot—which demanded a certain amount of strength and physical engagement, and introduced an element of real-time activity that is seriously risky for live theatre—Eurydice had to

---

5 In some sense the only exception is Henryk Vogler's review (1959) titled 'Orfeusz zgwałcony, ale niedopieszczony' [Orpheus raped but not fully caressed]. This apparently 'frivolous' title clearly points to sexual connotations that are present in the text and can lead to specific conclusions. Read literally it refers to Grotowski's textual and theatrical (but still homosexual!) 'rape' of *Orpheus*.

grind the carrot, and this action had to take as long as it took. Above all else, this created a realistic effect that contrasted with the overly poetic elevations and words developed in the next scene. Eurydice sets the plate on the table, and 'Orpheus utters a bombastic monologue about the solemnity of poetry, while eating grated carrot' (Flaszen 2010: 58). Aroused by his own speech, Orpheus would at times point at the audience with his spoon, and bits of carrot flew through the air and likely landed on spectators.

Quiproquo with Death

After Orpheus's attack on the audience—during which Eurydice sits by the wall clearly distancing herself from her husband's outburst—both take their places at the table and resume conversation. The words that followed would eventually be printed beneath the next photograph in the performance booklet: 'EURYDICE: "If I were dead you wouldn't notice it." ORPHEUS: "Without noticing it, we *were* dead" ' (Cocteau 1961[1926]: 15). These lines were uttered in a very ordinary, everyday way, in strong contrast to the showy finesse of Orpheus eating carrots to the left, and once again going down on one knee in a dynamic pose, and Eurydice on the opposite side calmly painting her nails. Here is a common scene from everyday life in which words about being dead sound false because they are uttered by someone eating, and thus seem to illuminate an everydayness stripped of meaning. Caricature and absurdity coexist in this almost literally expressed image, describing the futility of everyday life.

The conversation between Eurydice and Orpheus ends with the latter exiting, heading towards the town in order to enter a poetry contest organized by the bacchantes. The Horse dictated to Orpheus a phrase that Orpheus considered to be genial. The Polish phrase translates to 'A deceased road will return an angel.'[6] This was in some way an obscure foretelling of Eurydice's impending fate, and also a literary joke because in the Polish original the first letters of each word spell out a vulgar

---

6 In the English version, this 'famous sentence' reads 'Orpheus hunts Eurydice's lost life', creating an acronym that reads *O, hell* (Cocteau 1961: 13).

word.[7] It is worth noting that later on in the play the bacchantes consider this to be a dire insult and decide to punish its author.

After Orpheus leaves, Eurydice's ally Heurtebise visits her. In this role, Zygmunt Molik wore a dark-grey blouse with light-blue inserts on the left breast, and trousers of the same colour with similar inserts on both sides. Horizontal black clasps give the coat the appearance of a uniform—albeit less militaristic and more comical in character. It looks like the sort of uniform a lion tamer might wear. In his comments, Flaszen interpreted Heurtebise as 'the personification of rational order' (Flaszen 2010: 58). In Cocteau's play Heurtebise had some metaphysical aspect, and was—to put things simply—a poetic variant of a guardian angel watching over the love of Eurydice and Orpheus. In Grotowski's version the character was transformed to represent a 'rational order'. But Józef Kelera in his review of the Opole *Orpheus* interpreted Heurtebise as 'an Enlightened Genius, also a Genius of the Theatre' (2006: 108). It seems that the Opole production portrayed Heurtebise as also having some kind of ruling power, as someone who knows more than the rest of the characters. Furthermore, he can be seen as a representation of the director himself—a theatrical device, I later show, that is quite common in Grotowski's performances.

Eurydice and Heurtebise form a conspiracy to get rid of the Horse. Heurtebise brings some poison from Aglaonice—the leader of the bacchantes with whom Eurydice was once associated. From a queer perspective, one can clearly see that Eurydice's relationship with the bacchantes has a homoerotic aspect, while her departure to live with Orpheus can be seen as a rejection of this sexuality and a return to heteronormative life. This perspective gives a very different tone to Orpheus' misogynistic shouts. The scene in which they attempt to poison the Horse is depicted in a photograph, also included in the performance booklet. The photograph shows an image dynamically composed of the actors' bodies. Eurydice kneels on the table with her other leg stretched out towards the floor while her right hand—holding a sugar cube—reaches towards

---

7 The acronym in Polish '*Droga umarła powróci aniołem*' spells out the word *Dupa* meaning 'arse'.

the Horse. Heurtebise serves as a linear extension of her body—he sits on the edge of the stage with his right leg bent at the knee and his left leg pointing downwards, while his right hand reaches out towards Eurydice. The two bodies thus form a strong line that cuts across the image diagonally and clearly enhances the sense of tension developed in this scene.

Eurydice does not succeed in her attempt to poison the Horse, and instead she herself will die—poisoned duplicitously by Aglaonice. Knowing how little time she has left, she moves soberly to the room next door as she entreats Heurtebise to run and get Orpheus.

At this moment Death (Rena Mirecka) appears. Her dress might have been considered elegant,[8] but critic Bożena Zagórska ruthlessly deemed it a 'horrid, half red satin circus gown, embroidered here and there' (1959: 3). Two assistants accompanied Death—Azrael (Antoni Jahołkowski) and Raphael (Tadeusz Bartkowiak)—whose overalls with black lines painted across them echoed the cracked walls of Orpheus's apartment. Across the lower half of their faces they wore black triangular kerchiefs like those worn by cowboys. The upper halves of their faces were hidden behind helmet-shaped masks with large, black eye sockets reminiscent of insect heads. On the whole, Death's assistants gave off an impression of stiffness and a lack of even proportions.

The whole trio entered the stage with a dancing gait—which can clearly be seen in a photo printed in the performance booklet. It is not clear what sort of music accompanied this entrance. Three reviewers wrote about jazz, and two others—whom I consider to be attentive and reliable critics—wrote about 'sacral Afro-American music' (Korewa 1959: 5) and 'New Orleans pre-jazz rhythms from a mass for the Black Christ' (Danowicz 1959: 7). Jerzy Kaszycki who chose the music was a pianist and composer from Polish Radio in Kraków. He was quite well known at the time as one of the radio presenters popularizing jazz and Western pop music, previously banned in Poland. It is very likely that he would have encouraged Grotowski to use some gospel songs because this is the kind of music that reviewers seem to describe—albeit imprecisely.

---

8 Danowicz wrote that Death is a 'beautiful, distinguished dame' (1959: 7).

22 · DARIUSZ KOSIŃSKI

The dance performed to this score by Mirecka and her companions had a certain erotic character. It is probable that the actors performed movements associated with sexual gratification and depicted Death as a 'lecherous whore'—an image associated with 'her' during the Middle Ages and into modernity. The low-cut red dress must have aided this impression. If, in line with information provided by Aleksandra Korewa, we recall that the scene was 'almost sang', then we can imagine a sequence that is very much internally conflicted, grotesque, and evocative of cabaret. Dancing, Death sings a reminder to her assistants—those bugs—a message that the 13 Rows printed as a caption beneath a photograph in the programme: 'I demand order and the sort of cleanliness you'd find on a ship' (*Materiały i Dyskusje* 1959, VOL. 1: 8).[9]

A look at another photograph featured in the booklet shows two parts of the Death scene in stark contrast to one another. All merriment is gone. Death is sitting on a little stool at the edge of the raised stage—with one leg resting on the auditorium floor and the other bent over it. With this stiff, crossed-legged pose Death creates the impression of a very pragmatic, domineering young woman who takes her task seriously. Raphael further enhanced this impression by standing nearby—brandishing scissors and bent over. Death rests her left hand on the stool next to her thigh, and holds a hand-driven drill erect in the air, and in her right hand she turns a toothed wheel—which drives the drill-bit but which is not in place at this time. Seen from afar, the drill looks like a sceptre, a slim and dignified object, and it is only upon closer examination that one realizes it is a common household tool. Though it is not clear in the photograph, the position of her hands makes it seem like Death is tightening a line attached to the drill—the other end of which seems to be held by Azrael. Raphael is poised to cut it with his scissors . . .

---

9 *Materiały i dyskusje* [Materials and discussions] was the title of a series of publications by the Theatre of 13 Rows. Each issue of this quasi-magazine was published on the occasion of a new premiere, from *Orpheus* until *Kordian* (later the theatre had no money for the publication). Each issue included basic information about the performance, along with commentary by Flaszen, and also some additional materials—excerpts from the reviews of earlier productions, some general commentaries, etc. When referring to a programme of performance or booklet published on the occasion of a premier, I mean a specific issue of *Materiały i dyskusje*.

After they complete the 'operation', the mood of cabaret-like merriment returns. This scene is most likely presented in the third photo preserved at the GIA (inv. nos 13–15) featuring Death and her helpers. All three stand with Death in the centre. She dons a pair of narrow sunglasses with pale frames and waves a distinguished goodbye to the audience. The assistant standing to her right is also waving. The second assistant is giving a thumbs-up—evidently letting the audience know they have been good to the players.

This Death scene was undoubtedly one of the most important in the performance. The dynamic and grotesque play of contrasts—which was the basis for this scene's composition—took on a new dimension as it referred to the key philosophical question of the whole work. If we assume, with some simplification, that Grotowski's performance emerged out of an experience of facing death then playing this sequence in the way described above allowed the company to extract an ambivalent approach to it. Fascination, fear and something akin to disgust were feelings Grotowski allowed to enter his stage while wanting to tame them, looking for a plane within which they could coexist.

It is interesting that the ensuing sequences crucial to the Orpheus narrative are not described in the literature—for example, Orpheus setting off to seek Eurydice and their return home together, her dying once more, and Orpheus waiting to be torn apart by the bacchantes. Critics rarely mentioned them, and instead focused on a later scene: the investigation and interrogation of Heurtebise. This seems strange because the sequences after Eurydice's death are very important. And we can already say something about them based almost entirely on photographs, especially those included with captions in the performance booklet.

The first of these photographs presents Orpheus setting off to find Eurydice. Kurczyna stands by a silver curtain—which imitates a mirror—with his left hand reaching towards it as if in a moment he is about to go right through its surface. Behind him, Heurtebise stands looking at the audience and probably speaks the lines printed beneath the photo: 'You only have to watch yourself all your life in a mirror, and you'll see Death at work like bees in a glass hive. Good-bye. Good luck!' (Grotowski 1956).

Orpheus sets off. In Cocteau's play two short scenes follow, featuring a Postman who came to Orpheus with a letter and from behind a closed door asked if the happy couple were home. Heurtebise replied and told him twice that they were asleep. Interestingly enough, Grotowski did not delete this seemingly minor scene, although he probably staged it very differently from the original. In an unpublished interview found at the GIA by Agnieszka Wójtowicz, Barbara Barska recalled that 'the scene was so funny: Zygmunt asked: "Is anyone home?" To which Adam and I replied: "No, asleep" ' (Barska n.d.). Perhaps the actress could not recall the scene in full because the cast includes the Postman's Voice, which was performed by Tadeusz Bartkowiak, and so it wasn't really Molik (Heurtebise) who asked the question. However, it is hard to think that her memory failed her so much that she substituted herself and Kurczyna as the ones who answered 'Molik'—when in reality it was Bartkowiak. If we accept her version it would mean that Grotowski set this scene in a tellingly different way than Cocteau. In Cocteau's text, the dialogue between the Postman and Heurtebise serves as a kind of interplay, a sort of surrealistic-poetic way of filling and marking the time that passes between Orpheus setting off on his journey and his return. If in the performance Eurydice and Orpheus answered the Postman, by then they had changed their death into some sort of practical joke, a folly, a game. They did not 'really' die but only 'imagined' it and 'played dead' as in a child's game.

This is the context in which we need to situate Bogdan Danowicz's comment: 'the young couple die [. . .] to the test', while '*quid pro quo* with the deceased, resurrected and once again dying Eurydice is a theatrical-philosophical projection of death, death not for real [. . .]' (Danowicz 1959: 7). This vividly theatrical game of death and resurrection was the first of several risky scenes negating death as an irrevocable end that Grotowski included in his early performances (see chapters on *Cain* and *Shakuntala*).

After the interplay with the Postman comes a scene in which Orpheus returns from the netherworld with Eurydice. The moment of their reappearance is shown in another photograph from the booklet. On the left side of the stage, close to the audience, Orpheus stands in a dynamic pose. His left hand rests on his hip, and with the right one bent at the elbow he seems to point to the two characters behind him on the far side of the stage. These are Heurtebise, who sits on a stool, and Eurydice, who has just emerged from the mirror and stands next to him. Her appearance is the most interesting aspect of this scene. Barska is wearing the same costume as before but she looks different. Her hair is down, without the stiff pigtails. She is no longer wearing her soft shoes but instead high heels—which appear to be red—in the black-and-white photo. On her right forearm she has some white fabric that is hard to identify—perhaps a shawl. But the biggest change can be seen in the actress's posture—she is no longer the girl from the earlier scenes. She is now a mature woman, proudly erect, aware of her beauty and value. She is still young, though much more self-assured. Once again the reviewers do not seem to notice anything although it seems obvious that Grotowski's Eurydice returned from the other side changed—older and more experienced.

Here the well-known part of the myth begins: Orpheus is forbidden from looking back at Eurydice else he be punished by losing her, and yet he cannot restrain himself, and finally steals a quick look at his wife, who once again vanishes. But all these scenes are absent both from reviews and the photographic 'summary'. This is surprising, especially because in Cocteau's *Orpheus* this is one of the most interesting sequences in the play. Perhaps this sequence was not sufficiently developed in the performance, and hence those writing about the show skipped it over? Or maybe the absence of photos from this scene convinced them that the sequence was not so important?

The next photo from the performance program shows the scene after Eurydice has disappeared, and Orpheus prepares to die at the hands of the approaching bacchantes. The caption beneath it states: 'HEURTEBISE: "You frighten me." ORPHEUS: "What are the thoughts of the marble from which a sculptor shapes a masterpiece?" ' (Grotowski 1956). The photos that show this scene present Kurczyna standing downstage left just next to the mirror and gesticulating dramatically, performing gymnastic exercises—even seeming to 'show off'.[10] With his hands behind his head he seems to lean to the side—a typical sports exercise from school. While no one has described this scene, one possibility is that the pose where he placed his hands behind his head might have been intended to encourage associations with iconic angels and their wings. The shadow he cast on the wall behind him—clearly visible in one of the photographs—invites this interpretation.

The scene in which the unseen bacchantes approached and later tore Orpheus apart was to be accompanied by a 'moving jazz choir'. According to Konrad Eberhardt's review, 'a menacing musical rhythm completely substituted for the gaggle of voices or other realistic sounds' (Eberhardt 1960: 6).

In Cocteau's version, after Orpheus is killed, his head is thrown onto the stage, and he *then* proclaims his monologue—begging to have his body back. In Grotowski's version, the terrified Orpheus—his head cut off—calls for Eurydice. Eurydice then emerges from the mirror, takes her husband by his invisible hand and vanishes with his head into the mirror. A photograph in the programme shows this moment, confirming that Eurydice underwent another transformation—she appears here wearing a white dress and a long, white caftan with clearly visible black stripes—identical to those worn by Death's assistants. She is bent over, as if aged. Only Grzegorz Sinko noticed this change, and wrote about it as a 'very moving second return from the netherworld in the form of an aged woman' (Sinko 2006a[1959]: 111). Barska later confirmed that by her acting she had intended the audience to see the character ageing: 'The role of Eurydice demanded femininity be shown all the way from youth to old age. [. . .] It was necessary to reach deep down inside and experience life as if down to the very last moment' (Barska n.d.).

---

10 Three surviving photographs can be found at the GIA: two black-and-white (inv. nos 5, 7–9) and one colour (inv. no. 2). All three show the same scene in three variations with Kurczyna doing different postures and gestures.

This confirms the idea that Grotowski treated Eurydice's departure and return not as scenes of return from the netherworld, but rather as a synthetic representation of dying understood as a process that fills the entirety of our lives. Orpheus's wife died in the play text and returned to her husband from the other side—but on Grotowski's stage she slowly approached death through the act of ageing.[11] As a result it is possible to interpret her death as a process we are all born to experience rather than as something extraordinary. This shift turned the unique mythical events reinterpreted in the text into a completely ordinary—though no less moving—human experience. Importantly, this key element of the performance was completely handed over to the actress without being in any way verbalized, signalling one of the most important methods Grotowski utilized—constructing a staged montage through actors' 'subscores'.[12]

After Orpheus dies and departs with Eurydice, police officers enter their home. This scene is scripted as a sort of cabaret but was transformed by Grotowski into a clown show. The Police Commissioner (Stanisław Szreniawski) and his Assistant (Antoni Jahołkowski) wore striped, narrow trousers, identical hats with narrow rims and each had his face 'powdered white like clowns' (Danowicz 1959: 7). Both looked like little boys dressed up as adults for fun. They tried to frighten Heurtebise. The whole sequence was enhanced by allusions to the actual context of the Theatre of 13 Rows. The Commissioner introduced himself as Jan Paweł Gawlik— a cheeky reference to a well-known theatre critic who opposed Grotowski's idea of experimental theatre. The investigation scenes were played for pure laughs. The Assistant constantly fell asleep, forcing the Commissioner to keep waking him up by firing a toy gun—he also fired it at the audience—and they both searched the apartment in an overly pedantic way.

---

11 It is worth noting that the sequence in which Eurydice ages has its fulfilment and echo in the final scene of lovers ageing in *Shakuntala*.

12 I am using the term 'subscore' in a way proposed by Eugenio Barba in his analyses of the actor's dramaturgy: 'The subscore is a technical element belonging to the particular creative logic of every actor. [. . .] The subscore is an inner support, a hidden scaffold which actors sketch for themselves without intending to act it out' (2010: 29–30).

And yet in this apparently humorous scene, some reviewers noted serious elements. Jerzy Zagórski explained that what he enjoyed most about the performance might have been the 'scene in which Heurtebise is interrogated', which he saw as 'being more alive for us' (Zagórski 1960: 4). Was that 'aliveness' not related to the means used by the secret police to transform an accident into murder, and someone innocent into a criminal? And were not echoes of the politically engaged Krakow *Orfeusz* present in these grotesque scenes?

Thank You, World

Grotowski resolutely followed Cocteau's framing in arranging his composition, and he set up his performance in a way that made its final scene key by allowing his audience to understand its message. It was introduced and announced as a message that did not belong to the original drama: 'The play is coming to an end. And now comes a moment of terror: actors announce honestly that at this point Cocteau's original text ends and they begin to recite an invocation penned by Jerzy Grotowski' (Zagórska 1959: 3).

Cocteau's play ended with Orpheus thanking God for the salvation of Eurydice and 'for having saved me because I adored poetry, and thou art poetry' (Cocteau 1961[1926]: 46). Grotowski replaced these lines with his own epilogue—different in meaning, but equally declarative:

We thank you world that you exist.

We thank you for being a dancer who is endless and timeless.

We thank you for dancing your chaos, a chaos which has visited us in the guise of the Horse

of the Absurd, and that we (grasping your chaos) can sculpt ourselves, our own freedom.

We thank you for dancing your own form of order: an order of your laws and order of our intellect, which is capable of grasping those laws; in a word: for what has visited us as Heurtebise and liberated us.

We thank you world for giving us consciousness which permits us to overcome: to understand our eternity contained in your eternity. And that love is in this a teacher, an alphabet. We thank you for not being separated from you, that we are you, that it is in us that you achieve self-awareness and awakening. We thank you, world, that you exist.
(Grotowski 2012: 158)

This text was proclaimed by actors seated on stage and raising a toast—shown in the last photograph printed in the performance booklet. The whole composition of the actors' bodies gives the impression that they were flowing from the stage towards the audience.

Andrzej Wróblewski wrote: 'This fragment represents a sort of bridge between the stage and the audience, meant to guide their thoughts as they flow from Cocteau's interpretation on the subject of the myth of Orpheus and Eurydice' (1959: 23). The audience was therefore invited to follow the process initiated on the stage and to complete it in their lives. So it is not without good reason that the final lines of the play were called 'an invocation' and not an epilogue. It was an invocation in the sense of calling upon a higher power, not calling for aid in creating a work, as it was in the epics crafted by Homer and his followers, but rather as a plea for guidance beyond art—in life itself. This is why it was addressed to the audience. It was also—not unlike Cocteau's version—a statement that summarized and clarified the play while also being a unique sort of expression of faith. Grotowski preserved its place and function in the structure of the whole while also achieving a definitive ideological substitution. He gave his performance a purpose by praising the dynamic processes of harmonizing apparent contradictions—which he perceived to be a secular version of salvation. His 'invocation' presents in abbreviated form the same convictions Grotowski formulated in his texts from the late 1950s—perhaps most clearly and completely in his essay 'Theatre and the Man of the Universe' ('Teatr i człowiek kosmiczny'), in which he presented readers with the following diagnosis:

Human beings—deprived of myths, 'naked'—stand somewhat face to face with the immensity of the universe; with the abyss the heavens and the abyss that opens inside the atom.

The death of the gods places human beings in a desert. Nothing—in the face of gods—is disallowed any more, but then so nothing—in the face of gods—is obligatory any more. And nothing protects us from the terror of the death.

Faced with this new psychological reality human beings are forced to either 'accept despair and loneliness' [. . .] or seek further escape, craft new stained glass windows out of smashed myths and faiths, or else open up before this limitless material whole, take root in it with all their minds, grow into it, in its powers and regularities of the personal 'I', interact with it as an extension of the self. There is in this solution—secular and without cutting corners—a new majesty of human beings, a majesty of human consciousness, the highest form of widespread evolution: the universe achieves self-awareness, knowledge of the self through human beings, through the human mind [. . .]. There is also a psychological opportunity here: elimination of the tragic aspect of death, leading to the ability to see that the universe is not separate from us. And the universe—in the broader sense we are here concerned with—does not surrender to death.

(Grotowski 2012: 122–23)

This project essentially proposes a new kind of secular 'salvation'. It involves a sense of immortality through connecting and becoming one with the universe or 'world'—which can only be achieved by piercing through apparent contradictions and grasping that those forces which oppose each other find their place in the harmonious dynamic of the world as it is.

The whole performance of *Orpheus* was meant to allow audiences to recognize and experience this truth, so that through the mechanisms of meta-theatricality they could look at their own lives from a necessary distance. Danowicz saw and described this intention: 'Contrary to the

Master's epilogue, Orpheus and Eurydice then descend back down to earth!—Their death was an attempt to interrupt their existence, but also an attempt to judge this existence from the perspective of contemporary values, and not *SUB SPECIE AETERNITATIS*' (1959: 7). This attempt to interrupt and at the same time judge their existence is what the Theatre of 13 Rows' *Orpheus* was all about. This production was performed on the stage but was also meant to encourage the spectators to perform similar attempts, and to reflect on their existence in their own lives.

However, problems arise when we see that this contemporary re-evaluation of existence was not fully realized but was instead expressed as a declaration of faith. This declarative resolution was resoundingly criticized by some reviewers—most severely by Aleksandra Korewa:

> Grotowski ends the play by using his own words in the invocation to express his personal attitude to the problem. [. . .] Passing over the very nature of the invocation, which comes across as a very flat sort of prayer and is simply bad literature, I think that ending the performance with any sort of summary is unnecessary, because the value of the performance is in the provocation, in the way questions are posed. It is the audience who should find rational answers to these questions. (Korewa 1959: 5)

Korewa very much valued and precisely described the rhythmic organization of the performance, its complexity and multi-layered meanings, and could not accept Grotowski's 'invocation'—which really is 'bad literature'. Her criticism is important in that it emerges out of a deep reading of the dramaturgical framework of the performance. From her perspective, the finale came across as a discursive and declarative statement overwhelming all earlier efforts intended to present ideas that were not verbalized but played out on stage in a theatre context. She believed in human intelligence and freedom of thought, and was convinced that the audience should have been allowed to creatively extract their own conclusions from the game of oppositions on which the performance was based. This sounds somewhat paradoxical, but the critic seems to believe more strongly in the power of the theatrical experience than did the director, who seems unable to resist the temptation to directly lecture the audience. Her negative opinion about the finale Grotowski proposed for *Orpheus* is also a protest against reducing the experience of change-ability and complexity hinted at in the show as a 'rule of the world' to a declarative 'unity'. Luckily enough, Grotowski—an artist who was adept at learning from his experiences—drew his own creative conclusions. The self-parody with which he ended his next performance proves that he understood Korewa's and other critics' comments (see Chapter 2 for details). At the same time, he did not abandon the game of oppositions or the grotesque. Instead he crafted subsequent farce-mysteries with his Opole company and went on to develop something almost forgotten today—an original theatrical and philosophical project that is a lot closer to our contemporaneity than the famous 'ritualistic theatre' with which he is usually associated.

A Game of Multitudes

Korewa's review is an important document because it provides us with one of the first attempts to fully describe the way the actors of the Theatre of 13 Rows performed. It is based not on a psychological interpretation of text and character, but on an analysis of the consciously constructed composition of rhythms in the performance. Her review is so important that I will now quote it at length.

> Every sentence, almost every word has its own internal rhythm. The action is set to a rhythm not unlike a musical score. But it is not just movement, a slowing down or speeding up of the action, which is subject to firmly fixed rigours. Equally it is the stage image that is governed by the rules of rhythm and com-position. It is not an unimportant matter as to whether partners talking sit or stand, whether one of them is sitting down while the other is standing up. An actor is then not just an instrument upon which 'psychological etudes' are played, instead becoming an element within the play such as a colour or a sound, an element that is capable of constantly reinventing itself. Conflict or tension that emerges between people, as a result of the drama

narrative, is underscored by the situation, gesture, actors' mimicry, intensity, and timbre of voice. All these elements create a general atmosphere and tonality that arouse in us certain associations, certainly not demanding we know our psychologies, in the way that an abstract painting can create the impression of a woman without actually possessing any aspects of what we would consider to be elements of the female anatomy. […]

Ceaseless contrasts and their sharpness, presenting problems from numerous sides by using new formal means—force us to review our ideas. We are used to thought patterns and even if an idea is new, though served up in a traditional format, it can easily evade our perception. In Grotowski's theatre this is, however, impossible. Hence the formal assumptions of this theatre become more valuable, because they do not address new affairs—life and death, crime and punishment, responsibility, love, individual happiness, and so on. To find the correct, contemporary and truly theatrical shape for this sort of narrative seems to be an appropriate ambition. The premiere of *Orpheus* at the Theatre of 13 Rows evidenced that these assumptions are not just hollow phrases and useless theoretical chatter, but quite the opposite—they function as they should as specific forms of creative expression. (Korewa 1959: 5)

This was an extraordinary review, able to perceive the innovative offering made by the Theatre of 13 Rows. The majority of critics—even those writing about *Orpheus* in a complimentary way—made a point of undermining its innovative spirit, writing that it was merely a good performance, that the director had remained faithful to Cocteau. Instead, I have tried to show that Grotowski made no attempt to obscure his intentions when he stated that Cocteau's drama was only a pretext, and that he rightly considered the displacements and adaptations he performed to be radical. The issue—and likely the source of misunderstanding—was that his interventions as a dramaturg and director were precisely 'displacements within their own sphere'. He did not change the course of action, context or environment of the original, but by small interventions he twisted and distorted the meaning of Cocteau's drama. Sometimes the interventions were so slight that they were neither noticed nor appreciated.

The quality of the literary material might also have played a part here. Reviewers resoundingly noted that Cocteau's text was anachronistic and substandard from a literary perspective—while Grotowski would later on often repeat that the role played by a drama text in his theatre is one of a partner in the encounter, and that it therefore cannot be weak—because only a strong text can provide the required motivation for the company to work with. In this context he also likened the function of a 'strong text' to that of myths in the theatre of antiquity (see Grotowski 1968a: 55–60). From this perspective, one could propose that certain misunderstandings and troubles related to *Orpheus* emerged simultaneously from the weakness of the literary material and the lack of resonance the myth itself inspired in audiences. Grotowski seemed to confirm this years later in conversation with French critics when he referred to the myth of Orpheus as an example of a 'dead' myth, and compared it with the living 'myth of Christ'.[13] Grotowski considered the myth of Orpheus to be 'dead' because no one believed in the reality of the mythical hero, and instead treated him only as a cultural 'symbol'. On the other hand, many people still believe that Jesus Christ is a real God. For Grotowski—living in a Catholic country and being a deeply engaged Catholic in his early youth—the difference was obvious. It resulted in the conclusion that it was not possible to provoke a strong resonance in the audience with a dead myth. To get the strong reaction for which he aimed, Grotowski had to recall the 'living myth'. And this was exactly what he would do in his later performances, starting with *Forefathers' Eve*. Perhaps the reference he used in the Paris interview was related to conclusions he drew from the inaugural performance of his Theatre of 13 Rows—which was not completely understood, because the audience was unfamiliar with the theme of the basic myth of Orpheus.

---

13 'There are dead myths, such as that of Orpheus, which no longer arouse any emotional responses. They are now no more than metaphors' (Grotowski 2012: 302).

The game in which Grotowski asked spectators to take part—with all those circus and cabaret angles—was not designed to mock Cocteau or to provide entertainment. Rather, it was in fact an attempt to realize the programme Grotowski had tried to formulate in the texts written when he began to work with the Theatre of 13 Rows. Here is a fragment from an aptly titled essay of his—'Dialog z widzem. Między "zabawą" a postawą wobec rzeczywistości' [Dialogue with a spectator: Between a 'play' and an approach to reality]. Probably written in 1959, this is a telling commentary on the ideas presented in *Orpheus*.

> In terms of theatre as a 'dialogue with an audience' what matters most is of course [. . .] direct 'clashing and discoursing' of the 'content' of the theatre with the 'content' of the audience [. . .]. One of the forms this kind of dialogue could take might be the confronting of the 'content' of the theatre with the 'content' of the author of the drama (a show constructed as a polemic with the dramatic text itself). We should in this process clearly stress that if 'contrasting contents' does not also mean 'contrasting forms', we will cease to be dealing with a phenomenon which is artistic in nature. And one of the most 'aggressive' forms of 'dialogue' with the audience, and especially polemics with the text, could be (among other things of course) the grotesque, ridicule, 'frivolity'. In a certain sense we would in all this be dealing with a 'play', with an acute, philosophizing 'play', which is not fun for fun's sake, but a form of 'setting the self up', 'taking a position' in relation to the world, to objective reality and—at the same time— in relation to one's own life. (Grotowski 2012: 174)

In his thinking about theatre, Grotowski, from the very outset, placed great importance on something that today is usually called performativity—by which we mean seeing the performance as an encounter, an event. According to the theatre-oriented understanding of performativity developed by Erika Fischer-Lichte (see 2008: 24–37), a performance is rooted in the process of constant exchange between performers and audiences. While its aim is not the transfer of some aesthetic image or ideological statements, the effective use of theatrical means as tools opens up the audience to the play initiated by the performance. What is at stake in the play is not pleasure but, rather, a change of perspective and life attitudes.

Bogdan Danowicz defines the essence of *Orpheus*. In summarizing his impressions and reflections on the play, he proposed a formula that Grotowski would soon adopt and transform into an essential part of his work:

> The author of the new script [Grotowski] offered us a sort of new and very short tragicomic mystery-play based on the theme [of *Orpheus*], developing in the direction of theatre buffo. There was some formal logic in the performance, something of an account of probability in a defined human biography, but the sums did not add up. The stage smelled of the grotesque, persiflage, some sort of intellectual and artistic circus. (Danowicz 1959: 7)

The connection Danowicz draws between 'mystery play' and 'theatre buffo' makes its earliest appearance in descriptions of *Orpheus*. These early comments show that between 1959 and 1960, Grotowski resolutely produced a defined program of artistic and intellectual sensibility. The performances that followed in his theatre represent attempts to develop this connection on the stage more precisely.

Critics writing about *Orpheus* tended to see this aspect of the performance without fail, and taking a lead from Flaszen's explications, they wrote about a clear attempt to maintain throughout the show the attitude of an intellectual grotesque with a deeper philosophical background. Critics inferred that this grotesque aspect was understood as a way of developing the performance out of contrasting elements. This was most clearly seen in the tension between the gravitas of the themes being addressed of death, love, the meaning of human life and the 'unserious', parodic, circus-like aesthetic. Critics understood the grotesque rather broadly and did not define the term—even Grotowski himself never did so. And yet, critics pointed out links to versions and variations of grotesque theatre found in history. In this very context critics made mention of *comedia dell'arte*, medieval farces, buffooneries and—in stark contrast—mystery plays. A few critics also made connections between the grotesque presented by 13 Rows and other modern ideas and practices. In this respect, the review by Jerzy Zagórski seems especially valuable and meaningful. Zagórski quickly associates the performance by the Theatre of 13 Rows with, 'which years ago was shown at the Cracow Cricot,[14] and even earlier than that by Meyerhold in Russia' (Zagórski 1960: 4).

Zagórski was unlikely to have been aware of the fact that in 1959 Grotowski had been powerfully influenced by the theatrical practices developed by Vsevolod Meyerhold. Grotowski discovered and studied Meyerhold's theatre during his stay in Moscow and was deeply influenced by it. This influence is visible in Grotowski's use of the grotesque at the end of the 1950s—so close to that which Meyerhold had written about in his famous manifesto, *The Fairground Booth*:

> Without compromise, the grotesque ignores all minor details and creates a totality of life 'in stylized improbability' (to borrow Pushkin's phrase). Stylization impoverishes life to the extent that it reduces empirical abundance to typical unity. The grotesque does not recognize the purely debased or the purely exalted. The grotesque mixes opposites, consciously creating harsh incongruity and relying solely on its own originality.
>
> [...]
>
> The grotesque has its own attitude towards the outward appearance of life. The grotesque deepens life's outward appearance to the point where it ceases to appear merely natural.
>
> Beneath what we see of life there are vast unfathomed depths. In its search for the supernatural, the grotesque synthesizes opposites, creates a picture of the incredible, and invites the spectator to solve the riddle of the inscrutable.

---

14 We are dealing here with the Artists' Theatre Cricot—an avant-garde company active in Kraków between 1933 and 1938, directed by the painter Józef Jarema. It was one the most important Polish avant-garde theatres, and combined inspirations from Dada and Surrealism (mostly Jarema) with those of the Russian constructivists—mainly the performances staged by a sculptor Heryk Wiciński. Its traditions were upheld by Cricot 2 Theatre, where Tadeusz Kantor got his start and then led.

[...]

The basis of the grotesque is the artist's constant desire to switch the spectator from the plane he has just reached to another which is totally unforeseen.

(Meyerhold 2016[1912]: 164–66)

This is a programme that I suspect Grotowski could call his own, and as I will come to argue, he presented it in his own way. This Meyerhold reference seems particularly relevant to *Orpheus*, as well as to Grotowski's later characteristic attempts to immerse theatre-goers in the contemporary and the everyday—even as he desires to 'denaturalize' the quotidian. In the *Orpheus* based on Cocteau's *Orfée*, Grotowski and his actors tried to surprise the audience by shifting from one position on stage to another, using stage-craft to express the 'supernatural', and presenting an experience of a different view of the everyday—stripping it of all marks of the obvious.

In his statements and text from 1959, Grotowski spoke about his strategy of rapid dramaturgical shifts using the phrase 'pulsing of form'. He used this phrase to describe the rapid changes in aesthetics, the sharp contrasts between 'buffo' and 'serio', and the special version of grotesque developed more boldly in subsequent performances by the Theatre of 13 Rows. But it would not just serve as an artistic device—a brand of aesthetics adopted by Grotowski and his company. As in the case of Meyerhold, Grotowski supported this artistic device with a specific sort of philosophical grounding related to thinking about reality as a layered whole in which each unity is an illusion, or else the outcome of a simplifying, pragmatic operation produced by the human mind. Death is a name for—and also the final confirmation of—the unity that Grotowski challenged. He did so by using his theatre to share experiences of changeability and diversity, experiences that were a part of the 'world's dance'.

Dariusz Kosiński

CHAPTER TWO

Alpha, Omega and That Which Is In-Between
Cain after George Gordon Byron

Dramatic Score

The Theatre of 13 Rows' production of *Cain*, based on the drama by
Lord George Gordon Byron, premiered on 30 January 1960. Unlike
Orpheus, we do luckily have access to a copy of a stage script for *Cain*
written by Grotowski. In earlier studies of the Opole *Cain*—limited as
they were—this stage script was not referenced. These studies occurred
before Rena Mirecka found the manuscript in her home and handed it
over to the GIA in 2015. Thanks to Mirecka's donation we can better
understand how Grotowski thought about *Cain*, and also take a closer
look at his dramaturgical process and practices.

Reading the script, one quickly discovers that the general confident
opinion of the critics that Grotowski shortened Byron's text is untrue.
Of the 1,936 verses found in the Polish translation of Byron's drama by
Józef Paszkowski, Grotowski removed around 450—which is more or
less one-quarter of the original. Many of these deletions increased the
dynamics and cohesion of the whole. Others made the text more contemporary, more suitable for an age when older characters onstage no
longer used expansive rhetoric with long and elaborated sentences.
Grotowski also removed expressions he considered anachronistic.
However, some of the phrases retained in verse were meant to stand out
as pompous and false.

40 · DARIUSZ KOSIŃSKI

A large and important part of Grotowski's deletions is the elimination of the opposition between Lucifer and the Angel of the Lord who represents God, a key concept of the performance. In the script, and subsequently in the performance, these figures were substituted for by Alpha and Omega—hence Grotowski's removal of such words as 'God', 'Jehovah', 'Creator', 'Satan', etc. References to traditional religions were also erased and replaced. For example, all references to Jesus Christ were deleted.

More important than these deletions were Grotowski's changes to the structure of Byron's drama: cutting the whole into dozens of scenes, giving them all different titles and also providing instructions about the rhythm and style with which they should be performed. Grotowski maintained a three-act structure related to the three stages of the narrative: (1) Cain's conflict with his family and meeting with Omega; (2) his journey; (3) his return and murder of Abel. In his script, Grotowski made the three-act structure less important by dividing the drama into short scenes, and using them to create a 'pulsation of form' that became a general mechanism for his future stage compositions. He described it clearly for his actors in 'a working note' typed at the beginning of the working script—'pay attention to the pulsation of form (systematic, sharp change of formal convention from scene to scene)' (Grotowski 1960a: 1). This means that at the preliminary stage of the production—the writing of the script—Grotowski was already considering performance dramaturgy and theatrical conventions. In this sense, the *Cain* stage script is analogous to a musical score in which each individual theatrical scene is assigned a title that indicates the tempo in which it should be performed—*allegro, largo, adagio*, etc. Grotowski of course jots down other indicators related to what he calls 'formal convention'. I will return to this phrase in a moment—but for now, suffice it to say that by introducing each scene in his script to his actors, Grotowski included information on the way it was to be performed, and that this became a general practice Grotowski followed in later productions.

With this in mind, one might note that the differences between the sequences are much more stark in the written text. Grotowski indicated additional shifts with powerful graphic signals—the numbering of subsequent scenes, the placement of underlined titles in the middle of the page, the inclusion of technical pointers beneath the titles and an empty space between individual 'scenes'. This dynamic 'pulsation' likely vanished in the performance. No review revealed an awareness of the existence of an interior division into 33 scenes—which most probably means that the differences between scenes were wiped away and did not exist for audiences. Nevertheless, it seems important to examine this structure to see what kind of dramaturgy Grotowski designed on the page before he entered the stage.

According to the script, the Opole *Cain* opened with an 'Introduction' that Grotowski created as a prologue:

> The curtain is drawn. A scream (from behind the curtain—seriously): 'Mystery play!' A scream (from the doors leading to the audience—ironically): 'Mystery play!' Shout (from behind the curtain—questioning): 'Mystery play?' (Abel and Cain calling out). Abel at the door takes up a wild song. He carries through the audience a black ram, the curtain parting once he reaches the stage. Adam, Eve. Abel enters, places the offerings upon the altar.
> (Grotowski 1960a: 1)

This meta-theatrical scene announced and at the same time questioned what was about to happen. As we will see, Grotowski very often introduced similar meta-theatrical games in his performances. However, it is telling that his 'Introduction' was a kind of 'declaration of uncertainty'—the creators of the performance refusing—to some extent—to take up the position of ones who know what they were doing, and thus revealing that they are not certain what kind of performance they had just launched.

The next scene titled 'Ritual' was introduced with information guiding the performance style: 'Alpha's music, Pompous and pathetic declamation of the text'. It featured the prayers of a group of characters, and ended with a sacrifice offered in the name of Alpha by Abel. 'He kills the ram (the animal howls), penitent voices: "Praise to you." Music ends' (2).

The third sequence titled 'Interrogation' was played in naturalistic fashion. Adam interrogated Cain—with some help from Eve. Adam asked his first-born why he was not taking part in the ceremony put on by the rest of the family. According to the script 'Cain answers, standing next to the doors to the auditorium: dialogue through the auditorium' (2). And so, the plan here was to stage a version of the scene that included the audience in the action. At the same time, this sequence introduced a clearly defined distance between Cain and the rest of his family, and exposed the basic conflict of the drama. This theme continued in the next scene 'Pressure through humility' in which Cain's sister, and wife Adah puts strong emotional pressure on Cain to accept the rules of his parents and family. At this point, another shift of theatrical convention took the performance from naturalism to a rhythmic recitation of the text.

Once Cain was left alone, the sequence titled 'Definition' began. Cain completed the scene with a monologue in which he expressed his bitterness and rebellious desires. According to Grotowski's script, Cain 'talks with the audience, walking between the chairs towards the stage' (4). The dramaturg quite clearly blurred the borderlines between stage and audience, and established—for the first time in his theatre—a kind of united theatrical environment. If we wanted to define the initial meaning of this move, we would need to admit that blurring boundaries between stage and audience in *Cain* consisted of a union of doubts and questions. In this context, Grotowski aimed lines composed of tricky questions and uncertain answers directly at the audience.

Scene 6 was marked by the appearance of Omega. The theatrical convention of the scene was defined by the handwritten words added beneath the title of the scene: 'logic, rationalism'. Omega presented himself as 'Alpha's antithesis' and as able to free people from death using the knowledge he could pass on to them. The philosophical and rather heavy-handed dialogue between Omega and Cain was interrupted by a scene added by Grotowski, titled 'Promenade of Philistines'. Its subtitle describes the scene: 'Adam and Eve: couplets, dance, grotesque'. This interlude contrasted in style with the preceding and subsequent scenes.

It depicted the first parents as Philistines, and as representing a vivid answer to the call for rebellion formulated by Omega. Instead of rebels fighting for truth, the audience saw grotesque and jolly parents, the first human beings ever, representing a living resistance against the desire for knowledge.

After the 'Promenade'—in a scene once again titled 'Dialogue', and performed in 'rationalistic' way—Cain asked Omega about his parents' temptation. Omega's answer was derived from the words Byron used in the second act of his drama about sexual desire. This shift indicates a rationalization of 'temptation' and primal sin—both of which, lost their theological aspect and became, above all, biological. This marked the appearance of sexuality and the procreative process associated with it, shown as a 'proliferation of death' and a tool for ruling over human beings. This important theme usually went unnoticed by commentators. From this point of view, the sequences described here give us a very clear message. The end of Scene 6 with its call to rebel, Scene 7's grotesque parade of the first-ever parents and the start of Scene 8 with a tale about the sexual nature of temptation all point to desire as the power that stops us from controlling our own lives, and therefore stops us from becoming truly free. It is desire and reproduction that lead humanity to fall to the level of philistinism. This was the lesson Omega tried to teach Cain.

Another important subject of Omega's pedagogy was also introduced in the same scene—death. Like sexuality, death both intrigued and repelled Cain. Following Byron, Grotowski firmly accentuated the fact that until the killing of Abel, death was unknown to human beings— even if it had been foretold. Omega—as in the case of sexuality—connects death with Alpha. Omega calls Alpha 'destroyer', and concludes that 'he only creates in order to destroy' (11).

Filled with doubt, Cain is ready to surrender to Omega, who promises that if Cain follows him he will discover the secret of his existence. Adah opposes Omega, and the discussion between the two fills the next three sections of the script. As in Byron's version, this debate focuses on love in all its dimensions, and Adah defends love as a good thing regardless of its nature. Grotowski retained Adah's fiery and provocative defence of incest as the highest form of love—which is rejected by Byron's readers, Grotowski's audiences and most cultures. The dispute is related to the human right to love and to freedom, and the chance to achieve happiness. Omega constantly points to Alpha as the cause of divisions—claiming he is a god incapable of loving and possibly even opposed to love itself.

In the end, Cain goes away with Omega and leaves Adah desperately crying the name of her husband, brother and lover. This made it all the more ironic and bitter when the whole act ended with another sequence of the 'Promenade of Philistines' that featured Adam and Eve singing grotesquely joyful couplets. Grotowski accentuated this dissonance in his script by interrupting their performance with 'Alpha's music', which 'rising gradually drowns out Adam and Eve, as they sing voicelessly. Music culminates. Curtain' (23).

The second act of Grotowski's version—much like the second act of Byron's drama—was based on a journey taken by Omega and Cain. But, what for Byron was a journey through hell—clearly inspired by Dante's *The Divine Comedy*—became for Grotowski an expedition into outer space, a sort of sci-fi fantasy based on contemporary conceptions of the 'space race' and the supposedly imminent conquest of the universe. At the very start of the act, Omega announced that he will show Cain 'globes / beyond your own globe', and led his co-traveller through the vastness of a universe where the Earth became only one among billions of worlds, and not the only inhabited planet by any means. This was a key change because it replaced the hierarchical arrangement of traditional religions—which was still the convention in Byron's times—with a modern conception of the universe as an unimaginably vast, limitless array of planets and galaxies.

The first scene of the second act was titled 'Theatre of Silhouettes' and the script calls for it to be performed with a 'rhythmic, quick scansion'. A little later the action moved to the audience. According to Grotowski's script, 'Omega and Cain walk among the audience, conducting an aggressive, predatory dialogue with the spectators. For Omega individual audience members are Cain, for Cain they are Omega' (25). This sequence featured the literal inclusion of viewers into the circle of questions and provocations by Omega as well as Cain's answers. As a result of Omega's provocations, Cain recognized the absurdity of human existence when ruled by desire and procreation—which are both the cause and the consequence of the fall of humankind. This recognition became essential to Cain's attitude and future fate. The strategy of involving spectators in this specific fragment was not accidental. Rather, it was a kind of confrontation with something that those in the auditorium represented by their very presence. They were a living denial of Cain's rebellion and disobedience. So what Grotowski achieved was not to create some kind of unifying experience, but quite the opposite—he wrenched the audience from their culturally defined roles and forced them to experience a sense of duality—to recognize the absurd, and deny it by the very fact of being alive. The actors' attack seems to serve an ambition to strip the audience of their privileged position, and also to open them up to feelings of uncertainty.

The next short sequence was titled 'Discussion' and described as a 'continuation of the previous scene'. Grotowski set the scene 'on the very borderline between the stage and audience' (27). Building on the previous scene's audience interaction, this scene continued as a form of discussion between the two characters while involving the audience. The text of this scene represents another stage of moving away from Earth, strengthening the experience of its evanescence, and at the same time introducing the next stage of the journey, which Omega precedes with a question: 'Do you want to see the human beings of the future?' (28). This point, in the journey from earth, was accompanied by the next argument to convince Cain that life and the world are not governed—as he believes—by harmony and beauty. Omega promises his 'pupil' Cain that they are rather governed by that which, once discovered, will terrify him.

The next sequence was titled 'The Flight'. Its staging instructions read 'darkness, quick rhythmic scansion', which is further elaborated in a handwritten note: 'as if suspended in a void' (29). On the one hand, this reflected a continued distancing from the limited perspective of the Earth. On the other hand, this was a foretelling of that which Omega and Cain were striving towards. Supposedly, this sequence was meant to create a soundscape of a journey through the universe.

46 · DARIUSZ KOSIŃSKI

The fifth scene introduced a change of theatrical convention to naturalism, and at the same time a move away from verse. It was titled 'A Pantomime of Lit Matches'—likely referencing a design concept, and its character and mood were described by Grotowski with the words 'Dialogue—intimacy'. In Byron's version, this was a scene of entering hell—seen as a realm of death ready to consume all of humanity, and not just the damned. Grotowski changed the meaning of the scene. Most prominently, Cain's legacy—which lies in the future for the hero but in the past for the audience was manifested in 'voices recorded on tape, bickering, conflicted'. The text used for this sequence reads as follows:

> *Cogito ergo sum—cogito ergo sum*[1]—man is a thinking reed[2]—
> God is nature—existence determines consciousness[3]—there is
> no God but Allah[4]—it is easier for a camel to pass through the
> eye of a needle[5]—cast down into existence, condemned to free-
> dom—essence precedes existence—existence precedes essence—
> existence in the self and existence for the self[6]—for whom the
> morning sun rises[7]—those who rise early are awarded by them-
> selves[8]—panta rei.[9] (33)

---

1 Latin 'I think therefore I am', a famous thought by René Descartes written for the first time in his *Discourse on Method* (1637).

2 A phrase by French philosopher Blaise Pascal, taken from the 347th paragraph of his *Thoughts* (1670).

3 A shortened version of Karl Marx's idea from his book *A Contribution to the Critique of Political Economy* (1859): 'It is not the consciousness of men that determines their being, but, on the contrary, their social being that determines their consciousness'.

4 The first part of Shahadah, the testimony of the faith in Islam.

5 The first part of the sentences said by Jesus to his disciples: 'it is easier for a camel to pass through the eye of a needle than for a rich man to enter the kingdom of God' (Matthew 19:24).

6 A series of thoughts and phrases describing the main ideas of the philosophy of existence of Jean-Paul Sartre, which was very popular in Europe in the late 1950s.

7 The transformed version of the initial verse of a well-known Polish religious hymn written at the end of eighteenth century by Franciszek Karpiński. The original goes: 'When the morning sun rises / The whole Earth and the sea All that lives sings: / Be praised O Great God!'

8 An altered Polish proverb that originally says, 'Those who rise early are awarded by God.' It is equivalent to the English phrase 'the early bird gets the worm'. The difference in Grotowski's phrasing introduces a crucial difference in meaning.

9 Greek for 'everything flows', a statement by ancient Greek philosopher Heraclitus expressing his idea of eternal change; this phrase was added in handwriting.

This cacophony of voices was a real mess of well-known sentences, both philosophical and religious. While it was meant to create a rather simple aural presentation of antagonized humanity, at this point in the script the cacophony importantly accomplished another 'secularizing' shift. The realm of death to which Omega brings Cain is a realm of human thoughts and beliefs reduced to argumentative gibberish. At the start of the 1960s, there was a widespread conviction that human culture and thought is nothing more than a collection of mutually opposed elements, that it is worthless because it did not save millions of humans from evil and annihilation. In this scene, Grotowski was not contributing anything original to his audiences. Nevertheless, he achieved a vital reinterpretation of the sense of Cain's journey of initiation.

The central point of this journey is found in the next scene titled 'The Extermination of Mars', and subtitled 'A Lecture'. In the course of the journey, Omega explained the cause of the fall of the glorious creatures who existed before humans. In Byron's drama they lived on Earth, while in Grotowski's version sentient beings were based on Mars but also explored Earth, presented the lecture. These creatures were completely wiped out because of an uncontrolled desire, one that also endangers humankind.

Encountering this perspective led to the next scene in which there was another shift of mood and convention. It was titled 'A Mutual Confession' and was to be dominated by 'honesty, sadness, poetic lyricism', 'stability' and 'darkness'. Once again, the audience was to become scene partners with Cain and Omega—but the manner of their involvement was not precisely described in the script. It is however possible to assume that the lack of specific instructions meant that they maintained the previous form of addressing questions and answers directly to the audience. These included questions about the point of being alive and the root of evil—which led to a questioning of faith in the value of life and love, and then to 'Cain's attack' in the very next scene. Here 'vocal dynamism links up with dynamic movement. "Ballet". Physical actions line up with a poetic dynamism' (39). In this scene, Cain asked Omega about the state of 'natural innocence' and suffering caused by thinking. This is a well-known motif that was very popular in the Romantic era. Grotowski gave it a more modern meaning—sharpening it with both a clear tone of ridicule and a total demythologization of 'natural' life. Cain was not so much ripped from some 'blessed natural state', as he was unable to accept it. He declared his love for Adah but wasn't able to live by her side on a daily basis. And so, he seemed to be a man caught in a trap between two impossibilities, two negativities.

Their return to Earth—according to the scene's stage directions—was a 'Theatre of silhouettes'. Beneath the primary stage directions as typed, additional directives such as 'the voices hurry', and further below, 'rhythmic scansion' is added in handwriting. This 'return to earth' sequence summarized the whole 'educational process' to which Omega subjected Cain. We can easily pinpoint elements of secular ethics in Omega's teachings that were close to the views Grotowski held at the time, and are familiar to us from the aforementioned text, 'Theatre and the Man of the Universe'. If we assume that Omega's 'commandments' and Grotowski's diagnosis are similar in key aspects, the third act of *Cain* is a step further, functioning as a way to check how the philosophical proposition can work in practice, what forms its realization might take and what sorts of consequences might follow.

The first scene of the third act occasioned a return to 'grotesque—irony', and the sequence appeared under this title in the Opole script. The instructions concerning the performance style called for 'the application of formal poetic rhythm' and 'clowning' (45). In this way, Grotowski wanted to show the familial idyll enjoyed by Adah and Cain as they bent over their sleeping 'sweet babe' Enoch. This picturesque moment transformed into an argument between Adah and Cain. Rebellious Cain finally rejected the happiness of home, and declared outright that it would be better for every human being to die than to live in suffering and unhappiness.

In this mood, Cain met Abel who had prepared two sacrificial altars, one for himself, and the other for his brother. However, Cain had no intention of making an offering. Another scene begins, this time bluntly titled 'Interrogation'. It is staged in a 'naturalistic convention'. Cain refuses to make a sacrifice, and Abel aggressively questions his brother. Cain wants to avoid a dispute with Abel, and asks to be left alone. However, Abel continues the argument with his brother in the following scene titled 'Pressure without humility'. This short fragment of brotherly dispute maintained the scene's 'naturalistic convention', the scene ending with Abel insisting on a shared sacrifice.

A quick transformation brings us into another scene of the 'grotesque' that calls for a 'rhythmic drumming out of the text'. In this very short sequence Abel intoned a thankful prayer to Alpha. The words he chanted provided a grotesque and pompous contrast with the brutality of the death being inflicted: 'Abel uses a long knife to penetrate the black ram. The animal screams' (54).

Cain answered Abel's prayer and sacrifice in the next scene: 'Rationally. By the means of reason' (56). Cain's response was a declaration and also a manifestation of his otherness. Grotowski shortened and modified Byron's text. Cain's rejoinder was not a declaration of rebellion or independence, but a way to recognize his dependence on an incomprehensible and unclear force. In his monologue, Cain developed a series of questions concerning the power on which he felt dependent, and wondered if killing was a way to secure its support—he reasoned that this force had to be connected with death, not with life.

The answer to Cain's provocative questioning comes in the next scene titled 'Sacrificing', which was scripted to be performed as 'Pathos Motivated by Indignation'. In this scene, Abel's murder is played out as a kind of metaphysical experiment. At the start of this sequence, Abel states that Alpha rejects his brother's offering. Cain accepts this answer and draws the conclusion that Alpha is a force that desires death and destruction. Cain's deadly act emerges from this recognition. Grotowski dramatized this sequence differently from Byron. In the original drama, Abel essentially died by accident while defending the altar as Cain tried to demolish it with a log. Grotowski changed this scene in a meaningful way. Cain says 'Take life to your Alpha / who likes lives', and then the stage direction: 'Cain pierces Abel with a long ritual knife. Abel's scream is identical to that of the previously slaughtered animals' (56). Thus, the act of fratricide became an ambivalent act of ritual slaughter. It was both an expression of rebellion, and of capitulation, because in the end Cain fulfilled the will of Alpha, who Cain saw as a god desiring death and incapable of feeling love.

The verses from the original text that Grotowski deleted were in opposition to this construction—they highlight Cain's despair and lament, and present a dialogue in which Abel forgives his brother. Of these numerous verses from the original, all that remained in Grotowski's version was a six-line fragment of Cain's monologue expressing his surprise at the blood spilled on the grass, and most importantly, the line that ends the scene: 'Death is in the world!' (57).

Grotowski did not let up the tempo and did not tone down the contrasts. Right after the dramatic death scene, he staged another 'Promenade of Philistines' with Adam and Eve performing couplets. They danced and sang, and emphasized the duality of the whole sequence—thereby giving these scenes of terror and despair something of a grotesque cabaret feel.

Perhaps the next two sequences featuring Cain and his family were to be performed in the same tone—but sadly we cannot say this with any certainty, as the manuscript is missing the relevant four pages. The last of these probably included the title and directions for the next scene contained in the surviving script—that of Alpha-Omega's appearance. This scene is the penultimate sequence in the play, and is otherwise mostly preserved in Mirecka's script.

The first part of the final scene of *Cain* is essentially in line with the biblical telling of the story and even takes lines from scripture. 'Where is thy brother Abel?' 'Am I my brother's keeper?' Alpha condemned Cain to exile, and to prolong his suffering, Alpha put a mark upon Cain that was to protect him from the death Cain so desired. The stage directions then tell us that Alpha vanished. Thus began the final scene which was written almost entirely by Grotowski:

ONENESS

(*When Alpha finished his 'judgement' the actors turn towards the audience.* CAIN, ADAH, ADAM, *and* EVE *have* ALPHA-OMEGA's *faces (masks are donned). Even* ABEL's *corpse, even trees, even various objects don* ALPHA-OMEGA *masks. There follows a semi-delirious rhythmic movement by* ADAM *and* EVE. *A sonorous scream is heard—a grotesque lamentation. During the whole scene lights pulsate rhythmically.* CAIN *and* ADAH *act naturalistically. Music ends.*)

ADAH: He vanished. Let's go into the world! I can hear my tiny Enoch crying in our cottage.

CAIN: East of Eden we will turn back. Only the desert is right for me.

Oh Abel! Abel!

ADAH: Peace be upon him!

(*Alpha's and Omega's music overlapping. Darkness.*)

CAIN's VOICE (*shouting over the music, rationally clearly*): And what about me?

(*The curtain is drawn. Alpha-Omega's music turns into jazz. Verging on the ecstatic and elemental.*)

VOICE (*over the music*): Pantomime about the oneness of the world.

(*Music, song. Verging on the ecstatic and elemental. The curtain parts—Cain's decorations invisible, the space empty, a dancer wearing an Alpha-Omega mask pantomime about the oneness of the world.*)

(61–62)

The final scene clearly references Grotowski's formative journey to Soviet Central Asia in 1956, which he undertook mostly for health reasons. At the end of the text, *Mim i świat* [The mime and the world], he recounts his experience on the trip.

> Between the old Turkmenistani town of Ashgabat and the most westerly enclave in the Hindu Kush mountains—a chance meeting with an elderly Afghan by the name of Abdullah who demonstrated to me a family tradition called 'the pantomime of the whole world' [. . .]: 'The pantomime is like a giant world and the giant world is like the pantomime.' I had the sense then that I was listening to my own words being said back to me. Nature—changeable, mobile and yet eternally singular—always seemed in my imagination to appear as a dancing mime—singular and universal—hidden beneath the twinkling of numerous gestures, colours and life's follies. (Grotowski 2012: 117)

The final scene of *Cain* was a staging of this experience—a philosophical image of oneness hidden beneath the changeability of forms as well as conflicts between superficial contradictions.

If we are to look at the 'dramaturgical text' of Grotowski's *Cain* as a whole, it turns out to be—with all its changeability and striving for pulsating forms—coherent and constructed in an entirely traditional way. The three-part composition, with two 'earthly' acts that frame the central cosmic segment, resembles a triptych and at the same time can be seen as analogous to a three-part ritual process of separation, liminality and inclusion in a new order. From this perspective, *Cain* as a script is a story about a human being who trusts and pursues his feelings of disagreement and alienation and goes through a process of initiation. The knowledge he gains as a result makes him a rebel—but his rebellion becomes a tragedy. Cain's rebellion is a tragedy not because Cain murders his own brother but because in the final reckoning he turns out to be a tool. As a tool, his actions serve the will, and confirm the rule of the force against which he rebelled, which turns out to be the same force that supported and taught him. Cain's tragedy is simultaneously a means for the realization of Alpha-Omega's plans and an expression of his disagreement with their dominion.

The final sequence represented the totality of Cain's tragic fate. If the world is unified by Alpha and Omega—and Cain is a part of this unification—then conflicts and disputes turn out to be only superficial misconceptions, the binds from which we should try to free ourselves. The game of opposites, and the pulsation of form present throughout the script, can be seen from this perspective as a 'pantomime of oneness' played out by actors and prepared for audiences, and the final image provides the unique synthesis of a 'mystery play'. Cain's dilemmas are irresolvable within his world, and therefore find resolution on a deeper level in relation to Grotowski's Alpha-Omega structuring of reality in the play.

This sounds like a repetition of the lesson learned in the Theatre of 13 Rows' previous performance, *Orpheus*. Indeed, in a comment published before the premiere of *Cain*, it was announced as a 'continuation of the philosophical discussion begun by the Theatre with Cocteau's *Orphée*' (*Trybuna Opolska* 1960). It would therefore be a specific sort of sequel in terms of ideas—a polemic with the same approaches and conducted with the use of more or less similar tools, albeit with a different text, cultural context and religious background.

It was possible that Grotowski, as dramaturg and director, also started working on the script intending to continue the conversation inaugurated by his staging of *Orpheus*. But during the working process, new elements appeared that thoroughly altered the meaning of the Opole production of *Cain*. The idea of the oneness of the world appeared with greater complexity than before.

A Jester's Mass

Renowned Kraków-based artists Lidia Minticz and Jerzy Skarżyński were responsible for *Cain*'s sets and costumes. But it is hard not to suspect that that the staging concept—or dramaturgy of the space—was Grotowski's doing. Certainly it was he who decided this would be the first attempt to remove the separation between stage and audience. He mentioned a few years later that it was this second performance by his Theatre of 13 Rows, that began his search for a way to get rid of the stage itself (see Grotowski 2012: 226). This does not mean it was completely removed. The photos that document the performance clearly show a low, podium stage similar to the one used in *Orpheus*. It was however present only as a small step in a space that was otherwise not designated solely for the audience, or solely for the actors. The script itself made it clear that some of the sequences of the performance were to take place among the seated audience. The merging of stage and auditorium was also made clear through the placing of some decorative elements along the walls of the room. Archival photos show that to the right of the audience the wall panelling bore different schemes and designs, while on the opposite wall, sheets of thin, apparently grey fabric were hung and draped to resemble fishing nets, or ginormous spider webs. These 'nets' held round and semi-rounded objects—impossible to identify from the photographs. But they had to have more specificity, and therefore meaning for attendees, because critic Andrzej Wróblewski wrote that this wall was 'covered with the material remains of our ancestors' (1960: 23).

A few years later, Eugenio Barba explained this 'extending of the scenography to the audience'—likely basing his explanation on Grotowski's comments, since Barba himself did not see the performance. According to Barba's explanation, the spectators watching *Cain* were treated as 'the descendants of Abel's killer, present though also distant, almost inaccessible' (2014[1965]). This formula means that the audience created a sort of additional dimension to the history of mankind retold and re-performed by the Theatre of 13 Rows. While Omega presented Cain with the past of pre-Adam generations that were annihilated, Cain experienced and represented contemporaneity with the birth of humankind, and the audience was the embodiment of the future—the distant descendants of Adam's firstborn son.

Grotowski himself presented this union between the actors and the audiences from another perspective—one close to the dialectic he discovered and formulated later—that of apotheosis and derision. In his first auto-commentary written in 1962, *A Possibility of a Theatre* (*Możliwość teatru*), he interpreted the space composition employed in *Cain* as an 'ironic paraphrasing of "scene" and "audience" in the Roman Catholic mass'. According to his explanation, it was to be '"a black mass":

stage = sacrificial altar, audience = nave of believers, Actors = "priests-offerers", who talk with the audience, trying to provoke in terms of some "black liturgy"; there is in it a sense of playfulness, almost a cabaret' (Grotowski 2012: 233–34).

Allusions to the Mass were meant to give the play a sacrilegious feel. Grotowski would go on to use this trick numerous times. One such allusion can be found in the most important element of Minticz and Skarżyński's scenography—the triptych built on the central stage, which was a transformation of church architecture.

Its central 'altar' was constructed in the form of a monstrous egg—cut down the middle and emptied of its insides, leaving a recessed niche inside it. A giant metal funnel hung upside down pierced its top, most likely concealing a light source. The bottom of this 'altar' was made of a sort of low box similar to an altar base and in its upper section there were massive tree branches—perhaps an allusion to paradise, its tree of knowledge, good and evil. This central mansion was indeed used as a place of ritual sacrifice—this is where Abel placed the ram. Later the body of Abel will also be placed at the foot of this altar.

On each side of the altar sits two three-dimensional constructions made to look like sculptures of significance. They symbolize the two antagonistic powers ruling the world—Alpha to the audience's left side of the altar, and Omega to the right. The statue symbolizing Alpha was constructed of three egg-shaped masses, one on top of the other—two larger ones and a third, smaller 'egg' slightly flattened between the two others. The lower egg was decorated with an ankh, an Egyptian cross and a symbol of fertility, the shape of which suggests a woman's womb. The upper egg featured the Greek letter alpha and two realistic 'human' legs attached to it—the legs pointed upward and gave the egg the appearance of a female body turned upside down. The central, oblong egg sandwiched between the other two eggs contained a naively kitsch mock-up of a fish—which in the context of the cross could be seen as a travesty of the ancient Christian symbol.

Omega's sculpture was made up of what appears to be the bottom half of a nude, male statue cut off at the waist, its upper half replaced by blocks of various sizes stacked atop one another. These boxy shapes strike a precarious and uncanny balance. The Omega sculpture's angular forms provided sharp contrast opposite the rounded shapes that dominated the Alpha sculpture. The rule of opposition characteristic of the two main forces was thereby resolutely and precisely reflected in the scenography.

This scenography created a backdrop for the first and third act. In the second act, the central altar was covered with a giant, circular map of the universe—stretched and fastened to a larger circular, wooden frame. This may be interpreted as a visual sign of another important opposition—between the mortality affirmed in lethal sacrifice, and the might of a universe that 'does not surrender to death'.

An important aspect of the performance is revealed in the costumes and masks that gave each character an individual look. Never before and never again did the Theatre of 13 Rows use such refined and rich costume designs, and never again would they use so many rich and expressive masks. The masks worn by Eve (Rena Mirecka) and Adam (Antoni Jahołkowski) were the most grotesque in the production, almost offensive, and yet also clearly funny. They were reminiscent of clown masks and make-up. The lower parts of their faces were covered in white paint, and they covered the upper halves with masks that were also white—though Eve's cheeks were reddened with rouge. The masks' eye openings were clearly outlined. Adam's eyes had striped rings around them and flower petals framed Eve's eyes. Eve's face was 'adorned' with a round, potato-shaped nose whose pronounced nostrils gave the appearance of a pig snout. Adam had a long, phallic nose strangely placed perpendicular to his face resembling a huge, phallic nose moustache. Both their heads were covered. Adam wore a tall, soft, yellow-and-black fabric hat with a narrow brim. Eve wore a wig closely fitted to her head that appeared to be made of fake fur. The 'fur' formed a thick, white band around her hairline, and darker, more ruffled hair grew out of the top with some feathers protruding.

Eve and Adam's costumes were a wonderfully grotesque variation on the theme of the first parents' freshly covered-up nakedness. Both wore tight, flesh-coloured tricots theatrically symbolizing their nakedness. Atop their tricots they wore costume elements that toyed with 'paradise' iconography, and the tradition of regulating desire through covering and uncovering the body. One such element of Eve's costume was two small, 'naked' breasts made of papier-mâché and attached to Mirecka's costume. Mirecka and others referenced them numerous times in various gestures throughout the performance. This bust also functioned as a prop separate from Eve's costume. I found film footage of the first of *Cain*'s 'Paradise Dances' in a short fragment from the Polish Film Chronicles (1960). In this footage, the bust was connected to a wire hand—which at its bottom had a huge lengthwise leaf. Eve held the wire hand in her hand. This allowed her to operate the breasts as a *lorgnette* or a fan. The photographs of some later scenes show that Eve's fabricated breasts became an element akin to a caduceus[10] of female sexuality.

The remaining elements of Eve's costume included dark gloves and tights fastened with lacy black garters reminiscent of cabaret. Dark fabric resembling a bustle covered Eve's buttocks. The contrast offered by these elements helped enhance the tricot 'nakedness' of the rest of Eve's body—especially her underbelly—which in some scenes was covered by a comically oversized leaf attached to the costume.

Compared with his wife, Adam was quite thoroughly covered up. He wore a striped top—yellow and black like his hat—that extended only as far as his lower ribs. He wore dark gloves, calf-length, leather boots and striped socks held up by garters. His nether parts were covered completely; his groin and belly were masked with a monstrously grand leaf, and an old tin pan covered his buttocks. It is not clear how the pan was attached to the rest of his costume—it was probably held up by braces concealed beneath his striped top. This particular element of the costume drew audiences' attention to the body parts it covered up, and thus paradoxically helped to highlight what it otherwise served to hide.

---

10 I termed this branch a 'caduceus' because of its shape, reminiscent of a snake wrapped around the mythical stick—the symbol of Hermes.

The ridiculous costumes worn by Adam and Eve featured elements present in their iconographies: for example, their newly discovered awareness of nudity and Eve's ability to play with it. They also clearly referenced traditions of cabaret, circus and even *commedia dell'arte*, and the folk mime farce from which it emerged.

Abel (Stanisław Szreniawski) wore a mask that resembled those worn by his parents, although his costume was quite different. His face looked very much like Eve's and also resembled a clown—with his white half-mask, the rest of his face painted white and his potato-shaped nose. Associations with a clown were strengthened by his straw hat which displayed three dark circles at its front, a pair of two-toned shorts held up by suspenders and his light-coloured top. But most reviewers focused on another association entirely—one suggested by Ludwik Flaszen—namely, that 'Abel is presented as a thick-headed boy, like a kind of member of the Hitler Youth' (Flaszen 2010: 61).

Adah (Barbara Barska) wore a costume featuring elements that connected her to the costumes worn by the other members of the family. Just like Eve and Adam, she wore a flesh-coloured, tightly fitted tricot with additional elements attached. The key addition was a kind of soft, black corset with a long, white gusset that started at her rounded collar, wrapped round her neck and ran down the centre of her torso, widening as it extended between her legs and reached her knees. Several black buttons line the centre of the gusset just below her collar, and three more buttons adorned the portion that covered her genitals. All this gave a geometric appearance to the costume, accentuating the actress's shapely figure, especially in scenes featuring physical movement.[11] Other parts of the costume were reminiscent of birds and contrasted with these geometric elements. Adah's wig, formed from glued-together feathers, was especially avian. The design of the eyes in her mask further accentuated this avian feel, a 'birdness' also enhanced by feathers attached to her waistline covering her buttocks. This costume effectively reflected Adah's complicated

---

11 This can clearly be seen in the photograph showing the actress, taken by Mirosław Kopydłowski (inv. no. 62).

character, characterized by critics as a 'house hen' capable of transforming into two different birds: a predator, as in the fight scenes with Omega over her husband, and a seductive 'bird of the night' in a dialogue with Omega (see below).

Adam and Eve's masks and costumes remained in close stylistic harmony with Enoch's. Enoch was 'dressed in a pink tricot with a bib and a mask with an upwards pointing nose and a dummy, holding a rattle' (Wójtowicz 2004: 38). He had inherited his Grandmother Eve's bulbous nose and her rouged cheeks. His hair was also completely covered with a cap. As a result, he looked more like his grandparents than his parents did. Adam Kurczyna played Enoch. He was a tall, adult male, and therefore all the elements of his costume had to be enlarged, turning him into a comic 'giant babe' relative to other characters.

Kurczyna also played the sacrificial Lamb that appeared at the beginning and end of the performance. The colours and shape of his costume made the Lamb one of the 'family group'. He wore a white shirt with short sleeves, short white trousers and black gloves, just like Adam and Eve. In rather unclear photographs, we can also see something like a fur tail attached to his costume. The Lamb's face was covered with a horned, white half-mask.

Interestingly, Omega (Zygmunt Molik) was also dressed in a basic costume similar to that worn by the first family—a tight-fitting, flesh-coloured costume with dark patches at the knees and sides of the hips, and dark gloves. When Omega found himself next to Adah or Abel, he outwardly resembled them. And much like the others, he stood out thanks to the elements attached to his costume. The most visible distinguishing element was a long, possibly red belt made of shiny material, which in the photos looks like the kind of rubber used for medical or slaughterhouse aprons. It formed a stiff collar beneath his neckline, falling down past his torso, all the way to his feet. Interestingly, at chest level there was an object attached to the belt: a tobacco pipe. Omega's light-toned mask was emblazoned with a thick, black, T-shaped insignia across the forehead and down the nose.

Of all the characters in the play, the one who stands out the most is Cain (Tadeusz Bartkowiak). He was the only character not to wear a mask or a wig, which immediately gave rise to interpretations of his character and his place in the world. For example, Andrzej Wróblewski wrote that the unmasked Cain is 'like a human thought which cannot be hidden' (1960: 23). Instead of a mask, he had an upwards-turned moustache painted onto his face. His costume consisted of a shirt, a blazer and trousers—all of the same light colour. Dark lines were sewn onto the trouser legs, blazer sleeves, across the chest and high up beneath the neckline, giving the impression of a faux uniform akin to those of hotel workers or circus performers. Along with the moustache, these lines made the costume seem less serious while making his body appear more symmetrical. This effect was strengthened by a dark belt that joined the two sides of his grey blazer right across the neckline, running shoulder to shoulder, and forming a T-shape with a black vertical line running down Cain's torso—the same shape found on Omega's mask. Another grotesque element of Cain's costume was a paper heart attached to his blazer's left breast. Red lines painted across the heart mimicked bloodlines. In this way, Cain's romantic emotionality was quite literally externalized as a stereotypical symbol.

This precisely composed visual aspect of the Opole version of *Cain* represented not only a 'theatrical backdrop' and a way to organize the stage space, but above all a collection of interconnected signs that created a performance 'subtext'. The visual elements still basic in *Orpheus* exploded in *Cain*. It's even possible to imagine that one of the most important theatrical elements of Grotowski's experiment undertaken here was the use of visual signs to construct a fundamental layer of meaning not directly conveyed, but communicated through the iconographic allusions and symbolic accoutrements described above.

I point this out because in subsequent performances more frequently discussed in the literature, scholars tend to focus not on scenography but on the architecture of space. Clearly, Grotowski's collaboration with Jerzy Gurawski, starting from *Shakuntala*, focused on the theatrical space and not the set, and on architecture, not visuality. But we should not forget that the 'scenographic subtext' remained equally important, even in the later era of 'poor theatre'. Recalling the values of Grotowski's theatre, it is also useful to take a closer look at its scenographic aspect so clearly visible in *Cain*.

Mystery Play! Mystery Play?

A fragment recorded by the Polish Film Chronicle (1960) shows that the performance began with the line 'Mystery play!'—also included in the script—shouted out in a range of tonalities by actors behind the curtain, within the audience and outside the door of the theatre. Then followed a sacrifice of the Lamb, which presented and resolved a problem in a telling way. According to what Adam Kurczyna told Agnieszka Wójtowicz many years later, 'the Lamb entered the stage via the auditorium, tied to a rope and led by Abel [Stanisław Szreniawski]. I sang this terrible song: "You want a song, you have your song. A bloody sacrifice, a terrible sacrifice." Abel killed me and I was to lie there dead through five acts of poetry' (Wójtowicz 2004: 195).

For the actor this was unsurprisingly hard to bear, and so, Kurczyna asked Grotowski to somehow be removed from the stage.

> Grotowski and Flaszen then started to try to work out how to get out of this bind and came up with a solution in time: 'Ours is the kind of theatre where anything is possible, so you will come off the stage'. After the act of sacrifice a mighty voice sounded off stage: 'Lamb! Let it leave!' And then I stopped being a corpse, majestically heading towards that voice. (Wójtowicz 2004: 195)

In spite of the anecdotal genealogy, this sequence is important enough to make the scene involving the calling of the Lamb off stage a very risky, complex and ridiculous variation on the theme of resurrection. The 'innocent Lamb' rose from the dead on the command of a mighty voice not assigned to any character. If we are to read the first sequence as a kind of prologue, a term favoured by Grotowski, then we have in it a foretelling of the finale which is at the same time a recasting of resurrection and a defeat of death itself *in life*.

After this complicated prologue and its grotesque game, there likely followed the first of three 'Paradise dances', which were cabaret vaudeville couplets belonging to Adam and Eve. In the script they were more meaningfully titled as *Promenades of Philistines*, an appellation that in the final *Cain* script did not appear until much later. The first Paradise dances sequence served as an interlude that interrupted the first conversation between Cain and Omega. In the course of rehearsals, Grotowski presumably changed the order and the scene's function within the actual performance. Here, Adam and Eve—by singing their couplets at the very beginning—continued a type of exposition that clearly introduced the play's version of the first biblical personages to the audience.

In the first scene of Paradise dances, Eve entered the stage riding on the back of Adam, who was moving along on all fours. They both sang a couplet about a seductive snake to the tune of Charlie Chaplin's 'Titine' from *Modern Times*. The proto-parents then declared their sexual and reproductive capabilities. Because humanity was waiting, and the world needed to be peopled, they got 'to work'. In this last commitment, they quoted the refrain of a well-known Stalinist work song from the 1950s which the Opole actors sang to the same tune. Thus Grotowski, Mirecka and Jahołkowski showed Adam and Eve as sexual *stakhanovites*[12] who, thanks to their output, were able to people the entire Earth. This grotesque, cabaret-style presentation of endless copulation as some sort of achievement stripped it of modernist elation and mystery. Copulation here represented the source of physical pleasure and yet a rather ancient carnival tradition. It was connected with the need to produce new human beings and they performed it mindlessly.

---

12 *Stakhanovite* is a Russian term referring to the workers who, in a course of 'socialist competition', took a challenge to work more and produce more than normally required. It comes from the name of Aleksei Grigorievich Stakhanov, a miner who mined 102 tons of coal in less than 6 hours (14 times his quota) on 31 August 1935. A subsequent stakhanovite movement of competitions was supported by the Soviet Communist Party, first in the Soviet Union and later in the countries it controlled during the Cold War, including Poland.

It is likely that after this Paradise dances sequence, Cain made his appearance on stage. Tadeusz Bartkowiak played the scene in a way that displayed both sides of the battle between the actor striving for the 'Big Serious' and the director's attempts to subvert the seriousness and 'honesty' in the character's reactions and emotions. Many years later, the actor himself recalled working on the Cain character as a ceaseless friction between these two tendencies. Bartkowiak was a young and handsome actor with fine stage manners who dreamed of playing heroic roles, while Grotowski was more interested in the grotesque.

> Work on this role gave me a lot of hope. At times I was able to play naturalistically, behave like James Dean's cinematic 'rebel'. But instead I was dressed and made to look like a jester, which is how I behaved during this performance. Grotowski's great strength was his ability to precisely follow an actor and see the changes in him: he enthusiastically received every idea involving comic forms of playing this role, all the way through to jester-like behaviours. (Bartkowiak 2001: 65)

We encounter here a reflection of the director's consistent and very important personality trait. Grotowski was unusually wary of all sorts of aesthetic and ethical 'props', all cultural 'readymade' solutions, and items of cult worship protected by rules governing indecency, religious feelings and so on. He immediately recognized them and mounted attacks to test their value. He did not trust any 'tradition' or 'heritage' that people cherish only because it is considered the duty of a 'cultured person' to do so. He challenged rules and conventions with apparent relish—wilfully ridiculing and provoking, not because he was a nihilist but because he did not want to be one. Critically appraising Cain was not about questioning his position. On the contrary, it was an act of stripping him of all the poetic, 'romantic' and emotional simplifications that Byron and Bartkowiak, each in their own way, used to build into the character of Cain.

According to the script, Cain was to enter through the audience, and it is likely that this was done in the performance. Following a short monologue, Omega appeared suddenly next to Cain. This sudden appearance caused Cain to manifest excessive fear, which can be seen in a fragment of the film I mentioned. Cain jumped up from his bench and took on a pose of abject terror—his arms bent at the elbows in a way that forced his hands to dig into his armpits, and his arms mimicked the wings of a bird about to take flight. Omega declares, 'I am Omega, Alpha's antithesis.' When he utters his own name, he is brightly illuminated from above.

Zygmunt Molik was generally praised for the way he played Omega—with intelligence and cultured verbosity. This allowed his Omega to not be blandly boring, though he did remain 'mean and distant' (Wróblewski 1960: 23). As much as it is possible to say anything about the way the role was played, based on photographs and short film fragments, we can surmise that Molik's Omega was above all alienated and distant.

Notable breaks from this construction of characters were scenes of closeness that verged on intimacy. Grotowski planned the first of these moments to occur in the dialogue between Omega and Adah in the tellingly titled Scene 11: 'Dialogue—Intimacy'. The scene can be viewed in two photographs. The first was printed in the booklet accompanying the performance. It shows Omega seated at the end of the bench, while the rest of the bench is almost completely occupied by Adah's loosely-stretched-out body (GIA inv. no. 56). Adah reclines and rests her head on Omega's lap. Omega slumps over Adah's head with his right forearm across Adah's chest, his right hand on her breast. With his left, Omega holds the tobacco pipe to his lips. The whole image gives the impression of a couple that feels comfortable together, caught in a moment of privacy. Cain provides a stark contrast to the tableaux. He stands aside, erect, uncomfortable and turned slightly away from them, like a boy who does not want to interrupt his parents 'caught' in an intimate act. A surprising kind of understanding between Adah and Omega is even more clearly seen in the next photograph, which shows them in a close-up (inv. no. 64). Adah is still reclining but propped up on her elbows with her neck and head resting against Omega's chest and arm. His right arm snakes

ALPHA, OMEGA AND THAT WHICH IS IN-BETWEEN · **65**

around her neck as in the previous picture, while his other hand grasps her shoulder. Adah's face is turned to the audience with a coquettish delighted half-smile. In his 'pulsating form', Grotowski planned this unconventional duel scene as an intimate coming together—apparent enemies close to understanding each other.

This 'coming together' would be torn asunder in the dispute over Cain that followed, which was played as a tennis match. As we can see from the archived photographs, this tennis match was markedly theatrical (inv. nos 55, 57, 58). Adah and Omega adopted tennis-player stances that were very clearly 'biomechanical', and yet the two conducted the discussion with their faces turned theatrically towards the audience. Flaszen formulated a rather clear position in his comments with respect to these and other sports contests used in the show: 'When the clash of ideas takes place (still alive yet indifferent to our current sensitivities due to its pathos), the staging uses parody to distance itself from the issue by turning the conflict into an almost physical battle: tennis, fencing, wrestling, or boxing' (Flaszen 2010: 61).

Flaszen's words suggest that using sports as a device meant abandoning emotional depths in order to make world views more legible. These world views related to a question that was essential to the show and is captured in a challenge uttered by Omega: 'Choose betwixt Love and Knowledge—since there is / No other choice [. . .]' (Byron 1821: 1.429–30). If Adah in this scene was the embodiment of love in all its complexity and came to its defence, then Omega represented reason and the knowledge it delivers. The tennis match included in the first act was therefore a staging of the basic conflict around which Grotowski constructed the whole performance. Thus, it makes sense for the whole scene to set Cain between the posing opponents, watching the game with interest.

But Adah lost the match. Finally, Cain decided to follow the promise of more knowledge made by Omega and criticized his parents for not learning anything while allowing themselves to be tempted. It was clear that both would set off on a journey. Standing 'on the bench, slowly, step by step they moved their feet on the spot, making a great effort to overcome resistance, Adah bid them farewell by waving a kerchief'

66 · DARIUSZ KOSIŃSKI

(Wójtowicz 2004: 36–37). This moment is presented in one of the photographs published in the performance booklet (inv. no. 53). The whole group facing the same direction to the audience's right creates an aesthetically composed and rhythmic image, almost relief-like in effect. Cain and Omega are walking away. Adah waves goodbye . . .

After the main characters depart, the script makes plans for a second sequence of Paradise dances. Two photographs from the GIA show Adam and Eve in a dynamic pose. Adam is standing, holding up and embracing Eve who dips into his arms, arches her back and kicks her downstage leg up, her knee pointing to the ceiling, and her other leg firmly planted between Adam's (inv. nos 72, 79). This is a well-known cabaret pose suggesting sexual intercourse. In this way, Grotowski composed a frame for the first act, beginning and ending it with scenes of the first-ever human couple engaging in an erotic dance.[13]

In line with the script, Act 2 included the initiatory journey of Cain who, following Omega, seeks the secrets of the universe and the history of creation. Its first stage was the audience. This stage had to be important to the creators of the performance as they published two photographs from the scene in the booklet accompanying the premiere. The first photo shows Omega and Cain talking with audience members sitting closer to the left side of the auditorium—'Alpha's side' (inv. no. 74). Omega leans over a woman audience member sitting on a chair and explains something to her, while Cain tries to explain something to a man sitting in the same row. It is very likely that the photograph does not come from an actual performance, because the remaining seats in the auditorium are empty. The couple in attendance—if my eyes do not deceive me—are Irena and Ludwik Flaszen. The second photo might actually be from the performance itself. It shows a dialogue on the opposite side of the auditorium, 'Omega's side', with Omega standing over four audience members who focus on him as he points towards one of

---

13 According to the information printed on the *Cain* poster and in the booklet, these dances were choreographed by the actors Rena Mirecka and Antoni Jahołkowski.

them. Cain is standing farther upstage, away from the audience and closer to the stage podium (inv. no. 70).

Returning to the podium, Cain and Omega continued their journey in a scene titled 'The Flight'. This scene was perhaps described best by Jan Paweł Gawlik,

> Cain and Omega are marching against a backdrop of an expansive firmament among their own drifting voices, unimportant at this point, broadcast from a speaker and marked by the silent journeying characters—the form takes on the cognitive functions of the content, pushing them towards a distant, inaudible level, creating a wonderful artistic mirror of philosophical values, a wonderful synthesis and also a symbol of as yet an inaudible text. (Gawlik 1960: 9)

Grotowski used rhythm, movement and lighting tricks to create this sense of deadness and unimportance, the experience of which was one of the key elements in the educational process to which Omega subjected Cain.

The journeying Cain and Omega finally reached their destination. In Byron's version, this destination was hell, but for Grotowski, this destination was the paradoxical world of human civilization—as yet unborn for Cain and already devolving for the audience. 'Cain facing the audience took on the theatrical persona of a poet—standing erect, he reached a hand out—pausing a moment in order to sing an operatic line: "Enormous vapours roll Apart—what's this?"' (Byron 1821: 2.198–99). Omega bent in half, in a subservient pose [. . .] whispered: 'Enter' (Wójtowicz 2004: 37). The scene here described by Agnieszka Wójtowicz can be seen in a photograph kept in the GIA (inv. no. 49). The Opole actors performed a kind of parody of Byron's romantic spectacle by imbuing their words and actions with an exaggerated pathos that are odd and out of place on the small stage in Opole.

In fact, upon completing their journey, there was no place to enter. In response to Omega's invitation, Cain sat on a bench beneath an illuminated map of a planet (inv. no. 50). Omega picked up a pointer and began a 'lecture' about the 'annihilation of Mars'. In the performance booklet, beneath a photograph showing this scene, the following caption appears:

CAIN: Why did they fall?

OMEGA: Ask the Destroyer.

CAIN: But how did they fall?

OMEGA: Through mutually widespread destruction. Through the mixing of unchecked atoms.

(*Materiały i dyskusje* 1960, VOL. 5: 7)

It is, however, necessary to note that the records of the actual performance are not aligned with the scene in the script. The film made for the Polish Film Chronicle recorded the words printed in this photograph caption being said in a completely different scene. The film shows Cain and Omega rhythmically swaying with their hands up in the air, and a brightly lit map of 'Mars' in the background—a real theatre of silhouettes, dynamic and oneiric—as far as possible from a conventional lecture. The film seems to be the more trustworthy record, because the photographs' captions could have been moved around and placed beneath photos from different scenes.

Upon learning that humanity is condemned to disaster and destruction, Cain began to resist and tried to defend the value of human life, beauty and love. Alternately, Omega resolutely sought to prove the worthless futility of Cain's attempts. Cain therefore went on the attack and asked about the relationship between Omega and Alpha. 'The conversation then became a sudden argument, culminating in an arm-wrestling match' (Wójtowicz 2004: 38). This scene can be viewed in a performance photograph featuring the two characters arm-wrestling against a backdrop of a large, dark, circular map of galaxies (inv. no. 48). An extension and escalation of the duel between Omega and Cain was a scene in which they fenced with reflectors. In the opinions expressed by fascinated reviewers, this scene seems like a prophetic prefiguration of the 'lightsabre' battles known by all fans of *Star Wars*. 'In the tense dialogue between Omega and Cain there appear lines of light emerging from the characters' hands as if they were long, lit-up swords as they cross them, imperceptibly moving to the rhythm of a duel which synthesises the rhythm of their argument' (Gawlik 1960: 9).

This scene was the culmination of their space journey and of Act 2. The next act began with a radical change of mood. The first scene of Act 3 was a grotesque and audience-pleasing sequence involving a family idyll with Adah, Cain and Enoch. After speaking to Adam Kurczyna, who played the 'babe', Wójtowicz described it thus:

> Enoch lay on a bench in front of the triptych, his head resting on Adah's knees, Cain standing behind her. The audience could hear some quiet snoring—this was Enoch [. . .] sleeping. Adah was humming a lullaby. Cain spent a long time looking dead ahead, silent, placing a finger upon his lips from time to time. This was a sign asking the audience not to disrupt the 'infant's' sleep. 'The introduction of this "lovely babe" played by a two-metre-tall man wearing pink tricot' during the more sentimental sections (Sinko 2006b: 118) caused the audience to roar with laughter, noise which—as Grotowski had planned—would then wake Enoch. He would then rise and stretch, allowing the audience able to see the massive body in all its glory. He towered over both Adah and Cain. Sitting on the bench between his parents he would then lip-sync a song with the words 'there was a snake a cruel snake, my grandpa he would lead astray'. In fact Enoch recited the words of the song loudly, with a strong voice that almost did not change pitch. Adah and Cain shyly took up the tune. They started clapping. (Wójtowicz 2004: 38)

This description of the opening scene is confirmed by a photograph in the GIA (inv. no. 47). Enoch is lying stretched out across the bench, and his head rests on the lap of Adah, who is seated on the left. Cain holds a dynamic pose and stands behind the bench over his wife and son.

This idyll was interrupted by the appearance of Abel and the brothers' quarrel, which then turned into another stylized sporting contest: a boxing match. Thanks to two preserved photos of the scene, it is possible to see just how choreographed and biomechanical their poses were (inv. nos 75–76). The brothers stood far from each other at either end of the long bench—Abel on Alpha's side and Cain on Omega's. From this distance, Abel moved as if to launch his right fist straight at Cain, who moved in such a way as to appear to absorb the blow by turning his body in the appropriate direction.

Next came a scene of fratricide, key to this act and to the performance as a whole.

> Cain pulled out a knife (the same knife with which Abel had killed the Lamb in the first scene). As Abel was saying the words: 'I love Alpha far more / Than life', Cain grabbed him by the neck and plunged the knife into his back, singing operatically: 'Then take thy life unto thy God, / Since he loves lives!' (Byron 1821: 3.315–17). Cain's gestures were exaggerated, clearly played out, rankled with its artificiality . . . and comical.[14] (Wójtowicz 2004: 38)

If the information about the 'operatic' style of performing the sacrificial song is true, then while working on staging the performance, Grotowski changed the 'ritualistic' element of the sacrifice written into the script. In his staging we see a clear theatricality that gives the murder a humorous feel. It is as if during the process of work, Grotowski slowly backed away from a serious treatment of the ritual, and also strengthened meta-theatrical elements. In the performance programme, the photograph of the fratricide scene appears alongside another photo with the caption 'The third Paradise dances', which shows the two proto-parents dancing a lively cancan with their legs stretched out and raised high (*Materiały i dyskusje* 1960, VOL. 5: 15). A similar scene can be seen in another photo preserved at the GIA in which Adam is raising his leg up high—seemingly leading the dance—while Eve seems poised to start dancing (inv. no. 71).

---

14 This description is partly based upon a photograph included in a performance programme, with the caption featuring a line from Cain quoted by Wójtowicz (inv. no. 43).

ALPHA, OMEGA AND THAT WHICH IS IN-BETWEEN · 71

If we are to assume that the couple performed this cancan next to the corpses of Abel and the Lamb, and also next to Cain, who is shocked by his own act,[15] then this scene becomes a far stronger proposition than what is found in the script. A lively dance performed by the proto-parents confirmed that Cain's murder of Abel—intended as a rebellion against Alpha—was in fact a confirmation of Alpha's rule, and therefore a confirmation of that which Adam and Eve worshipped. In this context, Cain turned out to be a truly tragic figure. He tried to escape from the world of his parents, the power of the desires to which they bowed. But in fact, he confirmed the rule of this power and at the same time surrendered to it.

This interpretation is confirmed by the final scene—distinct from the performance's finale—of Cain's drama as staged by Grotowski: the Alpha-Omega triumph revealing Alpha-Omega's unity and dualistic identity. We know the sequence of this scene from photographs and a short film clip. At first, Eve cursed Cain in a sequence that can be seen in the performance programme (*Materiały i dyskusje* 1960, VOL. 5: 17). On the two furthest ends of the stage, we can see Eve to the left (Alpha's side), posing like a showbiz diva who had just finished a triumphant performance, and Adam to the right (Omega's side), with his hands bent awkwardly, seeming to clasp his own neck. Adah is seated closer to Eve, and her face is turned towards the central altar. Cain is seated beside her, closer to Adam, slightly stooped, his hands folded and resting on his knees. Abel's 'corpse' is seen lying between the spouse-sibling couples, while Alpha-Omega stands erect on the main altar. Fragments of this scene were recorded for the Polish Film Chronicle. In these recordings, we find a different composition of the sequence described above. Adam, Eve, Adah and Cain are found in the same places as in the photograph. Abel's corpse can be seen in its place, the Lamb resting on the main altar, and Alpha-Omega sitting on the ground leaning against the bench

---

15 This conditional is due to the fact that in both photos of 'The third Paradise dances' the stage is empty: there is no Cain and no Abel, nor anyone else. One possible explanation for this contradiction is that the photographs were taken during prearranged sessions, a practice long maintained in the Theatre of 13 Rows. Therefore it is possible that the photo was taken without the presence of other actors who were actually on stage for this scene during performances.

between Adah and Abel's corpse. From a seated position, Alpha-Omega says very slowly 'Cain, Cain! Where is your brother Abel?' Adam and Eve accompany the slow speech by singing a wordless liturgical tune. They both stand to the side with arms raised and sway slowly to the rhythm of their singing like trees moving in the wind. Cain firmly and slowly answers Omega: 'Am I my brother's keeper?'

The film confirms that they played the scene in a quasi-ritualistic convention as an 'awaited act'—the aim of Alpha-Omega's actions. This is what Alpha-Omega sought to achieve. Humankind is embodied by Cain and Adah as the second human family and the second set of proto-parents, who, just like Adam and Eve, were themselves marked by sin and cast out 'to the east of Eden'. Performing the scene as a specific sort of liturgy accentuated this aspect of the repetition of the first exile from the Paradise. At the same time, it connected the themes of sin and guilt with cultish consequences involving surrender and obedience. In the finale, the cult was affirmed and strengthened through sin, which the cult itself provoked. Cain turned out not to be a rebel who undermined the system but, rather, an element predicted by it—his rebellion ultimately reintegrated into the whole.[16] The use of liturgical song and biblical phrases accentuated the scene's sense of repetition, a return to the previously well known.

It appears that this return was crowned with a lament sequence recorded in the script and present in the performance, though only marginally perceived by the audience, perhaps because it was very quickly overwhelmed by the music of the finale. And yet, the insightful and sensitive critic Tadeusz Kudliński wrote that what remained 'in the end in the ears' of attendees was 'the despairing and staggering scream of

---

16 To explain it for a contemporary reader, I will allow myself to recall the well-known analogy from pop culture: the same sort of relationship between the rebellion and the system is depicted in *Matrix Reloaded* (2003), the second part of the *Matrix* trilogy directed by the Wachowski brothers. In the film's finale, Neo manages to reach the Architect who created the Matrix only to discover that his rebellion is merely one in a series of exceptions predicted by the system, and its prediction of dissent allowed the Matrix to reactivate itself and ensure its own survival.

Polish peasants: "Olaboga!"[17] uttered by Eve' (1960: 4). Kudliński's note confirms the tragic tone of the 'ritualistic' return to the previously established order of death and exile that once again struck Eve.

The last scene of the performance differed strongly from 'the pantomime of the whole world' planned in the script. The solo ritual dance recalling some ancient practices and images was replaced by a noisy and fierce dance, featuring all the characters wearing Alpha-Omega masks. A fragment recorded in film allows us to see that the dance was really very dynamic. It was performed to boogie-woogie music played on a piano accompanied by hoots and shouts. Even today, the group of bodies wearing close-fitting, flesh-coloured costumes shaking chaotically makes an impression. This is not an image of some sort of unity or oneness but a scene of unbridled passion that is perhaps even reminiscent of—and this seems rather important—the earlier Paradise dances. In a sense, the finale would constitute the fourth of the Paradise dances, which suggests that we should take a certain degree of care when formulating simple, optimistic interpretations of the finale.

The formulation of a kind of closing statement in the finale also suggests that we should take care. This 'invocation' was written by Grotowski and displayed in large format on a panel above the stage during the finale.

> Alpha = Omega = world, you know, hey!
>
> The world is oneness after all, which is danced unendingly, you know, from the elements to the thinking mind, which means from Alpha to Omega. From parties to pain too, you know.
>
> It lasts, and it's rather fun if you don't part from it, you know, so you don't turn your back on it, pardon. And don't believe in ghosts. And giggle at your own pain as it happens, you know, hey!

---

17 This common scream expresses strong feelings of a different kind. It was also used as a form of lament usually heard during folk funerals and in the moments of deep grief. It was probably created by combining and shortening the words 'O dla Boga' meaning 'Oh, for God's sake'.

13 Rows[18]

(Grotowski 2012: 65)

In its style, format and graphic design, this linguistic parody is almost impossible to translate. It references Polish futuristic poetry, and the linguistic jokes played by the avant-garde writer and philosopher Stanisław Ignacy Witkiewicz. The writing is crooked, as if it was written by a child and appears to be in draft form, with corrections, marginalia and small sketches appearing alongside. The document's illustrations include an arrow piercing a heart, a sun, a half-moon, a cat, a flower and a pair of eyeglasses—perhaps those of the director himself?

The final text that appeared in *Cain* was clearly a parody of the final 'invocation' in *Orpheus*, which happened to be a sincere kind of philosophical statement or secular prayer. But the 13 Rows presented *Cain*'s invocation in a light, joyful tone. The contrast between the two paints a picture of the creators of the Theatre of 13 Rows laughing at themselves for having been so serious.

This parody meant a withdrawal—or at least a distancing from the straightforwardly optimistic mood of *Orpheus*. Multiplicity, diversity and the dynamics of opposites within the world played out in *Cain* were not harmonious but, rather, a collection of dissonances. Cain—the rebellious hero of discovery—found himself in a trap in the finale of his own drama. His rebellion turned into a crime and an affirmation of the rule he wanted to escape. All the characters wearing Alpha-Omega masks presented an all-pervasive oneness. They lost their identities in the name of that 'god' of sex, fertility, death and conformity. This emphasized the essential failure of Cain and the human race that emerged from him, the audience among them. The finale's chaos did not propose a liberation from opposites but a surrender to them—a surrender to the world of disorder and desires.

---

18 The original version is written with a lot of spelling mistakes, clearly seen in the signature in which even the name of the company is spelt wrong: '13 Żenduff' instead of '13 Rzędów'.

The Edge of Modern Eschatology

Flaszen attempted to define the philosophical aim of *Cain* from Opole.

> For Byron, human existence is tainted with an absolute condition of 'no-exitness'; there is only a tragic pathos. Grotowski processes this tragic aspect of human life through the filter of derision and self-irony. This seems to be the result of knowing our own relativity and understanding the fact that a human cannot live isolated from the powers of nature and interpersonal relationships. Thus the pathos of absolute pessimism, just like the pathos of absolute optimism, deserves derision. Therefore the form the staging takes is unstable and changeable, moving from seriousness to mockery, from tragedy to the grotesque.
>
> Grotowski's desire is to show spectators their own anxiety, their hunger for answers, their disdain for morality and faith-based solutions. After a while, verses of solemn despair are ridiculed and turned into wailing about the nonsense and 'no-exitness' of existence. (Flaszen 2010: 61)

In *Cain*, there was an attempt to create a certain union of contemporary experience to facilitate a collective self-diagnosis. Or, put more carefully, *Cain* presents a synthetic experience of one's own situation in a world stripped of protective layers. Flaszen's take on this indicates that for the first time—although far from the last—the Theatre of 13 Rows intended to affect the audience not through an idea but by summoning into the theatre that from which the audience hides. That which the audience does not recognize or which they do not want to admit was literally presented and made visible: anxiety, hunger for answers, and disdain for morality and faith-based solutions.

Some critics perceived a deep sadness beneath the farcical, in the gaps and inconsistencies between numerous explosions of the director's ideas, and they extracted worrisome questions from the performance. Zofia Jasińska—the author of one of the most interesting reviews of *Cain*—wrote:

A mask of gross laughter and vulgar ugliness pulled over everything. So that no one would ever come to guess that we have
doubts, that we think, that sometimes we suffer. A characteristic
fact. Eve and Adam's 'Paradise dances', cabaret-style interludes,
even those most parodic [moments] did not raise many laughs
among the audience. Quite the opposite. They became a kind
of dissonance, deepening the sadness blowing in from the stage.
Yes, sadness. Because this galloping range of effects gave the
impression of some sort of inner tension, unease. [. . .] Ending
with Cain's words 'And what about me?' made a lot of sense
and clearly emerged out of the whole show. (Jasińska 1960: 151,
153).

The intellectual meaning of these racing ideas was also perceptively recognized by Jan Paweł Gawlik, until recently the number-one enemy of
the Theatre of 13 Rows. He perceived the 'Value of the Opole staging—
and Grotowski's strength' in the director's

ability to extract questions, gathering them together, conden-
sations and formal layerings, presented in an interesting shape
of the performance which was full of cross jumps and contrasts.
This shape so saturated with endlessly changeable situations
and incessant pulsating of form becomes all the more arbitrary,
until it finally amplifies the intellectual contents of the play,
thereby becoming in some way the philosophy and ethics of
this drama. [. . .] The stage frenzy, a frenzy of form which is
not necessarily rational [. . .], but seemingly total and sensual,
turned out to be stronger than all the discursive intentions and
it was that frenzy which by an almost irrational metamorphosis
showed us in this performance the edge of modern eschatology.
(Gawlik 1960: 9)

In *Cain*, we therefore see a use of theatre as a tool and space for dramatically and aesthetically conducting an experience prepared for all its
participants. Its aim was not—contrary to the audience's and critics'
expectations—to communicate some kind of truth, or a polemic with a

programme, or a way to support an idea using theatrical signs that demanded careful reading. Rather, its aim was to initiate a process lived through 'here and now' by the actors and the audience. This process was essentially philosophical in nature. It led audiences to recognize the illusory partiality of binary oppositions, and guide them towards an experience located beyond and between opposites, hence in some ways beyond aesthetics and ideology.

Gawlik saw in this 'edge of modern eschatology' an elegant and puzzling formula. In order to understand it, we have to enter a realm until now barely touched upon and mostly passed over: the religious and theological context of the performance. Overall, the Opole performance was based on a text that critically reinterpreted one of the most important fragments of the Book of Genesis, a fragment that explains the origins of evil and sin. Byron, in the spirit of romantic rebellion, conducted a defence of Cain and simultaneously, to a certain extent, a defence of Lucifer. Grotowski admitted a few years later that he sharpened Byron's attacks, adding that the basic 'archetypes' he attacked in his *Cain* were 'biblical myths'.

> The 'dialectic of derision and apotheosis' works on two layers here. Firstly, as a perverse and sarcastic theology (atheology? antitheology?) assigning to Lucifer the attributes of wisdom and light while Jehovah is presented as the spirit of darkness; in the end Jehovah and Lucifer turned out to be identical. Byron himself led towards such a reading ('Byronic irony') while also defending Cain and accusing Abel. (Grotowski 2012: 217–18)

One could reduce Grotowski's self-interpretation to a very simple formula: through the dialectic of apotheosis and derision, God was shown as identical to Lucifer. This revelation led to the conclusion that Cain's rebellion against Alpha, in the name of the values he learned from Omega, was pointless and vain. True opposition would need to be more radical—a fight for being absolutely free from the game of desires and the progeny it promises. To be such a radical rebel, Cain would need to rise up against the rule of prolonging life.

What I find interesting is that the reinterpretation of Cain's rebellion suggested by Grotowski was not far afield from those developed by the Gnostics of antiquity, especially so by a radical sect of Canaanites. They considered the biblical Jehovah an evil demiurge, and a demonic creator and lord of the Earth whose rule had to be challenged in order to attain salvation. Thus, everyone who rises up against this force—even if, like Cain, they commit a crime—becomes a holy rebel and is associated with Jesus as seen by Gnostic reinterpretations of the son of God (see Jonas 2001). I recall this not to suggest that Grotowski was a Gnostic but to show that beneath his experiments with conventions, he posed an eschatological question so perceptively noted by Gawlik, a question about the possibility of salvation.

He did not pose this question discursively but, rather, played it out in a dialectically dynamic experience. In this context, what seems particularly important is the 13 Rows' reference to the Catholic Mass and church architecture as templates for a way to organize the space and the whole performance. Grotowski's theatre, generally associated with a stereotypical 'rituality', was modelled on the Mass understood as a composition of symbolic and performative actions and gestures, which in effect represents the experience of 'actualization' known in liturgical theology as *anamnesis*. Liturgical dramaturgy is a process that, to some degree, can be reduced to a regularly renewed experience of being in the eternal here and now. It is not some sort of reconstruction in which, in order to honour an important event, someone puts on a costume representing a hero and mimics the hero's gestures, words and actions. Rather, it is about the actualization of mythical events and hence a real activity that reveals the everlasting and permanent presence of God among and within the faithful.

I have to stress that here I am not talking about an attempt to create some kind of 'other' Mass but about using a defined cultural dramaturgical model that references direct experiences. Just as the aim and the point of the Mass are to rise above natural experience—beyond its time and space—so the aim and sense of a performance utilizing this model are to create a dramatic and theatrical means (a vehicle) of discovery. That which is thus discovered is not any kind of God but an experience that is clearly human even if, as Gawlik suggests, it leans towards some sort of eschatology understood as a way of explaining the deep meaning of human life yet transcending all values and the aims of each individual existence.

Trying, in spite of all, to answer the question of what sort of eschatology is present in *Cain*, we do well to quote Flaszen.

> The issues in Byron's drama deal with religious mutiny, but Grotowski's production treats them on purely secular grounds. God is replaced by a blind and ruthless Alpha, personification of the elements, and the automatism of nature's powers. Instead of Lucifer there is Omega, personification of reason, the anxiety of the human consciousness. Forms of a cult and cultish ethics are brought to the level of the absurd. (Flaszen 2010: 60–61)

Those interested in the work of the Theatre of 13 Rows and the Polish Laboratory Theatre are known to adopt a conditional approach to ritual in performance—that, if it is to be a ritual, then it will be 'secular', and that if salvation is sought, then it is in the secular sense of the word, and so on. To a certain degree, the recurrence of this secular proviso took on a tactical character and aided 13 Rows in their games with representations of Communist authorities' striving towards a 'secularization' of life and culture. But this does not mean that the ideas expressed here should not be taken seriously. Grotowski really wasn't interested in creating a new religion, sect or monastery. He faced such accusations when it was supposed—correctly—that what he was trying to do was challenge the Church. But the core of Grotowski's competition with the Church was not that Grotowski tried to create his own church or brotherhood, but that he had always strived resolutely to help people find their way to salvation outside of any religion. I have been saying for years that this was the aim of his efforts: to build a road leading to the experience of liberation from the rule of death and time, and to the experience of eternity, which tends to be associated with religion but instead is located completely beyond it. Grotowski was searching for precise and practical ways for human beings to achieve a state in which they could feel themselves to be a part of eternal life, live that eternal life consciously here and now, and then live life with the memory of this experience—instead of faith in a promise made by some god.

In his attempts to achieve this secular salvation, Grotowski constantly battled despair, and the mighty forces of desire and death. Many times in his performances, he seemed to lose all hope in confrontations with them. But he always left some kind of a chink, a crack, a scratch . . .

If we take the secular aspect of *Cain* seriously and consider Alpha-Omega to be the embodiment of the forces that rule the human world, then the parodic insufficiency of the finale—especially Cain's closing question and his whole attitude—takes on the character of such a scratch. Though not very large, this chink in the armour of death and desire does eat into the ruthless mechanisms of totalitarian rule that depend upon the unity within supposed opposites. Cain, in some way, surrendered to the mighty forces governing humankind but, at the same time, did not seem to belong fully to their order. In this sense, he remained independent and retained his own place from which he could ask the question 'And what about me?' This question remains secular in its own way because there is no hope for religions to give any other answer than a demand of subservience to their commandments and faith in their promises. It also remains irrational because Cain's process of finding proof did not leave any doubt as to who rules the world. But despite all knowledge about desire and obedience to its rules, the first murderer and prime rebel called to the stage by the Theatre of the 13 Rows remains where he was at the beginning of the performance—still asking the same troubling question without an answer. His question can be seen as the very 'edge of modern eschatology'. From within the scratch, as small and minimal a space as it is, a different sort of tale can develop.

This minimal yet essential space is also—let me add this at the end—theatre. In this space, it was and is still possible to hold the mechanisms of desire and death at arm's length and to ask fundamental questions about ourselves.

Dariusz Kosiński

CHAPTER THREE

Farce-Mystery, or There Can Be No Other Socialism

Mystery-Bouffe after Vladimir Mayakovsky

Editing Mayakovsky

Mystery-Bouffe—an Opole performance based on texts by Vladimir Mayakovsky—premiered on 31 July 1960. It is one of Grotowski's earliest and most important theatrical achievements, a fully conscious and complex artistic statement ably summarizing his theatrical experiences and non-theatrical activities, including political ones. If his following production, *Shakuntala*, was considered by its co-creators and historians to be the opening of a new chapter in Grotowski's research, then *Mystery-Bouffe* should be considered a synthesis of his work up until that point.

In order to grasp this synthesis, we will first delve into Grotowski's script and later into some other materials: the programme booklet printed for the premiere as the next issue of *Materiały i Dyskusje* and photographs from the archive. I will use these to reconstruct the performance, gauging how it differs from the script. But first, let us see what Grotowski did with Mayakovsky.

The only surviving copy of Grotowski's *Mystery-Bouffe* script was prepared for censors at the time and unfortunately is incomplete. Even so, it represents a remarkably valuable source for studying Grotowski's dramaturgical work. The director not only made a range of cuts and crucial changes to Mayakovsky's *Mystery-Bouffe*—as he did with Byron's *Cain*—but he also added to it numerous elements from *The Bathhouse*, another drama by the Soviet futurist and framed the whole with a Prologue and Epilogue. Grotowski created his own script which was far more original and complex than those we have dealt with thus far.

82 · DARIUSZ KOSIŃSKI

Mayakovsky's *Mystery-Bouffe* can be described in brief by its subtitle: 'A Heroic, Epic and Satiric Representation of Our Era' (Mayakovsky 2014). Written between 1918 and 1921, it is a theatrical synthesis of the history of common people called the Unclean. Since the dawn of humanity, the Unclean have been exploited by the rich and powerful. The first act presents the beginning of this exploitation with allusions to the biblical flood. Then the history of humankind is presented in a dynamic, virtuoso shortcut version as a series of conflicts and frauds, with the ones who seized power exploiting the people's anger and hunger for justice. Mayakovsky shows, even if not directly, all revolutions as vain attempts to change—including the Russian Revolution of 1917, which he depicts as unfinished and therefore as yet unsuccessful. In the last three grotesque and poetical acts of his *Mystery-Bouffe*, Mayakovsky leads his Unclean out of history, taking them to other dimensions; first to Hell, then to Heaven—which cannot satisfy them—and finally to the future. In the future, the Unclean finds a Communist paradise with no alienation. The workers find harmony with the Things, tools for production, and no exploitation. Mayakovsky's drama ends with a hymn to human labour and true revolution.

Grotowski took this scenario and followed the demand Mayakovsky stated on the title page of his drama: 'In the future, all persons performing, presenting, reading, or publishing *Mystery-Bouffe* should change the content, making it contemporary, immediate, up-to-the-minute' (Mayakovsky 2014). Of course, in 1960, Grotowski was not in a position to make the play show a dreamy, Communist future. He knew all too well that what Mayakovsky dreamt of in 1921 was not accomplished at all and that his ideal world without exploitation was destroyed by totalitarian rule that cost millions of lives, including that of Mayakovsky. Grotowski's dramaturgical talent was proven here by the way he created his 'up-to-the-minute' version. He neither wrote anything new nor used texts by other authors. He simply inserted fragments of Mayakovsky's *The Bathhouse* (1930) into the frame of *Mystery-Bouffe*. Written shortly before Mayakovsky's suicide, *The Bathhouse* is a fierce satire of the post-revolutionary bureaucracy seizing power in the Soviet Union. Like *Mystery-Bouffe*, *The Bathhouse* ended with the vision of a bright

Communist future. The true revolutionaries fighting for the better life of all people were taken to this future by a time machine that no autocrat was able to enter. Grotowski inserted long fragments of *The Bathhouse* into his *Mystery-Bouffe* to show what 'real Communism'—that he and his audience knew all too well—really looked like. He also changed the basic composition of *Mystery-Bouffe*, adding a Prologue and an Epilogue.

The Opole *Mystery-Bouffe* script opens with a text Grotowski probably penned himself.[1] The sequence is spoken by a Promoter[2] who introduces 'a play not frivolous yet amusing, / where jokes blend with the serious'. He encourages the audience to laugh as much as they want but cautions them to maintain a readiness and an ability 'to consider the truth / which hides beneath the surface' (Grotowski 1960b: 1). After his introduction, the Promoter presents a 'very, very sophisticated' Prologue composed from an old Polish text. It is based on a morality play from the sixteenth century, titled by its discoverer and editor Julian Lewański as *Starzec ze Śmiercią* [The old man with death] (1959), in which a character known as the Old Man, tired of his incapacity and powerlessness, carelessly calls Death to come and claim him. When Death appears, the Old Man uses a trick to prolong his life: he asks if he can finish reciting the Lord's Prayer before Death takes him. Death agrees and the wily elder stops his recitation midway, leaving Death unable to claim his life. Yet, after some time passes, he forgets and recites the prayer all the way to the end. Death appears instantly, triumphantly taking the Old Man away, reminding him that this is what awaits everyone. Grotowski cut a lot of the original text but retained the final sequence of events—Death declaring its power over everyone and everything. Grotowski prefaced the Prologue's finale with a short scene in which the Old Man manifests the dramatic tension between his desire to end his suffering and his fear of dying.

---

1 Here I deal with the script. There were serious discrepancies between the script and the performance, including the order and content of some of the scenes, especially the Prologue and the Epilogue. I will address these discrepancies when I write about the performance.

2 The Polish word for promoter is 'promotor', which includes the word 'motor', literally meaning 'the engine' in Polish. So in the name itself, there was an aspect of the dynamic force that was important for Grotowski. He even played with the name in his script. He spelt it 'Pro-motor', which, when translated from Latin, reads 'someone who inspires movement'.

Following the Prologue, Act 1, 'The Earth or Hell', is identical to the opening of the first act in Mayakovsky's *Mystery-Bouffe*. The ensuing scenes also maintain Mayakovsky's structure of ideas and narrative for the duration of the first act. The material that Grotowski cut from the first act was not substantial and was generally deleted for the sake of economy. Having a small company at his disposal, Grotowski combined several characters from the original play and deleted many secondary characters. He also changed his approach to the historical characters that Mayakovsky used for political satire, instead opting for generic character names. For example, instead of the original character of the French Prime Minister Clemenceau, Grotowski simply introduced a 'Frenchman'.

Grotowski composed Act 1 using two threads, biblical and historical, both taken from Mayakovsky but reinterpreted. The first biblical thread is the story of the Flood sent by Jehovah to destroy humankind.[3] The historical thread is an allegorical summary of three political systems, each created to save humanity from hunger and catastrophe: a monarchy, a bourgeois republic and a dictatorship of the proletariat.

After Act 1, Grotowski introduced a short sequence titled 'Hell Interlude', constructed from fragments of Mayakovsky's Act 3. The interlude presents the arrival of a group of abused and exploited Unclean in Hell. Having tasted the cruelty that humans inflict upon one another on Earth, the Unclean laugh at the punishments that Hell's devils brandish. Undeterred, the Unclean proceed to demolish the kingdom of Satan.

What follows is Act 2, titled 'Earth or Purgatory'. Grotowski based this sequence on fragments from the second and third acts of *The Bathhouse*. The very first scene, taken from Mayakovsky's second act, presented the rule of a Communist bureaucrat named Optimistenko, who scorned the Unclean petitioners who relied on him for necessary and important signatures and approvals. Grotowski gave the petitioners the same name Mayakovsky used for all exploited people in *Mystery-Bouffe*: the Unclean. In so doing, he clearly suggested that in 'the peoples'

---

3 It is worth noting that the Flood that opens *Mystery-Bouffe* follows Cain's murder of Abel as the next major, well-known biblical story. Thus Grotowski's choice to follow the biblical thread in Mayakovsky's drama can be seen as a continuation of *Cain*, in a way its sequel.

democracy' the old hierarchical systems of rule and exploitation remained. This presentation of bureaucratic rule was developed and magnified by combining the two bureaucrats from Mayakovsky's drama, Optimistenko and Pobiedonosikov, into one named Optimistenko. By bringing two roles into one, Grotowski created a kind of super autocrat, embodying all the sins and crimes of 'real Communism' that his audience knew very well from everyday experience. This combination worked especially well in the final scene of Grotowski's Act 2 which featured fragments from Act 3 of *The Bathhouse*—the scene in the theatre. The dramaturg retained this scene almost in its entirety. This resulted in a satirical and meta-theatrical sequence in which the dull bureaucrat Optimistenko represented all opponents of engaged and experimental theatre.

Thus, the second act of Grotowski's *Mystery-Bouffe* was biting, remarkably amusing and also a theatrically striking sequence. It presented a grotesque, risqué and wickedly accurate image of the post-revolutionary world. Seen from a larger perspective, this sequence could have been interpreted as a commentary on the Polish Communist reality: the revolution took place but it did not change the mechanisms of exploitation.

Act 2 was followed by 'Paradise Interlude'. In this sequence, when the Unclean raid what appears to be a Christian Paradise, the Christian saints welcome them. 'Paradise Interlude' presented a shortened and modified version of Act 3 of Mayakovsky's *Mystery-Bouffe*. Among the scenes that Grotowski shortened were the saints' preparations for the arrival of the Unclean. In this version, the Unclean encroached upon Paradise, singing the most rebellious, indeed blasphemous, song:

We ourselves are Christ and Saviour!
We ourselves are Christ
We ourselves are Saviour
(Grotowski 1960b: 49)[4]

---

4 In Mayakovsky's drama, the Unclean sing: 'Make your rifles shout! / Make your cannons roar! / We ourselves are Christ and Saviour!' (Mayakovsky 2014). Grotowski takes only the last verse, making the entire three-verse rebel song of it.

As was to be expected, heavenly pleasures did not delight the rebels and the interlude ends with them destroying Paradise.

Act 3, mostly made up of fragments of Acts 5 and 6 of *The Bathhouse*, followed the interlude. It is important to note the manner in which Grotowski used these fragments to construct his third act. He did not take entire scenes from the play as before; instead, he composed the third act using elements taken from various *Bathhouse* sequences. And yet he retained the original's narrative thread of a Time Machine journey undertaken by a chosen few into the bright future promised by Communism. The Phosphorescent Woman, who in Mayakovsky's *Bathhouse* travelled from the future to retrieve the elect from the present, was replaced by the Promoter.

As with Pobiedonosikov in the original drama, Grotowski's Optimistenko and his comrades also tried to enter the Time Machine but were thrown out of it. Stage directions in the script have Optimistenko and his cronies, denied access to the future, leaving the performance space via the audience—thus remaining in the 'real' life outside the theatre.

Unfortunately, the surviving *Mystery-Bouffe* script does not tell us how the script ends. Page 58 and all pages after 60 are missing. The final surviving pages, 59–60, contain fragments from Act 6 of Mayakovsky's drama. It was set in a Communist 'Promised Land' where the Unclean make peace with Things, the means of production from which they are no longer alienated. In Mayakovsky's play, after this scene, the Unclean and the Things tried to start life anew without owners and possessors, and the play concluded with the 'Internationale', the triumphant hymn of international Communism. It is hard to believe that in 1960 Grotowski would finish his script with the song that became the official hymn of the Stalinist authoritarian regime. It was certainly not in his performance. If Grotowski's *Mystery-Bouffe* was intended to reveal some non-faith-based vision of a grand future, it was almost certainly deleted.

The Dynamics of Metamorphosis

In the *Materiały i Dyskusje* issue published on the occasion of the *Mystery-Bouffe* premiere (1960, VOL. 4: 1), one can find a humorous attribution: 'STAGE DESIGN: Hieronymus Bosch in association with Wincenty Maszkowski'. The note is not precise because Maszkowski also created some elements of the stage design that had little to do with Bosch. The majority of the scenes were performed against the naked theatre walls and simple, wooden planks that covered up two windows. These panels were constructed so as to leave rather wide gaps and allow light to seep through the window behind them. The planks and the light rays coming through their gaps and cracks were not taken from Bosch; they are more in the spirit of abstractionism and are expressionist in style. They are clearly visible in photographs; there can be no doubt that they were used for a purpose. This choice indicates that it was for the first time—though not the last—that the Theatre of 13 Rows offered itself stripped bare to audiences. Couldn't Bosch, in collaboration with Maszkowski, paint fantastic canvases to cover the bare walls? Surely he could, but evidently the director did not ask him to do so.

In some scenes, the 13 Rows did hide their naked theatre walls and covered windows according to a Bosch design with a curtain that Maszkowski painted. This was essentially a screen that most likely slid across the stage cutting the shallow platform in such a way that when in place, all it left was a narrow strip of proscenium on which only a small number of actors could perform. This was used as a backdrop for the Prologue and the Epilogue and for the scenes in which Optimistenko was thrown out of the Time Machine with Belvedonsky and the Lady. It has long gone unnoticed that Maszkowski painted on the curtain his own version of Bosch's famous *Ship of Fools* (*c*.1490–1500), which is on display at the Louvre. In fact, it is hard to think of a more apt and less accidental choice. This painting was supposedly inspired by a popular poem by Sebastian Brant about fools sailing to Narragon, a fool's paradise. This is an ironic and remarkably accurate commentary on the journey of the 'Unclean, or Simpletons' to their 'Paradise'.[5] It is also worth noting

---

5 'The Unclean, or Simpletons' is what Grotowski called the Unclean in the list of characters at the beginning of the booklet created for the premiere.

88 · DARIUSZ KOSIŃSKI

that the title 'fools' given to those on the ship is not solely pejorative. It belongs to a carnivalesque and utopian tradition that in a grotesque way—and therefore in the way of Grotowski—expressed the desire felt by people deprived of all rights to find a different world and a different life. The Unclean are fools but only in the sense of the famous words of Saint Paul: fools in the eyes of the world (2 Corinthians 11:16–33). In fact it is they—crazed by the desire to stand up to the world as it is—who have a chance to change it.

Bosch also 'painted' another key element of the stage design: a panel that served as part of the Time Machine which was built using a wooden ladder, representing a simple and humble version of a space rocket. The panel stood vertically on the stage floor supported by the ladder and featured a very well-known fragment of 'Musicians' Hell', one of the Bosch paintings that make up the triptych *The Garden of Earthly Delights* (*c*.1490–1510), at present in Madrid's Prado. On this panel, Maszkowski combined a monstrous musical instrument, a primitive apartment akin to a cave, and a pale-faced man in a hat that is widely acknowledged to be Bosch's self-portrait. This painted collage referencing Bosch thereby gives the Time Machine a dual meaning. What in Mayakovsky's drama was a vehicle to a future paradise bore infernal associations in Grotowski's performance.

Another element created by Maszkowski in the style of Bosch was a series of boards on which he painted the characters' names that the corresponding actors used during the performance. The boards were painted with whole patches of colour. Each actor's board featured an outline of each character's figure and their name. The panels served as a simple tool to inform the audience about who was on stage in front of them. Some of these 'shields'—as Flaszen called them—were almost oval in shape and their dimensions large enough to allow actors to hide their upper bodies behind them, thus giving the impression of the boards moving about the stage atop actors' legs. Other panels were taller and covered the actors almost completely. Both types had openings cut into them that allowed actors to easily hold them. They also used panels as set pieces. To decorate walls, they were rested against them or left leaning against the bench. It is hard to interpret the precise meaning they had in such cases. Looking at photographs of the production, one sometimes has an impression that the panels serve as simple decoration, while at other times it seems the figures painted on them are 'witnessing' the scene.

Jerzy Falkowski, fascinated by the multifunctional dynamism of the shields' metamorphosis, wrote:

> Six actors play all the roles. [...] They present new characters by swapping shields with the required Boschesque painting and script. [...] The shields—used to represent the characters—need just to be turned around and held appropriately in order for it to be used in place of a machine gun or a painter's palette. If the passage of time is to be suggested—a night gone by—the method of showing this was a minute of a rhythmic floating of the shields above prostrate actors ... (2006[1960]: 130)

So the shields were used as conventional markers to signal the change of time, for example. They were also used as a clever way of getting out of the serious bind Grotowski faced in terms of casting. Even after deleting and combining characters, there still remained far too many roles for the tiny Opole company. The 13 Rows turned this limitation into a unique artistic proposal. Flaszen wrote that 'the actors speak on behalf of characters depicted on painted boards; these "shields" function as puppets in a Nativity play, at the same time illustrating one of the key ideas of modern acting—that the actor does not impersonate the character but performs "beside" the role—introduced in a provocatively literal way' (2010: 64).[6]

To this extent, the shields constituted a very simple element that opened up numerous possibilities and at the same time intelligently resisted theatrical classifications. What is the proper term for these

---

6 This comment is just the one of many signs and traces of the relation between the theatre of Bertolt Brecht and Grotowski's research. Some of them will be explored later in this book. There is no doubt that to Grotowski Brecht was an important and inspirational figure. The deep and precise study of the relation between Grotowski and Brecht by Zbigniew Osiński is unfortunately accessible only in Polish (Osiński 2009: 159–85).

objects? Were they props? Masks? Costumes? Set pieces? Maybe each shield was a kind of puppet or animated object? In fact, they seemed to be all those things at once.

The costumes accompanying the shields were a carnivalesque combination of circus tricots and clothing for practising gymnastics or biomechanics. All actors wore shiny shirts with long, short or no sleeves and shorts of the same sheen as their shirts. Optimistenko (Molik) and Belvedonsky (Kurczyna) had sleeveless shirts and they wore gloves that extended up to their elbows—Belvedonsky's black and Optimistenko's gold. Rena Mirecka was the only female member of the cast. She played the Dame among other characters and wore a one-piece, sleeveless bodice with the same sort of black gloves as Belvedonsky and very short shorts which almost completely bared her legs. The back of her outfit included a shiny, possibly gold, train which widened generously as it reached the floor. Optimistenko and Belvedonsky wore similar trains. They also wore sashes tied across their waists and in certain scenes, the sashes' ends dangled between their legs. The tricots were colourful and non-uniform and featured contrasting stripes or rhombuses made of shiny fabric sewed to their costumes. These thoroughly deliberated costumes, at times, brought about a very much humorous tone. This was especially true in the case of Optimistenko, who had a golden sun sewn on the back of his dark shorts that was very much visible when he did headstands with his back to the audience. Much like their shields, these costumes were tools with which the actors played.

Another series of elements important for the performance were simple props: the black bench familiar from *Cain*, a pickling barrel and a tin bath which 'depending on the way it was set up—could serve as an ark, a desk, a table in a theatrical foyer, [and] also a part of a complex time machine' (Falkowski 2006[1960]: 130).

All these metamorphoses involving objects would not of course be possible without a special approach to acting, something reviewers commented upon and complimented, even as they struggled to find some traditions that could help them articulate this odd approach. Janina Zdanowicz wrote that the acting is something completely different than that which we are used to seeing, but which we have also heard about when faced with avant-garde theories of the 1920s (such as FEKS).[7] The actor-acrobat operating a range of gestures "presenting" or "symbolizing" emotions or situations is a counterpoint to the so-called embodiment of a role. (Zdanowicz 1960: 10)

While rather laconic, this formula seems to me to be quite helpful for understanding the aesthetics of Grotowski's *Mystery-Bouffe*. This squarely places the performance in line with the Russian avant-garde that emerged in part from Meyerhold's experiments on the 'actor-acrobat' who 'operates' and does not only embody. In creating his philosophical theatre, Grotowski, like Brecht, did not want to 'cast spells' upon his audiences and yet, unlike Brecht, Grotowski did not want to lead them towards critical thinking per se. He rather strove to create a shared experience of a certain process with philosophical meaning, related not to some sort of 'life experience' or personal drama, but rather to a general attitude towards life. Through the very way in which they performed, Grotowski's actor-operators attempted to facilitate the experience of that which in *Orpheus* Grotowski called 'the dance of the world'. In *Mystery-Bouffe*, this 'dance'—understood as physical action subjected to intense rhythms—became the 13 Rows' basic rule for performing. The actors' performing style was based on the physical actions composed in a kind of choreography of gestures and movements involving props and their 'shields'. It was dynamic and far afield from the emotional 'experiencing', typical of the theatre at the time. It can instead be seen as a continuation

---

7 FEKS—abbreviation of Russian Fabrika Ekstsentricheskovo Aktiora (Factory of an Eccentric Actor)—an avant-garde group of Russian artists promoting so-called 'eccentrism'. FEKS was founded in Petrograd in 1922. Making use of various techniques, including vaudeville, *variété*, cabaret and slapstick, eccentrism postulated theatre which radically departed from life experience and strove for 'estrangement' (Rus. *ostranyeniye*)—which it achieved by shocking audiences with a range of tricks. According to Katarzyna Osińska, 'eccentrism meant ripping things, phenomena and human behaviors out of accepted contexts, showing them in a fresh light and connecting them to new rules. The aim of these practices was to constantly surprise the audience, challenging their perceptual habits' (2009: 166).

of the avant-garde theatre of the early twentieth century—especially Soviet constructivism, in which Mayakovsky played an important role.

It must be stressed that the 'dynamics of metamorphoses', which were the essence of *Mystery-Bouffe*, were not—as in the later performances from the period of the 'poor theatre'—a means of expression or a way to focus attention on the acting process. Rather, these 'dynamics of metamorphoses' constituted a theme in and of themselves, one more layer of meaning in the whole composition. Of course, we can interpret them in the context of the evolution of acting technique in Grotowski's theatre, but I would rather focus on how these dynamics had a different, important part to play, related to the experiences and the interests of the creator of *Mystery-Bouffe and* the preceding performances described above.

Images from a Journey into the Unknown

Jerzy Falkowski described *Mystery-Bouffe* as a 'whirling kaleidoscope of actors' incarnations' (2016[1960]: 130). In his review, he delights at the dynamic nature of this whirling. In order to stop audiences' heads from spinning and to help them grasp what it was they were seeing, the *Mystery-Bouffe* performance programme included the following 'mini-guide':

'MYSTERY-BOUFFE'
in 3 parts
after VLADIMIR MAYAKOVSKY
theatre script and direction by JERZY GROTOWSKI
CHARACTERS IN THE MYSTERY-PLAY:
Characters in part one:
a) in the Prologue: Promoter.
b) on Earth or Hell: Eskimo, Fisherman, Frenchman, Pole, German, Negus [African], Lady, the Unclean or Simpletons, Merchant, Priest, Promoter.
Characters in part two:
a) in the Interlude or in the Hell of the Faithful: Devils, Beelzebub, the Unclean or Simpletons.

b) on Earth or in Purgatory: Optimistenko, Lady, the Unclean or Simpletons, Nochkin, Belvedonsky, Director, the Ballet Master of the Grand Theatre.

Characters in part three:

a) in the Interlude or Heaven of the Faithful: Angels, St Peter, the Unclean or Simpletons.

b) on Earth or Paradise: Promoter on the Time Machine, the Unclean or Simpletons, Optimistenko, Lady, Belvedonsky, Things, or the Means of Production.

c) in the Epilogue: Old Man, Death.

(*Materiały i Dyskusje* 1960, VOL. 4: 1)

It is enough to look at the first item on the list to see how much, from the very outset, the performance differed from the script. In the list of characters in the performance programme's Prologue, there is only mention of the Promoter, while the Old Man and Death—who also made an appearance in the Prologue—appear on the script for the first time in the Epilogue. It seems that in the performance, Grotowski moved the old dialogue *Starzec ze Śmiercią* [The old man with death] to the end and in the Prologue, the Promoter made his announcement in a faux medieval style that exemplified the meta-theatrical convention so typical of Grotowski's work.

We can get a good sense of the appearance of ensuing scenes from the photographs. The first of these is captioned 'The ARK' (*Materiały i Dyskusje* 1960, VOL. 4: 2).[8] The titular vessel is constructed from props and the actors' bodies and set in the middle of the stage. The tin washtub Falkowski described as a multi-purpose prop and set piece served as its base. Tadeusz Bartkowiak—playing the role of one of the Unclean—sits on the black bench on the audience's right-hand side of the ark with his legs inside the tin tub. He holds his hands behind his head, so that his arms form triangular shapes on either side of his head. His body leans to the right and suggests a swaying motion, a rhythmic movement. On

---

8 This photograph taken by Leonard Olejnik is also preserved in the GIA (inv. nos 182–83). A very similar scene—which differs only in the body posture of Tadeusz Bartkowiak—is documented in other photos from the same collection (inv. nos 179–81).

the other side of the bench, there is a barrel upon which Rena Mirecka is perched—here probably performing another Unclean—bending her knees slightly and evidently making flowing gestures with her hands. Together they create a simple, human-object construction of a two-mast ship. The way they assemble the set design with bodies and simple props, recalls a play for children, in a way.

Other photographs from the *Materiały i Dyskusje* relate to Act 1 and show 'The Fall of Negus' (1960, VOL. 4: 4). The photograph shows a group of actors whose bodies are completely hidden behind the painted boards; we can only see their legs and hands sticking out through openings in their 'shields'. From the names painted across their panels, we know who these six characters are, from left to right: the Merchant, the Frenchman, the Dame, the Priest, Negus and the German. Negus is pictured at the front of the stage, on the edge of the podium, while the others are 'kicking him out' with their legs, the equivalent of throwing him overboard in Mayakovsky's drama.

The third photo published in *Materiały i Dyskusje* includes the puzzling caption, 'The Unclean, or the Simpletons. The Devil (Angel) and Beelzebub (St Peter)' (1960, VOL. 4: 6). The caption is puzzling because of the double meaning and multiple identities assigned to characters, who in different scenes appear according to these attributes in turn. The photograph shows Bartkowiak, Molik and Jahołkowski standing with their legs splayed. Each actor holds a posture that expresses determination—hands on hips and heads turned to the audience's left, looking at Rena Mirecka. With her hands together in prayer, her left leg bent at the knee and her foot resting against her inner thigh, Mirecka's stance is associated with angelic iconography. On the opposite side of the central three, Adam Kurczyna crouches, his hands resting on his thighs, one leg resting on the stage podium and the other lowered and resting on the auditorium floor. He is looking up from his low position at what is taking place centre-stage. If the photograph's caption placed the Angel on one side and the Devil on the other, then the matter would be simple. But this is not so. We know from the script and the information contained in the programme that there were two separate interludes and that the

Devil and Beelzebub took part in the Hell interlude, while the Angel and St Peter appeared in the Paradise interlude. It seems unlikely that the photograph shows two scenes on stage at the same time in the actual performance. The most straightforward solution is that, having so little space in the programme booklet, its creators included only one photograph, using the caption to inform readers that the actors they saw performed heavenly characters in one interlude while in the other they played devilish figures. Interpreted this way, the caption—and also the photograph itself—corroborates the information we read in the list of characters, which mentions 'angels and devils' in the plural. Meanwhile it seems that there was the one protagonist—Beelzebub/St Peter, most likely played by Kurczyna—as well as a one-person 'choir' played by Mirecka as Devil/Angel. The photo also supports the notion that both interludes were performed in the same fashion with the same triptych arrangement, the Unclean in the centre and representatives of Hell and Heaven on either side. If this is the case, then the performance would have been reinforced by the spatial composition hinting at the resemblance between Hell and Heaven suggested in the script itself.

The interlude visible in the photograph takes place in front of a drawn curtain. This decision allowed the preparation of the stage for the next sequence behind the curtain. It also allowed a very simple presentation of the final demolition of hell and heaven, signalled simply by the curtain opening.

The next photograph shows the sequence from *Earth, or Purgatory* that Grotowski constructed from *Bathhouse* scenes. This sequence is the most well documented with photographs. The first photo presents Optimistenko in his office using the Dame (Mirecka) as a telephone (inv. nos 176–78). The photograph caption reads, 'The Dame (as a telephone), Optimistenko, Noczkin' (1960, 4: 9). Mirecka sits stiffly on a bench positioned at an angle on the left side of the stage. She extends her left arm forward and bends it at the elbow, making a hard-right angle, her forearm pointing straight up. Optimistenko (Molik) holds her other hand like a handset to his ear and at the same time, leans over her in a dynamic pose while dialling a phone number on her stomach.

To the right of the bench, there is a desk fashioned from the tin tub set atop the pickle barrel. Noczkin (Antoni Jahołkowski) is standing in front of the desk.

The caption under the next photograph reads, 'The Dame (as a typewriter), Optimistenko (dictating)' (1960, 4: 11). The photograph shows the Dame in the same spot, this time with her right leg crossed over her left (inv. no. 184). Her right shin formed a horizontal line across her body and her right ankle rested on her left knee. Her legs serve as an invisible typewriter upon which the Dame—here a secretary—types out with wide-spread fingers a text dictated by Optimistenko. Optimistenko dictates to the Dame while standing on his head in the centre of the stage, his back facing the audience, the sun design on his buttocks on full display.

Thanks to a comment by Jerzy Falkowski's we are able to better understand Optimistenko's action here and in other scenes too: 'Citizen Optimistenko performs a handstand. Very much literally and acrobatically. He does so any time he expresses all his authoritarian opinions, dictating moronic trifles added to his lecture. Optimistenko [. . .] symbolizes [. . .] a Philistine repainted red and adorned with honorary titles' (2016[1960]: 130–31). Falkowski showed remarkable insight and courage, perceiving and reporting something that the creators of the performance seemingly wanted to conceal. He points to political allusions not overtly present in the text—which was censored after all—but that nevertheless came through in the performance, which was of course 'experimental' and 'extravagant' but also not that hard to read into. A Communist apparatchik standing on his head was an embodiment of the absurd aspect of a system that was turning the world upside down.

The final photograph from the third office sequence is mysterious (inv. nos 166–67). The caption reads: 'The Dame, Optimistenko and Belvedonsky—as monuments. An Unclean or Simpleton is laying there fainted' (1960, 4: 13). It shows the Dame, Optimistenko and Belvedonsky (Kurczyna) in poses resembling those of classic sculptures. All three stand with legs slightly bent and their torsos leaning slightly forward. Their arms are arranged in 'graceful' gestures—their right arms bent towards their chests, their left arms gently elevated and slightly bent at the elbows. All of them hold their hands turned slightly to the left. Their expressions display charmed melancholy, their eyes turned upward. The Dame and Belvedonsky are standing on the stage, while between them, Optimistenko is elevated, standing on the overturned tin tub atop the pickle barrel. Laying in the foreground in front of the scene's three central characters is an Unclean (Antoni Jahołkowski) on his back with his arms and hands spread wide. He apparently fainted and was just left where he fell.

The order of the scenes presented in the photographs differs from the order found in the script. According to the script, the dictation scene comes first, followed by the telephone conversation in Noczkin's presence. In the script, there is no scene involving the 'graceful' poses struck by the Dame and Belvedonsky. The only likely explanation is that Grotowski cut the earlier scene with Nochkin and created a series of scenes showing Optimistenko's and his court's bureaucratic stupidity. Then the inventor rushed into the office, only to learn that he has been refused permission to build a spaceship. Upon hearing the news, he fainted. Then the three characters, representing the new ruling power, constructed a sylphic triptych introducing the next scene. The Director's appearance at this point—and the removal of the fainted man—allowed a smooth transition to the next scene.

The second sequence in Act 2—Purgatory—features the character of the Director (Andrzej Bielski). The programme includes only one photograph of a scene including him. Its caption: 'Optimistenko (a speech about formalism), the Dame ('the play should reflect . . . a beautiful life'), the Director ('promises to change the staging')' (1960, 4: 15). The photograph shows the trio of actors (inv. nos 173–74), with Optimistenko leaning over and placing his hands inside the tub that serves as a desktop. He seems to be drumming on it, aroused by his own speech. The Director is downstage, on the audience's right side of the stage, opposite the side of the stage from which the photo was taken. A shield resting against the stage podium with his character's name on it reveals his identity. His whole body and gestures express humility. He bends his legs at the knees, his thin little legs splayed slightly to the sides. He is bent double at the waist, his head is bowed and his chin is raised slightly in order to look at the principals. His arms are bent, his elbows drawn towards his torso and his hands limp, fingers splayed and drooping towards the ground, like a little dog heeling behind its owner. His canine obedience gives the impression of something pitiful and repulsive.

Bielski's posture is even more pitiful when contrasted to the sweep and confident elegance of the Dame standing between the two men. Mirecka appears to be dancing, standing firmly planted on her slightly bent right leg, her left leg bent at the knee raised upward. Her left arm is stretched forward, her hand turned, so that her palm faces the audience. Her right arm extends laterally from her body, slightly bent at the elbow and her forearm points downward, parallel to the length of her body. Her arm is rotated so that her hand is turned and her palm faces backward. Overall, the image gives the impression of a precise composition based on contrasts.

It is easy to imagine that the scene featuring the Director was for Grotowski a sort of personal settling of accounts. Jerzy Falkowski read it this way, writing 'Optimistenko is [...] a real threat, his wrong taste— something the 13 Rows company knew all too well—can still be found in an arm's reach even when one thinks the "promised land" has been found' (Falkowski 2006[1960]: 131). Grotowski staged a surrender to the will of 'aestheticians', shown as unlearned petty bourgeois, thereby parodying their ideal form of theatre. It is as if he was saying: this is what it will look like, should you win.

The final part of Act 3 before the Epilogue, titled 'on Earth or Paradise' in the performance programme, centred around the Time Machine. This can be seen in three photographs included in the programme. The first one is captioned 'Promoter and the Unclean or Simpletons on the Time Machine. The Dame and Optimistenko are attempting to board it also' (1960, 4: 17). The photograph shows a simple, A-frame wooden ladder, perched atop a bench and set up in the centre of the stage (inv. nos 164–65). Uncleans climb up both sides of the ladder, Tadeusz Bartkowiak to the audience's left and Andrzej Bielski to the right. Holding onto the ladder they both watch the Promoter (Antoni Jahołkowski) standing between them underneath the ladder. The Promoter is probably standing upon the bench, though his legs—and indeed the lower part of his body—are shielded by a Boschesque panel featuring fragments of *Musicians' Hell*. His face is obscured by a strange contraption—a ribbed tin wheel attached to a long, cast-iron pipe, running from the centre of the wheel down to the ground and anchored below. It looks like some sort of odd, cast-iron washbasin, with a drain pipe.[9] The contraption affixed to the head of the Director looks like a tuba, or some kind of astronaut's helmet. Optimistenko and the Dame stand together beside the whole Time Machine assemblage, trying to push shields with their names on them into the Time Machine, in this way, trying to join the group's journey into the future. Their stances—legs bent and bodies leaning forward—give the impression of a wily and false humility.

Their attempt to board the Time Machine was not successful. Their failure is shown in the next photograph from the programme, captioned 'The lament of the Dame, Optimistenko and Belvedonsky, who were swept away by the Time Machine' (1960, 4: 19). Importantly, this scene takes place in front of a drawn curtain (inv. nos 189–91). Optimistenko is sitting on the stage podium in the centre of the stage and the Dame is sitting on his knees. He appears to be gently stroking her outer thigh with his left hand. To their right, Belvedonsky is bent over on all fours—as if walking on his knees—and straight, stretched-out arms. All three of them have sad, disappointed expressions on their faces, clearly expressing defeat.

According to the script, a scene with the Things came next, an alleged apotheosis. Bogdan Bąk—the only reviewer who mentioned the scene at all—considered it to be the weakest fragment of the whole show (1960: 6). Although the next photograph in the programme should in fact show this scene, it does not. Unfortunately, aside from the programme and Bąk's comment, we don't know much about this scene. The next photograph in the programme is captioned 'The Promoter led the

---

9 It does not seem to be the tin bathtub, previously used as a desk and an ark, because the one in subsequent photographs from this part shows the bathtub hanging up on a back wall. It is polished silver with the word 'EARTH' written on it.

Unclean to the Promised Land. Optimistenko despairs—he did not make it there' (*Materiały i Dyskusje* 1960, VOL. 4: 21). The photograph shows the Time Machine standing in more or less the same place, although no longer set atop the bench but on the ground (inv. no. 163). It had to have been taken down and the bench removed during the last closing of the curtain. Its front is still covered up with the Bosch-inspired construction and the Unclean are still perched atop the ladder. Meanwhile, the Promoter is in what looks like a very uncomfortable position. He lies on his back on the narrow, top step of the ladder—his back arching strikingly. His legs bend backward and his arms thrust straight down to the frame of the 'Time Machine' ladder to support his body weight. His head is bent back and hanging upside-down facing the audience. To the right, in an equally challenging position, Optimistenko is doing a handstand on the pickle barrel, thereby somehow manifesting his own analogous Machine.

Falkowski described this final scene: 'Optimistenko—for the last time—butts into the dialogue being conducted by the "Unclean" with the "Things". He once again does a headstand and asks the well-known question: ". . . are you trying through this to say that I and those like me—are not necessary for Communism?"' (2006[1960]: 131). This key exchange suggests that what is taking place on the Machine is a discussion between the Unclean and the Things, voiced evidently by Jahołkowski. Or maybe not only voiced but also embodied? Maybe his odd position meant that in this scene—like Mirecka earlier who 'performed' the telephone and typewriter—he too became a 'hybrid' actor performing non-human characters such as the Things? Was he, in this character, using Mayakovsky's text to ask the workers for forgiveness?

At some point—though we don't know when precisely—the dialogue with the Things was interrupted by Optimistenko speaking the last words of *The Bathhouse* which, in the original, were uttered by Pobiedonosikov: 'What have you been trying to say here? That people like me aren't of any use to Communism?' (Mayakovsky 2014). In Mayakovsky's version, this question was answered almost immediately on the stage, because Pobiedonosikov did not travel to the future, losing

FARCE-MYSTERY, OR THERE CAN BE NO OTHER SOCIALISM · 101

both his position and his allies in the present. In Grotowski's version, the opposite! If Optimistenko really did butt into a conversation between the Unclean and the Things as Falkowski suggests, then he was in some way, present in the future. It is true that the caption states clearly 'he did not get in', but the audience saw something different: the Unclean, the Promoter and Optimistenko were all on the same stage. The presence of the bureaucrat was a clear sign: You're not going to get rid of me that easily. The answer to the closing questions was far from optimistic. Optimistenko did not seem to be losing power at all.

The performance ended with an Epilogue constructed of fragments from the dialogue *The Old Man and Death*. This finale is shown in a photograph from *Materiały i Dyskusje*, captioned clearly: 'EPILOGUE: Conversation between the Old Man and Death ("so that you take death into consideration—and not live life in vain")' (1960, VOL. 4: 23). Against a partly closed curtain, standing next to the Boschesque Time Machine, is Antoni Jahołkowski lying on his back in a dynamic pose suggesting terror (inv. nos 186–88). Rena Mirecka stands behind him with her hands raised above her head, clasping a stick or rod, ready to strike the prostrate man. This is the scene in which the Old Man is killed, ending his dialogue with Death.

But this doesn't seem to be the end of the performance! The words seen in the caption have yet to be uttered. Who recited this admonition addressed to the audience? In the Prologue, this line belonged to the Promoter, but that was the Prologue. If I am right in thinking that Death killed the Old Man—played by Jahołkowski who also acted in the role of the Promoter—then there are at least two possible solutions. Either the Old Man said those lines, or Death said them. The first option seems to me odd, because it would mean that the character who had just been killed suddenly stood up and spoke, while the second really does fit. It is Death who has the right to take death into consideration.

Grotowski closed this historical and political grotesque performance with an Epilogue, in which Death itself reminded the spectators that no one will be able to evade death. This concluded an important theme in the performance—the idea of change, of metamorphoses, represented by the Promoter in all his incarnations, performed by Antoni Jahołkowski, who then played the Old Man killed in the Epilogue. If we read Jahołkowski's appearances as a continuum, then the final death would mean that the revolutionary dynamic of constant changes is not the highest power. The finale would therefore be a challenge to one of the most important elements of Grotowski's earlier personal and artistic belief: his faith in the dynamics of life and its eternal 'dance'. It is not the last time when the artist challenged himself, questioning something that just before had seemed to be the core of his Credo.

Engaged Theatre

After describing Optimistenko's handstand and his Time Machine at the end of Act 3, Jerzy Falkowski continued:

> By moving a few scenes from *The Bathhouse* into his *Mystery-Bouffe* Grotowski broadened the scope of his charges, attacking contemporary masks of opportunism. These are rather wonderful fragments in the show from a staging context. Optimistenko [...] was ridiculed along with the rulers of the 'Clean', with the Angels and the Devils. But he does not represent an outdated prop; he still acts upon the 'Earth or Purgatory' [...]. Optimistenko is therefore a real threat [...]. (2016[1960]: 131)

If theatre aims to conceal the critical message being sent in the performance—as *Mystery-Bouffe* does, according to Flaszen—then Falkowski unmasked it, providing the key to its meaning. It rests in the composition of events and in Optimistenko, who—with his bureaucratic pomp and stupidity and with all his bourgeois ethics and aesthetics—is a figure representing post-revolutionary political power, another incarnation of a system of suppression and oppression. He was the very power the revolution was supposed to get rid of—reborn. Not reborn, but never dead: the show clearly highlighted that in the future this power would not disappear.

Grotowski's performance did not contain even a shred of political hope, a hope one may find in even Mayakovsky's bitter, satirical dramas like his *Bathhouse*. The Russian poet could still laugh at Communist apparatchiks in spite of despair. Grotowski in 1960 was not in a laughing mood. Everyone in Poland was by that time aware that the hopes aroused by the October 1956 political 'thaw' had proven futile. Although Stalinism did not make a return in its most totalitarian form, the ideas and goals Grotowski fought for as an activist in the radically anti-Stalinist organizations he co-founded in the late 1950s,[10] increasingly appeared impossible to achieve. By 1960, Communist Party apparatchiks had taken over, suppressed popular rebellions and couched the suppression as a strategy to achieve 'minor stabilization'—using concern over privacy as a pretext to maintain power, by ensuring people that only the Party allows them to live relatively peaceful and comfortable lives.

It is fitting at this point to refer to fragments of what may likely have been Grotowski's most important political statement, 'Cywilizacja i wolność—nie ma innego socjalizmu' [Civilization and freedom—there can be no other socialism). The published statement was a speech Grotowski made during the Constitutional Congress of the Socialist Youth Union in Warsaw, 25–27 April 1957. The speech read in part:

> People must understand that if they do not stop messing about and do not on a daily basis take part in the affairs of their nation; if they do not activate and take active part in these affairs whenever and wherever possible, everyone within their own realm, then we can be heading for a catastrophe, blood, ruin, years of despotic triumph.
>
> [...]

---

10 In late the 1950s, Grotowski was very active in the anti-Stalinist movement among young intellectuals and workers. In November 1956, he co-founded the organization Rewolucyjny Związek Młodzieży (Revolutionary Union of Youth). Then in March 1957, he became the leader of Polityczny Ośrodek Lewicy Akademickiej (Political Centre of Academic Left). In the late spring of 1957, Grotowski stepped back from political activity because he realized that it was impossible to achieve his goals. More information may be found in my book *Grotowski. Przewodnik* [Grotowski: A guide], forthcoming in English.

The direct responsibility for the difficult reality of the Polish experiment falls in a very substantial way upon the passivity and the lack of political engagement [...]. Passivity is fertiliser for despotism. The passivity of the masses is a gesture of surrender to poverty, ignorance and economic regression.

[...]

Bread, civilization and freedom are all things others cannot provide for us. We have to bake bread, fight for freedom, create civilizations. It is not true that we can sit in the comfort of our own private affairs and 'live on somehow'. There is no escape from poverty and despotism. If we cannot overcome the passivity of the masses, one day our streets and our homes will be visited by a wave of violence, lawlessness and despotism.

[...]

The heroes of this country are not those who tear at their robes, driven by historical negations, never getting their hands dirty doing any work. The heroes of our nation are the mothers who feed their families from meagre incomes. The youth of our land is often attacked, disoriented, dismissed from workplaces for 'deviations'. They lack the fair apportioning of state-built homes, bonuses, professional opportunities. The rights of the young are often taken away or actually ignored.

In our country the youth are longing for civilization, for a decent standard of living, for justice, for the chance to make choices about their own fates, for technological progress. This longing shows us all the way forward. Civilization and Freedom. There can be no other socialism [...].

(Grotowski 2012: 74–75)

I quote this text for two reasons. First it shows that the young Grotowski was politically and ethically radical. His conclusion is straightforward: there can be no other socialism than the socialism of freedom and civilization. In 1957, this statement was a call to effort and work and in subsequent paragraphs, Grotowski presented his programme of actions. In

1960, on the stage of the Theatre of 13 Rows, under his direction, one could clearly hear this 'there can be no' and it sounded more serious and more accusatory than in 1957. By 1960, it was clear that what the Communist Party was reconstructing was not a socialism of freedom and civilization, but rather a tyranny.

Yet, there is another reason to return to Grotowski's 1957 text: his conviction that despotism, violence and catastrophe threaten us ceaselessly and will become fact if people do not take active part in changing the world, if they do not engage in a struggle for the common good, if they do not stop 'messing around'. Grotowski's 1957 speech reveals a different, political aspect of the struggle with 'commonplace existentialism' discussed so far in this book. One might say that in 1957, Grotowski tried to challenge this trendy existentialism as supporting a return to despotism, through the propagation of elegant and intelligently motivated indifference, of withdrawal, of messing around, indeed.

As a theatrical artist, Grotowski did not turn his back on the struggle to achieve what was for him, the most important political goal of all: to overcome civic passivity and to provoke audiences—not in order to insult them, to preach to them superficially, or to distress them, but rather in order to engage them. In a review of *Mystery-Bouffe*, Janina Zdanowicz provides what is possibly the most insightful articulation of this aim and of Grotowski's strategy for achieving this aim. Zdanowicz wrote of the performance, in terms of the company's engagement in contemporary problems, emphasizing that 'Grotowski deals with these problems in a thorough way, striving to "build" conventions of a theatre which philosophizes, engaged ideologically in a desire to engage the audience through adequate forms of expression, aided in this by a faultless, super rich imagination and staging skills' (1960: 10).

I include this statement here because it shows that the Theatre of 13 Rows, when seen close up and in terms of its own time rather than in retrospect from the vantage of its further evolution, already *was* the poor theatre with all its mythologized anthropology and 'rituality'. It was a thoroughly contemporary theatre, relevant, engaged and engaging. *Mystery-Bouffe* presented a particularly vivid vision of this aspect of

Grotowski. Its bitter and serious diagnosis did not lead to capitulation, because essentially, the performance was an appeal to the public. This appeal was voiced with the words recited at the end of the performance: 'so that you take death into consideration—and not live life in vain'. While this recitation was not as declarative as entreaties in earlier productions, Grotowski used the frame of the performance to find subtle ways of influencing the spectators, arousing their sense of engagement.

It is often repeated that Grotowski did not create political theatre. I would like to challenge this by referring to Paweł Mościcki's dual definition of the two kinds of effective political theatre. The first is 'engaged theatre', which 'entails the artist speaking out on important political and social questions, but also the creation of messages that will respond to the current situation, problems and tensions' (Mościcki 2015). Mościcki called the second type 'engaging theatre', explaining that it emerges out of a broad, contemporary understanding of politics.

> If we utilize the general conception of the political as the sphere of conditions for the emergence of particular political figures, subjects and opinions, then each revolution in the sphere of perception, each reformulation of the pathways of our thinking, seeing, hearing and speaking, has a deep political dimension.
>
> Insofar as engaged art is a declaration on the subject of disputes already laid out in the field of politics, *engaging art has thus far attempted to imagine new lines of division, allowing positions to be taken that until now have appeared impossible. It doesn't respond to political demands or problems, but creates new questions and formulates previously unknown demands.* (2015; emphasis in original)

During his first season at the Theatre of the 13 Rows, Grotowski created the second type of political theatre, synthesized and summarized in *Mystery-Bouffe*.

What Mościcki would call 'engaging theatre', Grotowski understood as a continuation of his political engagement. In 1966, the editors of

Współczesność—an important weekly publication of young, political and cultural reformers—asked Grotowski to speak on the subject of the 'generation of 1956'. He presented in great detail his theatre programme, by then already well known, centred around the ideas of poor theatre and the complete act. He placed this presentation in a framework that allowed him to explain what this all had to do with the generation of 1956 and the anti-Stalinist revolution in which he himself was engaged.

Ten years ago, we experienced something which can be termed an eruption of the possibilities of talent, misunderstandings, false and tested expectations; it was a vortex which mixed up existing perspectives and opened up new ones in all the areas accessible for us to act in on our national territory. It seemed for a moment, that we had found ourselves facing the birth of a completely new reality: depending on age and personal circumstances, we watched this space opening up with excessive hopes or with excessive scepticism. This was also the time when the surface of public life was tread by previously unknown young people, who appeared in this tempestuous civic reality with their readiness to act, or the willingness to develop their potential in some sort of defined expressive discipline, profession etc.—thereby earning themselves the moniker of the 'generation of 1956'. This term was not only informal but, above all, rather hard to verify. It was not until the period of stabilization, which formed itself around 1958–59 and helped define the framework and realistic facility to act that we saw the verification of the value of the energy contained in individuals who were entering public life around the year 1956. As a result, it verified the value of this 'generation'. This is because people show their true colours not in moments of eruption, but when they spend a long time clashing with barriers set in their path by everyday realities. That is when they form their place in life—their professional calling and ability to define their own perspectives, not from the outset and not in a 'philosophical' sense, but as if from grassroots level, hence as a result of experiences born out of long-term activities.

Members of the generation 1956 passed their test in as much as they were able to go from dreams about changing the world in a grand style to long-term activities encompassing their everyday lives. They did not pass the test in as much as feel disappointed that eruptions are not lasting things and do not take the responsibility to act on a daily basis and slip to the sidelines—claiming that reality had severed their abilities, or that only scheming and brilliant cunning pay off and give results. Their success and perspectives are decided by the question of whether they are capable of moving on from revolutionary acts involving all the world's affairs to the courage to take up an uncompromising duel involving their own personal challenges. (Grotowski 2012: 285, 291)

The dates mentioned in the text support the theory that in Grotowski's case, this crucial turn from revolutionary fervour to everyday activities was manifested in his directing career beginning with the first season of work with the Theatre of 13 Rows. Perhaps this is a far-reaching conclusion, but it seems that this switch from 'revolutionary acts involving all the world's affairs' to 'uncompromising duels involving one's own personal challenges' was fully realized with *Mystery-Bouffe*.

A Timeless Treatment

Work on this performance allowed Grotowski to condense his first whole theatrical programme—which he wrote in 1960 and then distributed among the closed circle of those keen on theatre. He titled the work *Farce-Mystery* (*Farsa-misterium*) and produced it a few months after the premiere of *Mystery-Bouffe*. It was here that Grotowski rather clearly described what it was that he sought with his actors in the process of working on Mayakovsky's dramas.

His original doubts centred on the sense of working within the theatrical medium. Grotowski dissected this question into two further questions:

1. What sort of genre of the arts could—in a secular sense—satisfy the excesses of the imagination and unease exploited by religious doctrines?
2. What is the essence of theatre? What is the unique element which decides whether something is theatrical or not? What would remain if we eliminated from theatre all the things which are not theatre (literature, visual arts, journalism, theories, the copying of reality)? What element could not be taken over by any other cultural genre (such as film)?
(Grotowski 2012: 191)

Considering that the answers he sought could only be practical, he wrote:

By our practice I attempt to prove that the listed questions are relatively speaking their own answers. I am assuming that the essence of theatre is capable—in a secular sense—to satisfy certain excesses of the imagination and unease exploited in religious ceremonies. I am at the same time assuming that what could be a secular substitute for religious rituals is the essence of theatre as an art.
(Grotowski 2012: 191)

As we know, for Grotowski this 'essence' was always an encounter between audiences and actors—a shared life and a shared experience. Not random meetings, but encounters consciously directed and led, while at the same time, spontaneous and organic. Grotowski's sense of theatre's 'essence' was therefore not any transcendental experience but, instead, an effectiveness in bringing about a prepared collective experience. As Grotowski stated:

Theatre was (and partially has remained) something of a collective act, a ritual game. In rituals there are no actors and no audiences. There are some key participants (such as a shaman) and additional participants (such as the crowd who watch the magical actions performed by the shaman and respond with the magic of gestures, song, dance, etc.).

The rule of taking part, a shared ceremony, a system of signs which assists in the creation of a certain specific collective psychological aura, concentration, collective suggestion—organizes the imagination and subjects unease to discipline.

Reconstructing in theatre partial elements of a 'ritual' game, meaning restoring to theatre its essential foundations, would be one of the main aims of our practice.

The thesis (about the collective usefulness of this sort of research): 'rituality' in theatre as a counter-offering in relation to ritual forms of organized religion.

[...]

In antiquity, in Greece similar forms of theatre, figuring of course on the borders of rituals involving the god cults, were called 'mystery plays'. The only difference was that in ancient Greece (much as in later similar examples from the Middle Ages) the mystery was found somewhere 'beyond' the participants—in divine characters and evil spirits etc.

'The Mystery' of modern mystery plays would however have to be something directly connected with the participants (through the fact that we are not seeking anything outside of them, nothing beyond the human being). That which is thought of as a collective 'mystery' involving the participants in a theatrical play, therefore their fate and the structures of their lives seems to be an obvious fundamental aspect of the mystery play. (Grotowski 2012: 192–93)

It is worth making an effort to understand this 1960 fragment from Grotowski's synthesis of his dramatic trajectory *Farce-Mystery*: the aim of refreshing the essence of theatre as a collective event is itself a shared experience of human fate and a 'structure' of human life (which also includes its sense being understood dynamically). Achieving this aim is possible, in as much as one creates a counterproposal to religion, a search for a fate and structure beyond human life. This is a fragment that, perhaps as precisely as possible, describes the meaning of *Mystery-Bouffe* as an attempt to call up a collective experience that can lead us to

FARCE-MYSTERY, OR THERE CAN BE NO OTHER SOCIALISM · **111**

learn the immanent sense of human life. If this is so, then Grotowski essentially protested alongside Mayakovsky against fideistic religion, but also stood against Mayakovsky, who, as another sort of 'believer', promoted the mystery of the Communist religion promising future victory over all forms of oppression. Optimistenko's closing words, with all their satirical and acute relevance, pose retrospective questions to the transcendent faith Mayakovsky had in a kind of socialist salvation: that the necessity of the troubles of his time would be rewarded with humanity's future happiness. Grotowski did not believe in this bright future; not because he was disappointed with socialism, but because he did not see the need to project value upon a distant future reality. His mystery play was meant to drive towards a discovery and an experience of immanent value in life, here and now.

However, I do repeat, this rituality was not connected with discovering and learning one sort of truth. Grotowski linked this form of action exclusively to religious rituals:

> Religious rituals have magic functions. Shamanic spell and sacred gesture made by a priest aim to secure a helpful contact with divinities (demons, ancestral ghosts).
>
> The function of theatre as a game of 'rituals' is of course different. Religious rituals are a form of magic, the 'ritual' of theatre—a form of play.
> (Grotowski 2012: 194)

It seems that we have too easily and quickly forgotten this proviso, this obvious distinction and thereby turned Grotowski into a serious and initiated 'shaman'—or perhaps he allowed himself to be turned into such a figure. Meanwhile, in *Farce-Mystery* he obviously considers the 'ritual' of theatre to be a sort of playing. He also declares that there is something within theatre that has a special value.

> I would be willing to connect the playful function of theatre, at least in my own practice, with the idea of infantilism, child's play, games with conventionality.
> [...]

We play and so we seek diversity—that which is unexpected, reversed, which is a 'bit of fun'. The form pulsates, splits; the commonplace conventions are smashed, unexpected connections and similarities being born. Grotesque = seriousness, parody = tragedy, intellectual constructions = spontaneity (buffo), ceremonies = acrobatics. The dialectics of form and in this a dialectics of the psychological process, convictions, ways of perceiving.

In this erroneous mobility, mobility not related to situation but achieved through the fluid aspect of conventions what mattered would be the aspect of play, of surprise, of perversity, in a word—some sort of specific transgenre aspect of the farcical, of some sort of hyper-farce.

'Dialectical farce'. 'Secular mystery play'. We are discussing theatre for which we still have to come up with a name ('farce-mystery'?).

(Grotowski 2012: 194–95)

The dialectics of psychological processes, convictions and ways of seeing are to be experienced through dialectics of form, initiated through play and games. This experience of diversity, changeability and opposites that fit together because they are all part of life is almost impossible in linear, verbal constructions. But it is possible through playfulness. If we assume that successful functioning in everyday life is about ordering things, creating hierarchies and eliminating that which is unnecessary, then the theatrical play Grotowski is talking about would be excluded from this process—and opposed to it, a celebration of diversity and harmonized dissonances, a liberation from the routine and an act of agreeing to difference and opposition. The heart of such an experience is more related to play than ritual. The collective experience made possible through theatre—thanks to performative means such as mystery plays—allows us to discover something inaccessible through everyday life processes and almost forbidden in religious rituals—practical knowledge of multiplicity akin, in a philosophical sense, to examples set forth in the philosophies of Gilles Deleuze and Felix Guattari (1987).

Retrospectively, applying Grotowski's thesis about the 'farce-mystery' to *Mystery-Bouffe*, allows us to connect individual threads—especially the political and the eschatological. I find that in *Mystery-Bouffe*, the Theatre of 13 Rows exploded religious maxims like *memento mori* and revolutionary slogans like 'We have been nothing, we will be all!'[11] Grotowski questioned both religious and political transcendence and focused his engagement on the immanence of life and the world. In performance, he found this immanence to be dynamically changeable, diverse and existing in the multitude. In other words, he saw it as something 'timeless'—the direct experience of which is possible through games and fun. The ethical value of this experience was to be based on turning towards life, against denying it in the name of any sort of promises that go beyond it. In this sense, *Mystery-Bouffe* represented an attempt to put into practice 'the secularizing function of theatre'—which in the language of another epoch could be called an attempt at liberation.

Dariusz Kosiński

---

11 This is the English translation of the final verse of the first stanza of the Communist anthem 'International', written by Eugène Pottier in 1871. The French original reads 'Nous ne sommes rien, soyons tout!'

CHAPTER FOUR

Indian Erotica

Shakuntala after Kālidāsa

Playing at Shiva

On 13 December 1960, Grotowski premiered *Shakuntala*, based on Kālidāsa's Sanskrit play (fourth–fifth century CE).[1] It was Grotowski's first play to secure a lasting place in the artist's own narrative about the evolution of artistic research at the Theatre of 13 Rows. Several years later, in a very important statement titled 'Theatre and Ritual' ('Teatr i rytuał'), Grotowski spoke about his search for 'the possibility of creating signs in European theatre', and his attempts to 'discover a system of signs, appropriate for our theatre, for our civilization' (Grotowski 2012: 366–67). For Grotowski, this was the most pressing cause of the performance of *Shakuntala*. In his own estimation, his efforts ended in failure because he created fake signs. But *Shakuntala* was important because of its failures. Unable to create a stage code analogous to the Indian system as he was imagining it at the time, Grotowski entered a long phase of research.

Researchers of Indian culture and literature see Grotowski's production of *Shakuntala* in a very different way. They consider it significant that the not-yet-famous Polish director worked on a classic Sanskrit

---

1 The full original title of the drama is *Abhijnanashakuntalam*, usually translated into English as *The Recognition of Shakuntala*. I am using the shortened version, following the Polish translation by Stanisław Schayer that was used by Grotowski and the long European tradition of using the shortened title to refer to Kālidāsa's drama. The same title was used by Arthur W. Ryder whose English translation I am quoting from (Kālidāsa 1999).

114

drama. Krzysztof Maria Byrski—a leading Polish researcher and expert in Indian culture, who also knew Grotowski personally—wrote a pioneering work on Grotowski's attitude towards the cultures of Asia, in which he posed a thesis that still holds today. Byrski argues that Grotowski used Kālidāsa's play because one of the aims Grotowski set for himself was

> freeing the actors from the overwhelming influence of the literary text, which in contemporary Euro-American theatre actors abide by with great faith and humility. [...] Grotowski was not so much looking for a drama but for a score the company could interpret with the freedom to apply their own 'instrumentation', meaning the choice and ability to use the full means at the actors' disposal. *Shakuntala* happens to be such in its original intention. [...] The search for a score led Grotowski for the first time—at least in his theatrical works—to Indian theatre. (Byrski 1979: 86–87)

It is hard to disagree with Byrski, and yet I note that, at least in some of his statements, Grotowski treated earlier texts as 'scores', and therefore could have been led 'to Indian theatre' by something else, especially as the production of *Shakuntala* was his second creative encounter with the story.[2]

Some lovers of Indian culture and philosophy go so far as to suggest that the only real achievement Grotowski has to his name is that he discovered Indian traditions and transferred them to the West. In their interpretations, *Shakuntala* is an almost secret text, whose complete elements emerge and can be explained as a transposition of Indian philosophy into drama.[3] These types of generalizations make it harder for us to understand the important connection between Grotowski and India, and do not help us describe it in greater detail.

---

2 In 1958, Grotowski directed a radio adaptation of *Shakuntala*, produced for Polish Radio in Kraków.

3 A clear example of this perspective coming out of Poland can be found in Kołdrzak 2014.

116 · DARIUSZ KOSIŃSKI

It is not possible to understand the influence India had on Grotowski's thinking and work, if one does not first conduct extensive and competent studies covering what can be called his philosophy. He formulated this philosophy both in his numerous statements—we should probably start with these—and in the experimental forms his practice took in his theatre and post-theatre performances. Until such a field of studies is set up, we are just meaninglessly invoking various concepts and referring to them as 'source' and 'fundamental'. In fact, Grotowski's importance as a thinker and a practitioner comes from the fact that he used a range of inspirations in his own fashion, not merely linking them together, which led both to an eclectic practice and an original system. Thus, reducing Grotowski's importance and influence to him being a conduit of Indian philosophy and Indian theatre to the West is a far-reaching simplification and falsification of his achievements.

Paradoxically, the limitations of this reductive approach can be found in a text that represents one of the pillars of Grotowski's 'Indian aspect', the essay 'Playing at Shiva' ('Gra w Sziwę. Przypisek do praktyki'). This text was most likely written in the early autumn of 1960 as part of Grotowski's theatre school thesis, 'Między teatrem a postawą wobec rzeczywistości' [Between theatre and an attitude towards reality], which he successfully presented to the examination board at the Higher State Theatre School in Kraków.[4] Importantly, this document was not attached to the theoretical part of Grotowski's project which dealt with the philosophy of Grotowski's theatre, but instead was an introduction to the 'practical work on directing' required for the diploma. Most likely, the School authorities forced Grotowski to stage a text far from his interests, a classic Polish salon comedy from the first half of the nineteenth century, Aleksander Fredro's *Maidens' Vows*. 'Playing at Shiva' served as a theoretical introduction to Grotowski's staging of *Maidens' Vows* which meant to model the type of theatre required by the assignment. This strange connection allows us to read this 'Footnote to Practice' not only as a document that evidences inspiration and a fascination with India, but

---

4 The Higher State Theatre School awarded Grotowski his diploma on 10 October 1960.

also as an early attempt by Grotowski to explain his basic ideas. Therefore, I place this work in the context of the chronologically subsequent manifesto by the artist discussed in the previous chapter—*Farce-Mystery*, written the same month that *Shakuntala* premiered.

In 'Playing at Shiva', Grotowski presents the same idea of playfulness found in *Farce-Mystery*, but using slightly different figures, images and associations.

> If I had to define our research in a single sentence, the one term I would refer to is the myth of 'The Dance of Shiva'; I would say: 'we are playing Shiva', 'we are playing at Shiva'.[5]
>
> There is in this an attempt to absorb reality as if from all its sides, in the whole spectrum of its aspects, and at the same time as if remaining on the outside, at a distance, a marked distance. By which we mean—in other words—the dance of forms, the pulsation of forms, a fluid spreading into diversity of theatrical conventions, of styles, of traditions of playing; constructing opposites: an intellectual game in spontaneity, seriousness in the grotesque, ridiculing pain; the dance of forms which smashes apart the illusory nature of theatre, all life probabilities, and at the same time it aspires (though never fully achieves) to absorb, to embrace THE WHOLE, the whole of human fate, and through this WHOLE 'reality in total'; and at the same time winking, subtly smiling, keeping a healthy distance, aware of the relativity of all things. Shiva's Dance. This is us playing at Shiva.
>
> [...]
>
> The attempt to grasp and contain within the self THE WHOLE (questioning human fate and the human condition). Multifacetedness. Being at a distance. The performance must become a collective 'gesture of synthesis', 'dancing' reality, 'ritual'

---

5 In the Polish original, Grotowski uses two different phrases: 'gramy Sziwę' and 'gramy w Sziwę', because Polish differentiates the verb *grać*—to play a role, as in theatre, film, etc.—and *grać w*—meaning playing a game like football, etc. The difference—important for Grotowski—is hard to translate into English, because 'playing at' often means 'pretend to be' rather than to simply play a game.

118 · DARIUSZ KOSIŃSKI

game. Rituality which of course was created as a certain kind of religious psycho-technique should here crystallize into secular psycho-technique, into a pseudo-ritual, into a GAME.

'Ritualistic game'—like 'masquerade game', like 'game of football', like 'puzzle game'. A form of psychological training. We do not demonstrate an action to a viewer, but we invite the thoughtful viewer to enter the game of total conventionality, to take part in 'share-shamanism', in which the living extemporary presence of the audience is part of a game of theatre.
(Grotowski 2012: 180–81)

Much like 'farce-mystery', the formula 'playing at Shiva' does not relate solely to existence, but also—or perhaps above all—has epistemological meaning. It is a certain tool for discovery, which is also, at the same time, its subject.

'Ritual' games, the way we would imagine them in an ideal process, playing—using once again a mythological metaphor—at Shiva, at Shiva's dance, is in fact a therapeutic process, psychotherapy. We are simply seeking a certain method of working with the psyche, a method which would draw out 'eschatological' insecurities (connected with the fragile nature of life), usually compensated for through religion, into the surface of consciousness and (at least potentially) allow to discharge them in artistic play, and therefore on the territory—let us call it this—occupied by secularism.

We superficially 'heal ourselves' with tautology: the need to die is explained by the need to die, the flow of reality through the flow of reality, human fate through human fate. But tautology is superficial, because between the question and conclusion, the perspective of seeing has transformed. Now we are trying to perceive as if 'from the outside' and as if 'from all sides'. And at the same time, we are trying to comprehend our own everyday relativity.
(Grotowski 2012: 181)

In order to define the function of 'ritual games', Grotowski uses the phrase 'psychotherapy'. It seems an unfortunate use in this context, and I am not surprised that the artist eventually stopped using this term. For we are not dealing with psychotherapy here, but with an active, lived-through, embodied philosophy. In the context of a post–Second World War experience, and its attendant ideological chaos, to heal means to restore one's place in the world without questioning and disabling reality's changeability and multidimensionality, and without forcing it into any single dogma.

The figure used to capture this experience in the essay cited above was Shiva, who embodies a paradoxically engaged distance. Shiva is the cosmic dancer and, at the same time, a distanced observer. For Grotowski, playing and acting as such, like Shiva's dance, simultaneously absorbs the whole and remains distant from it. He defines the role of spectator not as an audience member drawn in various ways into the action as with Augusto Boal's *spect-actor*, but rather as an actor. As a person acting, the spectator can constantly keep observing their own actions. Such an approach, as is clear from Grotowski's statements at the time, would be the aim of his theatrical 'therapy'. To be an actor in the full sense also meant to be an active spectator, aware of the relativity of all things.

For Grotowski, such modes of activity meant engaging contemporaneity, fulfilling the social function of theatre:

> 'Playing at Shiva', playing at the multifacetedness and distance in seeing reality, we perceive ourselves in the aspect of general processes, most of all in interpersonal processes, in the 'dialectics of reality'. Questions about human fate, if they are meant to be asked by thoughtful human beings, have to be associated with contemporary forms of thinking, living, responding emotionally, etc. The same is true of 'ritual' games, their rules and conventions.
>
> This is a result of theatre's social engagement (in this very context) being necessary not only in an ideological sense, but also in the sense of skill and technique.
> (Grotowski 2012)

One of the fundamental problems Grotowski tackled was finding ways to impact society—or put another way, finding ways to work on the performative effectiveness of his theatre. He was, above all, concerned with finding in practice, contemporary ways of leading audiences to experience this philosophical game.

Archetype of Love

But this still does not explain how 'Playing at Shiva' was connected with Grotowski's staging of *Maidens' Vows*. According to Grotowski's comments, 'Playing at Shiva' was to be based on 'theatre assumptions' he sought to express 'in full', in his 'Footnote to Practice'.

Grotowski explained the basic idea of his interpretation of Fredro's comedy:

> In line with accepted assumptions, I am not trying to establish the 'main aim' of the play, but I am reading the text to attempt to work out what formal oppositions (the main formal opposition), which target the centre of the 'eschatological' problematics, can with any hope of success be adapted based on materials taken from this text. In *Vows* [. . .], I would say the main opposition can be found between the 'romantic beauty' of Fredro's text and the 'Arcadian' quality of the scenography on the one hand, and the ballet-pantomime of brutal sexual nature (even if artificially composed) on the other. The formal opposition we are dealing with would:
> —distance the audience from the action taking place; provide extreme distance, seeing 'from outside';
> —strike at the point of contact between life conventions and biology; split this connection; reveal the workings of two extreme aspects; give a thoughtful audience the sense of their own limitless relativity. This sort of cruelty is therapeutic in character: providing *catharsis*.
> (Grotowski 2012: 183)

Here, Grotowski clearly shows his fundamental method for treating literary texts. He does not read an overriding task into it, a lead theme that would be extracted through staging, or give it coherent form and unity. Instead, Grotowski treats the text as source material in order to conduct on the stage, a process that reflects a dialectic of opposites seen from an 'eschatological' perspective—a perspective key to his thinking at the time. This approach resulted in the salutary experiencing of one's fate as a convention, and the simultaneous ability to see it from a distance but without becoming inactive. This does not mean Grotowski abandoned the text. Nevertheless, in seeking 'the central formal opposition' in the play as his main focus, Grotowski refers, not so much to the structural composition of the play, as to ways of living and acting that, when revealed on the stage, encourage audiences to perceive, understand and overrule the dramaturgy of human existence that living with others imposes upon us—to develop a sense of distance towards it, and thus restore a partial or temporary rule over the self.

With confidence, Grotowski used *Maidens' Vows* as material to explore oppositions between the social and biological dimensions of the erotic, while also considering these in an 'eschatological' context. Grotowski was deeply concerned with these topics at the time. Obviously, this interest was connected to his work on *Shakuntala*. Grotowski says as much in a text he wrote two years after the *Shakuntala* premiere—*A Possibility of a Theatre* (*Możliwość teatru*). In it, he interprets his earlier performances from the perspective of the 'dialectic of derision and apotheosis', a process involving 'archetypes'. Notice how Grotowski thought this played out in *Shakuntala*:

Archetype:

HE—SHE

Archetype of love 'through predestination', out of 'magnetism of the heart' (a poetic model as seen in the legend of Androgyne)

'The dialectics of derision and apotheosis' was based on counterpointing the poetic archetype with that which is its physical foundation, with the eroticism of the biological sphere, with the sex act of human beings shown as spasms of birds or insects, with movement which by the unconscious associations reveals its physiological sources; even the construction standing in the centre of the stage evoked the associations that can be called— Freudian [. . .]. The performance ended with the characters visibly aged, quickly so, right before the audience's eyes. The end of biological strength—the beginning of elder knowledge. (Grotowski 2012: 220–21)

The average educated Pole would straightaway recognize the phrase 'magnetism of the heart'—which both appears in the first line of the Grotowski's essay and is the subtitle of Fredro's comedy. This also serves as further evidence of a very close connection between the staging of Grotowski's production and his *Shakuntala*. They are connected by the theme of love. The multi-layered complexity of this theme is activated by contrasting the clash of 'animalistic' desires with cultural creations, which both tame and obscure desire according to social conventions.

It is worth comparing this description of *Shakuntala* with Grotowski's use of 'key formal opposition' in his *Maidens' Vows*.

Act 1, I would suggest, should be staged as a faithful copy, a conventional staging of *Vows*. Of course, for any intelligent audience member, the parodic aspect of this copy should be easy to read—though through context and not a 'parody' style of acting.

[. . .]

Act 2 and Act 3 (meaning the end of the first part of the play and the start of the second) should be treated as the key opposition.

The text should continue this 'copy', while the action on stage should be composed as a ballet-pantomime focused on the animalization of human archetypes, animalization which is artificial, as if automated [. . .]; the pantomime should not be played for belly laughs nor in a pornographic style. It should be cold, be like a description of the sexual act demonstrated by a professor in a medical academy.

Act 4 should of course return to the form of 'copy' (in order to allow the audience to rest).

Act 5 should develop like Act 4 in order to, at the very end, land with a strong effect of the type found in Acts 2 and 3, with the proviso that at the end of the performance the rule of deformation should also encompass the word [...].
(Grotowski 2012: 184–85)

It is not hard to notice the similarities between this description and the way in which Grotowski described his staging of *Shakuntala* in 1960. In that performance, he made use of a paradoxical transposition of 'biology'—sexual desire in an animalistic or mechanical sense—into a firmly formalized 'ballet'. In it, he also provided precisely planned sequences, lyrical and poetic in style, with comments interspersed throughout.

In my opinion, Grotowski's staging of *Maidens' Vows* could actually be treated as a unique instance that sheds light on the compositional method utilized in his staging of *Shakuntala*. The similarities between them allow us to propose that the fundamental raison d'être and most important accomplishment of this production is that, thematically, eroticism is seen to be as 'sacred' and 'ritualistic' as death or the human subjection to cosmic and historical forces. This was not that obvious in 1960, nor is it obvious today, when eroticism is treated as a commodity. Grotowski, meanwhile, seems committed to placing eroticism in the network of forces ruling over human fate—forces towards which we ought to maintain an 'eschatological' distance. Put more simply, for all its playful aspects, *Shakuntala* was Grotowski's attempt at a game of love—just as *Mystery-Bouffe* was a game of history, and *Cain* was a game involving the universe and the place of humans within it. In spite of what has been written about *Shakuntala*, it was neither the actors' experience, nor India, that mattered most. It was love.

The Audience, Ambushed and Shocked

Shakuntala was the first performance for which the stage space was designed by Jerzy Gurawski—25 years old at the time and fresh out of the Department of Architecture at Kraków Technical University. Fascinated by the achievements of the avant-garde, Gurawski devoted his diploma thesis to researching 'space' in experimental theatre. Many years later, he recalled how he conducted a 'quite comprehensive analysis of spatial relationships in theatres through the centuries' (Gurawski 2015[1984]: 87). The outcome of this research was

> a theory of dependency that exists in the theatrical space and that influences the spectator. I believe that the space is influenced by light, color, sound, and movement, and by the sphere that I regarded as the most essential and the most 'magical'—that is, by the space of intuition that surrounds a person beyond their fields of sight.
> (Gurawski 2015[1984]: 87)

Gurawski aimed at creating 'new possibilities in accomplishing the previous idea: to draw the spectator within the theatre event and make them co-creator of the performance' (Gurawski 2015[1984]: 88). It is therefore not surprising that, motivated by such needs and ideas, the architect very quickly found a common language with Grotowski.

> The first play for which I designed the theatre space was the ancient Indian erotic drama, *Shakuntala* by Kālidāsa, as adapted by Grotowski (1960c). I received permission to implement the theory of the back and central stage areas and opposing auditoria. So we made a new theatre space by removing the raised stage and a few platforms that were in the auditorium. We created a space solely for this particular theatre performance.
>
> The central stage was equipped with phallic symbols—Grotowski's idea—which were quite a literal display of Hindu eroticism. Two stage areas behind contained less defined forms on which the Yogis sat. The opposing auditoria constituted two

gatherings places—one for the Court and the other for the princess [Shakuntala].
(Gurawski 2015[1984]: 89)

Looking back at the production years later, and informed by subsequent experiences, Grotowski reflected on the space created for *Shakuntala*:

> This was a rule of the centre stage adapted already—along with the auditorium—for the structure of the way the performance was to be staged. The 'dialectics of derision and apotheosis' was to be presented among other ways through the clash of Kālidāsa's sublime love poetry ('taking place' on the centre stage) with the drastically specific advice and prescriptions involving sexual activities (taken from the *Kama Sutra*) offered by 'yogis' (hence 'holy men' with a sacral vocal intonation) from both sides of the hall coming from behind the audience. [...] In this way, the central stage was completed through micro-scenes—behind the spectators backs (they could see only one side at a time) and through the isles between rows of seats. In practice the stage ambushed the spectators; and when the spectators were thrown into being given roles, in some way absorbed them.
> (Grotowski 2012: 235–36)

It is obvious from both comments that Gurawski's main theory—what is most important and most 'magical' is invisible because it happens 'behind people's backs'—lost its importance. The back stages, occupied by the Yogis, were used for traditional and conventional functions, as a place 'aside' (literally). They were on the periphery of the central action which they commented on. Even this contrast between peripheral commentary and central action is congruent with ancient convention. Asides—especially in comedy—should be the opposite of what is being said right out.

Despite the fact that the entirety of *Shakuntala* was presented in a playful mood, audiences did not necessarily leave the theatre convinced that they had taken part in an experiment in, what Grotowski himself described as, the 'magical ritual' of theatrical play. And yet, Gurawski was very pleased with the effect of the experiment, and years later, still held the opinion that in *Shakuntala*, 'the testing of [. . .] theoretical hypotheses' went smoothly, and that 'the spatial solutions turned out to be useful and worked well' (Gurawski 2015[1984]: 89).

The two auditoriums facing each other, as well as the rear stages, were only one of two key spatial and scenographic interventions. The second key intervention came about via a construction set up centre stage, with a dual meaning and provocative aspects described best in a report written by censors.

> The decoration placed centre stage presents two hills and a rounded column rising up between them. Looking at it, no objections come to mind. The 'initiated' however know it represents a phallic symbol, and though awareness of this fact did reach us, we still however do not have any justification for intervention.
>
> (quoted in Wójtowicz 2004: 151)

The set pieces imagined by Grotowski and constructed by Gurawski were visual designs, almost abstract and stripped of any realism. They suggested rather than presented, and yet at the same time, they embraced the origin of the text and referred to Indian symbolism. As a result, the censors could not intervene—though it was obvious to them that many ordinary spectators, not just the 'initiated', would know what they were looking at: *Shakuntala* was performed on and around a giant, erect phallus. Of course, it is possible to associate this huge phallus with Shiva, and to conclude that the phallus present in Grotowski's *Shakuntala* was meant to represent an Indian lingam. However, I argue it could be equally interpreted as an ironic representation of male dominance in the script, an ironic counterpoint to the lyrical love story.

Let us try to engage our imaginations and see things from the perspective of Polish audiences of the time, who, in December 1960 or January 1961, chose to attend the performance of an 'erotic' ancient Indian drama staged by the Theatre of 13 Rows. They would have been seated in a way that enabled them to see the other spectators, while exposing them to their own gazes. This was not something they were used to. Audiences found themselves in a situation where they were distanced, able to watch themselves watching. They were also continuously confronted with the central, provocative erection, and with their own gaze watching it. During the performance, a portion of the auditorium was lit further, engaging the spectators in the action. At this moment, Opole audiences lost the comfortable position of being hidden observers—one of the pleasures of conventional Western theatre. The spectators' theatrical voyeurism was exposed, because what they were watching was clearly erotic. At the same time, the male gaze was one of the main themes being played out before them: Dushyanta falls in love with Shakuntala while stalking and spying on her. Drawing the audience into the action is one thing—but Gurawski's design solutions also exposed the spectators *as such* to themselves and to one another. This effect was retained in subsequent 13 Rows productions.

Among the visual aspects of *Shakuntala*, it is impossible not to mention the costumes,[6] which came to garner the status of legend. Creators of the performance reported that the costumes had been designed by 'children'—in his commentary published in the programme, Flaszen even added that 'this is apparently the first such experience in theatre' (2010: 66). After managing to contact Wincenty Maszkowski— *Shakuntala*'s costume co-designer—Agnieszka Wójtowicz reports that the costumes were created by young adults, not children. Maszkowski described their work on costumes:

> In the end, it was decided that my class and I would design the costumes. I have to emphasize that this was a group of high-school students, but 'children' sounded better. Work on the costumes with them was very different than the usual costume-making process in theatre. Usually the scenographer has the text and instructions from the director, and then proposes something in line with what the director wishes. On the contrary,

---

6 Because they are complex and were changed in the course of action I will describe them in detail while describing the performance later in the chapter.

these were lessons I could lead in accordance with tales I had been told about the characters. The costumes were to show Indian influences. I therefore lectured about Indian paintings [...]. Our aim was to create costumes that reflected traditional Indian art elements. We took a long time working on sketches during lessons in drawing and painting. Many drawings were thus created—Grotowski chose the most interesting ones. [...] The costumes were then produced by tailors in town.
(Maszkowski quoted in Wójtowicz 2004: 214–15).

The creative process was so original, why, then, mislead the audience by suggesting children as the costume designers? Besides, the obvious marketing ploy—attributing the work to children—was also probably an attempt to create a contrast, which Grotowski himself presented directly.

Another layer of dialectic 'clash', 'vibration' of archetypes, was contrasting Kālidāsa's refined texts and love rules with the childishly naive costumes, designed by children from the Fine Arts School in Opole (class led by W. Maszkowski).
(Grotowski 2012: 221)

'Childishly naive' imaginations set against the play's mature lyricism and eroticism added another layer to the performance. Naive and innocent children were surreptitiously and scandalously included alongside (un)hidden erotic fantasies.

Apparently, no one has noticed that the *Shakuntala* costumes challenged gender conventions through cross-dressing. Men wore skirts, or blouses with extended tails, while Barbara Barska acted in close-fitting trousers, performing a boy. Also, no one noticed the degree to which the actors' bodies were exposed.[7] In the first part of the performance, all the women wore small tops, little more than bras, their midriffs exposed up to their bust lines. The legs of two women were also completely exposed. The actresses performed a range of intensive physical activities in their provocative costumes. No doubt, the spectators'—especially the

---

7 A key exception were Yogis wearing clothes that concealed their bodies entirely, looking like fancy clerical habits.

males—surprising close-up encounter with scantily clad performers amplified the erotic atmosphere of the performance.

The recollections of Ewa Lubowiecka, one of the actresses in *Shakuntala*, add another layer to the games Grotowski played with the costumes and the bodies of the performers.

> *Shakuntala* was constructed around the idea of breaking down our sensitivity. A sensitivity which for Jurek [Grotowski] did not exist. It was a bourgeois sensitivity, hence it had to be eradicated. Wincenty Maszkowski designed the costumes. I wore a pair of greyish galligaskins and a short bra top. During one rehearsal, Grotowski came up to me and cut my trousers so that I was suddenly left wearing a pair of tiny pants. I felt horrible. I was a fine-figured young woman, but this sort of costume only served to deform and ridicule the actor. I had to really struggle within myself, to overcome my own limitations. Today, this might seem ridiculous, but back then, I saw things very differently. [. . .] We played among an audience that was embarrassed, while texts from the *Kama Sutra* were recited by Andrzej Bielski and Adam Kurczyna, playing Yogis. All this meant that *Shakuntala* was perceived to be pornographic, a performance which outraged and scandalized.
>
> (in Wójtowicz 2004: 207)

The confluence of these various forces constitutes a clear attack on collective and personal shame, which in 1960 was a lot stronger than it is today. The act of Grotowski cutting those galligaskins to reveal Lubowiecka's thighs shows that he really was a co-designer of the costumes[8]—focused not on any idea of 'ancient India', but rather on erotic attraction and provocation. India was for Grotowski a mask behind which he hid and justified his erotic operations and provocations, targeting conventions and the audience's sense of shame.

---

8 Not only as the one who cut her pants, but also as the one who earlier chose which of the designs produced by the youth would be given to the tailor.

130 · DARIUSZ KOSIŃSKI

Grotowski did of course have a broad knowledge of India studying Sanskrit and Indian philosophy since his school days. That is why he felt he could fully and freely play with India and its stereotypical images. He used them to dramatize and stage a completely different topic. If he had staged *Maidens' Vows* in the way he had envisioned stage design in his diploma thesis, no one would have any doubts as to what the show was all about. Playing out this same conflict between biology and culture—between desire and sublimation using classic Sanskrit drama and Indian stylization—displaced even as it referred to that which was literally placed in the very centre of the performance: a phallus.

I Am Talking to You Shiva

As in the case of previous performances, surviving source materials allow us to get closer to a show from 60 years ago. In the case of *Shakuntala*, we can luckily read an original script drafted by Grotowski in 1960 and compare it with a recording of an audio version of the same play, which he directed for Polish Radio in Kraków in 1958.

The theatre script opens with an invocation and a meta-theatrical prologue, followed by two acts split into scenes—the first into four, the second into five. Act 1 takes place entirely in Kashyapa's hermitage where King Dushyanta and Shakuntala fall in love, ending with Shakuntala leaving to meet her future husband. Act 2 begins at the royal court, where Dushyanta—under a curse—does not recognize his beloved. Act 2 continues with a flight taken by the King and his Clown[9] and ends with the reunion of the estranged lovers, Dushyanta and Shakuntala. Act 1 is therefore the history of the birth and blossoming of love, while Act 2 tells the story of that love's collapse, followed by its miraculous restoration. Act 1 of Grotowski's adaptation encompasses Acts 1–4 of Kālidāsa's drama, with almost the entire original Act 2 deleted. Grotowski's Act 2 is made up of smaller or larger sections of Kālidāsa's Acts 5–7. Grotowski also added many non-Kālidāsa texts—fragments

---

9 The Clown (in Polish 'Wesołek') is a character introduced by Grotowski as the servant, a kind of counter-point to the serious character of the King. The Clown replaced all the other servants and helpers of the King from the original drama.

from the *Laws of Manu*, the *Kama Sutra* and other texts described in detail below.

Grotowski's choice of first words for his *Shakuntala* gives us insight into his approach to working with these ancient texts. Grotowski replaced the original benediction by Kālidāsa[10] with a Polish translation of the last three of the *Six verses on nirvana*—an eighteenth-century hymn by Adi Shankara translated in 1950 by Wanda Dynowska.[11] Grotowski changed the rhythm of Dynowska's translation by adding text. Every verse began with the call 'Shivoham, Shivoham—I am HIM', and after this first line, in each verse, Grotowski added the words 'Shiva, I am myself alone'. In this way, he strengthened the independence of this text—it is not assigned to any character—and needs to be taken literally, this is Shiva speaking to us. This Shiva is, however, not a Hindu god but an avatar of a character who, breaking boundaries and bringing together opposites, appears in earlier Theatre of 13 Rows performances as Alpha-Omega and the Promoter. He reveals himself, here at the outset, as a force with which all characters will reckon in due time; the one to whom the show will return at the end. This form is very characteristic of Grotowski's theatre, literally exposing characters and forces present in the performance itself, but at the same time put outside it, and in some way creating it. One could almost call this force the director, a figure of Grotowski himself, written into the play. At the same time, this meta-theatrical aspect presents a perspective that can be called philosophical, if not metaphysical.

---

10 Eight forms has Shiva, lord of all and king:
And these are water, first created thing;
And fire, which speeds the sacrifice begun;
The priest; and time's dividers, moon and sun;
The all-embracing ether, path of sound;
The earth, wherein all seeds of life are found;
And air, the breath of life: may he draw near,
Revealed in these, and bless those gathered here.
(Kālidāsa 1999: 3)

11 Wanda Dynowska (1888–1971) was a famous Polish philosopher, yogi, pupil of Ramana Maharishi, translator and specialist in Indian culture, who, from 1935, lived in India under the name Umadevi. For more information about this fascinating woman, see Tomaszewski 2013.

In Kālidāsa's *Shakuntala*, a meta-theatrical framework is imposed by the script, in the form of a conventional Prologue that precedes the three verses of translated Shankara hymns. The Prologue consists of a conversation between the Theatre Director and an Actress, on the theme of the play about to start. For performances of *Shakuntala*, Grotowski not only retained the Prologue in full, but also expanded it by adding the following instruction for the audience:

Dear Venerable People!

The main action takes place on a stage. However, actors are also seated behind your backs. Those of you who will be seated with your backs to them do not have to turn around. All that which is said not on the central stage but here and there is meant to be heard, not seen. Let's try. Here you go:

MAN, the period of whose life is one hundred years, should practise Dharma, Artha and Kama at different times and in such a manner that they may harmonize and not clash in any way. He should acquire learning in his childhood, in his youth and middle age he should attend to Artha and Kama, and in his old age he should perform Dharma, and thus seek to gain Moksha, i.e. release from further transmigration. Or, on account of the uncertainty of life, he may practise them at times when they are enjoined to be practised.[12]

Oh! You see? You can listen to them without turning around. I will add that they play the roles of yogis, but not just that. They play many characters, a whole crowd of them. Sometimes they are this, at others that. Do not be surprised.
(Grotowski 1960c: 2–3)

This is, of course, an instruction related to the specific shape and function of theatrical space prepared for *Shakuntala* by Jerzy Gurawski. It seems to have been the first time Grotowski so directly explained to audiences the rules of his performance.

---

12 This is a fragment from the *Laws of Manu* (Vatsayana 1883: 11).

The first scene of Act 1 in the script opens with King Dushyanta's hunt. It develops in line with the original sequences in the drama, and only minor deletions and changes were introduced to simplify phrases not easily translated from the original. More interesting than the cuts Grotowski made are the additions he wrote into his script. The first is titled 'The Song of a Dancing Girl' ('Pieśń tancerki'),[13] which appeared at the point when Shakuntala and her companion enter. The song exalted the joy of being a young girl—'Oh what joy it is to be a girl dancing, / is there any fate in the world more beautiful?' However, the Yogis negated this sentiment in the final verse, singing 'And I would rather be clay by the roadside / than a pitiful dancing girl' (Grotowski 1960c: 6–7).

The next fragment Grotowski added appears during the dialogue between Dushyanta, Shakuntala and the young women accompanying her. Shakuntala expresses how embarrassed she is by the King's overbearing attention. Two Yogis then recite a fragment from the *Kama Sutra*, describing in increasingly explicit detail the sexual foreplay of a woman trying to arouse her lover. The Yogis' erotic description appears after Shakuntala's reaction, and so, does not seem like a sort of choral 'inner voice' expressing her innermost desires. In fact, this voice belongs to two male Yogis reciting fragments from a book on love written by another man. If we are to consider the Yogis' pejorative intervention in the first song of Act 1 as disagreement with the 'selflessness' of the young women's dance, then this interjection can be interpreted as a voice calling for the 'usefulness' of female beauty and erotic charms—of course, its 'usefulness' for men.

The fact that Grotowski left Act 1 of Kālidāsa's drama almost unchanged is a strong contrast to how he deleted almost all of Act 2, leaving only the words recited in its closing intermezzo. One has the

---

13 'The Song of a Dancing Girl' ('Pieśń tancerki') is the first of several fragments Grotowski added to Kālidāsa's text that come from sources I cannot identify. I did hope that the poem was taken from Dynowska's anthology or another collection of Indian poetry accessible to Grotowski, but I was unable to find it. When I asked for his help, Prof. Krzysztof Maria Byrski wrote to me saying that, in his opinion, this is not an Indian work, and that—much like all other remaining unidentified fragments—it was likely written by Grotowski himself. For now I must content myself with not knowing for sure.

impression that the director is acting here in a 'Western' manner: from the perspective of European conventions and customs, Act 2 appears to be dead weight, not adding much to either the action or Shakuntala's character. On the other hand, Kālidāsa's second act contained the second *sandhi* ('segment') called *pratimukha* ('facing'), directly in line with the conventions of classic Sanskrit drama. The theatrical convention exemplified here is used to tie up sideline actions that deviate from the main narrative, actions that show that some intrigue that had begun would not be developed further (see Byrski 1979). Grotowski cut all of this act and went straight to Act 3, which he retained with almost no changes. First, after his long monologue about being in love, the king listens in on a conversation between Shakuntala—who is weakened by love—and her female friends. Finally, he reveals himself. Then comes the next big change Grotowski made to Kālidāsa's Sanskrit text. After Shakuntala expresses her jealousy—'Oh don't detain the good king. He is separated from the court ladies, and he is anxious to go back to them' (Kālidāsa: 32)—comes a montage of fragments from Lesson 3 of the *Laws of Manu* (*Manusmriti* 2019: 12).[14] These are pieces of advice given to a young man wishing to marry. The first Yogi recited ten types of families whose female offspring should be avoided—such as those 'who have thick hair on the body'—and indicates the kinds of women who should not be married. In reply, Yogi II drew the image of a perfect wife. In this way, the ensuing lyrical delicate love scene was interrupted by the clearly male voice of a 'salesman' with extremely detailed, 'practical' advice. The Yogis functioned as commentators who, with pragmatic poise, demolish 'romantic' visions of emotional ties.

---

14 I do not know which Polish translation Grotowski used. As far as I know, no one has asked this question thus far—perhaps because finding the answer is so difficult. No Polish translation of *Laws of Manu* existed prior to 1960, nor was there a Polish commentary from which Grotowski could have sourced the quoted fragments. So what did Grotowski use? Maybe the Russian translation published in 1960? Or a French version? Or else maybe he translated it himself using help from Fr. Franciszek Tokarz, his Sanskrit and Indian philosophy teacher? I do not know. It only seems certain the fragment of *Laws of Manu* used in the script are not quotations but rather a collection of summaries.

After this intervention, Grotowski's script returned to Kālidāsa's drama, until a scene featuring the successful courtship. Two minor changes involved adding lines for Shakuntala—whose friends left her 'all alone' with Dushyanta—relating to the presence of people watching. She twice expressed her fear regarding how 'they watch here' (Grotowski 1960c: 29, 30). Finally, the lovers decided to be wed 'by a simple voluntary rite' (Kālidāsa 1999: 34). Grotowski deleted the rest of the act. He did exactly the same thing in the radio performance in which, after the lovers exchange their final words, music was to be played to signal sexual intercourse. In the Opole script, instead of using music, dimming the lights or any other conventional way of suggesting sex, Grotowski had the Yogis recite a prayer to Shiva:

> YOGI I: I am speaking to you, Shiva,
> you who are lecherous fire shaping nature,
> divine shapes, symbols of death, and human desires:
> the cause of changeability
> organs of reproduction and skeleton bones and the warmth of
> love.
>
> YOGI II: I am speaking to you Shiva,
> you who are the lord of delight and despair,
> the lord of deadly pestilence and lord of blessed delights
> who guide the flow of heart and blood,
> whose touch drives passion, whose gaze destroys;
> in the cold and warmth of your lightest breath
> there is the embodied might of Delight and Death.
>
> YOGI I: Strong and quick is your temple Shiva,
> rushing like human beings in their unending run
> towards a limitless sea of eternal snows,
> yours is the source and yours the Might
> that pushes nature to unending struggle
> and your image is death at the gates of life
> (Grotowski 1960c: 30–31)

This dialogue has a totally different character than the earlier Yogi interventions. It neither interrupts nor wrecks the loving mood, but instead deepens it by introducing a philosophical and 'sacral' understanding of love and desire. In reading this scene, it sounds very serious. It represents a culmination of the whole love narrative in which, the voices and scenes previously opposing the Yogis to Shakuntala now come together in harmony and fulfilment. This effect is enhanced by a sequence from the *Kama Sutra*, describing the gentle and subtle caresses of lovers following love-making. It helps to build a mood of calm. The textual montage of the final sequences in Act 1, Scene 2, almost flawlessly dramatize rising desire. Its culmination climaxes in the image of Shiva as 'death at the gates of life', finding a calm resolution after the climax.

The next scene was presented from the perspective of Shakuntala's female friends and is key to the narrative in which the anger-prone sage Durvasa curses Shakuntala, because she was thinking only about her lover and did not recognize the sage, failing to welcome him in accordance with custom. As a result of the curse, Shakuntala was to be forgotten by Dushyanta, the one who caused her inattention, leading to her insult Durvasa. Shakuntala's friend Anasuyah, terrified, ran after the sage asking him to reverse the curse. She softened Durvasa's judgement. He said that the curse would be broken at the sight of the signet ring Dushyanta gave to Shakuntala.

The last scene of Act 1 is constructed mainly from Act 4 of the ancient drama. Grotowski's Act 1 finale is further augmented by sequences of Shakuntala bidding farewell to the hermitage, receiving advice from her adoptive father Kastapa as she sets off. In the 1958 radio play, Grotowski deleted the whole of this act—while in the 1960 script, he not only restored it, but also turned it into the finale of the first part of the performance. Seen from the perspective of Shakuntala and Dushyanta's love, this is a scene of secondary importance that extends the action, but essentially lacks any narrative importance. It is therefore unsurprising that Grotowski removed it from the radio play. But why did he include it in his stage script?

Perhaps, the most important reason appears on page 42 of the script where—in place of the original advice from Kashyapa—Grotowski inserted a series of commandments that demand the complete and unconditional subjection of women to men—a text created from fragments of the *Laws of Manu*, mainly from Lessons 5 and 9. The text Grotowski assembled is spoken by the Yogis who continue to function as a choir voicing male dominance over women. The Yogis' position is revealed here, with all its ruthlessness, creating a powerful contrast with the lyrical scene of the farewell, advice and blessing. In my opinion, it was exactly this contrast that interested Grotowski.

The first scene of the second act presents a conversation between the King Dushyanta and the Clown, oscillating around an unclear recollection and an incomprehensible longing aroused in Dushyanta by a song about a bumblebee. This dialogue dovetails with earlier mentions of the insect: Kālidāsa used a bumblebee as a metaphor for the love between Shakuntala and the King.

In the act's second scene, Shakuntala arrives at Dushyanta's court, but he does not recognize her. Grotowski left out statements made by members of the court as well as Shakuntala's companions. None of these characters appear here in his 1960 script, because the dramaturg/director changed the scene in such a way, that only the King and Shakuntala appeared. The members of the audience—already divided by the organization of the performance space into two groups—'performed' the accompanying personages to whom the King and Shakuntala turned when addressing appropriate lines. In the script, this dialogue was developed by changing grammatical forms and by adding the necessary verses to what the King and Shakuntala say, so as to craft a 'dialogue' with their respective audience members who, of course, remained silent.

The lovers' moment of encounter, strained by forgetfulness, is staged as in the original. Shakuntala reaches for the ring only to discover she's lost it. She realizes that her lover has forgotten her and that she has no way of restoring his memory. It is in this dramatic moment that she utters another fragment added by Grotowski, a monologue characterizing human beings as toys in the hands of Shiva.

138 · DARIUSZ KOSIŃSKI

> Like a puppet made out of wood, oh, King, [Shiva] moves its
> limbs,
> That is how here on earth everything moves that lives.
> Like infinite space, that is how, oh, King, Shiva
> Permeates persons himself and assigns good and evil,
> Like a pearl on a string or an ox roped by the nose
> We do what Shiva wants: he created and drives us!
> We humans do not rule over death: we all find death
> Falling like trees growing on a shore, captured by the river's
> flow,
> And the way grass blades surrender to the might of hail,
> That is how all creatures surrender to Shiva's might.
> Look at the illusory charm Shiva has created for himself:
> Bedevilled by this spell, human beings kill each other!
> And as Shiva wants, he unites or divides us.
> Like a small child playing with toys, this is how he plays with
> creatures,
> Oh, not like a mother and father Shiva deals with us,
> But like someone riven by fury, like an alien and an enemy.
> My maddened father Shiva.
> (Grotowski 1960c: 48)

This interpolation appears at a key moment in the script, after the initial hymn and the dialogue of lovers who refer to Shiva as a force that rules the world, including the world of the performance.[15] This image of Shiva

---

15 For a long time, I was unable to confirm where this image was taken from, even after consulting Professor Byrski. Its origin was uncovered by Wanda Świątkowska—who has an abiding interest in the image of the world as theatre. She confirmed that the basis for Shakuntala's monologue is Book 3, Chapter 30 of the *Mahabharata*, the 'Vana Parva', where Draupadi talks about Shiva manipulating human beings like wooden puppets: 'As a wooden doll is made to move its limbs by the wire-puller, so are creatures made to work by the Lord of all. O Bharata, like space that covers every object, God, pervading every creature, ordains its weal or woe. Like a bird tied with a string, every creature is dependent on God. Everyone is subject to God and none else. No one can be his own ordainer. Like a pearl on its string, or a bull held fast by the cord passing through its nose, or a tree fallen from the bank into the middle of the stream, every creature follows the command of the Creator, because imbued with His Spirit and because established in Him. And man himself, dependent on the Universal Soul,

becomes ever more layered and wrathful with each addition of this kind. In Shakuntala's despairing monologue, Shiva's dark and dangerous side is revealed. Shiva, who in the *Invocation* is presented as a figure of complete awareness and then as a figure with a 'lecherous fire shaping nature', now appears as a ruthless ruler playing games with the fates of humans, creating seductive illusions that push them towards violence and murder. In the guise of Indian and mythological references, this is the same topic Grotowski introduced in all his previous performances: the ambivalent nature of the forces that rule reality.

Shakuntala does not abandon Dushyanta at the court but is kidnapped right after leaving the room. The King listens to the Yogis' reports about this event with astonishment and also leaves, ending Act 2, Scene 2, in the script.

Scene 3 faithfully follows Scene 1 of the original's Act 6, in which two palace guards grab a fisherman who they suspect of stealing the valuable ring. It turns out to be the very 'fatal ring' Shakuntala lost. It reminds Dushyanta who Shakuntala is, but too late. The whole scene gives the impression of the folk-style comedy that Grotowski used in the radio play, showing that he already planned to use folk traditions in his Opole staging.

Scene 4 was based on materials from Act 6 of Kālidāsa's drama. Grotowski shortened the scene, leaving only Dushyanta's and the Clown's lines, but adding three fragments from the *Kama Sutra*, recited by the Yogis. They incorporate a kind of imaginary reconstruction of the experiences of love presented in the first part of the drama. The first fragment describes an erotic geography of kisses: 'The following are places for kissing: the forehead, the eyes, the cheeks' (Vatsayana 1883: 39). The second fragment relates to signs of love that help to arouse desire: 'The

---

cannot pass a moment independently. Enveloped in darkness, creatures are not masters of their own weal or woe. They go to heaven or hell urged by God Himself. Like light straws dependent on strong winds, all creatures, O Bharata, are dependent on God! [. . .] And the Supreme Lord, according to his pleasure, plays with His creatures, creating and destroying them, like a child with his toy (of soft earth). O king, it seems to me that God does not behave towards his creatures like a father or mother. Like a vicious person, He treats them with anger!' (Vyasa 2019: 894).

love of a woman who sees the marks of nails on the private parts of her body, even though they are old and almost worn out, becomes again fresh and new [. . .]' (43). The third, and longest fragment, describes sexual violence: 'Sexual intercourse can be compared to a quarrel, on account of the contrarieties of love and its tendency to dispute. The place of striking with passion is the body [. . .]' (49). This fragment refers quite clearly to sexual climax, in which delight merges with pain in line with Dushyanta's memories of his 'wedding' with Shakuntala.

Once the *Kama Sutra* recitation ends, Dushyanta deliberates about the causes of his forgetting Shakuntala and how it came to be that the ring was lost. He finally contemplates a picture of his beloved which, in this scene, functions as a stand-in for her. Grotowski retained Kālidāsa's scene in its entirety, thereby setting a calmer tenor supporting the next sequence's evocation of desire, when Dushyanta recalls love scenes from Act 1 with nostalgia and melancholy.

The King's longing love scene was then suddenly interrupted by a divine messenger attacking the Clown. In the original, Indira sent Matala with a message for Dushyanta, but in the script, Grotowski replaced Indra with Shiva, and Matala with the Clown. Just as in Act 1, Scene 1, Dushyanta sets out on a journey, and much like the first journey, it ends at the hermitage where he was to find Shakuntala. Grotowski conducts this very subtly and without any emphasis, and yet it is apparent that the composition of his script has a symmetrical character. Scenes from Act 2 that follow the loss of Shakuntala represent a sort of return to the actions of Act 1, which are symbolically evoked here in reverse order— first, the love experience, then the journey. Placing the Clown on the flying cart instead of Matala, visually illustrated this symmetry.

Scene 5 in the script is based on Act 7 of the Indian drama. The scene begins with an airborne journey showing the King battling demons. Dushyanta defeats them and journeys on to the hermitage where he finds Shakuntala and their son. Grotowski shortened this sequence, turning it into a series of lyrical exclamations that represented the joy and surprise felt by the lovers upon rediscovering one another after many years of being apart. These edits however are very small, compared to the change Grotowski introduced in the finale of his script. He ends his version of *Shakuntala* right after the two lovers reunite, removing everything that follows this moment in Kālidāsa's drama, deleting nearly the entirety of Kālidāsa's second act. Grotowski's final scene represents his largest cut of the original text. The content of this final deletion has large implications for the interpretation of the whole work. Grotowski removed scenes in which Kashyapa explains the logic of what happened to the story's heroes, thereby liberating them from their sufferings.

Instead of the original drama's explanation and conciliation, Grotowski ended his version with four mysterious verses whose literary source remains unknown. Dushyanta and Shakuntala recited them in unison:

> I will now devour you whole, father Shiva,
> Seeing as I was born under a dark star
> And the one born so is said to be destined to devour one's father.
> Now I will devour you whole, father Shiva.
> (Grotowski 1960c: 72)

Truly surprising words! At first glance, it seems like these words are related to the two lovers' romantic history. But after careful consideration, a hidden narrative thread emerges that is connected with Shiva as a force, not a god. The play's final intonations are linked to earlier fragments invoking Shiva made by the Yogis in the love scene from Act 1, Shakuntala's monologue from the court scene, and above all, the *Invocation* that opens the play. Although the closing words are assigned to Dushyanta and Shakuntala in the script, it is hard to imagine that these characters from Kālidāsa's drama would say these words. The words are spoken in a voice that is hard to assign to any character or figure. Just like the words spoken at the beginning, they seem to belong to some hidden subject of the whole script. It would be a simplification to assume that it is the voice of the creator of the script, Grotowski. Maybe, it is better to say that the voice does not belong to anyone, and is the voice of the performance itself.

A Thirsty Bumblebee and a Doll Made of Wood

The cover of the fifth issue of *Materiały i Dyskusje*—published to celebrate the premiere of *Shakuntala*—featured a photograph of Rena Mirecka and Zygmunt Molik in extraordinary, almost acrobatic, poses. The first in a series, this photograph shows the start of the performance. The caption:

DIRECTOR: Shivoham, Shivoham—I am he, Shiva
The Fulfilment of Being-Happiness-Awareness.
MAIN ACTRESS: Like a puppet made out of wood, oh, Lord Shiva
moves its limbs,
That is how here on earth everything moves that lives.
And as Shiva wants, he unites or divides us,
Like a small child playing with toys, this is how he plays with
creatures
(*Materiały i Dyskusje* 1960, VOL. 5: 1)

If the caption is not a montage used only for the programme, then it seems that in his show, Grotowski changed the 'Invocation', and at the very beginning, contrasted the hymn of Nirvana and Self with the image of 'a puppet made out of wood'. Hence, the image of Shiva as 'the Fulfilment of Being-Happiness-Awareness' was immediately juxtaposed to the opposing vision presented next—that of a ruthless lord and manipulator who teases creatures defenceless against his might for fun. Instead of a 'cult' act of placing the divine figure of Shiva in the position of a single voice initiating, and in some way, delivering the drama, at the start of the show we instead have a dialectical double voice showing two different ways of seeing the relationship between humanity and the transcendental force ruling over our lives.

The meta-theatrical Prologue is also represented in the photographs reproduced in *Materiały i Dyskusje* but, strangely enough, these do not appear right after the 'Invocation', but instead half-way through the script in-between photos from Act 1 and Act 2. The notion that Grotowski moved the Prologue to the beginning of Act 2, thereby adding something of a second meta-theatrical frame to the second part, is tempting. And yet, this seems improbable, because no report from the performance mentioned such a scene in the second part, and the photograph shows Mirecka and Molik wearing costumes from Act 1. It seems more likely that the arrangement of the photographs in this case does not follow the arrangement of scenes in the performance.

The photograph in question shows Mirecka sitting on a boulder at the foot of the phallic column with her legs bent hard at the knees and crossed at the ankles (inv. nos 136, 137). Her arms are raised, bent at the elbows, her palms are pressed together as if in prayer (but she holds them behind the top of her head) and her lips are wide open as if singing. Molik is standing behind Mirecka smiling, with his arms splayed and raised upwards, slightly bent at the elbows, his hands forming a gesture resembling an Indian mudra. The photograph gives the impression that he is showing off his pupil's skills with pride and joy. My impression seems to be confirmed by the photograph's caption.

MAIN ACTRESS (sings).

DIRECTOR: Bravo, dear lady, bravo! The whole audience became
    as if a painting, fixed still with delight.
(*Materiały i Dyskusje* 1960, VOL. 5: 8)

In Grotowski's script, the Prologue ended with a 'rehearsal' intended to show the audiences that they need not turn around to hear the Yogis speaking behind them. It is written in a way that clarifies the shape of the space designed by Gurawski, and hence, we can imagine that it was created at a late stage of work on the script. The Prologue's ending also has a clearly theatrical character. Thus, it is rather strange that no reviewer mentioned it. It seems that it should have drawn attention to itself through its uniqueness and by the very fact that it was staged at the very beginning. Who knows, perhaps it was ultimately deleted?

After the Director announced the play's title, Act 1 begins with a scene in which King Dushyanta goes for a hunt. Zygmunt Molik played the King. His costume was made up of a long-sleeved shirt, cut so as to expose most of his torso, and a long, ankle-length skirt slightly widened at the bottom. On his head, he wore a simple, round cap reminiscent of a kepi—though without a peak. The whole costume was singular in colour, though from the black-and-white photographs, it is hard to tell what that colour was (perhaps green). The costume was decorated with several unique elements. A small, dark shape was attached with tassels at the breast where the two sides of the shirt joined in the middle, the dark material and tassels reminiscent of an insect with many pairs of legs. The skirt had thick strips of fabric stripes sewn into it, alongside each leg on the front of the skirt, starting at the hem and shooting up towards the waist. Both strips featured text painted on the fabric. On the left-hand side, the text reads 'Theatre of 13 Rows' and on the right, it probably read 'Shakuntala' (inv. nos 106–8). A piece of fabric with an obscure face painted onto it is affixed to the waistband of the King's skirt, just below his navel. It is unfortunately difficult to tell from the photos what it is exactly. The King's costume is completed with simple make-up: dark lines follow his eyebrows and nearly meet at the bridge of the nose, then continue downward along the sides of his nose following the contours between the edges of his cheeks and the corners of his lips, before joining beneath his chin. His make-up strongly defined his facial features, as it did for Shakuntala and the Clown.

As we know from the script, in Act 1, Scene 1, King Dushyanta sets off on a hunt. This sequence can be seen pictured in the second photograph in the series, included in *Materiały i Dyskusje* (inv. no. 120). It shows the perversity and sense of humour conveyed through creative staging in *Shakuntala*. On the central boulder, the King and the Clown— who this time serves as the King's coachman—use their bodies to manifest horses, a cart and hunters. This happens in a very simple way. The Clown (Antoni Jahołkowski) kneels upon the boulder and leans his whole body forward. He stretches his arms far behind him and grasps the King, who holds onto the Clown and leans far back. This forms a dynamic pose clearly reminiscent of a charging war or hunting chariot.

However, the most interesting aspect of this photograph is the third person in the frame, Ewa Lubowiecka. She is standing on the floor in front of the semi-sphere and the charging chariot. Her legs are slightly bent, and she seems to be moving them as if at a trot. She holds her arms out to the sides, bent at the elbows, her fists bunched and lowered towards the ground. She holds her head high, and her face looks as if a mask of fear. That she appeared in the photograph as a fleeing animal is confirmed by the caption.

> KING: Ha, ha, my coachman, how far our chase has brought us in the hunt for this gazelle!
>
> CLOWN: Oh, my eternal sir! The horses are racing, their ears perked up, as if ashamed of being outrun by a gazelle.
>
> GAZELLE (Out of a snout tired from running—Spilling blades of un-chewed grass).
>
> (*Materiały i Dyskusje* 1960, VOL. 5: 3)

In this scene, then, Lubowiecka played a Gazelle pursued by the hunting King. As we will soon learn, this was not the last animal the actress would come to embody while working for the Theatre of 13 Rows.

Upon a warning from Yogi I (Andrzej Bielski) that he is approaching a sacred hermitage, Dushyanta interrupts his hunt and enters the hermitage, where he meets Shakuntala. It is possible to imagine—though I have no proof of this—that the entrance of Shakuntala and her female attendants was set to 'The Song of the Dancing Girl' that appears at this moment in the script. As I have already mentioned, the three female characters that appear in the first act were dressed in revealing outfits for 1960s Poland. Rena Mirecka wore a short-sleeved shirt that ended just below her bustline, revealing from her midriff down to her hips. It was lighter in colour than Dushyanta's outfit—probably light red—and decorated at the sleeves and neckline with strips of bright fabric covered in black dots. Two dark cups were sewn over each breast. Mirecka also wore a skirt decorated with dark spots, probably the same colour as her shirt. It was cut into several long, narrow strips of fabric that tapered to points. She wore dark shorts beneath the skirt—short enough to show her bare legs beneath her revealing skirt when she moved. She wore soft, light-coloured moccasins. Just like Molik and Jahołkowski, she also wore make-up that emphasized the lines of her face.

Lubowiecka appears in several photos that span the length of the play and dressed the same in all of them. She wore a dark short-sleeve crop top, cut just beneath her bustline, exposing her midsection. Her short, tight-fitting, light-coloured pants ended just above her knees. The first layer on top of her shorts was a pale miniskirt, and then a shawl tied below her midriff in such a way that it covered her buttocks and the backs of her legs. She wore the same footwear as Mirecka.

Barbara Barska wore a light-coloured crop top with short sleeves and a completely exposed lower torso in the same style as her friends. Barska's top, like the rest of her outfit, was brightly coloured (perhaps yellow or orange). Her legs were also covered completely by loose trousers that were somewhat darker than her blouse and cut like galligaskins but tied with narrow ribbons that cinched her pants both around her thighs and beneath her knees. Her trousers ended above her ankles. She wore almost the same footwear as Mirecka and Lubowiecka.

Dushyanta revealed his presence when Shakuntala was attacked by a bumblebee.[16] One of the photographs from the GIA probably shows this very scene (inv. nos 122–23). Shakuntala is clearly frightened as she crouches by the phallic column. On the column's other side, Anasuya stands, gesturing with her hands reminiscent of a mudra. At the top of the central copula, Lubowiecka stands leaning towards Shakuntala, her hands stretched backwards, staring at Shakuntala with a mean gaze, her pose suggesting gliding flight. Lubowiecka is partly obscured by Dushyanta, who is face to face with Shakuntala and is stretched taught like a string—his right arm raised upwards but his hand bent at a sharp angle, his extended first finger pointing in Shakuntala's direction like a poised scorpion's tail. His left arm is extended backwards, making a line with his right, while his left palm is angled upwards. My supposition that this is the scene in which Shakuntala is attacked by the bumblebee is confirmed by her expression of fear and the position of Lubowiecka, who here plays the winged insect flying towards the heroine. Molik's

---

16 'Bumblebee' appears in the Polish text; in the English translation, it is simply 'bee'. In keeping with the source materials, I will continue using 'bumblebee'.

pose and his gesture look as a sequence in which he tries to create an image of an attacking bumblebee and defending the young woman from the insect's attack, at the same time. If I am reading the photograph correctly, then, at this moment, Grotowski and his actors constructed a sort of embodied, gestural equivalent of a bumblebee, which Kālidāsa subtly deploys as a symbol of love and desire.

As stated above, Grotowski deleted most of Kālidāsa's Act 2. Surprisingly, he kept Act 2's closing scene where the Pupil[17] speaks with an off-stage Priyamvada. An explanation for why Grotowski retained this scene can be found in the arrangement of events from the perspective of the stage. The director used the Pupil's appearance in order to turn the audience's attention away from the young women and the King— who were exiting from the stage or were hiding in the shadows—before paying attention to them a moment later. Secondly, the Pupil engages in dialogue with a partner who is not present on stage. The actor performed the presence of his conversation partner by being 'responsive', and by directing his responses to the audience. In doing so, he also laid a foundation for later scenes constructed on a similar basis, to induce audience participation.

Scene 2 of the performance opened with a long monologue from the King in love. Unfortunately, we know nothing about how it was staged. The next scene, however, is presented to us with a photograph and a caption. Shakuntala, afflicted by a broken heart, is consoled by her friends. The heroine is lying on her back across the centre-stage construction with her arms raised and bent at the elbows, fingers pleated together (inv. no. 112). To her left, Anasuya sits, leaning against the edge of the copula and massaging Shakuntala's temples. On her right side, Priyamvada lunges towards Shakuntala, props up the heroine's bare leg on her bent knee and massages Shakuntala's lower leg. The photograph caption states:

---

17 In the Polish translation, the scene with the Pupil is the last in Act 2. In the English version by Arthur W. Ryder, the scene occurs at the beginning of the Act 3. We do not know who performed the role in the Opole production—maybe one of the Yogis?

ANUSUYAH: Shakuntala! I can't help thinking that you are in a state like that of a lady in love

SHAKUNTALA: Try your best to make the good King take pity upon me. If not, you will soon need to pay a burial offering for me.

PRIYAMVADA: She must write him a love letter!

(*Materiały i Dyskusje* 1960, VOL. 5: 5)

This is a shortened version of the ancient drama's dialogue where the King spies on the women's conversation (Kālidāsa 1999: 29–30). The King—who cannot be seen in the photograph—is most likely hiding behind a pillar.

The most important part of Act 1 was the love scene. There is a photograph of this scene included in *Materiały i Dyskusje*, with the following ironic and humorous caption:

SHAKUNTALA and THE KING (surrendered to love).

YOGIS (averting their eyes).

GAZELLE (standing there in melancholy).

(*Materiały i Dyskusje* 1960, VOL. 5: 7)

Centre-stage, the lovers stand with their backs to each other (inv. nos 106–8). Leaning backwards, their heads touch. As they arch their backs and touch heads, they hold each other by their hands. In this way, the lovers create an arch as they surrender to love. On the either side of the couple—more or less symmetrically—the Yogis turn away from the loving couple in embarrassment.[18] On top of the central copula, we see Lubowiecka leaning forwards on slightly bent legs, with her back to the lovers and her head turned slightly towards them. In the photo, her eyes seem shut—which lends her a certain melancholic appearance.

---

18 As far as we can tell from the creators' comments and critics' reviews, this appearance of Yogis on stage is exceptional. They otherwise mostly remained on the platforms at the back of two banks of seats. Maybe this composition was arranged only for this photograph? Another instance of their presence on the central stage can be seen in the next scene, with the commandments given to Shakuntala. So it seems possible that they entered the stage during the love scene—adding to its exceptional importance by their presence—and then remained on stage to deliver the series of commandments.

Interestingly enough, Lubowiecka is described here as performing Gazelle, not Priyamvada. By introducing Gazelle into the scene, Grotowski evidenced just how carefully he read the staged text. In Kālidāsa's version, the world of animals accompanies that of people providing love symbols that are subtly played out. One of these is the aforementioned bumblebee, a symbol of desire, as well as pain. Another is the gazelle—the appearances of which in the drama are uniquely identified with Shakuntala—as her ward, and as the animal the King tries to hunt down: a delicately suggested allegory of her youth and innocence, and thereby a counterpoint to the ecstatic act of fulfilment of desire, both overshadowed by melancholy.

The first part of the performance finished with the scene in which Shakuntala bids farewell to the hermitage and receives fatherly advice from Kashyapa. As we learned from the script, instead of the original drama's litany of advice, Grotowski inserted a series of commandments derived from the *Laws of Manu*. In the performance, the Yogis entered the central stage as the representatives of patriarchal power, to recite these rules of complete and unconditional subjection of women to men. The scene is shown most clearly in a photograph from the collection at the GIA (inv. nos 130–32). The Yogis are perched atop the copula facing Shakuntala, who kneels on the floor at their feet. Their poses spark associations of the casting of spells, rather than the giving of advice. Yogi I's hands are raised high up over his head, and Yogi II stands next to him in a confident pose, with his arms crossed over his chest and his palms turned towards Shakuntala, as if he were barring her from doing something. Shakuntala is kneeling to their left in a humble pose, with her head hung and her hands together as if in prayer—a pose that recalls images of penitents often placed at the edge of medieval and renaissance altar paintings alongside images of great saints.

Interestingly enough, at this point Mirecka is wearing a different costume than in previous scenes; she must have changed costume when Anasuya tried to convince Durvasa. The new costume makes her look like the Yogis. She wears a simple, ankle-length skirt, in plain colour that appears to be grey. It is stylized with two simple, white, horizontal stripes at the bottom of the skirt. The upper part of her body is completely covered with a simple, light-coloured tunic with wide sleeves. The tunic is so long it nearly reaches her knees and is decorated at the neckline with a strip of lighter coloured fabric that follows the length of her collar. She wears the same costume in Act 2.

The scene showing Shakuntala's departure from the hermitage at the end of Act 1 allowed the audience to engage with the narrative in a very simple and inventive way. After Shakuntala departed, the audience got up and left the auditorium for intermission—in a way, joining Shakuntala on her journey. Perhaps thanks to this device, the audience was prepared for the role they were to play in the second half of the per-formance.

The second act opened with a very short dialogue between the Clown and the King, as the King was being tormented by a longing he could not understand. The short conversation served as a kind of pro-logue, and also served to help the audience return to the world of the performance, in preparation for their imminent involvement in the action. In this scene, as in the rest of the second act, Dushyanta appeared in a different, richly decorated costume. Instead of the short shirt and skirt, his new costume (inv. nos 152–54) featured a cape sewn from a thick, reflective material and knee-length trousers made from three strips of fabric—each darker than the previous strip which then turned into a collage of shiny fabric serving as an ornate top. His pants and top were cut in such a way that the golden fabric around his hips and around his biceps was covered in dark rhombus shapes. Above his hips, in the centre of his midsection was a triangle filled with dark vertical stripes that were cut in places with fragments in the same horizontal stripes on the left (making it look like a blouse bound with a belt). The back of the overalls was decorated with a cape (probably red), that was sewn into the fabric across his shoulders and hung down to the King's waistline. The King's costume was completed by a sort of collar—a wide, golden triangle beneath his neckline, decorated with a dark ornamentation. Instead of a simple cap, the King wore a snow-white turban. His whole body was covered. As with Shakuntala's new costume, the King's hands and face were all that his new costume left exposed.

After the short preliminary sequence featuring the King and the Clown came a court scene featuring the spatial architecture designed by Gurawski. Here, only Shakuntala and the King were on stage. Shakuntala's companions and the King's court were performed by the audience. The roles were divided among the two groups of audience members that sat facing each other.

This is one of the two scenes from the performance upon which the director himself commented:

> The audience on one side of the stage were treated like royal courtiers: the King sought out advice from them, and shared subtle, discreet observations about their guests. The audience on the other side of the central stage were treated like the delegation from the hermitage. The King listened to them (silence commented upon by the King: 'and so you say' and so on), he chided them, making individual allusions and snipes at the expense of individual spectators treated as hermits (grey haired elderly man, elderly woman etc.). These persons were picked out of the audience by the actor playing the King based on contrast: a young woman for example 'played a role' of an elderly woman; 'picked out' meaning noticed and indicated by gestures to all those present. In this fragment of the performance the central stage remained unlit, but the auditorium—on both sides—was illuminated, or rather only a part of the audience was lit up: those who were 'actors' at that very moment. Work on this scene allowed me to understand that finding a shared spatial formula for the two ensembles was not so much a question of placing the viewers-actors in space, a system of placing them, but rather a specific staging process, creating a shared 'action' involving the audience and the actors and then letting architectural consequences emerge.
> (Grotowski 2012: 235)

152 · DARIUSZ KOSIŃSKI

This discovery had enormous consequences in subsequent performances by the Theatre of 13 Rows, especially for *Forefathers' Eve* and *Kordian*.

We do not know exactly what the next two scenes looked like. In the first, there is a farce of an arrest when a Fisherman finds the 'fatal ring', and in the second, a lyrical sequence communicates the love pangs felt by the King longing for his beloved. There are no photos of these sequences. In contrast, the 'attack' sequence of the messenger who challenges Dushyanta to fight demons, the fight itself and the subsequent flight from the scene of the fight, are very well documented with a series of photos showing the dynamics of the Molik–Jahołkowski duet. This series begins with a photo showing Dushyanta in what appears to be a dance pose. His right leg is raised and bent at the knee, his whole body lightly bent backwards. His head is tilted back, and his left arm is raised in the air and bent at the elbow, with his fingers spread wide. The caption reads:

> KING: My very palace is invaded by evil creatures
> (*Materiały i Dyskusje* 1960, VOL. 5: 13)

In Kālidāsa's drama, this is how Dushyanta reacts when Matala attacks him and the Clown's screams can be heard from offstage (Kālidāsa 1999: 78).

The next two photographs featuring Dushyanta and the Clown are connected to their fight with demons in the first part of Scene 5. These archival photographs show two stages of the same movement made by Dushyanta, who rolls over forwards on top of the copula, while the Clown stands next to him in an aggressive warrior pose—his right leg elevated, bent at the knee and tilted slightly, so that it crosses over the straight left leg on which he stood (inv. nos 127–28 and 129). His right arm appears above his head in a way that suggests he is about to strike a blow. This gesture indicates that this is a fight sequence and also, links this image to the scene in which the demons are defeated. Dushyanta's tumble could very well be the element completing this theatrical staging of a battle.

INDIAN EROTICA · **153**

There is no doubt that the battle between the King and the demons can be seen in a photograph printed in *Materiały i Dyskusje* (1960, VOL. 5: 11). Dushyanta is pictured sitting on the shoulders of the Clown/Coachman, who is pointing at something ahead of them with his left arm extended forwards (inv. no. 155). The King is also extending his left arm, but in a striking gesture with his fingers pulled in towards his palm. His right hand's fingers are curled inwards like his left hand, and drawn close to his chest just below his chin. The dynamic tension between his outstretched left arm and his right hand curled up and drawn near, makes it seem as if the King is poised to strike a blow. In *Materiały i Dyskusje*, the caption reads:

> CLOWN: And now we will descend to the trail of the clouds. Demon! Kill him!
>
> KING (shoots).
> (*Materiały i Dyskusje* 1960, VOL. 5: 11)

The scene involving the duo's return flight is represented by a photograph, also printed in *Materiały i Dyskusje*. It shows the Clown and Dushyanta as if in the final stages of their airborne fight (inv. nos 156–59). The King is still sitting on the shoulders of his servant, who is bent over the central copula in a way that allows Dushyanta to rest his knees and extend his arms upon it. Dushyanta's torso is straight, and his face expresses elation, or even, delight: eyes closed, mouth slightly open, the whole face raised. The photograph's caption speaks to this elation caused by their arrival:

> KING: It seems that we have descended into the region of the clouds.
>
> CLOWN: In a moment, oh, eternal, you will stand upon the Earth.
> (*Materiały i Dyskusje* 1960, VOL. 5: 15)

The central hemisphere stands in for the Earth in this scene, and the whole image is expressed by the caption, the final stage of cosmic flight. Yet, their posture is multivalent and ambiguous. At their resting point, the Clown's head is firmly pinned between the King's legs and up against the copula. The Clown extends his arms backwards, forming a set of 'wings'. While their posture fits the context of the scene, there is also something about this image that suggests homosexual ecstasy—as if an allusion to the stereotypical metaphor of riding or flying is a stand-in for sexual climax. The whole thing is played out subtly and seems to be a continuation of the previous 'ride' on the Clown, but at the same time, the photographed pose is reminiscent of standard images of homoerotic arousal.

The heroes' flight ends at the hermitage, where Dushyanta meets a boy playing with the lion. Soon, the King will discover that the brave boy is his son, Bharata, living in the hermitage with his mother, Shakuntala. Reading the script, one might rightly ask who played the boy and who played the lion which had the misfortune of becoming the boy's toy. It turns out that the answers to these questions can be found easily by looking carefully at two photographs from the GIA (inv. nos 114–16, 117–19). They show two images from the same scene. In both we see Dushyanta standing with his right leg planted on the ground, his left foot on the hemisphere with his left knee bent, and his body leaning forwards, up the slope of the copula. The lunging King is positioned next to the phallic post, and he holds a bulbous object that looks like a large rattle—but also seems to serve as a small, directional lamp that illuminates the two actresses on the central copula.[19] Ewa Lubowiecka is on her hands and knees atop the structure, while Barbara Barska towers over her and makes a triumphant gesture that summons images of an animal tamer. Importantly, Barska is wearing a costume similar to the one worn by Dushyanta, the only difference being that her turban is not white, but appears to be gold. It seems obvious then that what we see is the King's son (Barska) taming a wild Lion. The beast is played by Ewa Lubowiecka who performed all animal characters in *Shakuntala*.

The last photograph published in *Materiały i Dyskusje* shows the performance finale. Shakuntala and Dushyanta are standing on the floor next to the central construction. They look like they are dancing. They

---

19 An electrical cord can be seen dangling from the object in photographs 114–16.

lean sideways, with one of their arms drooping down the sides of their bodies, while their other arms are bent at the elbow and elevated, as if they are being raised up by an external force from above. Their heads fall with gravity towards their drooping side, their faces glow with happy smiles and their eyes are closed. The photograph was published on the back cover of *Materiały i Dyskusje*, accompanied by the four-line poem that appears as the very last lines of Grotowski's script, with one difference. On the back cover of *Materiały i Dyskusje*—unlike in the script—each line is given to a specific character.

SHAKUNTALA: I will now devour you whole, father Shiva.

KING: Seeing as I was born under a dark star,

SHAKUNTALA: And the one born so,

KING: Is said to be destined to devour their own father.

(*Materiały i Dyskusje* 1960, VOL. 5: 16)

Grotowski remembered the scene very well and commented on it with striking precision, more than thirty years after the performance.

The action shows a couple of lovers. They will be shown after the whole story comes to a beautiful conclusion, now as elderly people. There is now no joy of young age, no energy as there was before when they allowed themselves to surrender to Eros. Everything is now very old. It is the same action, a couple of lovers; they are taking up the same poses, saying the same lines of text, but now with aged voices. We can quickly deliver this using montage number one. In this case the pair's actions stop in a certain position, while they begin to act as elderly people, changing their postures, movements, voices, and yet maintaining their starting positions. For me this montage number one would never fit, it would be banal. Let us assume instead that they are half way through their actions and light is shone from the opposite side of the stage. There must be a natural reason for this, nothing at all which could cause an absurdist effect. Let us say for example that someone lights an oil lamp: this would be

enough. Here we have fire, which has the power of attraction. We look at the light while listening still to the ongoing dialogue. Yes, we recognize that this is a simple lamp. We look again in the other direction, but now we have two elderly persons standing there, finishing their sentence, half-finished when the light appeared. It is as it was in folk tales. The girl left home, lost her way, then met a witch and was led back home. She returns home and no one recognizes her. The people are different. She asks them questions, saying the name of her father and mother, but no one knows who they are. Then she mentioned her brother, her sister and someone answers: 'Oh yes! They lived here fifty years ago'. You can see how it is: in a short moment when the audience's attention was redirected forty years has passed [...].
(Grotowski 2012: 781–82)

Grotowski's commentary tells us something that cannot be seen in the photograph, about the shift that he made from assigning individualized verses to finally giving the entirety of the four-verse poem to Shakuntala and the King to say in unison. The fact that the finale features the pair of lovers as an elderly couple was reported in Flaszen's 'instructions for seeing'. Flaszen points to the importance of this element in a performance considered a study of the paradoxes of love. The precision with which Grotowski describes this scene after so many years is evidence of how important it was for him to show this—to show this image of instantaneous ageing. This was a key moment when the power of love—'Shiva's power' in the language of the performance—subsides. Seen from the perspective of the action, this was connected to the ageing of the characters, but from the perspective of the planned audience experience, it was connected with the experience of transgressing desire. If we can literally interpret the closing four-line poem about the devouring of Shiva in this context, then the scene manifests an externalization of desire— and its transformation—leading to an ecstasy very different from the erotic one. By letting the paradoxes of love play out, showing the creative power of desire and the rules that limit it, and exhibiting the power of forces that emerge from desire and its limitation, the director staged his own declaration of faith in his finale—just as he did in his previous performances. There was no mention here of any sort of 'dancing world', or about life lived for good reason. Grotowski's declaration was presented indirectly. And yet it seems that compared to previous performances, Grotowski's *Shakuntala* finale had longer-lasting and farther-reaching consequences. In short, in the finale of *Shakuntala*, Grotowski presented and played out one of the most powerful engines of his creative process: turning a sexual desire into a vehicle of transformation.

The Doubted Elephant

In proposing that *Shakuntala* is about desire, sexuality and their transformation, I sense I am on unsteady ground. The evidence is circumstantial, based on guesswork and my imagination, which inevitably contains a large dose of subjectivity. And yet, I cannot escape the thought that *Shakuntala*—which crowned the first period of Grotowski's collaboration with his company—was a very personal performance for him, in which many of his obsessions came to light. In *Shakuntala*, we find the themes and fantasies that remain present in Grotowski's work for the rest of his life, even if as spectres: femininity encompassing animal and sacred aspects; homoerotic tensions appearing in odd and unexpected cracks; masculinity producing a fear of one's own weakness; and holiness merged with violence. All these were expressed in *Shakuntala* as self-ridicule, parody and grotesque play.

This entanglement was received in an equally entangled way. The reaction to *Shakuntala* ranged from popularity—the entertaining and sexually charged performance was enjoyed by audiences—to criticism from those who created the show. An assessment written by Flaszen years later is a particularly apt example of the latter.

> *Shakuntala* [. . .] did not earn its place in the annals of the masterpieces of 20th century theatre. Grotowski himself treated it somewhat neglectfully, though he did admit its role in his (along with his company's) explorations. In fact, it was one of

158 · DARIUSZ KOSIŃSKI

those performance-laboratories, performance-hatchery, the significance of which can only be seen in hindsight. A similar
show—a few years later—would be the half-baked *Study on
Hamlet.*
(Flaszen 2014: 348)

This comparison with *Study on Hamlet*—a performance in which many
unexpected elements exploded and revealed themselves (see Chapter
9)—indicates that *Shakuntala* was a performance that also surprised its
creators and reveals something about a performance they did not see as
important, or simply did not perceive themselves. While I am hesitant
to jump to conclusions, I am convinced that the important yet uninten-
tional aspect of Grotowski's *Shakuntala* was the theme of desire as 'heavy
energy', to be used not in the process of creating signs, but rather in a
very specific theatrical process that would later lead to the discovery of
what Grotowski came to call the 'total act'.

In Grotowski's timeline, *Shakuntala* is still far removed from the
development of the 'total act'. And perhaps, I am unnecessarily reading
Grotowski's later work onto his earlier efforts. Perhaps, it would be more
honest to let the interpretation of *Shakuntala* be governed by two interpretations related to understanding and misunderstanding: the visible
and the invisible. Olgierd Jędrzejczyk wrote that:

in the Opole staging of *Shakuntala* there is not a jot of that
which theatrical reviewers often accused the Theatre of 13 Rows.
There is none of the infamous lack of communicability of which
Grotowski was so unjustly accused.
(Jędrzejczyk 1960: 6)

Another opinion comes from a fan of the Theatre of 13 Rows who would,
soon after *Shakuntala*, become one of the most frequently quoted commentators on Grotowski's work: the elderly intellectual and experienced
critic Tadeusz Kudliński. *Shakuntala* clearly baffled him, leaving him
uncertain about its meaning and the reasons for staging it:

Why was this modern theatre choosing to stage an ancient Indian drama of a different convention—a dance pantomime with words—it's character that of lyrical mood, ceremonial process, and religious karmic determinism? It must be in order to parody and ridicule this old-fashioned shape and narrative thread. [. . .] And indeed the heroic King-lover Dushyanta was turned into an almost clown, a jester, while his unhappy lover a frightened waif from popular theatre. Numerous interpretations of the text (faithfully lifted from Indian literature) try to discredit the high-brow and infuse the action with the everyday and the erotic. And yet in spite of this slight parody of the love-heroic narration, the show retains some lyrical charm and old-fashioned love and nature poetry. This is why on this one question I would agree with the 'instruction' written by my friend Flaszen when he claims that the play is a parody also of the creators themselves! What was done in the staging of *Shakuntala* reminds me of a line from the drama: 'like one who doubts an elephant / Though seeing him stride by . . . ' (Kālidāsa 1999: 91)

(Kudliński 2006a[1961]: 137)

Seen in the light of these two interpretations, the performance turns out to have captured—through the complexity of seeing and unseeing—something that the audience grasped and read into. It also captured something that does not want to be seen—something that appears but not in order to be understood—at least not within the framework constructed by its creators. In my opinion, in both cases we are dealing with the same topic, sexuality. The funny and attractive erotic play draws the audience in and also reveals a certain seriousness associated with sexuality. Beneath the superficial playfulness, something was hidden, something that was the essence of the performance: a completely earnest attempt to deal with the erotic as the fundamental power and energy of life.

It is very possible that the importance attributed to *Shakuntala* by Flaszen, in retrospect, was connected with the discovery that Grotowski made while working on the performance, but developed later—that taking on a serious topic like this has to be by means of sabotaging that which was close, tangible and part of our shared experience. *Shakuntala* was culturally so far from the Polish audiences' experience that its key and earnestly presented theme was not visible beneath the layers of grotesque games and pseudo-Indian dress-up. The director himself admitted as much.

> I noticed that the lack of a transplanting of Oriental love archetypes into a clearly European archetype, the lack of evident transplanting, of referring to—Adam and Eve? Romeo and Juliet? Something else?—caused a certain oddness in this performance; the play was successful with audiences and critics alike. But overall—sitting every day among the spectators—I could not lose the feeling that there is something alien in this playfulness, something 'not from our circles', 'not from around here'.
>
> (Grotowski 2012: 222)

The Indian elements were too arresting for audiences to accept the play as a study in the paradoxes of love, as a performance that related to them. Kudliński was right: Grotowski, Flaszen and the rest of the company so clearly stressed the Indian and ancient character of the source material, and devoted so much attention to the theatrical score, that sex—the 'elephant in the room'—went more or less unnoticed.

Dariusz Kosiński

CHAPTER FIVE

A Mystery 'in-yar-face'

Forefathers' Eve after Adam Mickiewicz

Forefathers' Eve as a Model of Contemporary Theatre

On 18 October 1961, the Theatre of 13 Rows premiered their version of *Forefathers' Eve*, based on the drama of the same name by Adam Mickiewicz. The premiere came just six months after that of *Shakuntala* and not quite 11 months after the premiere of *Mystery-Bouffe*. I am consciously juxtaposing these titles in order to highlight the contrast between the Opole company's earlier performances and their later productions— *Forefathers' Eve*, *Kordian* (based on Juliusz Słowacki's text), and *Acropolis* (based on Stanisław Wyspiański's play).[1] These later performances are all based on canonical texts of the Polish Romantic tradition. In selecting these texts, the Theatre of 13 Rows made a clear gesture akin to a manifesto—an experimental theatre specializing in provocative and profane games decided to play with the most revered works of Polish literature.

Grotowski did not announce at the outset that he intended to work on Polish Romantic drama. When asked about his plans at the time, he did not mention Mickiewicz or Słowacki. If he had continued with Romantics after *Cain*, one could see some logic in his choices, but *Forefathers' Eve* after *Shakuntala* seems incongruous.

---

1 I consciously omit the 'poetic evenings' that the company worked on simultaneously. In spring 1961, they created a programme of *Turyści* [Tourists] and *Gliniane gołębie* [The doves of clay] which premiered 31 March or 1 April). Soon after, they created *Pamiętnik śląski* [The Silesian diary] (premiere 9 July). Inspired, if not outright determined by the sociopolitical environment within which the theatre worked, these activities belonged to a line of the Theatre of 13 Rows' activities other than performances directed by Grotowski.

The question of why Grotowski worked on Mickiewicz's 'master-drama' in the spring of 1961 could be answered in a number of ways. Ludwik Flaszen once offered an explanation in a private conversation with me. 'Grotowski staged it because any self-respecting Polish theatre director has to stage the *Forefathers' Eve*'. Yet we should also keep in mind that Grotowski's decision to stage the most important title in the Polish repertoire—a script of innumerable performances of national identity[2]—was not just a personal gesture. It was also a manifestation of a more general need. The Opole staging of *Forefathers' Eve* should be considered not only in terms of Grotowski's creative path, and that taken by his company, but also in the context of broader cultural and social processes. Namely in the context of the need to reinterpret the Polish Romantic tradition in the face of radical political changes, social transformations as well as moral and cultural debates that emerged from the Second World War and its consequences. The political thaw that took place towards the end of the 1950s was the first moment—apart from a short period just after the end of the War—when it was culturally possible within Communist-controlled Poland to tackle in a relatively open way the philosophical and existential fallout from the War. This thaw featured the questioning of the Polish Romantic tradition as the foundation of Polish national identity, and occasioned that tradition's critical reinterpretation. This was one of the most important streams of Polish culture at the beginning of the 1960s, and it was especially created by a younger generation of artists at the time, for example, Andrzej Wajda and Andrzej Munk in cinema, and Sławomir Mrożek in drama. The Theatre of 13 Rows took a very special position in this critical movement.

In a conversation conducted a few months after the premiere and published under the title '*Dziady* jako model teatru współczesnego' [*Forefathers' Eve* as a model of contemporary theatre], Jerzy Falkowski—an important Silesian journalist, a cultural activist of the time and a truly important ally of the 13 Rows company—asked Grotowski 'Why did Mickiewicz appear in the repertoire of the Theatre of 13 Rows?'

---

2 For the explanation of the role and special position of Mickiewicz and his drama in Polish theatre, culture and history, see Kosiński 2019: 75–87.

Grotowski's answer was simple: 'Because Mickiewicz wrote good texts.' He also at once dismissed the notion that he was interested in ridiculing or parodying *Forefathers' Eve*. He declared that his version was driven by a fascination that 'did not manifest itself so much in piety, but in an attempt to use the possibilities contained in the text in order to build a shape of theatre with avant-garde ambitions' (2012: 204). Grotowski therefore separated himself from the typical motivations connected with the 'classic' aspects of *Forefathers' Eve* related to its meaning for Polish culture and identity. He turned Mickiewicz into his contemporary and connected him with the avant-garde.

Later in the Falkowski interview, Grotowski explained which elements of *Forefathers' Eve* fit the contemporary theatre he sought. He mentioned three: 'sorcery', 'superstition' and the 'Great Improvisation'— the most important monologue of the Romantic Hero. Grotowski continued, and connected 'sorcery' with the ritualistic aspect of drama.

> We are dealing here with collective surrender to rigors of 'rituality': nothing is acted, nothing presented, instead one takes part in a certain ceremony that liberates the collective subconscious. In *Forefathers' Eve* we finally eliminated the stage (we do not intend to return to it). The audience is dispersed throughout the whole auditorium. The actors also address the audience members directly—treating them as co-actors and even encouraging them to move in the space.
> (Grotowski 2012: 204)

The creators of the Opole *Forefathers' Eve* aimed to transform the staging of a drama into an experience that encompassed all of those taking part. They did so to such a degree that the events prepared by the artists— which featured the emergence of new characters and the development of sequences of activity—were intended to be perceived and accepted as effects of the psychological activity of the whole collective. The 'collective' in this case included those who came to the theatre as audience members. As a result, the performance would initiate a radical change in the conventional theatrical order of the time; what was initiated by the actors was to be accepted as called into being by the audience.

Flaszen presented this basic idea of working with the collective imagination thereby providing one answer to the question that I ask here again and again, 'Why of all things *Forefathers' Eve?*'

> Because the play clearly shows how theatre originates from ritual. In it, the fate of an individual human appears before a community who is actively engaged in the ritual: evoking, emanating, and judging. Releasing, with the help of sacred gestures, 'occult powers', the community creates its own, earthly image, transported into the world of folk myths, giving a tangible reality to its own moral concepts. [. . .] Not to show the world cut off from the spectator by the border that footlights make, but, together with the spectator, to create the world again, in which—surrounded by this mutual presence, stimulated by common participation in collective play—we will feel that we are the hosts. It is irrelevant whether Mickiewicz believed in ghosts or not; we are interested only in the human aspect of this faith. Thus, the ceremony is treated as a form of play. However, this playing is ambiguous, and has some serious meaning.
> (Flaszen 2010[1964]: 68)

These shifts in the understanding and practice of 'rituality' in performance proposed by the Theatre of 13 Rows were substantial. For Mickiewicz what mattered was the real existence of ghosts and the possibility of contacting them through theatre—at least in terms of contact through memory if not literally bringing the dead back to life. In Grotowski's performance the essence of rituality was the process of bringing people together in the realm of 'this world'. Flaszen's declaration clearly shows that for the creators of the Opole *Forefathers' Eve*, the ghosts were (or were meant to be) emanations of a collective imagination or 'mind' while the 'ritualistic framework' of the performance created a self-referential process of experiencing the way in which these emanations happen. No one was going to hide it. Quite the opposite, the communal process of creating figures of the collective and 'national' imagination was to be revealed and shown to the audiences as something that they too are a part of.

Some comments made by the performance's creators include phrases we might read as suggesting that their aim was to call together a united theatre community capable of experiencing rituals. But Grotowski knew all too well that this was impossible. Instead, he declared his desire to arrange a collective 'which will not be clearly divided between the audience and the actors, but rather consist of the leading and supporting performers' (Grotowski 2012: 204). In his comments and theoretical statements, Grotowski resolutely stuck to this differentiation talking about 'two ensembles' and the need to 'direct them'. I believe that this bringing together of 'two ensembles' in the staging of *Forefathers' Eve* and then in *Kordian* is tied to the essential themes of both dramas: collective imaginations and the processes of their development and externalization.

Grotowski told Falkowski about the kind of collective imaginations he was interested in staging in *Forefathers' Eve*. Grotowski also pointed to a second key reason to work on Mickiewicz's 'master-drama', namely to employ 'superstition as artistic material'.

> Through Mickiewicz's text we tried to find in superstition the grotesque in human judgements, a form of absurdist action, hence becoming tragi-grotesque. The chance to demonstrate how a collective can construct in itself an image of a supernatural world and perform itself out in front of itself, leading through the grotesque to an understanding of the truth about human ignorance and suffering.
> (Grotowski 2012)

I call this aspect of the Opole *Forefathers' Eve* a 'dramaturgy of superstition'. What was to be revealed and experienced during the performative process was the very mechanism of collective creation and of performing 'an image of a supernatural world'. This was not about unmasking a 'supernatural' image as an 'illusion' or as an 'opium of the masses'. Rather it was about revealing 'the truth about human ignorance and suffering', and therefore also about the human need for transcendence; and the sound logic in which this desire is rooted.

Grotowski was remarkably resolute in his work. He decidedly cut himself off from all confessional acts and negated the possibility of establishing the meaning of life through religion. He was determined to find alternatives, a non-religious foundation better suited to counter the dangers of absurdity and emptiness. Grotowski employed an almost scientific approach to the sense-making procedures that functioned in individual and collective lives. He treated them seriously and considered their usefulness, even if he questioned their obvious utility or doubted their ethics. For Grotowski, creating and performing a collective imagination—or perhaps creating it by and while performing it—was not achieved by way of cheating or manipulation. Rather it was achieved through a process connected to the very foundations of human existence. This process fascinated and occupied him not only as a subject for critical deconstruction but also as an expression of essential human needs traditionally met by religion. When he refused to accept the religious answer, Grotowski did not treat the need for an answer as some sort of 'false' aberration from which we ought to heal ourselves in order to live 'freely', a pleasant illusion suggested by today's consumerism and trivial 'secularism'. He tracked and researched this need and sought out not so much the psychological mechanisms of its production, but experiences or embodied memories capable of rooting the human community in something that transgresses and transcends the limits of individual and social lives. He used theatre to conduct this research, all the while trying to shatter unquestioned collective imaginations thus leading to their 'source': the non-verbalized desire for transcendence within human constraints.

In this search, Grotowski shared in a broader contemporary passion for unmasking constructs and processes that produce collective imaginations that determine people's lives on very basic yet deep levels. Grotowski resolutely explored these processes considering them to be inescapable aspects of being human. 'Inescapable' not because they could not be removed but because removing them would result in the ultimate fall of human beings as such. This conviction would be most fully presented—with all its ambivalence—in his *Acropolis* (see Chapter 7). But already in *Forefathers' Eve*, it was an incredibly important aspect: people create their own heroes and gods in order to then perform rituals that involve these creations because in this way people affirm the existence of the transcendent, and save themselves from fear, despair and death. This process is not only impossible to eradicate completely, it is also wrong to try and do so because it is born of the fundamental need and equally fundamental, extra-daily experiences to which Grotowski devoted many years of research.

It seems to me that the beginning of Grotowski's search is directly connected to his work on *Forefathers' Eve*. He began this project at time when attacks against the Romantics became increasingly bold. Ancient figures' powers and scripts were questioned and a palpable emptiness emerged in their place. This cultural context is illuminated in a very important fragment from the commentary on *Forefathers' Eve* published by Flaszen in 1964, well after the premieres of *Kordian* (1961) and *Acropolis* (1962). I quote it here because it refers to the 'dramaturgy of superstition' and the dark, anachronistic force that superstition evokes:

> Romanticism is an odd form of consciousness, balancing on the edge of madness and magic superstition. From the point of view of our sober age, it is grotesque. Yet from the perspective of the needs of the collective consciousness, mutilated by violent transformations, it is not alien to these values. In Romanticism, there is something of an archaic psyche, which would be glad not to distinguish between dreams and waking, between the individual and the community, between the soul and the world. Romanticism seems to see a guarantee of the preservation of the primal unity in magical procedures, as often identified with poetry. Contemporary man is a reasonable person, deeply rooted in reality, who has dispensed with childish illusions about his power—yet he is internally disintegrated and socially uprooted. In a naive way, Romanticism expresses a longing for a lost spiritual unity, for a feeling of being at home in the world. Naive—therefore funny; giving vent to an important longing—therefore uplifting.
> (Flaszen 2010[1964]: 79)

Seen in this way, Romanticism comes close to resembling something Grotowski studied intently in later years, so-called 'traditional cultures'. Grotowski and Flaszen are of course not so naive to consider the folk community created by Mickiewicz as 'authentic', and yet they do see it as a cultural product with considerable power. For them, Polish Romanticism, and especially *Forefathers' Eve*, emerges from the same source as the other cultural traditions and actions that they researched later especially in the context of the Theatre of Sources (1976–82). I am using a rather anachronistic analogy here in order to show that the games Grotowski played with Romanticism starting in 1961 were not just games played with the canon of Polish culture. Additionally, they were more general explorations of cultural creations that, according to Grotowski, drew their power from the human need for transcendence or, put more simply, spirituality.

The important example of such creation—one that plays an incredibly important role in Polish culture—is the Great Improvisation. This is a key scene in Part III of *Forefathers' Eve* in which the main protagonist, Gustaw-Konrad, performs a poetic monologue while trapped in a cell. He tells the tale of a journey to Heaven and a battle with God over the fate of Poland that ends with blasphemy, a fall from grace and madness. An opportunity to work on this scene was the third reason Grotowski gave Falkowski for wanting to work on *Forefathers' Eve*.

> The main idea of the performance is centred around the Great Improvisation. In a narrowed context we could talk about how suffering gives birth to a supernatural world and also about how solitary and all-encompassing rebellion is hopeless. A broader and overarching meaning could be linked with the fixed subject of our search—the one Władysław Broniewski (talking about *Shakuntala*) termed 'using voice and body to experience the substance of human fate'.
> (Grotowski 2012: 205)[3]

---

3 Władysław Broniewski (1897–1962) was a Polish poet and Communist activist who was very well-known and influential during Communist rule in Poland. He visited Opole in May 1961 and

For the time being I will leave aside the question of the way in which the Great Improvisation was performed. I will first inquire about the model of theatre that Grotowski tried to construct around this monologue.

Grotowski treated the Great Improvisation as the culmination and grand finale of his staging. This first of all meant that the dramaturgy of superstition showing how the odd forms of the supernatural world were born out of human suffering was above all related to that which 'is born' in the Improvisation, namely Konrad himself as the Hero of the Polish Nation, a metaphysical rebel and a martyr. The Opole performance showed Konrad in process emerging from the collective, slowly taking on heroic form culminating in his martyrdom. The fundamental aim of the performance was to create and play out an experience of the procedures and implications of national holiness embodied in a hero-martyr who saves the nation by sacrificing oneself.

This interpretation of the Great Improvisation implies a meta-theatrical character—an amplified mythical figure of the national hero played out by a delegate elected by the community. I understand the 'broader and overarching' meaning of the Improvisation as setting the standard for 'modern theatre' by 'using voice and body to experience substance of human fate'. This is a key development in Grotowski's theatre practice, sustained in all subsequent theatrical performances and even in his para-theatrical projects. It involved a clearly demonstrated process of embodying and gradually becoming—in a functional sense—a defined model character as was Gustaw-Konrad in *Forefathers' Eve*. Though at first this character appears to be an external entity most often suggested or imposed by the community by force, the model character later became a 'trampoline', a 'scalpel', or a 'vehicle' of discovery, his actions revealing the human truth of the performer, what is not only most important to

---

saw some performances of the Theatre of 13 Rows (*Shakuntala* among them). He was strongly moved by the performances and wrote an open letter with a very positive opinion about the theatre that Grotowski quoted many times, partly for political reasons. Broniewski had great authority and was acclaimed by the Communist Party as the most important revolutionary poet so quoting his positive reviews gave the company esteem and leverage with apparatchiks.

him but also only involving more than him.[4] This processual dramaturgy of embodiment in all its variants—from *Forefathers' Eve* to *Apocalypsis cum figuris* (1969)—is invariably presented by the creators as 'artificial', a clearly theatrical game. Grotowski resolutely avoids making the process of 'empathizing with the substance of human fate' any easier, and does not allow the use of what could be considered stereotypical authenticity effects or sublime conventions. This makes things harder for the actors by removing any potential supports, forcing them to make good use of contrast and dissonance. Grotowski uses parody, grotesque ridiculing devices, and at the same time places upon actors the obligation to craft a serious and complete act and to deeply experience the situation and state achieved by taking on external character archetypes. If this works, then a troubling discrepancy appears on a meta-theatrical plane. A dialectical movement complicates the simple situation of blasphemous laughing at a sacred figure. Even, in later performances, starting from *Kordian*, actually eradicating the grotesque, and strongly extracting the power of the source archetype. In this way 'manipulating the sacred' paradoxically leads to 'sacred acting' with its promise to save us from the hypocritical games we play in everyday life.

All of this will of course be developed in the years following the premiere of *Forefathers' Eve*. Reactions to the performance and statements made by the artists involved quoted in this chapter seem to indicate that these 'sacred' possibilities arose as a *result* of work on the performance rather than being its starting point. In this process, the Great Improvisation

---

4 I am consciously using only the male form because I am convinced that the male actor and hero was the central figure of Grotowski's imagination and practice. I do so not to indicate the secondary role of women in Grotowski's research, but to reveal it. Of course, the role and influence of women in Grotowski's practice is important. Female performers developed it in deep and creative ways, as did Rena Mirecka and Maja Komorowska in the Laboratory Theatre, and many women later especially in the Workcentre of Jerzy Grotowski and Thomas Richards (see Magnat 2015). But it was with male actors—from Zygmunt Molik to Zbigniew Cynkutis, and from Ryszard Cieślak to Thomas Richards—that Grotowski mainly worked to create the 'total act' and *Action*. Additionally, in Grotowski's earlier writings and speeches he used the male form while speaking about acting and performing. Later he often used the Polish word *człowiek* and would explain that it means 'a human being' in general without a determined gender— although grammatically this word is also masculine. See also Adamiecka-Sitek 2012.

was established as a kind of culmination and an effect of the entire dramatic process that examined the power of a national myth. The process facilitated the discovery of meta-theatrical possibilities and made possible the beginning of a planned and disciplined work on the theatrical use of the sacred. We can therefore say that Grotowski was right—*Forefathers' Eve* was a model for contemporary theatre—one that he himself was going to create.

Words by Adam Mickiewicz—Script by Jerzy Grotowski

The *Forefathers' Eve* poster designed by Waldemar Krygier highlighted a provocative yet precise description of the authorship of the performance:

WORDS BY

ADAM MICKIEWICZ

SCRIPT AND DIRECTION: JERZY GROTOWSKI

This simple gesture was almost revolutionary for the time in that it augmented the role of Grotowski as dramaturg and director, as the contemporary creator, and thereby diminished the status of the great master and author of a 'cultural centre-piece'. We should not forget that, in the 1960s, theatre was still perceived above all as a place to stage dramas, and so a performance titled *Forefathers' Eve* or *Kordian* would have been viewed and mainly judged as another iteration of the well-known source text. By distancing oneself from these texts with such a powerful declaration of independence and suggesting that Mickiewicz was only responsible for the 'words'—not even the 'poetry'—of the performance, Grotowski avoided a polemic on the (admittedly hollow) topic of 'faithfulness' to the source material. This of course did not save him from attacks initiated by literary authorities but it did mean that their attacks missed the point.

The poster's separation between Mickiewicz's 'words' and Grotowski's creative role also reflects the underlying approach taken throughout the performance. Grotowski further distances his production from the source text by eliminating those parts of the original text most popularly associated with the story. This applies above all to Part III, which nearly stands on its own.[5] Grotowski only retained the second scene, the Great Improvisation, cutting the rest which was very well known to audiences. This absence was part of Grotowski's design. By deleting the literary context and the historical context it contained, he uprooted the rebellion and sacrifice from its historical justification and thereby estranged it. In Mickiewicz's drama Konrad performs his final monologue of an imagined journey to Heaven and a fight with God as a reaction to the sufferings of an oppressed nation represented by students who had been arrested and detained by the Russian authorities occupying Poland and Lithuania, the author among them. The tale of the martyrdom delivered by Jan Sobolewski that precedes the Great Improvisation in Mickiewicz's drama compares the sacrifice of the young patriots to that of Jesus Christ. In Grotowski's version this comparison was retained and strengthened by stage images—more about this later—but without being situated in any historical context. In effect, audiences observed the Polish hero's rebellious and blasphemous transformation into the Polish Christ *as such*, and not as a reaction to specific events. When Grotowski jettisoned the historical background, the hero gained in his mythic and ritualizing power, and as such was subjected to a high standard of dramatic verification of his actions' strength and efficacy.

Thanks to a surviving copy of the script that originally belonged to Andrzej Bielski and is now preserved in the GIA, we can more closely study the scenario Grotowski composed using Mickiewicz's words. The surviving script is split into four sections, and therefore on first glance it conflicts with Ludwik Flaszen's report of a three-act structure (2010[1964]: 80–83). However, on closer analysis, it is apparent that the relatively shorter third and fourth parts of the surviving script were combined to form a single third act of the performance. At least at this stage of analysing the script I return to its original four-part division.

Each part of the script was loosely based on a different part of Mickiewicz's drama. The first part was composed mainly with words from Part II of *Forefathers' Eve*, the second part was based on Part IV of

---

5 *Forefathers' Eve Part III* was created as an almost separate composition. Mickiewicz wrote it in Dresden in 1832 almost 10 years after Parts II and IV were published in 1823.

the original, the third section was built with words from the unfinished Part I (see below) and part IV consisted mainly of the Great Improvisation (from Part III of the Mickiewicz).

As in the Mickiewicz, the script of *Forefathers' Eve* in Opole opened with a slightly shortened version of the poem *The Living Dead*. It is closely followed in the script by Mickiewicz's introduction to Part II, also somewhat shortened. Both these fragments gave the beginning of the performance a meta-theatrical character and frame. They served as a prologue or an instruction for audiences, clearly informing them about the two key elements of the performance: the central hero and the stage actions. The ontological status of the first element in the poem presents a problem. While the hero does not belong to the world of the living, he is also not entirely dead. He has returned to the world of the living in order to once again experience the fate of the unhappy lover. Although he is the 'living dead', he also calls to mind an actor—Grotowski strongly emphasized the analogy. Mickiewicz's introduction on the other hand indicated clearly that the thing the audience will experience is not the ritual itself but its imitation, and hence a re-performance.

The rest of the first part of Grotowski's script was based on Part II of the *Forefathers' Eve*, which presented a folk ritual led by the Sorcerer supported in his attempt to summon the ghosts of dead ancestors by a Chorus of villagers. Grotowski made relatively few cuts in this sequence; those he made mainly had to do with word economy and technical considerations. Of the 617 original verses, Grotowski deleted a mere 63. He also did not change their order, thereby confirming that for him the ritual was one of the key elements of his production.

Part II of Grotowski's script was based on the *Forefathers' Eve* Part IV, almost a one-man show where the hero reveals himself as Gustaw to his former teacher and friend, the Priest. Compared to Part I of the script, Grotowski made more cuts. In terms of length, Grotowski cut more than half of Mickiewicz's 1,285 verses. Generally, the cuts Grotowski made were dramaturgical and not ideological. His aim was to shorten the original text in such a way as to make it more or less equal in length to the first part of his script and to guard against it becoming too dull. It is also clear that Grotowski sought to make it more dynamic by removing segments that he considered to be too static and by moving in the direction of romantic love which seemed to be the most overt thematic aspect of this section. In this way the second part of the Opole *Forefathers' Eve* was closely related to *Shakuntala*, the previous performance of the Theatre of 13 Rows which centred on the 'paradoxes of love'. Grotowski once again showed love as an unbridled power with numerous aspects and colours.

The third part of the script was mostly Grotowski's own construction with the largest number of cuts and rewrites. The material Grotowski used to construct Part III of his script arose partly out of the rough assemblage of fragments pieced together and referred to as *Forefathers' Eve* Part I. Mickiewicz himself never actually finished these fragments or published them during his lifetime.[6] Scripting this sequence of loosely connected scenes did indeed demand courageous interventions. This may explain why in this sequence Grotowski was most bold in revealing his creative activities. An analysis of his decision-making processes will help reveal his general way of thinking and the basic rules he followed while working on the script.

Part III of the script opened with a return to ritual. The Sorcerer and Chorus appeared again in a dialogue that served as a sort of internal prologue to this section and at the same time was a short reminder of the ritual from the Part I. The Chorus reclaims its leading voice and comments on the events that had taken place in previous parts. The position the Chorus took with respect to prior events can perhaps best be characterized as 'nostalgic'. They desired a 'return to normal', and therefore a retreat into the past. The Sorcerer and the Elder distanced themselves from the Chorus, the former expressing the necessity of a ritual and the latter stressing the power of death. At the same time this sequence represented a sort of announcement and a frame for the upcoming fragment built around a 'Weberian' and 'Faustian' meeting between Gustaw and the devilish figure of the Black Hunter. In contrast

---

6 The fragments of texts often collectively referred to as *Forefathers' Eve* Part I were most likely penned in 1821 but not published until 1860 five years after the author's death.

with other fragments of Part I of the original that were radically shortened, the text of this scene was retained almost without cuts. It indicates that the confrontation between the hero and the diabolical Hunter was the most important for this part of the script, that this was above all what Grotowski was after. The dramaturg/director added to this scene a choral reprise of the last two lines of text in the Mickiewicz original: 'If you're steadfast in what you say ... / Dear God! What's that mean?! Get away from me!' (Mickiewicz 2016[1823]: 144). Thus, the third part of the script ended with a ritualistic chant from the Chorus. The 'Faustian' meeting with Satan represented something of a third station on the protagonist's journey that culminated in the Great Improvisation. The bulk of the material used for the fourth and final part of the script came from the Great Improvisation which was essentially kept in its original form.

Grotowski did not make any major cuts to the scenes he chose to use in his version. Many of the fragments he retained remained untouched. In seeking to increase the dynamism of individual scenes without making them any longer Grotowski tended to remove the more familiar fragments, as if thereby introducing into the script a game with telling absences, and at the same time most probably not wishing the well-known fragments to distract the audiences from observing and experiencing the whole he had constructed.

Community of Theatrical Experience

The most important element shaping the environment and audience experience of the Opole *Forefathers' Eve* was the way the 13 Rows constructed the performance space. It was surprising and innovative for the times but it was also recognized as being closely related to the general concepts of the production. Tadeusz Kudliński wrote that

> Grotowski abandons conventional staging and ramps, as well as decorations. Jerzy Gurawski replaced these with a multi-levelled performance space that encompassed the whole theatrical auditorium, hence including the audience seats, among which the actors circulate and where they do their acting. [...]

176 · DARIUSZ KOSIŃSKI

> Chairs were arranged in groups around the whole hall and at
> various levels, facing the centre. The actors were now addressing
> the audience directly, attacking them and drawing them into
> the forefathers' ritual, the performance itself. In this way a whole
> new situation is created: merging the stage and the audience
> into one community.
> (Kudliński 2006b[1961]: 139)

The creators of the Opole *Forefathers' Eve* did not at all ask themselves
what the visual 'frame' or 'stage' background would look like. Instead,
they completely moved away from thinking about the performance as a
two-dimensional image. This sort of thinking was still present in *Mystery-Bouffe*, but thanks to Gurawski it started to fade away in *Shakuntala*.
For *Forefathers' Eve* they worked on the architecture of the performance
space and created a three-dimensional 'environment'[7] common to all
taking part in the theatrical event.

The shape of this architectural work presented a visual effect that fit
into the dynamic vision of *Forefathers' Eve*. Gurawski developed this
point when recalling the performance:

> We built something strange, something that in no way—thinking
> logically—fits in with *Forefathers' Eve*, and yet was a system of
> certain layered steps. That was when I was [. . .] under great
> psychological pressure put on me by Grotowski and Flaszen
> who [. . .] filled my head with their wisdom, stupefying me
> completely, demanding I draw things from deep within, in order
> for me to do something. And after a while I began—departing
> from all those 'chapels' and 'non-chapels' which I associate with
> *Forefathers' Eve*—heading towards some sort of totally abstract
> form, because this reminds me of a sculpture by Jean Arp . . .
> this is a layering of steps—wooden, very much . . . brutal,
> arranged in odd shapes . . . building such a space. And suddenly

---

7 I am using the word consciously referring to the theory of environmental theatre created by
Richard Schechner and presented first in his seminal article in *TDR* (Schechner 1968) and
then elaborated in his book (Schechner 1973). The space created by Gurawski and Grotowski
was one of the main inspirations of the theory.

it turned out that this space somehow fit in with *Forefathers' Eve* and somehow became an equivalent of the multi-layered drama. It worked out . . . I think so right now. These were layers upon layers, the audience seated within them, scenes from *Forefathers' Eve* happening in various places.
(Gurawski 1992: 53)

This story suggests that regardless of the functionality of the performance space as an environment, Grotowski and Flaszen encouraged Gurawski to create something that would become a subtle visual metaphor for their understanding of *Forefathers' Eve* as a multidimensional and multi-layered work. The 'Arpesque' construction featured layered steps made up of curvy shapes. In Gurawski's sketch, his design looks like a fluid mass temporarily halted in place while at the same time stripped of firm outlines. Wavy lines demarcated places for people, and the different architectural levels gave the impression that they could simply melt into one another. This 3D sculpture visually represents the lack of stability in the drama and in the performance itself. But none of those who saw the show and reported their impressions interpreted it this way, perhaps because the structure was obscured by audience chairs placed throughout the space. And yet somewhat paradoxically the structure was a visual sign of the fluidity and instability of the production.

The audience was inserted into the spatial environment not only as participants in the ceremony but also as visual elements, as parts of the architecture. They belonged to individual 'layers' and spaces and were seen by other spectators. Considering this context, Gurawski's testimony claims that at first the audience was to be seated directly on the steps, and only in the later stage of the development of the performance—following theatrical convention—were chairs brought into the auditorium. Even with the introduction of chairs, the pre-arranged auditorium was maintained with individual spectators seated in pre-selected places.

This fluid and multi-layered space was organized around three places of particular focus that Flaszen called 'mansions': one in the centre and two on opposing short sides of the Theatre of 13 Rows' rectangular space (Flaszen 2010[1964]: 80). When thinking about the spatial environment we should not forget that *Forefathers' Eve* was originally performed in the theatre's small cramped room of 72 square metres. The whole construction described above should be imagined as pressed into this small space. This allows us to see the importance that proximity played in the performance. All of the action took place right next to spectators, sometimes close enough to raise the experience of proximity to a level as important as sight and hearing. The creators evidently wanted to maintain this proximity because while on tour even when performing in much larger spaces, they retained these spatial dimensions just as they were arranged in their own theatre. This can be seen clearly in photographs from a show presented in Wrocław.

Matters of visibility, spatial dynamics and the multiple vantages from which audiences saw the performance were also strongly influenced by lighting—or to use a more precise term—by a dramaturgy of visibility. Gurawski insisted that 'in *Forefathers' Eve* the lighting was extremely important [. . .], an obvious point' for Gurawski because of the 'action taking place among people' (Flaszen 2010). Though none of the surviving reports contain a precise description of how the lights were used, it is possible to deduce from these reports that there was minimal lighting in the scenes where ritual dominated, in the first and third parts of the performance. The lit places were strictly limited to the actors they wanted audience members to see in those moments. This first of all involved a dynamic operation with actors carrying electric candles to illuminate themselves and those audience members who at a given moment were illuminated by the candles and therefore included in the action. Other sources of light doubled as devices for developing the dramaturgy of visibility. Spotlights spread throughout the room lit characters emerging from the darkness. This is how the scenes involving the appearance of ghosts were staged. Additionally, special small spotlights were designed to make characters appear 'demonic'—lit from below—and 'angelic'—lit from above. Finally, lights were mounted in a central candleholder—a menorah—around which actors circled in scenes such as 'counting out the Living Dead'.

It seems obvious that all these uses of dynamic lighting effects imply that most of the theatrical space remained hidden in relative darkness. Why would the actors carry candles and raise them up in order to illuminate one another if other sources of light were overpowering their dynamic lights? Why would they include technically basic but inventive lighting design if not to successfully illuminate specific spaces using relatively limited and weak lights? It seems clear that especially in the scenes of sorcery—the first and third parts of the performance—Grotowski consciously used the surrounding darkness. The spectators only saw what the actors wanted (and were able) to light for them, while the rest of the set remained dark, unclear, worrisome—at times actually threatening. If we recall the meaning attached in this performance to the dramaturgy of superstition, and if we realize that one of the key themes of the performance was the process of emerging from the darkness, ignorance and imaginary fears associated with symbolic meanings, then we can clearly see that Grotowski established a relationship between light and darkness as a means for enhancing the power of the experience.

While the scenes of sorcery were played out in very tightly controlled lighting dramaturgy, the second and fourth parts of the performance— scenes involving the Priest and the Great Improvisation—were played with the lights up. Flaszen clearly reported that towards the end of the second part—when the Priest and the audience alike learned of Gustaw's status as one of the living dead—'the lights went down', implying that previously they were turned up. Before the Improvisation, 'actors switch all the lights on', and therefore they must have been turned off earlier (Flaszen 2010[1964]: 81). This means that, on the level of the dramaturgy of visibility, these two scenes were connected and, at the same time, in contrast to the ritualistic scenes of sorcery.

The precise relation between lighting and the actions performed by the actors represented a very important discovery for Grotowski. It allowed the attainment of a totally new centre of montage—which for Grotowski was one of the most important elements of the art of directing (see Grotowski 2012: 817–27). At the same time, it was another step on the path towards removing all that was external from the theatrical

180 · DARIUSZ KOSIŃSKI

space, all that was not linked directly to the work performed by the actors. Grotowski would make masterful use of this knowledge about the dramaturgy of light and darkness in *Apocalypsis cum figuris*.

Dressing Up as 'Great Theatre'

Alongside the carefully designed space—which drew the most attention from commentators and reviewers—another important and often-noted element of the staging were the unique costumes created by Waldemar Krygier. Flaszen described them:

> The costumes and props are designed to keep some connection to Mickiewicz's era, and at the same time to serve the game and the improvisation. Men wear nineteenth-century trousers, shirts, and cravats, yet without frock-coats or tails, with visible suspenders. Women wear fancy Empire-style lingerie, with curtains that look as if they had just that second been taken off curtain rails, draped over their shoulders in the shape of Romantic era robes. Gustaw wears a cheap rug, substituting for a Romantic coat, and the Priest is dressed in a quilt instead of a cassock. Household items are used, dressed up as 'great theatre'. The beauty of the stylish costumes is juxtaposed with the banality of underwear and prosaic everyday objects.
> (Flaszen 2010[1964]: 80)

This commentary published three years after the premiere focused on the dialectical rules governing the performance. In focusing on this dialectic, Flaszen elides what seems to be the fundamental point of thinking about the costumes, namely the idea of a homemade theatre. In a conversation with Grotowski on the subject, Krygier confirmed this as the source of the costume design. 'Finally, we agreed that the play was taking place in a bourgeois salon and the costumes would be improvised from curtains, bedding, drapes, tablecloths. The ladies disrobed' (Krygier 2001: 77).

The idea of creating such homemade/found costumes was a revelation in its simplicity. Already at the level of first impressions, the costumes established very potent and transparent signs related to key ideas of the performance: playfulness, distancing from historicity and the contrast between the highbrow and the ridiculous. These costumes also clearly signalled the meta-theatricality and rituality of the Opole staging of *Forefathers' Eve*. Important poet and critic Jerzy Zagórski recognized this:

> This is a play at mystery similar to the play at 'calling the ghost' that many years ago was organized in old mansions, forests, and cemeteries. For contemporary audiences this way of performing the Forefathers' sorcery is new and unknown. But I wouldn't be surprised if someone of my age recalled something like this from his or her childhood before the First World War. (Zagórski 1961: 4)

'Playing at mystery' and 'dressing up as great theatre' are more than just acting processes. They can also be seen in relation to how the creators of the performance worked. Grotowski and his collaborators played at creating a mystery play using repurposed everyday items in order to ape and mock 'great theatre'. The meta-theatrical aspect of the costumes—the characters were visibly 'playing dress-up'—was not designed to deride or sneer. Instead, according to the rule often applied to Grotowski's subsequent performances, the costumes paradoxically served as a means for challenging conventional theatrical mechanisms and aesthetic 'crutches'. Exposing the artificiality and the sociocultural construction of the performance served as a test even as it revealed the non-theatrical power of the performance. If despite a clearly visible theatricality certain reactions were still aroused in audiences causing serious tensions and leading to something of an emotional layering, then it would mean that the performance's effect on audiences function independently of theatrical conventions and rather belong to social life, not to art. The Theatre of 13 Rows used meta-theatricality in this way for the first time in *Forefathers' Eve*, with the costumes being its most obvious manifestation.

The costumes served another important function noted by reviewers: their adaptability and metamorphic possibilities. Tadeusz Kudliński wrote about this with great insight, reporting that

> the borderlines of serious and derisive notes were underscored by specific garments. They were designed with unexpected visual and metaphorical inventiveness. [. . .] Hidden allusions to the styles of the time, at times jokey and sneering, in certain situations in the play transform the general mood into a threatening one. In this way the costumes, make-up, and props are not a fixed part of a spectacle, but they perform, transform, and dynamically evolve. A sizeable achievement.
> (Kudliński 2006b[1961]: 140)

What a pity that Kudliński did not give examples of how costumes transformed the mood from jokey to threatening! But this does not change the fact that Krygier's costumes were designed in a way to work not only on the basic level of 'playing dress-up' but at specific moments to give rise to new meanings or effects almost physiological in character. Perhaps the best example of this was the costume of the Priest (Andrzej Bielski) who was 'dressed in a quilt, only his slim arms sticking out of it as he sweated from the heat, as well as out of fear of Gustaw's blasphemous attacks' (Wójtowicz 2004: 64). Other costumes also worked that way in subsequent sequences, revealing and activating different meanings and capacities without adding anything to costume itself. Here we find ourselves on the cusp of something that would soon enough become a rule of the poor theatre: 'magical' transformations achieved with minimal material resources.

One important question related to costumes that affects the whole performance has not been raised until now. In the report quoted above, Krygier noted briefly that 'ladies disrobed', and both this note as well as Flaszen's mention of the actresses appearing in their underwear have thus far been interpreted as simple consequences of the theme of 'playing dress-up' and the idea of a 'home theatre'. And yet this is not true. In photographs from the performance, we can clearly see that both Ewa

Lubowiecka and Rena Mirecka are dressed in a way clearly related to the shapes of their bodies. Ewa Lubowiecka wore shorts with frilly detailing that tied above her knees making her thighs appear larger than normal. Her costume further emphasized her curves with a very revealing corset of red, although it is hard to tell from the black-and-white photographs. This costume did not hide her figure which was decidedly more curvaceous than Mirecka's. Mirecka wore a similar corset and frilly, knee-length pants. However, unlike Lubowiecka she wore black stockings and a white costume. On Mirecka's slim body this costume had a substantially different effect than Lubowiecka's costume had on her larger body. Along with these form-fitting outfits the actresses wore light-blonde wigs with lengthy braids, a parody of the hairstyle favoured by Polish young women of the early 1960s.

Looking at both their costumes—and considering they were mainly acting in children's roles!—it is not hard to see that unlike the men's costumes the actresses' costumes had strong erotic overtones. The frilly additions to their shorts could have alluded to the clothing of the times of Mickiewicz. But equally and even more easily they could have represented erotic fantasies hinting at prostitution. After all, garments such as these are characteristic of 'bawdy houses'. If we also recall that Mirecka recited Zosia's monologue while wearing frilly pants,[8] sexual associations were an important part of the performance clearly revealed by the female actors' costumes.

The rules related to costumes—especially their multiple functions and situational changes—were also applied to props. The performance made use almost exclusively of everyday trivial objects. The most obvious and well-known example is the broom which first appeared in the second part of the performance as a branch, the 'best friend' of Gustaw, and which in the final sequences became a cross. The most multifaceted, most intensively used props were the enamel cooking pots the actors carried. These cheap and trivial domestic items served as ritual vessels.

---

8 Zosia is a ghost of the young girl who died as virgin. Because she did not accept any love proposals during her lifetime, she was sentenced to return to the world of the living to ask young men to interact with her.

184 · DARIUSZ KOSIŃSKI

Simply by appearing as such, they activated a derisive distance towards the idea of 'ritual'. Yet they also had other specific functions. The pots' reflective interiors strengthened the light of candles inserted into them making it possible to illuminate parts of the set without increasing the number or intensity of the theatre lights. When the candles were removed from the pots, the vessels functioned very well as sound and voice ampli-fiers-as in the third part of *Forefathers' Eve* when 'the chorus's solemn undertones are multiplied and deepened by the hollow echo of the sauce-pans which function as resonators' (Flaszen 2010[1964]: 81).

It is worth noting that the items used in *Forefathers' Eve* were not constructed but found, ready-made objects. They introduced meanings into the world of the performance that were connected to their everyday life functions—sometimes surprising, and even on occasion unrecogni-zable. This last remark relates specifically to the most important and lar-gest ready-made prop, the Jewish menorah that stood next to the central 'mansion'. Reviewers remained silent about it. Only Kudliński identified what he saw, writing that 'the seven-arm candelabra stood centre stage [and] created a ritualistic, celebratory feel' (2006b[1961]: 139). No one noted the Jewish context from which the menorah in the 13 Rows' pro-duction of *Forefathers' Eve* emerged, and yet it was fundamental to the performance. We have to wonder about this omission which lasted until Agnieszka Wójtowicz broke the silence in the 1990s when she recognized the cultural meaning of this 'seven arm candelabra' and the importance of placing it at the centre of the action.

> Grotowski carried out a blasphemous change of props—the menorah in place of a cross was the first sign of this change;[9] a sign which makes the space sacred, without belonging to the Christian tradition [...]. What besides 'creating a mood' could the menorah mean?—most likely a chosen people.
> (Wójtowicz 2004: 57)

---

9 In the renowned stagings of *Forefathers' Eve* directed by Leon Schiller with the set design by Andrzej Pronaszko—three subsequent versions in Lwów 1932, Vilnius 1933 and Warsaw 1934—three monumental crosses were an ever-present element of the performance, a kind of permanent visual metaphor for the entirety of it. The 13 Rows used the menorah in a similar way.

Wójtowicz does not give reasons for her theory about the menorah. As far as I understand, Wójtowicz's proposal could have emerged from the following thought process: the menorah is a symbol of the people of Israel, one of the oldest such symbols. Jews are seen as God's 'chosen people', and hence the menorah represents chosen-ness—which in this context could also refer to Poles. This connection can be made, but especially after the Shoah, the comparison is risky. Another possibility is that the menorah replaces the messianism implied by the cross, and, by placing it centre stage, messianism became the central object of derision in the performance.

There is another interpretation. If the menorah is not the symbol of a chosen people but rather simply represents the Jewish community, then its placement in the centre, and the failure of critics to read it correctly, is a dramatic symbol of how the annihilated Jews of Poland have been forgotten. Forgotten so completely that no one knows what the menorah is any more, and no one is bothered by it being a piece of furniture in a bourgeois apartment where young people play games trying to contact ghosts! The menorah—around which the actors perform a scene of 'counting out the living dead'—which I will describe shortly— also indicates that for Grotowski the ghosts (not) present in the very heart of Polish consciousness were not Mickiewicz's folk phantoms but rather the ghosts of Jews murdered on Polish ground. They are not yet referred to explicitly in *Forefathers' Eve*. It is not until *Acropolis*—the staging of which Grotowski was already considering in May 1961—that representatives of the victims of the Shoah will be inside the Theatre of 13 Rows confronting the audience.

Following this trail further, we can take an even greater risk and hint that the choice of the menorah as a substitute for the Christian cross can also indicate that Poles are being stripped of their position as unique victims of history. After the Shoah, Poles no longer have the right to consider themselves as 'chosen ones' in the sense established in nineteenth century by Romantic messianism—i.e. a nation specifically experienced in suffering and therefore destined to lead the world. Poland's Romantic era martyrdom shrinks almost to insignificance when set beside the horrors and sufferings of the Shoah, and thus also the rituals associated with Polish Romanticism are also diminished, insignificant and pitiful in comparison, and can only be performed after the Shoah as a sneering parody. If even today this perspective were to be emphasized and made visible, it would constitute a real national blasphemy in Poland. But no one who saw the Opole *Forefathers' Eve* articulated (or perhaps they just didn't take note of) this possible meaning behind the use of the menorah.

When writing about the menorah, it is impossible to avoid referring to its rich religious and cultural symbolism. A thorough study of the potential meanings of the menorah used by the Theatre of 13 Rows would need far more space and competence that I am able to give it here. But I will venture to indicate some basic points. The menorah is a gift from God who presented Moses with a detailed description of how it should be constructed (Exodus 25:31–40). According to the most popular ancient explanations by Philo of Alexandria and Joseph Flavius, it is the symbol of heavens with planets and the sun in the centre (see Ovadiah 2014). But it is also a symbolic representation of the burning bush, and hence a unique 'medium' of the manifestation of God's will. Symbolic meaning is also assigned to its six arms which represent the physical world created in the same number of days while the seventh, the central arm, is considered a symbol of the seventh day that God blessed and called holy. This idea developed into considering the menorah a symbol that shows the human capacity to triumph over darkness and evil. In photos from the performance where the menorah is clearly visible, its lamps seem turned off with the exception of two scenes in which one candle—the central candle—is lit. I do not have any firm proof of this, but I believe this is no accident. I think the artists responsible for the performance—especially Ludwik Flaszen (born into a Jewish family)—were aware of the religious contexts of the menorah.

Interestingly, the menorah is not visible in the sketches of the performance space made by Gurawski, including the one printed on the cover of the performance programme. This indicates that the idea of using a menorah instead of a cross did not come from the theatre designer.

Maybe Flaszen suggested this incredibly important element of the performance during rehearsals. If so, why did he never say so? In any case, even if Flaszen made the initial suggestion, there was only one person able to approve such an important substitution, Grotowski himself.

Calling Out the Polish Hero

In a conversation with Falkowski, Grotowski described the essential dramaturgical rules governing the first part of the Opole *Forefathers' Eve*:

> We had tried to reveal the connection between ritual and playfulness: actors begin magic ritual with something of a playful act. They pick at random one of the actors or audience members—using Mickiewicz's text—as the 'leader of the chorus' (a living dead, later to become Gustaw-Konrad). This game goes beyond anything 'sacral', participants calling upon the dead and then instantly playing them as roles. The act of taking a spectator who is expecting no such thing out of the auditorium as 'a shepherdess' haunted by the living dead is meant to be a return to theatre-ritual, to theatre-playfulness, almost cabaret-like.
> (Grotowski 2012: 204)

So, the frame of this part of the performance was to be playfully cabaret-like, while its inner sequences were to be ritualistic and performed more seriously, though in ridiculous costumes and with the use of 'poor' props.

It is not clear how or when the actors entered the room. This most likely took place right after the spectators took their seats assigned to each of them by Antoni Jahołkowski who acted as a room manager. Jahołkowski composed the shape of the performance space by placing audience members in it. In pictures from a guest performance in Wrocław, the actors can be seen entering the performance space as if in a procession, then immediately beginning to play at counting out the 'living dead'. As Flaszen described it:

The actors, holding hands like children playing, circle a tall candlestick [menorah] placed in the middle of the room and rhythmically chant a text from the part of the poem known as 'Upiór' […]. And, as in a children's game, they count Gustaw out of the group.

(Flaszen 2010[1964]: 80)

According to Agnieszka Wójtowicz—who based her research on conversations with the artists and audiences involved in the performance—'it was the Sorcerer who chanted rhythmically to select and point to Gustaw' (2004: 62). This sequence accompanied the following verse: 'Who—is—this—man?—The—li—ving—dead' (Mickiewicz 2016[1823]: 145).

The meaning of this scene was somewhat obscured by the authority of Mickiewicz's text. It is therefore all the better to get out from under its shadow. 'Counting out' was a social game, maybe even a prank. It led to one of the participants being selected and cast in the exceptional role of the living dead. Later in the show, the selected participant would become the hero of the collective, taking on a specific responsibility. Osiński noted that 'the scene in which spirits are summoned and Gustaw-Konrad is designated as saviour clearly echoes the scene in *Apocalypsis cum figuris* in which the Dark One or Simpleton is selected' (Osiński 1986: 62). And it is this perspective—this light cast backwards—that allows us to better understand what happened in the first scene of *Forefathers' Eve*. Here is Gustaw-Konrad—the Polish Chosen One—who was called out in the course of a game for fun, by accident and thereby completely stripped of 'missionary' pathos. This seems to mean that this hero could have been anyone at all. It was not any special talent or predisposition that designated him the embodiment of national myths. It was the community itself who created its own idols and supported them by enacting their roles.

After counting out the 'Living Dead', Gustaw (Zygmunt Molik) spoke the rest of the poem and told his story—the story of an unhappy lover who may have committed suicide and returns each year to walk among the living and seek his beloved. During the monologue, the ritual Chorus dispersed to prepare for the next scene. Then the Sorcerer

(Zbigniew Cynkutis) and the men helping him entered the central stage while Gustaw, the living dead, remained in the shadows. The Sorcerer's assistants (Andrzej Bielski and Antoni Jahołkowski) were dressed in black trousers held up by suspenders and white shirts with black cravats. The Sorcerer wore an identical outfit but with a 'cloak'—a thick, shiny quilt most probably gold-coloured-tied at the front of the chest in a way that ensured freedom of movement. A characteristic element of the Sorcerer's attire was a long but sparse beard, slightly twisted, reminiscent of Orthodox Jews. The beard was visibly attached to the young actor's face displaying its theatrical artificiality. The Sorcerer also had a black moustache styled with a slightly upwards twist.

The sequence of 'calling out' ghosts in *Forefathers' Eve Part II* involves three sequences of summoning and the appearance of three phantoms representing different types of the living dead bound to the Earthly realm, unable to reach Heaven or Hell for a range of reasons. These phantoms appear consecutively in Grotowski's script—first as innocent children deceased before their time, then as the cruel Evil Landlord burdened with many sins, and finally as the virginal Zosia who had never known sex. Photographs taken by Zdzisław Mozer show us the scene in which the first spells were cast (inv. no. 255). The group of men leading the ritual were located close to the central 'mansion' indicated by the menorah, and the Children appeared on the opposite end of the stage on a tall pedestal behind the audience seats. In accordance with Mickiewicz's text, there were two Children but only one of them, Ewa Lubowiecka, said anything. The actresses Rena Mirecka and Lubowiecka appeared conjoined as one grotesque creation. This can be seen in Mozer's photographs (inv. no. 215) and in a drawing made by Krygier printed in the performance programme (*Materiały i Dyskusje* 1961, VOL. 6: 9). Lubowiecka is walking erect, taller, bigger and decidedly towering over the slim Mirecka. Mirecka, leaning forward, seems to be attached to her partner's side in such a way that her head emerges from below Lubowiecka's arm. Lubowiecka's posture seems to suggest self-assuredness while Mirecka rests her chin on her hand appearing like a female version of the Pensive Christ.

Though no one has mentioned this, it is important to note that mature women performed the roles of these Children. Their physical attributes were not concealed but rather exposed amplifying the scene's grotesque contrast. Lubowiecka's appearance as the 'one-hundred-kilo Angel'[10] successfully undermined any sentimentality conventionally embedded in the scene where the Children's ghosts come to meet their mother.

The Sorcerer alone conducted the second 'calling out' of ghosts by stretching his hands over a cooking pot filled with 'vodka'. In this scene Jahołkowski and Bielski, performing his assistants, could not accompany him because they were engaged in 'producing' the phantom. Flaszen wrote that 'The Ghost of the Evil Lord is simply a voice and hands lit by a torch making desperate gestures from behind a black curtain just above the spectators' heads' (Flaszen 2010[1964]: 80). One of the actors voiced the ghost and the other most likely created a visual effect using his hands.[11] Apart from this, we know nothing more about the scene. I have found no mention of where they placed the curtain that hid Jahołkowski. Nor do we know what sorts of gestures he made—perhaps he used his hands to imitate birds? And all we can do is imagine who spoke the lines belonging to the Chorus of Birds, and guess from where they delivered their lines. In Mickiewicz's drama, the Chorus of Birds responded to the Evil Landlord with the story of his cruel crimes. In the typescript version of the scenario used by Andrzej Bielski, the name 'Ewa' has been added to this fragment of the text with an instruction to turn down the microphone written beside one of the verses marked with a cross. This indicates that the Chorus of Birds was voiced by Ewa Lubowiecka hiding somewhere in the dark using a microphone. It is interesting that no one commented on this: probably the last case of Grotowski using an electric amplifier for actors' voices.

---

10 This is Jerzy Gurawski's description. See Gurawski 1992: 54.

11 Jahołkowski who had a better voice and was more experienced probably voiced the ghost. Bielski started his theatre career as a puppeteer so it is more likely that he was 'animating' his hands. If so, Jahołkowski could have shined his flashlight on Bielski's hands.

Rena Mirecka played Zosia, the third phantom. Photographs showing her in the central section of the performance space give the impression that Zosia is quarrelsome or roguish. She looks like a child pretending to be a rascal, a far cry from the naively idyllic figure of the ghost of the 'Maiden' conventionally presented.

After signalling the end of the ritual, the Sorcerer sprinkled the audience with real poppy seeds.[12] These closing gestures were interrupted by the appearance of another living dead, Gustaw. He suddenly emerged from the depths of the auditorium and stood over a woman he had selected from the audience. He held his right hand over his heart, with his left hand held over the female spectator as if to curse her. In this way he cast her in the role of the Shepherdess, his former lover. The appearance of this uncanny figure that in the original aroused terror was here performed as a prank. As Jerzy Kreczmar commented:

> The Shepherdess who sat down on a grave was perforce performed by a female spectator, chosen at the beginning by the actor [Jahołkowski], who was sitting in the audience [. . .]; she knew nothing about her role and duties. 'What do you stare? What do you grin?' [Mickiewicz 2016[1823]: 170] the Chorus asks, and then its members lead the embarrassed woman out the door. Then comes an intermission, and the 'actress in spite of her will' returns to the auditorium to rounds of applause. (Kreczmar 1961: 23)

This is an obvious tension-creating cabaret device, connected to the fact that a spectator has been drawn into the play—no one is safe. Yet it offers relief—'they took her and not me'. Grotowski and his actors consciously and radically destroyed the solemnity of the original drama, thereby allowing the audience to exit for the intermission in a playful mood.

In my estimation the first part of the performances served as a sort of 'tutorial'. The change of impressions and moods from fun to mystery

---

12 In Polish folk culture poppy seeds are connected to dreams and death, and serve as food for ghosts. This is why the Sorcerer threw them around the space—to feed the remaining spirits.

and seriousness and then back to playfulness changed points of view, created aesthetic dissonances and lacked coherence and consequence. All of this presented the audience with a taste of what they would experience in subsequent scenes.

The second part of the Opole version was based on *Forefathers' Eve Part IV* in which an unexpected guest visits the house where the Priest lives alone with two children.[13] The guest is introduced simply as the Hermit but later turns out to be the ghost of one of the Priest's old students—Gustaw—who killed himself because of an unhappy love. He tells and performs his story by singing, and even doing some 'magic tricks' for the surprised Priest, who is strangely enough a rationalist who does not believe in folk superstitions. This nearly solo performance by Gustaw—composed by Grotowski using Mickiewicz's words—was the first attempt by the character cast in the role of the main hero by the will of the community to perform his role correctly.

This is the most troubling part of the performance from the point of view of the reconstructed description and interpretation because so little is known about the scene. There are no photographs and the reviewers almost completely ignored it. This might have happened because this scene was relatively ineffectively staged. It was all about acting—especially that of the Hermit-Gustaw (Molik). Critics—especially those limited by word counts—usually describe such sequences briefly or not at all. This is especially true when their attention is drawn towards more defined dramaturgical and staging elements, as was the case here. But it is also true that this drawing of attention away was steered by the creators of the show themselves. In their commentaries on the performance, they directed attention towards the first and final sections of the performance passing over the intervening portion of the production without comment. Flaszen writing several years after the premiere provides us with the main source of information about the scene. I am of the opinion that Flaszen's note is a 'side effect' of his decision to describe the entire performance in the order in which it was staged.

---

13 This suggests he was a priest of the Ruthenian Uniate Church whose lower clergy retained the right to marry and have children.

I emphasize this because the near absence of this fragment in comments, reports and source materials appears to me to be telling, especially in light of the attention soon to be paid to the acting process within the Laboratory Theatre of 13 Rows. Let us then put two sequences together as a provocation: the second part of the Opole *Forefathers' Eve* and Faustus' role in the Opole performance derived from Marlowe's drama that premiered in April 1963—almost two years later—which I describe in Chapter 8. Both are confessions of life, and both involve the main protagonist performing his own life 'using voice and body to empathize with the substance of a human fate'. The difference in effect between one sequence and the other is obvious and shows the distance Grotowski covered in the two years between being a dramaturg and director working with actors on texts and myths, and becoming a director-midwife working with the aid of texts and myths on actors as human beings. It appears that *Forefathers' Eve* might be the point at which Grotowski noticed this potential—not in Part IV of the text but in the Great Improvisation. For Grotowski Part IV was clearly not anything that could lead to a focus on the 'inner process' of his actors. It was something else—a spectacle, a showing off, but also a polemic against the attitude represented by the Priest.

Flaszen writes very clearly about the showiness of this scene.

Gustaw performs his drama in an ostentatious manner, as if to show off. When he takes pity upon himself with lyricism, his voice rises to the upper registers of *bel canto*, while his body takes on poses suggesting fainting. When he surrenders to despair and madness we hear him roar in a basso voice, making fearsome faces, his body suddenly striking odd poses, their strangeness designed to comically frighten his partners and audiences. When he disagrees with the Priest's Christian conformism, he goes as far as blasphemy: there is something to it that resembles the metaphysical pranks of Don Juan, a dark sacrilegious humour, set to achieve a very specific sort of effect. He recites poems melodically, angling towards singing, breaking into actual song in the culminating moments of his role.

> Pompous in his form of expression, there is a child at the heart
> of his performance. And similar to the Priest's children—laugh-
> able, and yet deserving of pity.
> (Flaszen 2010[1964]: 81)

Thus, his role was an obvious attempt to show off—a composition constructed from bright and stereotypical effects, and something that was
not hidden from view but rather ostentatiously exposed. Grotowski and
Molik made their version of *Forefathers' Eve Part IV* meta-theatrical by
bringing the 'theatre' down to the lowbrow level of an obvious act of
showing off.

The exaggerated performance by Hermit/Gustaw was juxtaposed
to that of the Priest—'a dull but good old soul; a philistine sermonizing
in a silly but good-natured way' (Flaszen 2010). The contrast between
the two was heightened by their costumes. Gustaw-Konrad was dressed
in a patterned cape 'substituting for a Romantic coat' (Flaszen 2010)—
while the Priest wore a satin quilt which seemed to envelop Andrzej
Bielski's slim body in a grotesque way. The Priest hence gave the impression of being in a 'fancy dress' costume analogous to that of the Sorcerer.
Both wore satin quilts—probably gold in colour—that in the language
of the performance were signs of a 'priesthood'.

The cuts Grotowski made to the text of *Forefathers' Eve Part IV*
mostly affected the lines spoken by Gustaw and also to a certain degree
altered the proportions between his and the Priest's parts making the
distribution of lines more equitable. While it is still hard to say that they
were equal partners, Grotowski nevertheless transformed the auto-per-
formance of the Hermit into a dispute based on their divergent attitudes.
Gustaw is dynamic, changeable, open and at times 'crazy', while the
Priest is orderly and focused on defending the mainstream, safe image
of the world. 'The key contradiction' in the second part of the Opole
staging of *Forefathers' Eve* thus referred to the tension between being in
the world and following the rules that govern it. Gustaw followed an
irrational, loving impulse that came across as pitiful and naive in accordance with his Romantic, theatrical posing; also, he did not have a language
to express his experience. At the same time however, this experience

protected him from being locked in a fixed social role as happened to the Priest.

Gustaw's pitifulness and childishness—an important aspect of his character as a creation-in-process—was exposed in the performance via the surprising link between the uncanny guest and the 'Priest's children'. Flaszen described Gustaw as being just as 'funny but pitiful' as the Priest's children. All three were to be 'poor, misshapen creatures, the pitiful work of God's hands' (Flaszen 2010).

It is necessary at this point to recall that Mirecka and Lubowiecka played the Children, and they probably wore the same outfits they wore in the first part. They were therefore not naive little girls but rather mature women dressed in a clearly erotic way in corsets and frilly shorts. Alas we have no photographs showing the Children with the Priest. We only know that they were not supposed to leave his side even for a second, and that together they formed an 'awkward, crooked group' (Wójtowicz 2004: 64). We may suppose that both actresses created a double figure similar to one they formed in the first part of the performance when they—we should also remember—appeared conjoined as a monstrous ghost. If this was the case, then sticking to the same cast and the same visual design of the Children could be interpreted as a sign of their uncanny status analogous to that of the Hermit. In addition, through their femininity and erotic appearance, the Children may also at times support Gustaw's performance of his love story by stepping into the role of his lost object of affection. All of this of course could have been subtly communicated without a heavy hand, suggested and performed in a strange, disturbing way.

In summary, we can say that the second part of the performance led to a clash of two attitudes. On the one hand, childish, emotional and yet uncanny, 'ghostlike' madness and on the other hand, a rational-empirical, adult, dogmatic, limited pragmatism. The Priest represented the one-dimensional world of compromised, 'reasonable' dogma. And Gustaw represented a complex, multi-layered vision of the world as a whole discovered through the madness of desire that goes against the rules of normalcy. Seen from this perspective, the performance Gustaw gave in the Priest's home was an example of a theatre of education or even a theatre of initiation. It was a theatre of a living dead man who returns to the world of the living and adapts their performance conventions in order to parody them to the level of pompous excess. By this he destroys them. This destruction reveals the world hidden beneath mainstream conventions, behind the 'theatre of everyday life', a transhuman whole. This transhuman whole is something Grotowski articulated in previous performances and texts like 'the Universe' as something that 'does not surrender to death'. In all of his early performances Grotowski aimed to encounter this transhuman whole, and to share the experience of this encounter.

The second part of *Forefathers' Eve* featured the Hermit as the central protagonist and was thus a presentation of a 'Universal' way of understanding theatre. And yet—and this seems to be a key aspect—the performance presented this vision from within auto-ironic, parodic brackets where theatrical conventions were ridiculed. The Hermit, played by the Theatre of 13 Rows' leading actor Zygmunt Molik, performed the role in an almost comic way and yet, at the same time, he did not nullify the theatre's desire for truth. Grotowski used this directorial strategy frequently. Sensing his own deficiencies and restrictions, he did not try to hide them but instead, he ridiculed them. For example, sexual desire survived not as an idea or a concept but rather as what Grotowski later called 'a central temptation'. This is the very gesture Grotowski used in *Cain*'s last scene ridiculing the pompous final toast from *Orphée*. Similarly in the second part of *Forefathers' Eve*, the parody of the theatre of total discovery where love is the main driving force could have been performed as a commentary on *Shakuntala* with Molik playing the protagonist-lover, King Dushyanta.[14] This does not mean that after *Shakuntala* Grotowski neglected the importance of love. Rather, it served as a way of freeing himself and his actors from the conventional forms of expression to which they were accustomed.

---

14 Another important example of this method can be seen in the process of creating *Apocalypsis cum figuris* which began by parodying and mocking the 'saint actor', Ryszard Cieślak. See Grotowski 2008[1969].

In the context of the entire performance, the second part of *Forefathers' Eve* contained the first appearance of the main hero. When Gustaw was picked by chance to represent the collective, he put on a theatre of revelation consisting of a play of contradictions, and thereby represented Romantic visions of the world as a harmony of multitudes, but Gustaw's performance was not successful. Gustaw did indeed defeat the Priest but did not conquer the imagination of the audience. In spite of his apparent efforts to 'show off' on stage, the hero did not capture the audience's complete attention and thereby did not gain authority. He did not find a permanent place for himself in the audience's memory. This failure is supported by the total absence of this sequence from reviews of the performance. It is hard to say now if it was caused by some weakness of the actor or if Grotowski planned this scene this way. But Gustaw clearly lacked something necessary to achieve success with his audience.

The Final Temptation

The third part of the Opole production of *Forefathers' Eve*—as I noted—was different from Grotowski's script. Originally, he planned two separate parts. But in performance these relatively short parts were combined. This meant that the Great Improvisation overshadowed the shorter third part in Grotowski's script. This is evidenced by the fact that critics who analysed the production paid much more attention to the Great Improvisation than to the material in part three of the script. I will now reassess these sequences in the performance, which till now have been largely neglected.

Once more I note that as a result of sizeable cuts from *Part I*, the most important event in this section of the performance was the conversation between Gustaw and the Black Hunter. A unique introduction and prologue to their conversation featured scenes with the Chorus which recovered momentary control over the theatre. The actions that followed were supposed to re-establish a common bond between the actors and the audience. The former once again began to address the latter, treating them as equal partners, as seen in a photograph by Ryszard Okoński (no. inv. 262).

The Chorus of Young Men performed verses from Mickiewicz's drama: 'Who sing grave-songs when young / And visits tombs and urns, / He never sings gay songs, / Nor to this world returns' (Mickiewicz 2016[1823]: 132). These verses introduced the meeting between Gustaw and the Black Hunter clearly informing audiences of Gustaw's uncanny status as a living dead. If someone who visits graves in his youth will not return 'to this world' then it seems clear that the next scene has to happen somewhere else, in some 'other world'. In a comment from 1961, Flaszen wrote clearly that the 'conversation between Gustaw and the Black Hunter was moved to the underworld because in the previous scene it turned out that the protagonist had committed suicide' (Flaszen 2010[1964]: 68). Three years later he changes his recollection slightly: 'Dusk. Gustaw getting lost in the wilderness. Its location is unclear, possibly the underworld' (2010[1964]: 81).

This lack of clarity and the uncanny character of the place was emphasized in this scene by a soundscape involving noises made by actors who were scattered throughout the dark auditorium. 'Gustaw's monologues [were] desperately accompanied by quasiforest sounds, swooshing and distant barking, coming from places in the room that [were] hard to distinguish: a mood of ironic and gloomy horror' (2010[1964]: 81). In Bielski's copy of the script one can see handwritten notes detailing these noises—'wind shshsh', 'drawn out ooh' and 'drawn out double aah'. It is not clear if these effects were delivered by all the actors or if the notes referred only to those assigned to Bielski. The latter seems a lot more probable in light of Flaszen's use of the term 'barking'. In any case, it was most certainly an attempt to use sound to prepare for the appearance of the most important person in this sequence, the diabolical Black Hunter.[15]

The Black Hunter was played by Antoni Jahołkowski—which seems logical when we consider the fact that the same actor delivered monologues as the Evil Landlord in the first part of the Opole production.[16]

---

15 It is worth recalling here an analogous scene in which Mephisto is summoned in *The Tragical History of Doctor Faustus*. The soundscapes of both sequences seem similar, and in both cases the 13 Rows created a sense of the uncanny through non-linguistic sound techniques.

16 The traditional Polish name of the character—Zły Pan—literally translates to 'the Evil Lord', and can serve as the name of the Devil himself.

The meeting took place in an atmosphere—half-darkness with sounds-capes setting a mysterious mood—that most probably dominated the whole third part of the performance. In two photos taken by Zdzisław Mozer (inv. nos 250 and 253) we see a scene involving Molik and Jahołkowski that is likely a part of this section of the performance. Close to the centre of the performance space we find Molik. In one photo, his back is turned towards us, and in the second, he performs what seems to be a dynamic dance movement with his legs crossed, his hands raised and his fingers bent. In both photos, Jahołkowski stands on a platform close to the Opole theatre's exit to the foyer with his back to the camera. He is dressed in a white shirt and black trousers, his arms are raised and his fingers are pointing away from his temples. His hands form what appear to be horns, perhaps a naive and playful hint at devilishness? The photos seem to indicate that both characters talked to each other from a certain distance, there was no physical contact between them.

The finale of this scene was clearly described by Flaszen:

> The Black Hunter, hanging onto the doors, under the ceiling, with a placid expression, makes monotonous movements with his hands close to his face, as if neurotically pulling at his beard and moustache, and monotonously whispers prophecies about Gustaw's secret destiny. And when Gustaw falls to the ground in a pose of artificial horror, the Black Hunter, with his index finger meaningfully stretched upwards, announces factually: 'A cell in the Basilian Monks' Monastery in Vilnius'.[17]
> (Flaszen 2010[1964]: 81)

This was to be a moment in which the living dead Gustaw is brought to the world of the living, this time as Konrad. Agnieszka Wójtowicz provides us with more details:

---

17 This exclamation is the shortened version of Mickiewicz's information for the Prologue to *Part Three*: 'In Wilno, near Ostrobramska Street, in the Basilian Monastery (transformed into a state prison)—a prisoner's cell' (Mickiewicz 2016[1832]: 174). The cell in the former Basilian monastery located in present-day Vilnius in Lithuania was the one in which Mickiewicz himself was imprisoned. It later became a mythical place in Polish culture usually referred to as 'Konrad's cell'. Though the original cell was destroyed in the course of reshaping the building in 1867, there is still a so-called 'Konrad's cell' in Vilnius with a small museum visited mainly by Poles.

Candles were lit, arranged in such a way as to compose Gustaw's stations of the cross. From behind the door to the foyer the Sorcerer pulled a broom (the same one Gustaw brought with him to the Priest). The Chorus then carried the broom like a holy relic and placed it on the back of Gustaw as he lay in the centre. Somewhere off stage there was the sound of nails being hammered. Gustaw was becoming Konrad. The Great Improvisation was beginning.
(Wójtowicz 2004: 66)

This relatively short scene was also very rich and is important for understanding the final part of the performance and therefore the entire performance. It is beyond doubt that Gustaw's meeting with the Black Hunter is a scene of Mephistophelean temptation which is also the way the scene is presented in Mickiewicz's original. But it is also reminiscent of Dante getting lost in the woods at the beginning of *The Divine Comedy*. Thus, this sequence represents both a temptation and an initiation that leads to a journey through hell as its first stage. The Black Hunter's stage directions tell us where the Polish Hero Konrad will be born. This implies that the devil was in control of the stage,[18] that he was the one who sent the hero back to the world of the living with a mission planned by the devil himself. The result is clear: the Great Improvisation—the 'foundational act' of Polish national identity—was shown as the devil's work: thus, the nation was portrayed as possessed by His Satanic Majesty.

But nothing is ever that simple when it comes to Grotowski. It is true that the living dead was sent by the devil, but it was the community that gave him the form and the role he was to perform. The Sorcerer brought the broom—Gustaw-Konrad's doppelgänger—while the chorus burdened the hero with it. In so doing, they transformed the trivial object into a stand-in for the cross and thus initiated the Passion of the Polish National Hero. The devilish figure thereby became the Polish Saviour.

---

18 From this point on, the figure of a devilish director reappears in all Grotowski's performances. Jahołkowski usually though not always (the important exception is *Acropolis* where the role of the 'director' was taken by Molik) plays these roles—compare Mephisto in *Tragical History of Doctor Faustus*, The King in *Constant Prince* and, the clearest and final example, Simon Peter in *Apocalypsis cum figuris*.

As the most important scene in the play, the Great Improvisation was frequently described, always in surprisingly similar ways. Commentators noted almost the same elements emphasized by the creators of the performance. Grotowski told Falkowski:

> Gustaw-Konrad's monologue was crafted to resemble the road to Calvary. Gustaw-Konrad moves—among the spectators— like Christ between the stations of his suffering. He carries a trifling improvised prop—a broom—using it the way Christ used the cross. His pain is genuine, and his belief in a mission to save humanity sincere, and even filled with tragedy, but his reactions are naive, close to a childish drama of helplessness.
> (Grotowski 2012: 205)

Flaszen added that Konrad:

> cruises around the whole space, from time to time falling under the burden of his banal prop, in iconographic poses of Christ on his way to Calvary. Christ, sometimes suffering in an inhuman way, as if senile, sometimes swearing at his cruel Father with a helpless shrill voice.
> (Flaszen 2010[1964]: 82)

In the often-reprinted photograph by Ryszard Okoński (inv. no. 263) and in three drawings by Waldemar Krygier printed in the programme (see *Materiały i Dyskusje* 1961, VOL. 6: 6, 14, 15, 16), we see the different poses taken by Molik. They resemble the iconic pose of Christ collapsing under the cross. This association is not however based on some precise copy or replication of the typical depictions of the Way of the Cross. Rather, Molik's poses in Krygier's drawings seem to give form to generalized allusions and synthetic symbols hinting at the event they represent.

These poses of the Passion stand in sharp contrast to the fact that Konrad—the 'Polish Christ'—carried a broom instead of a cross. All the reviewers read this link in the same way, recognizing its meaning the source of which was easy to pinpoint, namely the conviction that *Forefathers' Eve* is the fundamental text of Polish messianic ideology. According to this line, after the blasphemy with which the Great

Improvisation ends, and Konrad is healed and saved by the humble monk Father Peter, he began a process of spiritual growth that finally led to his transformation into the Polish Saviour, the new Christ of global freedom. Grotowski took all these convictions—popular beliefs arising more from an emotional and communal reception than any careful reading of Mickiewicz—and combined them into a single scene. Grotowski turned Konrad into a rebellious, blasphemous Polish Son of Man, one who is both an embodiment of and the ambassador for the whole nation.

This resulted in the activation of the first of many 'key contradictions' between pride and humility, between rebelling against God and humbly accepting belittlement. Józef Szczawiński wrote:

> Konrad—played by Zygmunt Molik—doesn't make us laugh, even though his pride is ridiculed. His suffering was shocking without taking into account the sources that caused it to happen. It expresses the fates of human beings who can only enter into a dialogue with infinity from the position of someone encumbered with limitations imposed upon them by their bodies and time itself, and above all by our own essential ridiculous natures. This is not a lesson in pessimism, but in humility as the author originally intended. Perhaps it is in humility—that is the ability to perceive proportions—and not in self-destruction that we finally see the greatness that is our shared humanity. (Szczawiński 1962: 10).

Szczawiński's interpretation is interesting. It leads to conclusions other than those put forward by other critics. The Great Improvisation staged by the Theatre of 13 Rows is not at all a manifestation of superiority and debasement but is rather a theatrical act that—through the clash of two ostensibly contradictory value systems—becomes a lesson in becoming human. The outcome of the lesson might be interpreted as the ability to see all that is funny, small, worthy of ridicule—in this case Konrad's buffoonery—and at the same time all that is serious, full of values, that gives the hero his greatness: suffering, rebellion and above all striving towards his goal at all costs. It seems to me that the three closing sentences from the Szczawiński review quoted above could be used without change to refer to later martyrs featured in Grotowski's theatre, especially Faust and Don Fernando. Who knows, perhaps in the finale of the Opole *Forefathers' Eve* Szczawiński intuitively spotted a grain of what would soon enough become the total act?

In this context it seems surprising and meaningful that the contradiction—or to use a term that Grotowski and Flaszen used more keenly in 1961 the 'dialectics of pride and humility'—did not seem all that important to the artists themselves. In his conversation with Falkowski, Grotowski said that

> in the Improvisation we were mostly focused on the 'dialectics of blasphemy and devotion', indicating both signs which were to introduce this dialectic: the female voices turn the insults aimed at God into the melody of the prayer of the matins, and the fall of Gustaw-Konrad under the burden of his blasphemies coincides with the sound of church bells.
> (Grotowski 2012: 205)

Flaszen wrote about the same elements:

> From outside come the melodies of matins: pious female voices chant blasphemous fragments of the Great Improvisation. Konrad listens intently, argues with them, picks up on their singing, as if imitating and repeating it. It has the mood of a holy service in the countryside; it all has something of a naive Passion Play about it. When at the end of the Improvisation, Konrad—clinging anxiously to the wall—shouts out his famous accusation against God for being 'Tsar of the world', he falls onto the ground in an act of weird humility mixed with blasphemy. The sound of a bell can be heard above a prone Konrad, as if during the Elevation [of the Host].
> (Flaszen 2010[1964]: 82–83)

204 · DARIUSZ KOSIŃSKI

The suggestions of both creators allow us to establish a slightly more solid foundation for the frequently repeated formula of 'the dialectics of derision and apotheosis' proposed by Tadeusz Kudliński in his take on the Great Improvisation:

> This is an act of typical and solitary romantic rebellion set against everything, along with the obsession of saving the world in spite of the established order. In this scene we also experience the culmination of the basic dialectics of derision and apotheosis, where grotesque buffoonery intermingles with tragically demonic martyrdom.
> (Kudliński 2006b[1961]: 140)

I have the impression that Kudliński's observation has been quoted so often that no one is surprised by his formulations. But what is this famous dialectic about which Kudliński writes? Is it not the very thing Grotowski called more directly 'dialectics of blasphemy and devotion'? Is it not most of all connected to his perverse use of elements taken from Catholic liturgy, condensed and recomposed?

In the scene featuring the Great Improvisation we seem to have allusions to the Lent devotions focused on the Way of the Cross. The Improvisation is a prayerful copy, a repetition of and a contemplation on the suffering of the Lord; hence a way of 'using voice and body to empathize with the substance of the human fate' of Jesus. Here we have melodies taken from the matins, and more importantly *Forefathers' Eve*'s final direct allusion to the Holy Mass liturgy, the Elevation of the Host. The Elevation is the culminating moment connected with the Eucharist. It is a moment in which Priests present the faithful with the bread and wine transformed during the Eucharistic prayer into the Body and Blood of Christ. It is also the re-actualization of Jesus' action of establishing this Most Holy Sacrament during the Last Supper which is interpreted as the prefiguration of the suffering and sacrifice of his Passion. Using the bell for the Elevation to conclude the Great Improvisation may be read in the following way: the community had been presented with the one who offered himself up in its cause and was transformed by it thereby repeating the sacrifice that had already been made and was already treated by the community as the founding act of its identity. Grotowski was fully aware of what he was doing when he used the liturgical dramaturgy of an action intended neither to change a social status—as a *rite de passage* does—nor to create something new. Instead, he used it to the reveal an eternal present. He made use of it not to ridicule the Mass or to sanctify something profane. Instead, he used it to strip away historical and literary costumes revealing a figure full of dialectical contradictions, a fantasy character capable of engaging the imagination, thought and ways of acting of the members of the community with which and for which he staged his *Forefathers' Eve*. Just as in the case of the Holy Mass, the performance aimed at an experience of meeting face to face with something unspoken and yet real, complex and capable of embracing contradictions, at the heart of a drama that Poles keep on playing out in their culture and their lives on a range of levels. However, this was not meant to be an experience of elation as is the Mass, but rather of a paradoxical contamination of the apotheosis' signs appearing over the one who (literally!) has fallen.

If I am right in reading this (anti)liturgical aspect of Grotowski's Great Improvisation in between the lines of Kudliński's review, then we should straight away say that he was the only one to have spotted this. The dialectics of blasphemy and devotion would become one of the most important aspects of Grotowski's theatre after *The Tragical History of Doctor Faustus* premiered two years later and the liturgical allusions finally exploded with the 'black mass' of *Apocalypsis cum figuris* in 1969. In *Forefathers' Eve*, Konrad's blasphemous rebellion was perceived as weak and rather pathetic, and because it overlapped with Christ's humble acceptance of sufferings, it was seen as a rather buffoonish gesture of self-justification. We are still a long way from Faustus, a holy rebel struggling against a Demiurge who rules over 'this world'.

Another aspect of the Great Improvisation—the hopelessness of the solitary rebellion-was broadly commented on by Flaszen with reference to another myth important for Polish Romanticism, that of Prometheus.

The heroic individual believes in his unique role. The poet, God's equal partner, despising everything except for the impulse to sacrifice, wants to lead the community to introduce order into the tainted reality that cannot be defended or justified by any kind of theodicy. Mickiewicz seems to trust the meaning of his hero's rebellion, yet he sentences him to defeat. His defeat, taking place with tragic solemnity, proves that a rebellious attitude is considered vital, even if it is to be overcome.

The modern director does not share this belief in the individual act's vital meaning. Thus, he sees Prometheus as being sentenced to a double martyrdom. The martyrdom of a prophet of a lost—from the start—cause, a Christ whose gospel will not become the foundation for any church. And the martyrdom of Don Quixote, torn between the bombast of his attempt and his complete lack of any sense of reality, a person exposed to the enlightened crowd's mockery. The cruel silence of someone who is ambiguous in his distance (possibly being ironic?) is an answer to the individual who thrashes around with noble zeal. Is humility accepted then as a proud defender of human rights, as Mickiewicz wanted? Humility, maybe, but a bitter and perverse humility. A world in which Prometheus becomes a helpless, crazy child, a prophet without any faithful, a commander without an army, is worthless.
(Flaszen 2010[1964]: 82)

This might be one of the most courageous, and also the most troubling comments ever written by Flaszen. In fact, what we have here may be knowledge gained from watching *Kordian*, the next Opole performance. However, I think it is possible to accept that the questions and dilemmas that formed the foundations for Grotowski's next Romantic staging were also present in his *Forefathers' Eve*. These were truly complex questions. For if we look past the beauty of Flaszen's phrasing, then we will be confronted with a truly despairing lack of answers and lack of faith which in the final scene of *Forefathers' Eve* was thrown right at the audience.

Contemporary people who have been through their own experiences of rebellion and battles to change the way the world works no longer believe in solitary rebellions and Prometheus' mission. Hence, we can think that his struggle might make sense if it were a collective effort instead of solitary one. Yet it was the community that selected and cast an individual in the role of hero and saviour, and in this way somehow condemned him to failure and freed itself from the burden of responsibility. The hero of *Forefathers' Eve* suffers a fate that is in some way that of a scapegoat, one that takes on the hungers and the guilt of the masses, is killed by them and is then beatified as the one who overcame the crisis caused by the desires of masses.[19] Therefore, there is no chance of his rebellion being supported by the community.

And yet the humility and resistance that Mickiewicz so venerated over and above pride are also questioned because humility assumes acceptance of the world and its rules as they are, thereby also accepting the value of 'humanity' and surrendering individual singularity. It seems clear that in 1961 the director and his co-workers could not accept such an attitude—that they ought to humbly serve the world surrounding them and its residents. The effect was a paradoxical and also terrifying character, 'The defiled Prometheus, whose mutiny has been deprived of any dignity, his blasphemy becoming either funny or pathetic in the end, is identified with servile prayer' (Flaszen 2010[1964]: 83).

In 1961 the creators of the Theatre of 13 Rows saw no other future for a Polish Prometheus than one of derision, pity or compromise. They found no hope in unclear prophesies and no chance of salvation. They found nothing more than a blasphemous bell rung for the Elevation as a sign of desperate recognition in spite of it all.

---

19 Of course, this is a very brief application of René Girard's theory whose basic examples can be found in his books (1977 and 1986). A clear example of the scapegoat in a dramatic scenario can be found in *The Constant Prince* (see Kosiński 2007: 436–38).

The Torn Books of the Past

The fate of the hero called to perform in the Opole *Forefathers' Eve* is a uniquely balanced deconstruction of the idea of a Polish Hero who proudly declared that he embodied the whole nation (see Mickiewicz 2016[1832]: 213–14). This national hero was cast down from his pedestal from the very outset. Gustaw-Konrad was a living dead—the sort any audience member could become—who lost his exceptional position, and was thus no longer the 'messenger' or the 'messiah'. The performance showed him to be a collective creation that arose out of the 'dramaturgy of superstition' and presented him in a clearly buffoonish way. The hero was called upon to reveal a different type of epistemic order, one grounded in the world as an undivided whole. This attempt at salvific action ended in vain. The hero returned to his demonic character and, even worse, was abandoned by a community that preferred to remain 'midway'. They left him alone and lost, and he surrendered to a devilish desire to rebel and thus became a 'demonic martyr'—a national version of the Antichrist—whose resistance turned out to be equally hopeless even if it arose out of authentic suffering.

On the surface all of this may seem to be an attack on sacred national values. The idea that the Polish Hero is a living dead, a buffoon sent to visit the nation by Satan, consists of a radical questioning of the Romantic paradigm that also underscores the paradigm's absurd and socially destructive consequences. *Forefathers' Eve* read in this way could be seen as one among many anti-Romantic attacks popular in Poland in the 1960s that aimed to prove the anachronism and counterproductivity of the Romantic ideals of rebellion and sacrifice. But Grotowski distanced himself from such interpretations; or rather, he placed the anti-Romantic polemics of his time in contexts that deepened and complicated this relatively simple interpretation.

One way Grotowski deepened the anti-Romantic critique of his time—which I discovered only in the process of working on the performance—was by gradually exploring and strengthening the aspect of personal suffering and engagement involving the hero. As I have already mentioned, *Forefathers' Eve* marked the first time Grotowski's theatre presented audiences with a drama involving a ridiculed 'Messiah' who turned derision into a challenge and a metaphysical provocation thanks to the power of his human act. It was achieved more fully in later versions of this basic dramaturgy, especially in *The Constant Prince* and in *Apocalypsis cum figuris*, thanks to the power of the 13 Rows' performers. But already in *Forefathers' Eve*, Gustaw-Konrad's poses were rooted in authentic suffering, and were no longer ridiculous even if the forms and images he used were anachronistic and laughable.

The second context Grotowski added to his contemporary milieu is perhaps more important, and represents a key theme of the performance: the relationship between the hero and his community. Seen from this perspective, the process performed in the Opole *Forefathers' Eve* can be stated in a relatively straightforward formula: the hero cast away from his community returned to it with a message formulated for its benefit as the fruit of his suffering, yet he did not regain his previous place among the others. Instead, they abandoned him.

The key thing is that when speaking about a community here we are referring not only to the group of actors that surrounded Konrad as the Chorus but also to the larger community of participants—including the audience—that was established in the first part of the performance. It is this community that distanced itself from the hero—the hero the community itself created. This dynamic was performed in the third part when the Chorus that previously supported the Sorcerer declined to attend the cemetery and expressed their wish to 'stand here in mid-road' (Mickiewicz 2016[1823]: 138). Later on, the community took part in the suffering and rebellion of Konrad—the Polish Christ—in the form of a Chorus of the pious 'faithful'.

The audience was also encouraged to get involved in a similar process of distancing not only from the hero but also from the collective experience. After joining the performance for a bit of fun they gradually returned to their role as 'viewers', and in the third part, the representatives chosen from the audience were addressed with rather soothing, 'normalizing' words and gestures from the Chorus: 'leave out your mourning, dry your eyes', 'cease yearning' (Mickiewicz 2016[1823]: 130, 131). In the finale, the audience attentively listened and watched amid a theatrical silence, ever so close to the unfolding action but no longer involved in it as participants.

The process of the audience returning to the position and the role of viewers—a process that can be seen as one of alienation and estrangement—can also be seen as a strategy that paradoxically strengthened the impact of the performance. If we accept that the myths and images under attack in the 13 Rows' *Forefathers' Eve* were ones that audiences as representatives of national unity used to think about themselves, then the goal of the process carried out by and in the performance was to estrange these 'beloved' images and tear down the comfort zones built around them. Decades later Grotowski, quoting Jan Kott, called this process 'psychomachia'.

> It seems to me that it was Jan Kott who, writing about *Forefathers' Eve* by Mickiewicz staged at the Laboratory Theatre, said that I applied psychomachia to my audiences, by which he meant actions which were radically doubtful, based on drawing them in to then attack them, not in the sense of physical contact, but a somehow hidden attack on stereotypes which they are in love with.
> (Grotowski 2012: 776)

I am not sure if Jan Kott did in fact characterize Grotowski's *Forefathers' Eve* as psychomachia, but nevertheless the formula quite precisely describes the process that took place in the Opole production. The playful first part of the performance drew audiences in only to then subtly yet decisively attack them through the very things they loved such as the glorified idea they had of themselves, that they were members of a national community. This process involved subjecting audiences' precious ideas and images to ridicule, characterizing them as anachronistic and buffoonish which forced them away from those ideas and images, and only then forced them to face a twisted apotheosis of what had been derided, despised and abandoned by the collective. Performing and experiencing this process somehow meant its reversal, reminding the community that it created its hero. Then—when the hero had taken up his role, the community abandoned him and thus condemned him to failure. The main thesis behind this sort of attack on contemporary Polish society seems to have worked as follows: in spite of their self-aggrandizing perceptions and declarations, they had nothing to do with that which they claimed to worship, and instead they laughed at it, saw it as pitiful and hopeless. And yet that which they laughed at, considered to be ridiculous, was what they believed, showing them that beyond any masks this very thing has an inner value that they celebrated, and that they saw as 'sacred'. In line with his 'farce-mystery' programme, Grotowski's dark liturgical games played on 'the mystery of Romanticism', the readiness to gain everything in spite of everything, and the maximalist programme of sacred madness rebelling against the world and even against God. This basic Romantic attitude, well-known from Mickiewicz's and Słowacki's works, widely believed in Poland even by children, consists of a refusal to be easily verbalized and changed into a clear social, political, or ethical programme. So, in some way this attitude also gives rise to the sacred mystery of community, and any attempt to call it by its name sounds pitiful and profane.

In his *Forefathers' Eve* Grotowski not only revealed this mystery but also forced audiences to confront this mystery as something alien to them. In this I see a truly political and contemporary aspect of the Opole performance that consists of questioning the 'obvious' relationship between Poles and Romantic collective rebellion, and the experience of truly collective values as something lost, something that in fact does not exist, and perhaps never existed in the first place. Rather than signifying a laugh at Konrad's expense, the joke on Konrad—a pitiful national saviour that no one believes in—turned out to be an accusation levelled at a society that after a period of revolutionary 'storm and stress' in the late 1950s entered a period of conformism and 'minor stability' in the 1960s. It is true that the performance was partly rooted in the attitudes of anti-Romantic derision very popular at the time in Polish culture, strong examples of which can be found in the works of Sławomir

Mrożek and the 'Polish film school'.[20] But showing the falsehood of the thoughtless apotheosis of Romantic heroes simultaneously revealed a pettiness that was the result of a society abandoning its radical attitudes. Grotowski did not give answers, but instead offered up a disturbingly discomforting experience, an experience that I argue was the goal and essence of his theatre. And it is exactly here that one can find the most literal interpretation of the *Forefathers' Eve* project as a model for contemporary theatre.

Dariusz Kosiński

---

20 For more information, see https://rebrand.ly/3a4m71g.

CHAPTER SIX

Polishness as Madness
Kordian after Juliusz Słowacki

Profanation and Pamphlet

Kordian was the second meeting with Polish Romanticism at the Theatre of 13 Rows—a performance based on the most popular work by Juliusz Słowacki, the great Polish romantic poet and dramatist, and a leading figure of Polish national culture. The 13 Rows premiered *Kordian* on 14 February 1962, and at almost the same time Grotowski published his short book, *A Possibility of a Theatre* (*Możliwość teatru*). It was his first attempt to summarize the experiences and results of his first period of theatrical research in Opole. It should be noted that the composition and character of the publication was similar to Grotowski's world-famous book *Towards a Poor Theatre*, published in English six years later. Alongside Grotowski's own commentaries and explanations, the 1962 brochure contained numerous quotations from his collaborators—mainly Ludwik Flaszen—as well as reviews and commentary from third parties. Grotowski presented the collection as an assemblage of notes on work of the Theatre of 13 Rows, and deemed the brochure to be 'a diary of searches, an example of certain possible solutions' (2012: 209). The collection offered a complete reinterpretation of his achievements thus far, and was Grotowski's attempt to make use of retrospective, ex post concepts and notions that occupied his mind while compiling the text. He connected them to his most recent performances as well as to his earlier ones. By reinterpreting his past work, Grotowski in some ways checked the usefulness and effectiveness of the ideas that had organized his thinking. Grotowski would come to use this strategy many times in the future.

He created key words or word tools, used them to analyse his own achievements, while stressing that we should not become too attached to words or see them as 'objective'. He did not become attached to the words themselves, and he would often completely abandon words that at one time seemed to be of utmost importance to his work; sometimes he would deny ever having used them at all.

This is the case with the word 'archetype'. Grotowski began using it as a key word at the beginning of 1962, between the end of the 13 Rows' work on *Forefathers' Eve* and the premiere of *Kordian*. At this time, Grotowski maintained his earlier thesis that the essence of theatre is the live co-presence of actors and audiences, and that the essence of performance lies in 'the contact zone between audience and actors' and in 'the spark that leaps between two ensembles' (2012: 211). Grotowski also stressed the need to avoid 'the situation in which this contact point between the two ensembles will become purely conventional (for example limited to appropriate distribution of people within the theatre space, or a shared moral, or joint play).' He was looking for a 'factor that could attack both actors' and audiences' "collective subconscious" in a way resembling what took place in theatrical prehistory, a period of vivid and "magical" community of all those present during a performance' (2012: 211). And the 'factor' Grotowski used to 'attack' actors and audiences in 1962 was 'archetype'. At the time, Grotowski defined 'archetype' as 'a symbol, a myth, a motive, an image rooted in the tradition of a given national or cultural or other sort of group which retained its value as a sort of metaphor, a model of human fate, of the human condition' (2012: 211).

Referring to his definition as 'kitchen-theatrical' and distancing himself from the Jungian understanding of 'archetype',[1] Grotowski described the mechanism of 'archetype' as a theatrical assault.

---

1 Grotowski's footnote to his definition is worth quoting: 'I am using the word "archetype" in a narrow context, without Jungian philosophical background, not assuming the unknowableness of the archetype, nor that it might have existed outside of history, etc.' (2012: 211).

By creating an archetype within a performance we are striking at the 'collective subconscious'—something then resonates, a reaction takes place, even if merely as a rejection, the sense that something has been profaned; we bring two ensembles closer together (the team of actors and the team of spectators) a little bit on the ground of provocation, while pretending that it is on the ground of 'magic', a 'magic' act, in which, as in the prehistory of theatre, almost everyone is taking part (the mystery play, archetype plays here the role of the mystery play subject).

The spirit of the time is secular and practical. We only grasp the essence of the things we consumed (we affirm only what we overcame).

Archetype will be revealed, captured in its very essence, if we 'hit' it, if we set it in motion, set it trembling, if we 'profane' it, bearing it in its contradictory aspects, through contrasting associations and clashes of convention. It is then that we can lead the archetype out of the 'collective subconscious' into the 'collective conscious', secularizing and utilizing it as a model-metaphor of the human condition. We will give it a cognitive, or even, perhaps, an utterly mind-liberating[2] function.
(Grotowski 2012: 212–13; emphasis original)

Grotowski makes sustained use of the word 'profanation' in *A Possibility of a Theatre* to describe this assault on archetypes, and he connected this word to others in his 'key word' vocabulary: utilization (and even consumption), secularization and mind-liberation. In writing about *Forefathers' Eve*, Grotowski claimed that the goal he sought through the performance was

---

2 The Polish word used by Grotowski—*wolnomyślicielski*—is very important here but hard to translate. In Polish, the word works both as an adjective derived from the noun meaning 'free thought' and at the same time serves as a synonym to 'libertine'. What's more, Grotowski uses it in a context that gives it a much broader meaning. That is why I decided to use the phrase 'mind-liberating'.

to find and shape in performance an archetype (that which in prehistory of theatre represented the subject of the mystery play, the 'magic' point of the union between all participants). To reveal the archetype's function in the 'collective subconscious', to 'strike' it, to set it in motion, to make it vibrate, to secularize it, to make use of it as a certain type of model—a metaphor of the human condition—to lead archetypes out of the 'subconscious and collective' into the 'collective conscious'.
(Grotowski 2012: 214)

This description surprisingly and yet also justifiably fits Giorgio Agamben's later description of the procedure of profanation. The Italian philosopher argued that 'if "to consecrate" (*sacrare*) was the term that indicated the removal of things from the sphere of human law' then:

'to profane' meant, conversely, to return them to the free use of men. The great jurist Trebatius thus wrote: 'In the strict sense, profane is the term for something that was once sacred or religious and is returned to the use and property of men' [...].

The thing that is returned to the common use of men is pure, profane, free of sacred names. But use does not appear here as something natural: rather, one arrives at it only by means of profanation.
(Agamben 2007a: 73–74)

Agamben continues following the lead of Émile Benveniste pointing to the possibility of achieving a shift from *sacrum* to *profanum* 'by means of an entirely inappropriate use (or, rather, reuse) of the sacred: namely, play' (Agamben 2007a: 75). This breaks up the unity between 'the myth that tells the story and the rite that reproduces and stages it' (2007a: 75). This happens through both *iocus* or 'word play' and through '*ludus* or physical play' that 'drops the myth and preserves the rite' (2007a: 75).

The activity that results from this ['*ludus* or physical play'] becomes a pure means, that is, a praxis that, while firmly maintaining its nature as a means, is emancipated from its relationship to an end; it has joyously forgotten its goal and can now show itself as such, as a means without an end. The creation of a new use is possible only by deactivating an old use, rendering it inoperative.

(Agamben 2007a: 86)

Grotowski designed and re-interpreted his performances as 'a pageant of profanations' (2012: 223), and quite clearly formulated his programme of activities with the aim of recovering defined procedures by desacralizing them. The tool he used in this process was 'the dialectics of derision and apotheosis'. In the context of Agamben's analyses, this tool can be connected with the drive to separate myths and rituals—means of action—in order to use a now purified praxis for alternative, liberatory aims. If we read this last formula in Agamben's terms—in the context of profanation as desacralization—then we can see in it the possibility of purifying 'archetypes' and restoring the possibility of using them in the long-term.

This project clearly has critical and pedagogical aspects. Grotowski sought to create a toolkit for audience participants to singlehandedly undergo the process of a profane purification that would allow them to use practices freed from sacred aims thus participating in a long-term, repeated procedure or chain of procedures.

> The 'dialectics of derision and apotheosis' 'striking' against an archetype sets into vibration a whole chain of taboos of conventions and sacred values. In this way the flickering of a performance is awakened: a pageant of profanations, subsequent stadia (or layers) of contradictions, subsequent and mutual antitheses, subsequent annihilations of taboos . . . which in effect reveal new taboos (*a rebours*); repeated annihilation . . .
> (Grotowski 2012: 223)

The 'dialectics of derision and apotheosis'—which emerged out of a search for 'play' in the context of *Farce-Mystery*—appear here as a relentless movement towards desacralization conducted with a clear awareness of the dangers of the reverse mechanism of exaltation and re-sacralisation of that which has been profaned and purified. A performance that is locked within time–space frameworks cannot be relentless. And so, in order to function as a 'pageant of profanation', it has to initiate a process that audience participants will take on at their own risk in their own life. 'Setting in motion' that which in the past was 'the subject of the mystery-play' seems to involve giving everyone the chance to use it in their own way. And this can only be achieved outside of the time and space of the performance.

This interpretation of the project described in *A Possibility of a Theatre* makes the brochure appear to be a radical programme of political theatre that aims to separate potentially effective social practices from anachronistic myths that render such practices ineffective. Applying this thinking to the specific 'archetype' subjected to profanation in *Forefathers' Eve* and *Kordian* we can then assume that the purpose of these performances was to make possible the use of sacrificial rebellion against the rules of the world, as in the finale of *Forefathers' Eve*, and was at the heart of *Kordian*, not as the object of a 'patriotic cult' and national myth, but as a political praxis.

From the perspective of the idea presented in *A Possibility of a Theatre*—a political, theatrical perspective—the key aspect of the performance was (perhaps paradoxically) the response given by the audiences, and the performance's actual engagement, that is, its tested and proven effect outside the theatre—namely, the profanation outlined above. In my writing about the finale of *Forefathers' Eve*, I saw in it an act of desperate and also helpless lack of communion between the mythical hero and the collective that creates and worships him. According to this analysis, the 'possibility of a theatre' that emerges out of this failure depends precisely on the profanation and desacralization of the national ritual, and the act of handing it over for public use as a political practice. It seems to me that this kind of attempt can be found at the very heart of *Kordian*, and that this aim made a decisive impact on the dramaturgy of the play.

In spite of many differences, *Kordian* is also similar to *Forefathers' Eve*. In fact, Słowacki used the dramatic form created by Mickiewicz to criticize his ideology—it was a truly hostile undertaking. Both dramas are considered to be among the most important works of Polish Romanticism, and both are bound by the topic of the solitary act of self-sacrifice and its position as a founding myth of the collective, even if Słowacki in contrast to Mickiewicz shows such attempts to be pointless leading to personal disintegration and catastrophe. Flaszen confirmed that this topic was important for the Theatre of 13 Rows when he stressed the hopelessness of solitary rebellion and its anachronistic character in the context of the time.

> [I]n the past the Theatre of 13 Rows has presented adaptations of some other literary works where the protagonist was a heroic individual, obsessed with the mission of saving others, with bombastic gestures and in the glow of sacrifice. Doesn't this traditional Polish stance, shaped in the period of post-partition despair,[3] seem incomprehensible and ridiculous in today's time of rationalism and empiricism? The director's intention was probably quite different. He wanted to confront the meaning of the grand individual act with the age of mass movements, organizations, and the tried-and-tested efficacy of collective acts. Anyone who on an individual impulse would like to save the world today would be considered childish or mad, and, in our critical times, it is doubtful that he would even have Don Quixote's charm.
>
> (Flaszen 2010[1964]: 74)

This fragment clearly indicates that *Kordian* as it was staged in 1962 was set in a specific social, political and cultural context. Flaszen accepts the fact that a saviour complex is a 'traditionally Polish attitude' and thus questions the 'traditional' gesture of projecting salvation onto a future that will never come, entailing its separation from the present and the

---

3 Flaszen refers to the crucial fact of Polish history: the three partitions of Polish territory that led to the destruction of the state. These partitions were the result of the deep crisis of the First Polish Republic and the growing power of Poland's neighbouring empires: Russia, Prussia and Austria. The first partition took place in 1772, the second (only with Russia and Prussia) in 1793, the third and final one in 1795. Because of the partitions Poland lost independence for more 123 years, regaining it in 1918.

everyday. He interprets Grotowski's intentions in a way that suggests that the director's aim was to question the utility of—and hence the ability to use—this Romantic attitude in the contemporary context of 'the era of mass movements'. In 1964, Flaszen commented on *Forefathers' Eve*, *Kordian* and *Akropolis*, clearly asserting that 'the modern director does not share [a] belief in the individual act's vital meaning' (2010[1964]: 82). Hence, his fascination with this attitude and his political interest in it could above all be connected with questions regarding its usefulness for collective action and the possibility of crafting social tactics around a desacralized, rebellious sacrifice. In this way, *Kordian* as staged by the Theatre of 13 Rows was crafted in the midst of debates about political strategies taking place at the start of the 1960s and in the shadow of attempts undertaken by the Communist state authorities to suppress the revolutionary and reformist movements that emerged after 1956.

Theatre critic Andrzej Wanat reflected on his personal experience of *Kordian* articulating its place in the aforementioned cultural context.

This was a show about the madness of Polishness, about the Polish complex. It referred to all those disputes, which were in fact journalistic. I do not know what came first, and what followed: *Kordian* or *Popioły* [The ashes] by Wajda.[4] I saw *Kordian* as taking up a position in the dispute about the nature of heroism. Meanwhile, I did not find the performance to contain some deeper anthropological or philosophical context. It was more of a kind of dispute with a certain model of Polishness [...]. This might have been one of the first clearly defined, extreme demonstrations, not so much of a uniquely Polish sort of madness, but of the essential madness of idealism. Kordian was a man who was possessed by an ideal and in some sense this context harmonized with or was opposed in its attitude towards a specific sort of 'ideology' dying down after October 1956 in the world that surrounded us.
(Wanat in Wójtowicz 2004: 225–26)

---

4 *Popioły* [The ashes] came a lot later. Andrzej Wajda's film based on the historical novel by Stefan Żeromski premiered 25 September 1965.

Wanat's interpretation of the performance is of great importance because it is independent of the mechanisms of censorship and self-censorship that impinged upon Grotowski's own explication. Wanat more or less contends that Grotowski created a performance firmly rooted in the historical experience of his generation. Hence, *Kordian* constitutes a political attempt to find a way to act in a situation involving increasingly 'rational' opportunism and conformity.

Directly after the premiere of *Kordian*, Grotowski in a radio programme prepared by Jerzy Falkowski (1962) formulated the essential problem inherent in the performance:

> Perhaps we should ask not whether Kordian is a tragic madman. Perhaps we should ask this: what kinds of people, what sort of generation, and I am here referring to our own generation, can think of Kordian—meaning the one who wants to offer his own life up as a sacrifice for others—only as someone to be locked inside an insane asylum. In essence this is a pamphlet[5] against our own selves.
> (Falkowski 1962a)

This statement is vitally important in helping us understand the meaning *Kordian* might have offered up in 1962 and how this meaning would later be forgotten for a range of reasons. Grotowski's idea of 'a pamphlet against our own selves' is a phrase that vividly formulates a specific political address related to the historical context and situation in Poland at the onset of 1962.

We must at this junction recall what this generation was like—the generation about which Grotowski so clearly cared and of which he was an important member. This generation was comprised of people born in the first half of the 1930s whose most formidable experiences involved the tragedy of war and military occupation. Grotowski himself was six years old at the start of the Second World War, when Germany and Soviet Russia attacked Poland in September of 1939. The wartime

---

5 I am aware that the word may sound strange for English readers but I insist on using it here as Grotowski used exactly the same word—*pamphlet*—in Polish

violence culminated with the Shoah followed by Stalinist terrors. This generation's public activities began when they were twenty, during the thaw of 1956, a time that offered some hope and was full of revolutionary fervour. These young people were not afraid of using grand words and acting with courage and, at least in their most active period, believed in the possibility and even necessity of implementing the idea of total revolution both in society and in thought. Convinced of the impossibility of returning to ancient systems of beliefs—the world before Auschwitz— they either lived in a shadow of despair and absurdity or tried to convince themselves that a new world could be created on pillars of 'civilization and freedom'. They tried in many different ways amid very difficult circumstances to broaden the domain of personal and social freedom and to create a new kind of society, a new collective life.

Historian and political activist Karol Modzelewski (1937–2019)— who devoted many years to the anti-Communist struggle and from the 1960s to the 1990s was one of the leading figures of the opposition— serves as an important witness who confirmed that Grotowski was an almost model representative of this generation. Modzelewski knew Grotowski well beginning in the 1950s, and created a bravura portrait of the soon-to-be director that placed him in his generational context.

Those of this same generation: Grotowski, Kuroń,[6] Pomian,[7] and I (I list co-partners in the same formation) experienced the following shift: we physically rebelled against the system which we had up until then trusted without limits. Why? Because we realized that the system in practice trampled the

---

6 Jacek Kuroń (1934–2004) was one of the leaders of the anti-Communist opposition in Poland, a co-organizer of student protests in 1968, and a co-founder of KOR (Komitet Obrony Robotników; The Committee to Defend Workers) in 1976. After the fall of Communism, he became the Minister of Labour and Social Issues and a member of the Polish Parliament.

7 Krzysztof Pomian (1934–) is a historian and a philosopher. In the 1950s and 1960s, he was a young activist of the Communist Party and in 1957–1958 found himself in conflict with Grotowski who was far more radical than Pomian and broke with leading role of the Party. Pomian later became one of the leading figures of the intellectual opposition. In 1968, he lost his university position and was later forced to leave Poland. After 1989 he again became active in Polish intellectual and academic life.

ideals that it purported to support in theory, ideals with which it had imbued us. We thus became heretics, or as the Party called us in their secularized language: revisionists challenging Communist orthodoxy. We were not only revisionists, but were radical in this revisionism, for we were young at the time. Grotowski was so radical that he was the one that officials from the Central Committee had in mind when they called us 'rabid'. (Modzelewski 2010: 69)

Our 'rabid' director clearly saw the opportunities opening up to him and his community, and was equally aware of the dramatic dangers involved. As we recall, Grotowski operated as a youthful revolutionary activist as early as 1957, warning against the terrifying consequences of social passivity which could lead to catastrophe and the 'long-term triumph of despotism' (Grotowski 2012: 75). In this context it does not seem at all strange that, as a theatre director, he was still connected with the political anti-Stalinist milieu. In his performances, he not only accused but also sought ways of interrupting the rising tide of indifference, the tendency for Poles to shut themselves up in their private lives.

Thus, if we insist on drawing a straight line between a 'political Grotowski' and a 'theatrical Grotowski' (a line continually interrupted and blurred later by the artist himself), we will of course be surprised when we perceive a powerful Grotowskian connection between the radicalism of a left-wing heretic and the madness of a romantic rebel. Karol Modzelewski concluded his recollection by asking a question that for him seemed to be the most important one.

Is this persona adopted by Jerzy Grotowski—persona of the revolutionary, who in recovering from ideological poisoning demanded the system deal with his demands, persona of someone behaving in essence irrationally—a mad romantic—is this incarnation in any way connected to his theatrical work? (Modzelewski 2010: 71)

In the context of Grotowski's *Kordian*—which was after all created a mere several years after the period of 'revolutionary madness'—the answer to Modzelewski's question seems obvious. In *Kordian* Grotowski's earlier political incarnation was confronted by the collective, a collective for which according to Modzelewski Grotowski was ready to lay down his life. Although by 1962 the revolutionary fervour of 1956 had died down, its strategies, aims and perhaps naive determination not to accept reasonable compromises did not.

Questions and Their Environment

Słowacki's *Kordian*—the poet's polemical response to Mickiewicz's *Forefathers' Eve*—presents us with events that feature a sensitive young man who searches for meaning in his life. First, he searches in his home, then travels around Europe to London, Dover, Italy, the Vatican and Mount Blanc, before finally returning to Poland as a patriot-conspirator. He finds his life's meaning in the act of sacrificing himself for the freedom of others, and so he volunteers to assassinate the Tsar, freshly crowned as the King of Poland. The attempt fails, the hero is imprisoned in an insane asylum and then condemned to death. In Słowacki's *Kordian*, there are indications that the hero will be pardoned at the last minute— but we do not know if this will happen, and the drama ends just before his imminent execution. This poetic and extremely complex text has been a key feature in the annals of Polish history and theatre as the source of a personal template for patriots and rebels who refuse to accept compromise. But this refusal is the very reason Kordian fails. The radical aspect of his attitudes becomes an obstacle that will not let him cooperate with others. Thus, in Grotowski's *Kordian* the director once again took on a drama that boasted a high level of cultural authority and was well known to his audiences: Słowacki's play had been and still is an obligatory read in schools for many years.

A typescript of the Opole *Kordian* kept in the GIA disproves the frequently repeated opinion that cuts Grotowski made to Słowacki's drama 'were so far advanced that it gave the impression of a certain massacre' (Wanat quoted in Wójtowicz 2004: 227).[8] Grotowski did make a key intervention by crossing out the remainder of the original text after a scene in a psychiatric hospital (Act 3, Scene 6). However, the other cuts were in no way radical and certainly did not rise to the level of a 'massacre'. Quite the opposite. Reading the script today one would be surprised by the retention of lengthy passages that seem to fit awkwardly within the general shape of the script. While in the case of his *Forefathers' Eve*, Grotowski did not shy away from very thorough edits and deletions—some of which might seem provocative—in the case of *Kordian*, Grotowski's approach to the original script was much more conservative.

If we attempt to summarize Grotowski's script as a text that is relatively autonomous, we might say that it presents a visit to the insane asylum by a person—the Doctor—bestowed with specific power or knowledge. This Doctor wants to meet and analyse a unique patient, Kordian. The Doctor's intentions are to stage Kordian's delusions in order to present to him his own psychological biography, to externalize his fantasies and to prove that his ideas are merely symptoms of a psychotic illness, that therefore they have no 'objective sense' or meaning. The source for this concept is the theatre of madness created by Słowacki in Act 3, Scene 6, of his drama. In this sequence, the Doctor undermines Kordian's conviction about his own uniqueness and presents two other patients—one of whom thinks he is supporting the heavenly firmament while the other believes that he is Christ's Cross. Grotowski amplified a possibility existing within the text by expanding the scene to become a frame for the entire performance: the Doctor stages fragments from Kordian's biography and shows the audience, and Kordian himself, that he is a madman just like the others. In Słowacki's drama the Doctor's attempt failed. But in Grotowski's script the Doctor succeeds. Kordian

---

8 Signature IG/R/80. This is a unique copy because the text is bound, featuring the cover of an authentic medical form with the printed title 'The Diary of Work and Procedures of the Medical-Dental Clinic', and the name 'Kordian' inscribed in the column reserved for the patient's name. The next page of the form—which was to be filled out by a doctor—was also retained. This copy was presented to the censorship offices in Opole, and also in Krakow and Białystok, where the performance was also shown as evidenced by relevant stamps on the title page.

admits that the patients with whom he has been presented are indeed madmen and, accepting the Doctor's diagnosis, he simultaneously judges himself accordingly. Accomplishing his mission, the diabolical psychotherapist leaves the hospital ward.

To present such an interpretation of *Kordian*, Grotowski needed to remove subsequent verses from Scene 6 (beginning at verse 801) as well as the entirety of the next four scenes, the final scenes of Słowacki's drama. In these deleted scenes, Kordian is forced to make his desperate horse leap through a wall of bayonets (Scene 7), he readies himself for death, and proclaims a heroic farewell to the world (Scene 8). The Tsar and his brother have a heated dispute over his pardon (Scene 9), and finally Kordian stands in front of a brick wall awaiting a firing squad while an officer runs to bring notice of a pardon (Scene 10). The curtain falls and we do not know if the commander of the squad received the pardon or if he gave the command to shoot. By deleting these scenes Grotowski removed the dazzling finale.

More than fifteen years ago I published my interpretation of Słowacki's finale.

> *Kordian's* greatness is contained in its obliqueness, which is founded on its open-ended finale. Every other solution would demand some form of closure, resolution, and hence knowledge or faith. Our hero even at his very end fails to achieve either.
> [. . .]
> *Kordian* is neither a scientific lecture nor a revelation involving prophetic visions. It is an invitation to experience a wild vortex of signs, each one arranging itself in its own order, thereby providing its own answers to the questions posed at each and every step.
> (Kosiński 2004: 184–85)

In constructing his script, Grotowski deleted the scenes that were considered by some interpreters to contain 'final' answers, especially the 'heroic' horse leap from Scene 7 and the monologues from Scene 8. He thereby amplified a specific potential contained in the finale of *Kordian* consisting of a possibility so keenly dismissed by various philologists and more or less ideological producers—namely that no answers can be found within the text as an 'autonomous structure'. Instead, those seeing or reading the play are to find conclusions *within themselves*. The Opole *Kordian* is not a message to be read or seen and accepted but rather a tool for those who read, see and perform it to research their own attitudes. From this perspective, Grotowski as the author of the performance was very faithful to Słowacki. Both Słowacki and Grotowski stripped the actions carried out by their protagonist from oversimplified justifications. In this vein, the point of Grotowski's performance was to confront the audience with some crucial questions about themselves.

Thus, the meaning of the Opole *Kordian* was based on decisions made by audiences during the inevitable confrontation between Grotowski's actual staging and the specific experiences of the spectators-participants. This really was a theatre whose essence was grounded in the meeting of two groups—actors and spectator-participants—in an environment created especially for this purpose.

Jerzy Gurawski recalls that during the period of his work on *Kordian*, Grotowski was focused on the possibilities for 'theatrical space' beyond its defined visual shape and its visual design. Grotowski wanted a space that made possible (or even intentionally imposed) a novel relationship between the people present and the environment surrounding them:

> We were in fact all the time fascinated by the notion of entering a new spatial arrangement, all the time, without interruptions. Grotowski met with different people, getting into individual conversations with each one of them. When he and I spoke, we would talk about what we could achieve with the space, how far could we push the limits of the contact between the audience and the actors, and how close the latter might come towards the former—could the actors take audience-participants by the hand or whether this would represent desecration? Would the actors desecrate themselves by taking the audience member by the hand? What would happen? And so on without end. And I

think that *Kordian* was this sort of performance on the borderline of the query: how far can we go?
(Gurawski 1992: 54–55)

Grotowski did not ask about architectural shapes but about spatial relations and the effects of different variations. He did not inquire into how
the space might look but rather inquired into how it could be used and
what experiences were possible within it. Grotowski continued to work
on 'a variation of theatre without a stage' that 'found its form in
Forefathers' Eve' (2012: 226). In this pursuit he developed a pioneering
form of theatrical ecology. This approach was a means of treating the
spatial environment in which relations between all its elements—and
especially between the actors and audiences—were thoroughly developed
from the very start. The environmental theatre character of *Kordian* was
less focused on striving towards illusionary immersion. Instead,
Grotowski created an insider game of changeable, accidental happenings
and specific applications of incoherent experiences along with the reactions they unleashed. Gurawski gives a telling example of an actor grasping an audience member by the hand. For Gurawski this gesture signified
a self-aware and powerful interference with theatrical convention through
its intersecting association with a medical, hospital-based procedure.
Actors are not authorized to interfere with spectators' physical space,
whereas a doctor is authorized to enter patients' physical space. The
actor in the role of the Doctor transferred to the actor the real-life permission afforded to the latter, and the actor made full use of it by intrud-
ing into spectators' physical space. In so doing, the actor provocatively
disrupted the order of established relations between actor and audience,
thereby bringing about the effect of realism relative to their fictional
character. The assumed fictional 'reality' of theatre was thus disrupted
through the shared physical reality of a hospital staged in a theatre.

Surprising twists like this played a key role in *Kordian*. They served
as tools to reinforce a basic performative transfer of responsibility for
understanding the meaning of the performance to the audience. In
Kordian, the audience was considered to be an almost equal part of the
human ecology as actors—though not as members of a ritualistic com-

munity as was the naive case with *Forefathers' Eve*—as participants belonging to the inner ecology of the environment that influenced events in the performance deciding how effective and meaningful they were.

The physical environment within which the Opole version of *Kordian* took place was very clearly defined and left relatively little room for creative expression. Instead of an abstract, Arp-esque construction of wavy lines, the *Kordian* 'set' conveyed the brutality of a run-down, 1960s mental hospital. Gurawski communicated some reluctance about this design when he wrote that 'what in *Forefathers' Eve* was very poetic, multi-layered, and far from obvious [. . .]—here [in *Kordian*] was all too literal' (1992: 54). Later Gurawski told Agnieszka Wójtowicz that

> the idea was very simple, and emerged solely from the staging. All one needed to do was build a space representing a madhouse with full facility for actors to work within this space. [. . .] This was attractive in that we used bunk beds such as are found in army barracks and hospital wards. We set up two or three levels. Why levels? Because the beds on their own would have been too brash, too literal. We wanted to create different levels of movement in addition to ensuring some sort of spectacle and making the whole scene more attractive.
>
> (Gurawski quoted in Wójtowicz 2004: 218)

The creation of the performance environment was organized in line with two simultaneously applicable paradigms: the literal presentation of the hospital setting and the literal reflexivity of theatre as a 'machine for performing'. Authentic furniture was transformed in order to allow them to be best used by actors and spectators. This was not about any sort of naturalism or naive authenticity. It was about giving both competing and co-existing orders of experience—that of the theatre and that of the hospital—an equally strong, tangible presence.

The fundamental element of the spatial construction was a number of platforms made from wooden boards and set up on simple struts that allowed both a differentiation of the levels on which the actors worked and a differentiation of the levels in which spectators were seated.

According to a sketch by Gurawski printed on the cover of the programme for *Kordian*, there were five such levels including the baseline floor level. The beds on which the actors were to perform and the seats for the audience were set up in a way that allowed better visibility. According to photos from the performance, the different levels and multiple beds presented a challenge for actors. They needed to be very attentive to avoid stumbling and wavering as they navigated the numerous steps, heights and gaps in the performance space.

Alongside the three tall bunks—one with three levels and two with two levels—four single-level beds were set up around the auditorium. Spectators sat on these four beds, in some cases interspersed with actors. There were also audience members seating on the bottom bunk of the two-level beds with the actors performing above them, on the upper level. Only the three tier beds had no room for audiences to sit. According to Gurawski, the 13 Rows first sat audience members directly on the beds but soon sought alternatives because 'the bed springs made an awful racket', and furthermore 'the audience was afraid, the experience it had was not nice any more and started being terrifying, terrible. And that was when we decided to remove the iron springs from the bedframes and inserted chairs in there' (in Wójtowicz 2004: 218–19).

We must keep in mind that this whole construction was erected in the relatively small performance space of Opole's Theatre of 13 Rows. This meant that both actors and audiences had very little room. The auditorium filled with beds and chairs was very cramped. The varied steps, levels and aisles created by the chairs, bunks and erected platforms only served to make this cramped feeling more palpable. This can clearly be seen in photos from very well attended guest performances in Kraków at the Krzysztofory Gallery (22 III–8 IV 1962). It is impossible not to notice that this was a risky enterprise—especially in scenes when actors move about the auditorium and physical interactions between actors and audiences were far from safely distanced.

This extremely intimate space must have been even more disconcerting for audiences than the actors—especially in performances when theatre was at full capacity. The experiences of spectators were unique in the sense that they were not just close to actors but also to one another, squeezed into chairs on both sides of a narrow 'corridor' left open for actors to move freely. Spectators were so close to one another that they could clearly see each other's reactions close-up.

In *Kordian*'s claustrophobic performance space the angles and points of view were more shocking and troubling than in *Forefathers' Eve*. Perhaps the worst off in this respect were spectators sitting on the bottom bunks of stacked beds because they were unable to see what was happening over their heads. They were only able to hear that something was taking place above them while feeling vibrations all along the wooden platforms installed in place of mattresses as the platforms for the performers. To see anything from the action taking place on the upper level, those seated on bottom bunks were forced to bend and stretch and at that they would catch only brief glimpses of bodies above them. For these spectators the surprising and intentional lack of clarity—which was a performative strategy—worked in a particularly powerful way.

Another tactic the 13 Rows adopted to further reinforce the jarring aspects of the performance space was a lighting arrangement different from the one they used in *Forefathers' Eve*. Instead of playing around with darkness and light or using dynamic spotlights, *Kordian* featured a relatively straightforward lighting arrangement with several strong reflectors arranged on tripods and set up at even intervals around the auditorium. They pointed these large lights upwards in order to use their theatre's white ceiling—painted white for this performance—to reflect the light. Based on photographs from performances both in Opole and in Krakow, I find it hard to agree with the opinion expressed by Wójtowicz that they used a 'surgical' style of lighting that evenly illuminated the entire auditorium (2004: 71). The performance space was brighter in places—especially the upper bunks—and darker in others. This allowed for a dynamic play of light and shadow according to the actors' movements and gestures as they performed. This lighting arrangement clearly signalled the beginnings of the 13 Rows moving away from technical stage effects and replacing them with a dramaturgy closely linked to the actors and their performances.

Flaszen wrote about a similar tendency when it came to the costumes:

There are no costumes in any theatrical sense of the word. The men wear everyday grey suits, the women ordinary grey dresses. Their garments are not rags; on the contrary, [...] their elegance is so sophisticated that it doesn't work and becomes pretentious rubbish. The actors' apparel mocks the formal outfits of the audience who have come dressed up for the occasion. The hospital personnel wear white overalls.
(Flaszen 2010[1964]: 84)

Insofar as the costumes ridiculed audiences' finery, we can see a sort of ironic take on the 'community' created in the performance, and on the ceremonial distance that accompanied the obligatory elegance of dressing up for the theatre in the 1960s clearly visible in photos from guest performances in Krakow. The 13 Rows' contemporary costumes of suits, dresses and medical gowns made it harder for audiences to keep the play in distant history, and thus the costumes emphasized the constant presence of theatre at a fundamental level.

The objects and props used in the performance can be divided into two groups each of which served a specific function. As Flaszen notes:

The props are also completely real. In the hospital scenes there are medical and everyday items: a real scalpel and a real straitjacket, real bowls, pots and towels. In the scenes that come from hallucinations the objects are taken from the theatre's prop store: a decorative tiara for the Pope and a shiny cheap crown for the Tsar; old-fashioned rifles for Grzegorz and Kordian.
(Flaszen 2010[1964]: 84)

In accordance with these differences, for the purposes of analysing *Kordian*, we should probably treat the terms 'objects' and 'props' not as synonyms but as two distinct types of items that correspond to two distinct types of scenes—action taking place in the hospital and action taking place in the hallucinations. The hospital objects were very much defined by their histories. They represented a truly brutal 'authenticity' in their ugliness and simplicity, hinting at the horrible reality of psychiatric hospitals at the time. These objects included 'tin bowls for letting blood, other strange devices, old syringes and terribly rusty tools for maiming and torture taken from old army hospitals' (Gurawski quoted in Wójtowicz 2004: 220). These items, marked by traces of suffering, were more than mere symbols of a reality beyond the theatre. They were elements of an environment that aroused a sensory impression of encountering something 'infected'. They cultivated an awareness that one was sitting on a 'real' hospital bed, and it left audiences feeling afraid and 'horrible' (as Gurawski put it). In the performance they let the blood of the Polish Hero into a battered medical bowl that might have actually been used once to collect blood or urine from real patients. Thus, they turned this simple, theatrical sign into a source of abject, affective disgust.

In turn, the banal and clearly theatrical props used in the 'hallucination scenes' served, paradoxically, to signify theatricality itself. The performance's creators used these blatantly theatrical props to underscore the reality of the theatrical environment they wanted to project. The costumes and objects/props conformed to a rule retrospectively articulated by Flaszen who noted that they were meant to serve 'the perverse interplay between authenticity and theatrical artificiality, reality and fiction, the literal and metaphor. The truth of the objects plays here with their own double meaning, absorbed within a stylistically poetic construction' (2010[1964]: 84).

Kordian inaugurated the Theatre of 13 Rows' next phase: the reduction of special effects and the turn towards the actors and their performances. Grotowski recognized this shift as decisive in a spring 1962 radio conversation with Jerzy Falkowski.

> We tried to give up everything when it came to staging *Kordian*. There was no stage, no lights, no music, no costumes, no sets. Who was there? Actors and audiences. And it seems to us that this was the most important relationship.
> (Grotowski quoted in Falkowski 1962a)

Wójtowicz was the first to recall these words (2004: 75). She astutely noted that this statement in fact contained the basic elements of what would be known as 'poor theatre'. I agree with her, adding that in the case of *Kordian* this 'giving up on everything' was not connected with a search for a 'new theatre' but rather it was connected to a drive towards solving a very specific challenge. If the audience's experience was of greatest importance for determining the effectiveness and success of the performance, then their experience—enlivened by their proximity to and relation with the actors—had to be located at the centre of the performance with all other elements supporting it. In other words, the 13 Rows' 'giving up on everything'—and the beginnings of 'poor theatre'—was developed in pursuit of a specific theatrical relationship to the audience.

Kordian's Performative Theatre

The *Kordian* programme instructed spectators about their roles in the performance even before they entered the auditorium. The programme was not a stylish publication—the theatre could not afford anything more than a simple booklet—but it gave the audience a unique 'map' of the production. Gurawski's sketch of the performance space published on the cover of the programme together with the commentary by Flaszen published inside allowed readers to prepare for what awaited them; and to develop some form of tactic for approaching the performance. Most importantly, the audience entering the performance environment was forewarned about its key elements. The creators did not rely on the audience's ignorance or want to shock them when they entered the space. If the audience experienced any difficulty in making sense of the performance space, the comments and information printed in the programme pointed them towards concrete interpretations and created a strong frame of reference for their experience of *Kordian*.

From the very start this theatrical experience was unique. The configuration of chairs on different levels was unconventional (to say the least), and offered different degrees of audience comfort. The reality of hospital beds, cramped and uneven floors, and unsteady floorboards used to construct the platforms almost instantly challenged images people might have had about a typical 'evening at the theatre'. The totally transfigured space introduced a range of sensory experiences such as physical movement and the appreciation of small details.

Gurawski recalled the very start of the show, which in his opinion was excellent.

> It started suddenly. Spectators hadn't yet sat down when their hospital for the emotionally disturbed was visited by the Doctor. And here comes a beautiful quote: 'You're free to visit any cell you wish,/ Madmen are here, madwomen further on . . . ' [Słowacki 2010: 98] These were of course played by the unfortunate audience members. And then, after a calm opening, the first scream was heard: 'I am no person, I turned into the cross a long time ago'.
> (Gurawski 1992: 220)

The opening of *Kordian* was brilliant in its simplicity. The Doctor (Zygmunt Molik) entered the room full of audience-patients, and was greeted by the Caretaker (Antoni Jahołkowski) with the words 'You've come to visit our insane asylum?' (Słowacki 2010: 98). This means that from the beginning, spectators lost their fundamental status. They were no longer viewers, but instead found themselves under observation. The Caretaker presented them as such, and at the same time gave control of the room—and control over the audience-patients—to the Doctor.

A little later the Doctor begins diagnosing individual cases. He initiated this process by asking a question of the first of two crazed patients. And here we have a puzzle—were the actors already in the auditorium when audiences entered? Or, did they all enter together? From certain perspectives the former solution seems more probable, especially when we consider the specific places and poses taken up by the actors, and the difficulty of climbing to the upper bunks with the audience in place. And yet when we look at a photograph taken by Edward Węglowski (GIA; deposit of Andrzej Bielski; inv. no. 2) we see two madmen standing up on the highest level of a three-tier bunk bed in poses that signify

236 · DARIUSZ KOSIŃSKI

their delusions—one with arms extended in a cross and the other with arms up supporting the ceiling that the patient imagined to be the firmament. It is rather hard to imagine them maintaining these poses for more than ten minutes which is the time it would take the spectators to take their seats.

According to Flaszen's description—which is confirmed by the aforementioned photograph—both madmen 'stay in strange catatonic poses high up beneath the ceiling; their positions express their heroic hallucinations. This is a mocking complement to further Kordian's drama' (2010[1964]: 85). If we are to believe the recording included in Falkowski's radio programme from 1962,[9] both madmen—the first played by Andrzej Bielski was convinced he was Christ's Cross, and the second played by Ryszard Cieślak was an Atlas figure—introduced a specific tonality and way of expressing ideas. Their short monologues were recited melodically in a way reminiscent of liturgical song but their recitations were not a precise copy of any particular melodies from the Catholic Mass. However, they clearly imitated Catholic traditions—especially the Gregorian chant—that use musicality and intonation to charge words with meaning beyond their definitions. The same sort of intonation was retained—though with obvious variations and internal differentiation—by Kordian and other characters in other scenes. The madmen's performances of quasi-liturgical songs contrasted with the Doctor's and Caretaker's calm, sensible, very defined and powerful ways of expressing themselves. This contrast was also retained in the ensuing scenes.

The end of the introductory sequence was composed using fragments from Act 3, Scene 6, of Słowacki's drama. Wójtowicz accurately noted that the Doctor punctuated this composition by uttering the word 'Yes'.

This 'yes' from the Doctor, a sort of magic formula, evoked and ended the scene of crazy visions in the performance. It was a

---

9 I am well aware that the recording doesn't fully reflect the live performance. Nevertheless, the same actors who played the roles on stage also played those roles in the radio version. Furthermore, the radio version was created in partnership with Grotowski—so we can assume that at least the key indicators related to actors' voices were more or less the same. Assuming such, I will go on referring to the radio recording as a relatively valid source.

sort of calling out that returned numerous times, splitting and crashing individual scenes into each other.

(Wójtowicz 2004: 74)

The Doctor's 'yes' separated the Opole introduction from the following sequence, which was based on the initial scene of Słowacki's drama that the poet titled *Preparation*.

This was the first of many scenes in which the Doctor evokes hallucinatory visions. Flaszen reports that at this moment the Doctor 'transforms into Satan and initiates a diabolic ceremony of the birth of the new era' (2010[1964]: 83). Various reports and reviews suggest that in this very scene the audience was attacked, and thus was transformed into the subjects of medical treatment. According to Gurawski, this worked particularly well in the course of the first presentations.

> The audience was very intensively attacked—attempts were made to let their blood (of course not for real) into a massive and terrible tin pan. Zygmunt Molik as a surgeon walked around causing consternation and terror ... [...] These were examinations. Doctor visits Kordian's cell and begins to examine everyone, meaning audience members, before they can find Kordian. There was a range of reactions, different behaviours, but none of them was especially interesting or valuable.
> (Gurawski quoted in Wójtowicz 2004: 219)

Wacław Kubacki who witnessed the guest performances of *Kordian* in Kraków in April 1962 reported that:

> the Kraków youth audiences were enthusiastic in their reception of being cast as patients, seeing it as an ideological game. Coquettish ladies allowed their little heads in stylish hairdressings to be touched by the people in white gowns. Young men smiled when presenting their wrists to the Doctor and the Caretaker for their pulses to be taken.
> (Kubacki 2006[1962]: 160)

Everything indicates that 'Preparation'—the very first scene of the drama staged in Opole—should be imagined as a scene linking Słowacki's text to medical procedures. 'The Preparation became a medical round of examinations—one madman after another. The sick sat in beds taking up odd poses' (Wójtowicz 2004: 75). And all the while the Doctor conducted various procedures upon them and the spectators.

Two photographs by Edward Węglowski pictured the Doctor's examination on Maja Komorowska as a patient (inv. nos 298 and 299). The photographs show the actress lying half-on and half-off the top bunk of a two-tier bunk bed. Her head, upper torso and her outstretched arms arch downwards over the edge of the top bunk. The Doctor—dressed in a white gown and wearing a doctor's mirror on his forehead—kneels on the bed, and hovers over her lower midsection. His right hand holds Komorowska's legs as her upper body cascades downward off the edge of the bed. The Doctor raises his left arm up with his index finger pointed at the ceiling, and lowers his arm towards Komorowska's body with his thumb, forefinger and middle finger extended indicating that he counted to three.

There is a high probability that the Preparation scene—along with the previous scene involving two madmen—functioned as a dramaturgical introduction to the essential context of the performance. In Słowacki's drama, the scene established a historiosophical framework for understanding Kordian's fate. However, in Grotowski's performance these introductory scenes consisted of a series of actions that established the hospital setting, and taught the audience the rules of the game: the hierarchy of authority, the development of the dramaturgy, and the transference between layers of reality and hallucinations. As such, these scenes represented the most literal preparation for 'the main action of *Kordian*' theatrically enabling audience identification with the protagonist's fate as experienced by Kordian himself.

The shift between the Preparation and subsequent scenes in the first part of the Opole *Kordian*—which was equivalent to those in Act 1 of Słowacki's drama—was marked with a fragment from Act 3, Scene 6.

For this shift, Grotowski employed a relatively simple yet incredibly astute theatrical device. Just as the Doctor's 'Yes' concluded the Preparation scene, and signalled a transition to the remaining introductory sequences, another 'Yes' from the Doctor signalled the end of the introductory sequences. After the Doctor's second 'Yes' the Caretaker provocatively asked 'which head of ours is maddest?' (Słowacki 2010: 98). As we can hear in Falkowski's radio recording, the Doctor clearly and pointedly answered, with his voice lowered, 'It's that one-Kordian'.

Thus, the Doctor introduced the main patient—Zbigniew Cynkutis as Kordian—and Kordian began his first monologue. Judging by the recorded fragment we can assume that he spoke it using a slightly mechanical, apathetic, melodic recitation, however not completely stripped of changes in tempo and intonation. After each change of tone and tempo, he returned to his naturally high-pitched voice which sounded simple, soft and naive like the voice of an upset little boy.

Kordian recited his opening monologue while performing acrobatic poses atop a three-tier bunk bed. It is very possible that he recited his monologue in a very odd and uncomfortable position, for example hanging upside down as seen in a photo by Edward Węglowski (inv. nos 294).

After finishing the monologue, Kordian sat on the third tier of the middle bed, and following the narrative line of the original drama, listened to his old guardian and servant Grzegorz tell fairy-tales and recollections from the Napoleon campaign in Egypt. According to a reconstruction by Wójtowicz, during this storytelling sequence

> Grzegorz stood right below Kordian, holding a gun. As he was telling the tale about Janek and recalling the Egyptian campaign, he performed a military drill. Kordian, as if hypnotized, did not take his eyes off the rifle he was carrying. As Grzegorz finished telling his story, Kordian (with emphasis and delight) said 'God! The old man's/ Afire with passion' while rising up off the bed very slowly.
> (Wójtowicz 2004: 76)

This report leads to questions about who would have been performing the lines of Grzegorz. In the programme, the role is listed as performed by Ryszard Cieślak and Aleksander Kopczewski.[10] However, Flaszen states in his commentary that it was the Doctor who 'in the garden scene [...] becomes the servant Grzegorz who presents to a day-dreaming Kordian a vision of raw military bravery' (2010[1964]: 83). Flaszen's testimony is hard to deny. And so, it seems that Molik (at least partially) took Grzegorz's lines. A photograph from the Krakow performances confirms that the Doctor does indeed double as Grzegorz: it shows the Doctor standing (alongside Jahołkowski) in a military stance and holding a gun as confirmed by Flaszen's report (inv. no. 319).

Directly after the scene with Grzegorz, a dialogue ensued between Kordian and his lover Laura (Rena Mirecka) in a scene all about unrequited love. The lovers deliver their lines in the same apathetic, naive and mechanical style with which Kordian delivered his first monologue. They speak as if they were sentimental wind-up dolls declaiming rulebook emotions rather than expressing true feelings. Laura speaks in a lower, darker voice, and Kordian speaks in his rather high-pitched, boyish voice. Their dialogue is instrumentalized to create the impression that Laura is more mature and superior to Kordian. At times Laura speaks to him as if to an uneasy and upset child who exaggerates, acting as if he is mad at the world.

A photograph taken by Węglowski shows Kordian and Laura walking down an aisle between rows of seats (inv. no. 312). Laura is wearing a light-coloured skirt with dark stockings, and Kordian is wearing a grey suit. Together they look like a couple on a date in the 1960s, two young people taking a stroll together. In another scene captured in several photographs,[11] the lovers are locked in an embrace backlit by a reflector placed behind them. Kordian leans on Laura with his whole body as she stands erect supporting his weight. Kordian's left arm is extended straight over her shoulder with his left-hand hanging limp and his head hanging

---

10 Kopczewski likely appeared in the performance only once, and left the company after the premiere his parts taken over by Andrzej Bielski.

11 One photo by Węglowski from the GIA (inv. no. 313), and two photos by Andrzej Moskwiak also from the GIA (inv. nos 320, 321).

over Laura's left shoulder. The whole arrangement suggests she is a more experienced, more mature woman supporting a sick, weakened man. Though both actors were quite young, the posture suggests—in line with Słowacki's drama—that Laura be interpreted as a figure combining lover and mother.

Wójtowicz reports that the finale of this scene between Kordian and Laura was singularly erotic:

> Laura uttered her monologue ('Kordian is not coming back...') half-lying down on a ground-level bed, in a cataleptic attack. The scene had a very erotic bent. Laura rose up on the bed— very slowly, sensually, appearing to be 'a little nymphomaniac'— as described by Maciej Prus. Grzegorz then approached her, sat on the bed, his line 'A tragedy! The master's shot himself! ...' sounding like someone trying to appease a sick, neurotic patient. (Wójtowicz 2004: 77)

In this very moment, the Doctor brought things back to the 'reality' of the hospital with his established verbal cue—'Yes ...'.

In the subsequent scene the Doctor takes a role of the Caretaker of James Park in London. And this is just about all that we know about this scene. Not even Flaszen described its inner meaning—he left it out of his list of the Doctor's roles. This seems strange because the scene is long and Grotowski retained Słowacki's original scene in full. And yet in the actual performance the scene could have in fact been deleted. The Romantic criticism of urban industrial culture in the original scene was not a topic that interested Grotowski and his actors. Perhaps we know nothing about it because it was eventually cut from the performance?

One reason Grotowski might not have deleted this sequence was his intention to separate two scenes featuring Kordian with the female characters, and this scene would have served that exact purpose. The next sequence featured Violetta, a courtesan played by Maja Komorowska. Unlike the previous sequence, we know a lot about this one mostly because it was one of the scenes to which the creators of the Opole *Kordian* drew our attention.

The scene between Kordian and Violetta holds this performance's poetic characteristics. Everything is done by the actors alone. In various situations, arrangements and formations of metaphorically dense speech, they even create sudden leaps in time and space. Kordian and Violetta, like a duet in classical ballet, with languid poses and passionate twists of the body—where they take it in turns to 'support' each other—perform a story of romantic passion, one minute tender, the next brutal. Galloping, they become kinds of centaurs, both horses and humans at the same time. They take it in turns to run across the room; their legs behave like horses while their heads and arms behave like riders galloping crazily, shouting to each other to go faster. As a result, these actors' shortening of a great adventure has the effect of being an ecstatic grotesquery.
(Flaszen 2010[1964]: 86)

This scene had two distinct parts: first, the lovers' ballet, and second, a brief horse ride. This latter part was important from the perspective of how the acting style of the Theatre of 13 Rows would soon evolve.

A photograph from the Krakow performance taken by Edward Węglowski helps illustrates the love scene Flaszen describes. Komorowska is bent over backwards in a dynamic dip with her left arm bent over her head (inv. no. 311). Cynkutis strikes a similarly dynamic pose. With his feet firmly planted one in front of the other, he leans forward with his upper body. He clings to Komorowska with his right arm around the small of her back resting his head against her bosom. His left arm is extended laterally and awkwardly bent back at the elbow towards his head. His left hand rests atop his own head. Komorowska's right hand grasps a bunk-bed post as if to stabilize their pose. This photograph of this so-called 'ballet of desire' confirms an important argument made by Wójtowicz:

This was not a scene featuring a harlot: Violetta and Kordian came across more as a mother with her son rather than lovers.

It looked as if Kordian had wanted to be a son, as if he had wanted to once again become an embryo, to return to the womb. (Wójtowicz 2004: 78)

Wójtowicz's interpretation suggests that this scene represents a continuation of the Doctor's ongoing unique psychoanalysis of Kordian. By this time the Doctor was taking on more dominant roles intended to influence Kordian's conduct—Grzegorz, the Caretaker and (in a moment) the Pope. The Doctor thereby enacted variations of a father figure. On the other hand, the female characters delivered two complementary variations on a mother figure, both arousing fascination and fear.

The next part of the dance—the brief horse ride—takes on a distinct mood and meaning when seen in this psychoanalytic context. This scene was constructed without regard for its counterpart in the original drama. In Słowacki's version the horseback ride is placed between two scenes of dialogue so it does not need to be acted out on stage. In order to understand the Opole version better it is worth quoting Eugenio Barba's description of the dance from an essay on 'Actor's Technique as Self-penetration and Artificiality' published in his *Alla ricerca del teatro perduto* [In search of the lost theatre].

In *Kordian* there is a scene featuring the protagonist taking a horse ride with his lover. In the performance the scene was 'reconstructed' as a wild chase: the actors racing forwards while shouting, thereby expressing a lust for life, their inner energy and passion. They next stop suddenly; the composition of their attitude reminds us of human-horses: one leg on the ground as if in stirrups, the other raised like the hoof of a galloping racing steed, one arm extended forwards with the fist clenched, holding the reins, the other arm raised upwards with the hand convulsively clenched in an attack of vitality.
(Barba 2014[1965])

Barba's description allows us to read the second part of this scene as a symbolic representation of a sexual act based in well-known metaphors and images. At this point in the performance Kordian's mad dreams reach their culmination in an image suggesting Oedipal desire—which occurred frequently in Grotowski's works over the years.[12]

The following scene, part of a series of hospital sequences, involved the Doctor and the Caretaker. The Caretaker questioned Kordian's diagnosis as the most crazed of all. In reply, the Doctor nearly drives the Caretaker to madness with the trick of using a coin to light a cigar. From that point on, the Doctor becomes the sole master of the room 'treating' Kordian without hindrance. In this respect, the scene seems to me to be more than just another interruption to help us remember that the main action of *Kordian* is all about the patient's madness. The scene additionally represents a key turning point in the dramaturgy of the performance. It is here—right before the crucial scenes in the Vatican and on Mont Blanc, and before descending into Poland—that the Doctor's analysis of Kordian's most personally intimate experiences end. Kordian leaves behind childish and feminine spheres, and is liberated from the mother's influence through incest. This journey leads the hero towards the Father, the Fatherland and towards social relations—a key theme in later parts of the performance.

The main target of the theatrical attack perpetrated by the Theatre of 13 Rows was the collective imagination or—as Grotowski called it in his radio conversation with Falkowski—'national madness'. We should wonder why almost half of the performance was devoted to something else: the analysis of Kordian's Oedipal tendencies and misogynistic fantasies. And yet this pattern falls in line with Grotowski's confrontation with the 'idea' or 'archetype'. His insistence that a radical analysis has to take place—which often included a shaming of the 'mythical hero's' pretensions—was central to both his earlier and later dramatic attempts at profanation and blasphemy. This is how it was with *Cain*'s family scenes—performed as a cabaret with obvious psychoanalytic aspects—and in *Forefathers' Eve*—for was this not the point of including Mickiewicz's

---

12 A unique reprisal of this sequence of *Kordian*—of course staged in another way—was the scene with Beautiful Helen from *The Tragical History of Doctor Faustus* in which Cynkutis played Faustus.

Part IV in the Opole version? This is also a tactic Grotowski later used in *The Tragical History of Doctor Faustus, The Constant Prince* (although here the dramaturgy of this process was less linear) and *Apocalypsis cum figuris*. In each case the hero's elated position is questioned, demolished and overextended by sequences that dramatize the hero's erotic relations with both women and men. These sequences triggered specific energies of taboo breaking that are then shifted into a phantasmal reality. The impossibility of satisfying erotic hungers becomes a driving force for metaphysical rebellion that negates all the values offered by this world, pointing towards something unnamed that refuses to be reduced to symbols and therefore must sought beyond their province.

Thanks to the études created outside the text in *Kordian*, the Theatre of 13 Rows discovered the possibility of playing out the drama of desire and energy through physical actions connected with actor's personalities and psychophysical activities. This is why the scene of Kordian and Violetta galloping was so important for Grotowski. In this sequence, we clearly see the seed of discoveries Grotowski followed clearing the way for a theatrical laboratory.

Interestingly, the next important scene—Kordian's meeting with the Pope—is not described by Flaszen. Thankfully some reviewers have described it, as does Halina Stankowska:

> The grotesque served well in the scene of Pope's audience where real props were used—a tiara and a cigar. The parrot's voice and the cigar smoked by the pope became the cause of constant distraction and dismay, with which Kordian listens to the Pope; and his words, a judgement expressed in a state of complete distraction [...], effectively reveal and accuse the highest representative of the official church.
> (Stankowska 1962: 3).

The papal tiara and the cigar were the first props Kordian used in his internal theatre of grotesque distraction. Both mutually questioned one another, causing the hero to become confused, as Stankowska notes. The tiara seen in the photograph of the Pope by Andrzej Moskwiak was obviously theatrical, a stage sign without efforts made to match reality (Zygmunt Molik's deposit, inv. no. 317). It was made up of three gold crowns set upon a tall, white, oval headpiece. The cigar on the other hand was very 'real'; Molik simply smoked it. If we add to this that Molik also wore a doctor's frock, sat on a metal hospital bed with its metal springs exposed and awkwardly bent over to keep his tall tiara from bumping into the ceiling, we find an image that is totally incoherent. The composition of this scene clearly points to the Vatican, and yet simultaneously ridicules such associations. Marta Piwińska—an important and intelligent critic—saw this scene as an example of crazed dreams put up on stage: 'we are watching what seem to be materialized fantasies, seen as if with Kordian's eyes' (2006[1962]: 149). The incoherent, disturbing images created by his disturbed mind are staged right before the spectators' eyes.

And not only before their eyes. The soundscape of this scene was incredible as well. Kordian and the Doctor somehow swapped voices. Molik spoke in a high-pitched voice reciting his lines in a semi-liturgical way hinting at the false treble used by Kordian in earlier monologues. Cynkutis' voice contrasted with Molik's, with low and warm tones though he still maintained the artificiality he used throughout the performance. Their conversation was interrupted by a Parrot's voice. One of the actresses called out the bird's lines, and ended the scene by 'Parroting' a scream—'Ha-a-allelujah'—which sounded like a sudden sneeze. The whole arrangement sounds evidences the obvious care the 13 Rows took with sound composition, just as important as the visual elements.

Stankowska's review clearly suggests that for Kordian's character this sequence was unclear and troubling. I think that the source of this confusion is the 'holy fatherhood' created through the confluence of three false figures: (1) the Pope, the Holy Father, the highest spiritual authority of the Catholic Church; (2) the Doctor, a medical authority, lord of the flesh; and (3) the phallus, represented by the cigar in a rather obvious way that hints at familiar images of fatherly dominance. One might also observe that the phallus was doubled and visually represented by the papal tiara. Kordian standing at the foot of the bed thus confronts the Father's power and authority. The Father does not totally reject Kordian but rather dismisses and humiliates him.

It seems that for Grotowski—more so than for Słowacki—the Vatican scene served as an introduction to the famous Mont Blanc monologue in which Kordian has a vision of sacrifice for the nation that he resolves to be his mission and main goal. This is how Flaszen describes the way it was staged by Grotowski:

> After visiting the Pope, Kordian stiffens in a sudden stupor and falls down torpid in the nurses' arms. They lift him up, rigid, mumbling text from the monologue, and holding him high, carry him across the room. They lay him down on the top bunk of one of the beds, tie him up, and take his shirt off. The Janitor[13] twists a thick rubber band round Kordian's right wrist and freezes there with a bowl ready for the blood. The Doctor lifts his lancet and stands still for a while: he aims precisely for the patient's vein. The cool, dexterous, and definite actions contrast with Kordian's desperate euphoria, for he is just about to make the most important choice of his life. At the end, his loud mumbling changes into a hoarse whisper. The Doctor puts his lancet into the patient and Kordian screams: 'People! Winkelried is alive! Poland is the Winkelried of nations!'[14] While he carries on, the Janitor's procedures suggest that the surgery is finished. Kordian wakes up from his mad dream and utters his famous invocation, 'Oh, Poles!', in a calm, tired voice.
> (Flaszen 2010[1964]: 87)

---

13 In the Gerard T. Kapiolka translation, the character is named 'Caretaker'. I use this name in my description.

14 This famous quotation recalls the legendary, national hero of Switzerland, Arnold Winkelried. In a battle, Winkelried grabbed several enemies' spears, thrust them into his chest and sacrificed his life for the victory of others. Słowacki is using this figure as a symbol of Poland sacrificing itself for the freedom of other nations.

Compared to this description, the photograph of the scene does not present so strong image.[15] Kordian is lying on the upper level of a two-tier bed that stood near the centre of the space. His right arm, held by the Caretaker, is wrapped with the rubber band. Next to the Caretaker, the Doctor holds a white tin bowl and lancet aimed at the Kordian's vein. The scene seems ordinary, stripped of the drama and pathos with which the great romantic monologues were usually performed on Polish stages.

But there could be no doubt that the Mont Blanc monologue was the key point of the performance for both the artists and the audiences. Flaszen was clear in stating that, for him, this was a 'crucial scene' (2010[1964]: 87). It was certainly so for Grotowski who indicated that this sequence contained essential elements of the performance. In *A Possibility of a Theatre*—which remember was written before *Kordian*'s premiere-Grotowski stated the key concept for staging this monologue:

> The Mont Blanc monologue in which Kordian offers his blood for the sake of the nation and the blood of Poland for all other nations (Winkelried archetype) is delivered during an operation—the doctor lets Kordian's blood while Kordian is in a state of hysterical shock. The blood sacrifice is a real letting of blood, hence it is ridiculed, shown as delusion, but it is also a 'demonic martyrdom', and hence it is affirmed, subjected to apotheosis.
> (Grotowski 2012: 223)

Grotowski's interpretation of the Mont Blanc monologue makes it into a meta-model of his *Kordian*'s fundamental dramaturgical rule, and suggests that the monologue served as this rule's most radical application. Years later Grotowski interpreted the effect of this sequence differently.

> Kordian makes a real sacrifice, his own blood given up for others, but given in line with old medical procedures: the doctor bleeds him. In this there was solidarity with Kordian and a sad

---

15 Photo of a guest performances in Krakow; GIA (inv. no. 318).

derision of the ineffectiveness of solitary actions: reaching the roots that define us—and struggling with them.
(Grotowski 2012: 223)

This sort of interpretation formulated at a later date—and of course following other experiences—represents a clear modification in relation to Grotowski's initial 'dialectical' motivation. The automatic repetition of the apotheosis and derision formula seems to me to be both unfortunate and inaccurate in relation to how this *Kordian* was staged, and, according to recorded impressions, the way it was received. The very word 'derision' as used in the context of 'bloodletting' seems inapt because the basis of this scene was to bring a highbrow metaphor down to the level of the physical reality of medical procedures. It involved profanation—not derision.

No one noticed that Kordian's blood sacrifice—just like the broom and Konrad posing with it in *Forefathers' Eve*—had a strong connection to Jesus Christ. I find the scene most clearly associated with Christ's Eucharistic offering, despite the Doctor's lancet and the involuntary bloodletting inspiring associations with the Passion. If we consider that the whole performance is delivered in the tone of a Holy Mass, then it makes sense that the medical procedure takes place halfway through the performance—almost exactly when the Eucharist happens in the Catholic Mass. This subtle and concealed allusion strengthens the profanation aspect of the performance. The placement of this bloodletting shows the messianic model of Jesus to be an example and a source of the political attitude and activities Grotowski clearly wanted to profane in order to make them available as a foundation for secularized political actions. This may be too bold a thesis. However, numerous references to Jesus encourage us to consider Grotowski as a precursor of secular political activities modelled on Christianity and connected with left-wing post-secularism. This interpretation would allow us to see Grotowski as striving towards what Alain Badiou (2003) calls 'the foundation of universalism' through his use of profane theatrical actions. In the 1960s such attempts would have constituted a political action by creating a community around a secularized and socialized act of rebellion and resistance against rational rules. This is precisely what Grotowski seems to be dealing with when he staged 'solidarity with Kordian' and the sadness of deriding his isolation.

After *Kordian*'s premiere, the bloodletting scene was similarly interpreted by the emotionally aroused Józef Szczawiński who wrote that

> the creators of the performance, faithful to their rule of erasing opposites—apotheosis and irony, truth and parody—tried to ridicule the situation, the pathetic aspect of the gesture, just as they did in the Great Improvisation. They were able to confront what was communicative during the Romantic period, and thus honest, about the hero's experience, which remains honest and communicative even today. Hence, Kordian expresses his monologue as a sick madman, bled by the doctor. Kordian is convinced the blood is for his nation and humanity. His suffering is real. His tragedy is true, something beyond the reach of the Doctor and Caretaker performing the procedure, but clear to the audience who are co-actors and Kordian's brethren. (Szczawiński 1962: 10)

Here Szczawiński touches upon the most important experiment in the Opole *Kordian*. The core goal of the performance was to encourage the hero's 'brethren'—who sense a sad anachronism and ineffectiveness in sanctified possibilities for everyday action—to seek out new forms, and to do so without betraying their sources. In this case, they were encouraged to reject and rebel against the world as it was and its rules as they were. Without this rejection they would be left with a fallow earth and social indifference represented by the hospital ward once Kordian was pacified.

The following sequence featured the coronation of the Russian Tsar as the King of Poland. Flaszen described its mood:

> The street scenes. The actors, scattered around the room, describe the coronation ceremony, talking about and commenting on what is going on in the crowd. A favourite directorial

device: creating a mass of people by boundlessly extending the acoustic environment. The mood of the crowd has little in common with horror or excitement. On the contrary, they speak like common observers who routinely ignore big events. Lots is going on but no one is surprised or excited.
(Flaszen 2010[1964]: 86)

This description is confirmed by the fragment recorded for the radio programme directed by Falkowski where the scene was preceded by a spoken description: 'An evening in the hospital. Madmen out strolling'. Individual actors speak reluctantly, as if asleep. They draw their sounds out as if telling stories to children in such a way that might calm the listener. All of their single-syllable sounds such as 'a' are drawn out, and they are sometimes swapped for the dismissive 'e'; in some instances, they are also drawn out as in the 'y'. The recorded fragment culminates in calls of 'Long live the Tsar' which in their tone recall the apathy of an official ceremony.

In *Kordian*, Grotowski put a societal soundscape on stage that depicts a community in dispassionate disarray. He portrays the 'masses' through an 'undefined broadening of the acoustic plain' which includes the spectators as members of a Polish society that no longer cares, that is immobile and collapsed due to passivity. This was the same Polish community that had only just been Kordian's brethren. This palpable change in tone should have led the audiences to recognize that these 'Poles' to which Kordian referred in tired tones included the spectators themselves. If understood, this instigation could have been experienced as a massive shock to their systems.

The remainder of the scene was interwoven with the song of a Stranger whose part was played by the Doctor.

The singing of a Stranger. The Doctor wails out of tune, like a street beggar. He forces the actors and spectators to sing. He watches out for any disobedience and threatens them by waving his stick at them.
(Flaszen 2010[1964]: 86)

Forcing a 'shared playfulness' may seem to mean a way of forcing a communion between actors and audiences. And yet the point of this procedure was in fact opposite. This was about using derision and bitterness to show how the Poles for whose salvation Kordian was willing to sacrifice himself joined a song inviting Kordian to 'go to sleep' without a whisper of complaint. After calming down the most acutely mad patient, the Doctor started to treat the rest of the people in the room. Reviewers of course could not write about this allusion to a mood of general compromise and resignation from the revolutionary forces that had led the charge of Polish, anti-Stalinist rebellion several years prior but had been quite easily silenced by authorities. Reviewers aside, it seems unlikely that audiences would not be able to read into this.

After showing off the extent of his authority, the Doctor was fully empowered to don a theatrical crown covered in tinfoil and declare himself the Tsar. Having performed this self-coronation, he sat on the top bunk at the furthest end of the auditorium—the same lofty perch he took up as the Pope—and turned his back to the audience seemingly withdrawing from the action.

The next scene presented a meeting of anti-tsarist conspirators in the basement of Warsaw's St. John Cathedral. In the radio version, this scene was announced as a part of the hospital routine: 'The patients are preparing themselves to sleep, washing their hands, rinsing their throats. The Doctor has handed over his authority to the Caretaker. He [the Caretaker] is the President of the conspiracy' (Falkowski 1962a).

Flaszen described the scene:

A dispute in the 'cathedral crypt' is stylized in the manner of the exaggerated, bombastic way of the Great Theatre. Voting: Kordian, dancing like a beggar, moves around the room holding a hat in his hand. Then, despite the vote's negative outcome, he decides to kill the Tsar, and in a prayer-like manner with the tone of a *yurodivy*[16] he announces his plan to sacrifice his blood for the nation. Meanwhile, the crowd gurgles loudly while clearing their

---

16 The Russian name of the holy fool.

throats—the indifferent patients make their usual evening toilet. A favourite directorial device: to juxtapose the grand with the trivial.

(Flaszen 2010[1964]: 86)

The notion of a 'pathetic representation of Great Theatre' is relative and situated back in history. Today, the Great Theatre as understood by Flaszen is more or less gone from Poland, and the emotional engagement audible in the President's voice on Falkowski's radio programme no longer sounds excessive.[17] In the radio recording, the Caretaker who acts here in the role of the President, speaks in a low, strong voice, using his voice more dynamically than the Doctor. And yet his voice similarly provided contrast to Kordian's weak voice. Kordian continued to deliver his lines in the same naive, mechanical style though this time he says them more calmly as if he was holding back. It is not until the vote results are announced and Kordian proclaims that the Tsar will die that his voice suddenly returns to its usual high pitch.

The finale of the conspiracy scene described by Flaszen was also recorded for the radio. Even today this recording remains powerful. Cynkutis whispers conspiratorially 'I'm on duty in the Palace tonight!' (Słowacki 2010: 87), and then sings this same line to the tune of a religious hymn. Next, Kordian sings his oath in the same semi-liturgical melody.

To my dear nation
I bequeath all I have: my blood and life,
And an empty throne to be shared by all.
(Słowacki 2010: 87)

In the background we hear water gurgling in the mouth of other patients: the nation is clearing its throats.

This sequence of Kordian's declaration that he will assassinate the Tsar contains within it a confrontation. But instead of a confrontation

---

17 An exception to this is the sequence when the results of the vote are announced. In this case Jahołowski does 'thunder' in an exuberant but false pathos.

between elation and the brutal force of political power it presents a confrontation between a semi-liturgical offering and the disdain of the masses. This contrast reveals the essential problem performed and analysed by Kordian: the lack of connection between the hero's sacrifice and the everyday lives of the people. The mass-like tonality in the scene emphasizes this contrast, and clearly confirms that there is no church for which Kordian could serve as Messiah. The diagnosis being played out here indicates the same thing that was the main subject of the whole performance: the necessity of going beyond binary oppositions between solitary, 'sacred' sacrifice and the heartless, everyday existence of the collective.

Directly following Kordian's oath the spectators witnessed his failed attempt on the Tsar's life.

> Kordian in a straitjacket, his hands tied behind his back which is attached to a rifle, as though to a torture post. He moves then stops in positions familiar from the tradition of paintings of battles: a marching grenadier, a grenadier attacking, a grenadier aiming, a grenadier falling. He is accompanied by Imagination and Fear dressed in the male nurses' medical coats. In a soft soothing voice, they describe Kordian's terrible ghosts; they keep an eye on their charge's every step, wrestling with him and restraining him. Cold professionals, medical workers, whose task it is to calm the patient down. Their professional gentleness is almost cruel. Horror, depicted with a patient kindness, turns monstrous.
> (Flaszen 2010[1964]: 86–87)

This scene is documented in several photographs that show Kordian in his straitjacket with a rifle at his back. The two male nurses Imagination (Ryszard Cieślak) and Fear (Andrzej Bielski) are dressed in white, holding Kordian upright and trying to soothe him. Fragments from the scene were also recorded for the radio. The nurses speak as Flaszen said, calmly and delicately. Kordian speaks in a manner typical of his character; we can hear him pronouncing certain letters with apparent effort.

The Doctor sat on a bed wearing the Tsar's crown, and Kordian approached him. Kordian delivers the final lines of his monologue culminating with 'Jesus, Maria'. The radio version follows his monologue with the ring of an alarm clock. This might have been meant to evoke the 'reality' of the hospital, but also serving to wake the Doctor who then faced off with his would-be assassin.

We do not know how this scene transitioned to the final conversation between the Doctor and Kordian. It is also unclear where their conversation took place. Photos published by Wójtowicz show Kordian in his straitjacket facing the Doctor who stood on an upper platform among the spectators leaning on a cane (2004: 70). In photographs from the Zygmunt Molik deposit at the GIA, Cynkutis appears to be leaning backwards—supported only by the gun that is strapped to his back (inv. no. 2). The Doctor sits on a bed behind him, hovering above the hapless patient. This second photograph clearly shows the contrast between both characters. The Doctor is calm, and rather disinterested; Kordian is still 'inspired' sitting in a very Romantic pose.

The final fragment of the conversation is included in the radio programme. The recording allows us to get the idea of its soundscape. The Doctor speaks in a low voice, sounding tired and calm, but not triumphant. His sadness confirms his authority. In certain moments Kordian uses a similar tone, for instance, when he argues for the meaning of martyrdom before he resumes his liturgical chant.

During the discussion, Kordian recalls his ideal of 'man-angel' ready to give himself up for others. In reply, the Doctor once more initiates the theatre of two madmen that began the performance. The same actors who just calmed Kordian as nurses—Cieślak and Bielski—played the madmen. We do not know what garments they wore. They probably did not have time to take off their nurse outfits so it is likely that they continued to wear them as they 'parade[d] one by one, endlessly mumbling some words about their own high mission' (Flaszen 2010[1964]: 85–86). If this was the case, then the scene became one of derisive triumph. The domineering quality of their 'parade' proclaimed the triumph of 'reason and order', and also underscored the futility of examining the patients. After all, these were two former madmen who had just appeared as the Doctor's aides. They retained their past craziness while distancing themselves from it.

Their declamations overlapped. Following a Christ-like cry of one of the madmen—'God, take this cup from me'—the Doctor turns to Kordian: 'You see he sacrificed himself for . . . ' Kordian replies in song 'He's gone maaaaaad . . . ' The two nurses then drag him out of the room. Having agreed that martyrdom is madness—and having rejected the words of the dying Christ—Kordian can leave the hospital, he is considered 'cured'.

The performance ends with the Doctor liturgically intoning 'Sleep people! Good night!' The sound and placement of this chant clearly echo the end of the Catholic Mass: 'Go, the Mass has ended'. The final sequence of the Opole *Kordian* constitutes a typical finale in Grotowski's theatre. The ending worked on three levels. It signalled the end of performance as if a curtain fell; it worked in the hospital context—ending a long day and saying goodnight to patients; and it worked on the level of Kordian's history closing it without clear resolution. On a hidden level of secular liturgy, the finale paradoxically endorsed collective passivity in the face of all that had just happened.

The quick shifts and confusing interplay of this final scene activated and reflected the ambivalence of the entire Opole *Kordian*. From the point of view of the final scene, spectators could look back and somehow recognize their own experiences and reactions anew. What was it that happened in that room? Liberation from mad visions? Did psychological torture break a fearless rebel? Was this a dramatization of a 'normalized' Poland? Was it a profane anti-Mass? Or maybe even a Black Mass intended to play out and sanctify the fate of a scapegoat? It seems to me that all these possibilities were indeed present to some extent, and so, the Doctor's last words 'Sleep people! Good night!' were a final address to spectators whose reactions had a crucial function in establishing the meaning of the performance.

Intensification of Possibilities

In his *A Possibility of a Theatre*, Grotowski comments on the development of *Kordian* in rehearsals. He explains the specific idea he had for seating the actors and audiences in a shared space, a hospital for the mentally ill.

> The dialectics of affirmation and overcoming, a dialectics of forms targeting archetypes and in some way stripping them down, was here based on one radical concept. The whole of *Kordian* was transported into the scene set in a hospital for the deranged: as a result of this rearrangement the text of this scene opens and closes the performance, and even as a leitmotif it returns, comes and goes throughout the rest of the performance.
>
> In this way the messianic formula became a mad dream, delirium, improvisation, and fiction experienced by the sick. But this delusion transports the reality to a slightly different dimension: suffering remains suffering, and the act of sacrifice, though made in a dream state, remains self-immolation, a blood sacrifice.
>
> (Grotowski 2012: 222–23)

It is hard to disagree with Flaszen when he argues that setting the entire drama in an asylum was not a change of 'the characteristic style of the literary original, but rather an intensification of possibilities [. . .] hidden in the text—a translation of the Romantic style into today's' (2010[1962]: 75). Grotowski defended the nineteenth-century Romantic attitude—which was seen in Grotowski's time as mad, crazed lunacy—not by fighting with its definition or retrospective accusations but rather by affirming and strengthening these critiques.

If the aim of the creators of the performance was to overcome the separation between 'dream' and 'reality', between the hero and the community, between Romanticism and contemporaneity, and thus enable a collective utilization of the Romantic attitude, then a key problem remained in the position and the experience of the community—specifically the theatre community, and in this case the *Kordian* audience and actors. Flaszen wrote that

Kordian is [...] a further experiment, aiming to turn the theatre into a homogenous community of spectators and actors. The whole theatre is turned into a 'mental asylum', and the spectators (not without the actors' schoolboy satisfaction) are forced to play the role of the patients ... The actors are also patients, only more active. Thus they are not distinguished by their clothes; they wear normal suits which mimic with awkward elegance the spectators'.

[...]

We are certainly aware of how often we are left wide open to pranksters' inventive jokes: 'tee hee, they make fools of people ... tee hee, it seems that they are fools themselves ... it's not a theatre, it's a madhouse' etc. We do not ban such jokes. We know from experience that an element of humour will, in any case, blast away any barriers.
(Flaszen 2010[1962]: 74–75)

We must straightaway note that giving the audience the roles of less active patients in this asylum—presented as a 'further experiment' on the route to renewing a 'ritualistic' community of audiences and actors—had a very different character than attempts to build community between actors and audiences in *Forefathers' Eve*. We can see in Flaszen's commentary a contradiction because how are we to speak about a 'united community' when the audience played the role of patients, and in this way became a specific group of characters in the performance? After all, the actors' roles included the Doctor, Caretaker and nurses who represented a very different attitude than the 'madmen', especially Kordian, the most deranged among them. Spectators playing 'patients'—and therefore also 'crazy' people—in fact occupied the same position as Kordian. This meant that audiences tangibly experienced Kordian's situation as their own. This experience was essential to the whole performance.

Flaszen clearly articulated this central component of the Opole *Kordian* in a later polemic with Wacław Kubacki.

If [...] Grotowski makes Kordian into a madman then it is not to ridicule him—but because modern audiences, being used to the common morality of their times, tend to see him as 'non-practical'. The fact that Kordian is today, *hic et nunc*, a madman sounds like a challenge addressed at the audience's sober, philistine morality—and a bitter complaint made towards our culture, in which the solitary act doesn't have causative power, and sacrificial drives do not correlate with a healthy approach to reality. This then becomes an acceptance of the audience's attitude—however in order to shake them out of their secure defences.

(Flaszen 2006[1965]: 164)

From this perspective, *Kordian* was not about establishing a 'ritualistic community' but was rather a dramatic interrogation of the obvious that was assumed by the 'cult' status of Słowacki's drama and his hero. Already in *Kordian*, Grotowski saw the paradoxical possibility of establishing a local, contemporary community by performing differences, distance and otherness, a strategy that he consciously utilized and tried to perfect in *Acropolis*. Above all however, Grotowski used theatre and the troubling, uneven results of his dramatic process as a tool to shock audiences, to provide for them an experience that would challenge their high-minded convictions.

Grotowski himself commented on a crucial opposition between Kordian and the Doctor that shows his *Kordian* was not at all a naive attempt to create ritualistic community.

So we thought: Let us confront Kordian with the Chief Doctor, who will represent common sense in its cynical, egoistic form— i.e. an individual is 'normal' when he gives his whole mind to his own narrow interests. The doctor was a 'normal' man, but his 'normality' was vulgar and dirty' and it was lower-minded than Kordian's craziness, and this was the second plane of the performance. For, finally, Kordian was wrong because he wanted to act in alienation, or isolation, if you prefer, but he was right

260 · DARIUSZ KOSIŃSKI

in wanting to do something of a higher value, to sacrifice his life and blood.

(Grotowski 1968b in Schechner, Wolford 1997: 49]

When the opposition between the two central characters is presented in this way, we see that they are far from tragic dilemmas and choice-less choices. Grotowski uses clearly pejorative words to define the Doctor's attitude. Thus he indicates that in his opinion Kordian is right, that Kordian's mistake is related to his 'alienation, or else isolation' and therefore also driving his course of action. We could perhaps draw the conclusion that Grotowski meant for the performance to overcome the division between Kordian and the community, a division embodied in those who came to see *Kordian*. Grotowski questioned Kordian's isolation by literally placing audiences and the hero in a common space, and on the same level as patients, though he also did so ironically and with some theatrical distance. Grotowski thereby forced spectators to experience themselves as allies of a noble madman whose madness was called into question. Logically, if Kordian's madness was evidenced by his solitary and isolated rebellion and sacrifice, then returning him to this community would mean normalizing and socially curing the hero, thus inverting health and illness.

Grotowski described the process he sought to bring to all participants experiencing the performance:

[...] in *Kordian* after Słowacki the whole theatre hall was converted into a mental hospital ward, the audiences treated as patients—every spectator was treated as such—eventually even the doctors, meaning actors, were seen as sick, everyone suffering from a great illness of a certain epoch, a certain culture, or rather possessed by tradition. But that which in this performance was of greatest importance was the fact that indeed the one who was supposed to be the most sick—Kordian—was sick with nobility; meanwhile those who were the least sick, especially the Doctor coordinating the treatments, was 'logical' and filled with 'healthy mentality', yet viciously so. This is certainly a paradox, or a contradiction, with which we are often

confronted in life: when we directly desire to make great ideals into reality we become lunatics, madmen, even if we retain our health; and if we desire to be too logical we are unable to make our values into reality, and so with all our sober logic we move down what seems to be a correct path, we are not mad, we are healthy, enjoying good health . . . and yet a cow too represents a healthy specimen.
(Grotowski 2012: 357)

The conclusion is clear: If the Doctor represents health, 'then it is better not to be healthy' (Grotowski quoted in Domagalik 1979). And if that is the case, then the unique pedagogy to which the spectators watching *Kordian* were subjected represents a warning about the norm and the normalization advocated by the Doctor, a persona who is both diabolical and representative of the highest form of authority. In the context of Poland's processes of political normalization and the gradual silencing of revolutionary moods post–1956, *Kordian* created by someone recently characterized as 'rabid' could have been read as an attempt to oppose the political dominance of that time. Viewers sympathizing with Kordian experienced a similar oppression as did Grotowski, and some of them would have experienced the ways that rebellious 'madness' was beaten down. Meanwhile, those who saw in Kordian an anachronistic and ineffective dreamer were confronted with the fact that their attitudes made them allies of a cold-hearted perpetrator, and thus they would question the ethics of their position. This meant that in some way all those present were exposed to a test, and introduced to a dialectical process the effects of which depended only on their personal choices.

The relations between the Doctor and Kordian represent a basic tool for building what Grotowski called 'a pamphlet against our own selves', and still serve as an interpretive key to unlock the political and actual dimensions of the performance. If we could simplify the question posed by the Theatre of 13 Rows in *Kordian*, we might formulate it as 'Which side are you on?' This question was posed in the context of the 1960s Polish state's repressive process of extinguishing political engagement and dampening people's participation in public life. The Opole

Kordian clearly informed audiences that by accepting this situation they were indeed behaving logically but at the same time surrendering to bitterness and powerlessness. On the other hand, by siding with Kordian and accepting his madness, they rejected philistinism, and perhaps even restored the communal dimension of individual 'madness' thereby curing it. In 1962, this interpretation might have sounded like casting spells on reality; but the twentieth-century history of Poland clearly shows that these sorts of unreasonable ideas led to the practical fight for the survival of freedom and its associated ideals. Two years after the premiere of *Kordian*, Karol Modzelewski and Jacek Kuroń wrote an open letter addressed to the members of Polish United Workers' Party and the Union of Socialist Youth working in Warsaw University.[18] On 19 March 1965 they were arrested for writing this letter, and in July of the same year Modzelewski and Kuroń were sentenced to 3 and 3.5 years in jail respectively. Their brazen public proclamations may inspire associations with the Romantic, 'mad' typology embodied by Kordian. But in the end, the two Romantic revolutionaries were victorious.

Grotowski and Flaszen did not follow in their footsteps. Their theatre became increasingly accepted by the Polish authorities which from the 1970s backed their activities as 'universal' and not connected directly to the actual problems of their homeland. I think, however, that in the 1960s we could still talk about a notable engagement of the company in addressing these problems. Each Grotowski performance could have been perceived as a political declaration emerging from its specific historical context. In the unique case of *Kordian*, the political interpretation I outline was in various ways suggested by the artists involved. This also happened to be a rare case in which Grotowski himself promoted a political interpretation of his work as a diagnosis of the current situation in Poland and an attempt to awake social and political engagement with the reflection on the consequences of a 'normalization' promoted by the authorities.

---

18 For more information, see: https://rebrand.ly/0wqbs75

While I emphasize the political aspect of *Kordian*, I must also announce straight away that I have no intention of accepting any battle-front legends of the Theatre of 13 Rows' fight against Communism. This would be a gross simplification of the complicated games Polish theatre played with the Party authorities.[19] But I do want to draw attention to the fact that up to a certain point Grotowski and those working alongside him did make direct reference to the historical situation surrounding them. But they would then loosen these social and political connections to accentuate and focus on other aspects of their work. The effect of this loosening of connections—a side effect perhaps, but certainly a quite clear effect—led to the generally held opinion that their performances were apolitical and 'universal'.

Kordian's creators were aware of a serious danger that threatened their mission: the idea that the theatre experience connected to the performance was purely aesthetic. When I read the precise and intellectually subtle comments written by Flaszen, I have the impression that the performance's creators tried to evade this danger by applying a special dramaturgical frame to the performance. Speaking in contemporary terms, their essential aim was to enhance the direct impact of the theatrical event on audiences while reducing its representational and spectacular aspects.

As in *Forefathers' Eve*, there was an attempt in *Kordian* to achieve desired affects by moving away from cohesion, by a constant change of perspectives and by creating a multifaceted theatrical structure. To a lesser degree this meant employing meta-theatrical devices. More so, it meant experimenting with alternating points of view. In his instructions for the audience published in the programme Flaszen accentuated this dynamic:

> The production was invented as a fusion, a mutual game between reality and fiction. Theatre is the reality on which the first level of fiction grows: all those present in the room are patients from the psychiatric clinic. Yet it is not a fiction that is faithful to the

---

19 For more on this, see Kosiński 2019: 191–99.

hospital reality in any literal sense; the hospital is intentionally weird, as if seen in a nightmare. The acting—'artificial' in its dancing and gymnastic character—is supposed to intensify this mood of unreality. Out of the hospital reality a new fiction grows: *Kordian*'s actual plot, presented as a collective halluci- nation that reveals the truth of human misery and greatness. (Flaszen 2010[1962]: 75)

A very important discovery is presented here, a kind of inner dramaturgy of an event which is not merely a theatre performance. Instead of 'rit- uality'—which was almost mechanically imposed upon *Kordian* as it was in *Forefathers' Eve*—we find a conscious building and projecting of multi-layered perceptions. On the first level—much as in the case in *Forefathers' Eve*—*Kordian* does not hide the 'artificiality' of its theatrical setting. This self-conscious theatrical element was not as strong in *Kordian* as it was in the staging of the Mickiewicz. Nevertheless, the audience in *Kordian* was once again able to look at one another. Furthermore, the clearly 'artificial' convention of the actors' performances in some scenes and roles combined with the overly emphasized theatri- cality of certain props—the papal tiara, the tsar's crown—repeatedly reminded the audience that they were 'only' in a theatre. This funda- mental and obvious tactic was contrasted by casting the spectators as patients, something Jerzy Kwiatkowski aptly declared was the equivalent of using 'extras' (1962: 4). Indeed, the audience were extras; they were given specific, simple instructions to be accomplished within the world of the performance. We can thus consider the viewers' role as an allusion to how ambivalent the position of ordinary Poles of the time had become. Instead of being active citizens, its members became extras in relation to the changes taking place around them.

But in the context of *Kordian*'s internal dramaturgy, it seems to be of utmost importance that both levels—the theatrical and the politi- cal—should function simultaneously. Put another way, the two should be dialectically combined in the frame of a single experience. That the spectators were treated as extras recognizing their own 'extra' status as part of the performance metonymically played out within the performance itself. Seeing oneself as a patient is not just an aesthetic experience. It is rather a way of stepping out of a role built on the need to live an everyday life, a stepping away we might characterize as a sort of 'estrangement-effect' relevant to the viewer's experience. There was of course the danger that instead of encouraging reflexivity the performance would turn into simple fun—which was also a pitfall of the cabaret-like first part of the Opole *Forefathers' Eve*. Built-in aspects of the *Kordian* performance were meant to guard against this pitfall, including the 'sleepy dream' aesthetic of the hallucinated scenes, and the odd, improbable and thus also unique and surprising acrobatics performed by the actors.

Actors' acrobatics provided a clear counterpoint to the seated audience members cast as extras. In a very literal sense it created a borderline of possibility between 'patients less mad' and those 'more acutely' crazed, namely the actors. The latter could look the same as the former but all the complicated poses, tumbles and falls that the performers executed set the two groups apart. In this way, the distance between the actors and the spectators in the performance was conspicuous, and may have caused the 'extras' to feel isolated and passive in relation to the events in the 'hospital'. And so, we could say that the estrangement-effect was achieved here based on rules and mechanisms quite different than those used by Brecht in his *V-Effekt*.[20] Instead of comments, songs and banners à la Brecht, Grotowski's *Kordian* featured performative actions using sensory experiences and intimate proximity that took audiences out of their defined role and gave an inner dynamic to their experience. In so doing, Grotowski created a situation of curious discomfort, where spectators were fascinated with what was taking place. This fascination could

---

20 'V-Effekt' is an abbreviation of the German *Verfremdungseffekt*, and is roughly translated into English as 'distancing effect', 'alienation effect' or 'estrangement effect.' It is a key concept of Bertolt Brecht's drama and theatre theory. Generally, it refers to the opposite of the illusions of the bourgeois theatre. Its goal is to push audiences not to subconsciously accept as obvious or natural the 'reality' on stage—especially not its ideological assumptions. The V-Effekt attempts to initiate audiences' critical thinking by helping viewers perceive the strangeness of the rules-conventions they had learnt to accept and obey. From different possible English translations, I chose 'estrangement effect' not only because I think it is the closest to Brecht's idea but also because I think it is the closest to Grotowski's tactic.

certainly include an admiration for the actors' circus-like skills and commitment. It could also unleash questions about the *raisons d'être* and goals of the performance.

Both actors' engagement with audiences and their acrobatics were related to the third level of dramaturgy indicated by Flaszen: Kordian's story presented through mad visions staged in an insane asylum. Concepts repeated in commentary at the time understandably related the performance to psychology or psychiatry. Reports used words like 'delusions', 'hallucinations', etc. but this emphasis seemed to mask the fact that the level of 'new fiction'—the insane asylum setting added to the 'actual narrative of *Kordian*'—represented an interior theatre being staged in the mental ward with the involvement of its patients and hospital personnel.

Acknowledging this level of the Opole performance's dramaturgy links all three layers of the performance. In this tripartite configuration 'reality' consists of the Theatre of 13 Rows performing *Kordian*, and is analogical to the third and highest level of the performances' interior dramaturgical framework: a theatre of 'delusions' enacts the actual narrative of *Kordian*. The performances' central dramaturgical level—the spectators being extra/viewers-participants—represents a locus of cognitive experience that links the 'reality' outside the theatre and the 'interior' theatre of delusions connecting Kordian's 'madness' to the spectators' existential predicaments. These two theatres illuminate each other and thereby call one another's singularity into question. They are unified by their porous borders, their blurred oppositions and their power to call into question distinctions between 'fiction' and 'reality'. Their unification provides a model for theatre pedagogy that Grotowski subsequently applied to all his performances.

Anticipating the further evolution of Grotowski's theatre, I would say that the two poles of the pedagogy he developed in *Kordian* and applied to subsequent performances are found in *Acropolis* and in *Apocalypsis cum figuris*. In *Acropolis* the particularity of actors' performances radically strengthened the dialectics of admiration and alienation. In *Apocalypsis cum figuris*, witnesses were encouraged to ask themselves about their position in 'life' outside the theatre in a game almost identical to *Kordian*—between the theatrical reality of the 'here-and-now' and the 'staging' or 'play' of action in performance. In *Kordian*, Grotowski discovered this mechanism for the first time, and used it to challenge viewers to recognize the ambivalence of their own attitudes and to feel discomfort in a theatre that related to their situation outside the theatre. 'Real' theatre was using a 'fictional' theatre in order to make audiences aware of their own place in reality, and at the same time to recognize the paradoxical sanity—and so the real usefulness—of Kordian's attitude. Grotowski disturbed theatre's internal division between 'reality' and 'fiction'. In so doing, he questioned the divisions in public life between that which is real and that which is not, and called into question political orders imposed upon society which can also be understood as questioning the space from which authority reifies political power and knowledge.

Seen from the perspective of this model of dramaturgy, the Doctor's character becomes especially important and meaningful. In his comments Flaszen clearly points to the Doctor as the director of the inner theatre that presents 'Kordian's actual plot [...] as a collective hallucination':

> The Doctor is the one who releases and organizes these hallucinations; he is helped by the hospital Janitor [Caretaker]. The Doctor—a figure combining the features of a psychiatric charlatan, a circus magician, and a 'real' devil—selects from among the spectators those people he needs for his actions, like a magician lurking for victims to be used in his experiments. By performing certain hypnotist's procedures over the chosen people, he induces their daydreams, which are immediately realized. At the same time, the Doctor himself joins in the action that he has triggered, taking on important roles in terms of their content.
> (Flaszen 2010[1964]: 83)

It seems telling that Flaszen—who usually wisely and carefully chooses his words—uses terms in this context that are related to different showbiz spectacles—fairground characters, tricksters, charlatans and 'magicians'.

268 · DARIUSZ KOSIŃSKI

Seen in this light, it seems that Flaszen describes the Doctor's actions as a cruel game of deception, seeing in the Doctor's demonstration of his 'incredible' skills an inquiry into that to which 'healthy reason' can fall prey.

In this context we may ask ourselves this key question: Why does the Doctor enact 'Kordian's theatre'? To which we might reply that he does so for the joy of presenting his dominant position, and to be admired. And if we superimpose a theatrical analogy onto the Doctor's motivations then we can read into his character an ironic comment by director Grotowski—who in this way exposes and problematizes his own position. This is not the first nor last time Grotowski interwove such an interpretive possibility into the 13 Rows' performances. The Promotor from *Mystery-Bouffe* and the Theatre Director in *Shakuntala*; a similar internal theatre director also appears and plays important roles in *Acropolis, Hamlet Study, The Constant Prince* and especially *Apocalypsis cum figuris*.[21] In each of these performances Grotowski depicts theatrical or theatricalized games as cruel fun motivated by dark and dangerous psychological powers thus linking sadomasochistic desires with erotic fascinations that are often homosexual. In *Kordian*—especially in the relation between the Doctor and Kordian described by Flaszen—similar elements appear that decidedly emphasize sadomasochistic games and toying with one's own power.

Percival's Mistake

The more I stress the meaning of audience reactions in determining the sense and meaning of *Kordian*, the more I feel sorry that there are not more source materials concerning the audience's response. What makes it worse is that the reports that exist either come from the time of the performance and are therefore marked by censorship and self-censorship, or were written later with faulty memories and fading recollections, formulated retrospectively, coloured by intervening experiences and so on.

---

21 In all three, Antoni Jahołowski plays the role of the 'director' who initiates and leads an 'inner theatre.'. In *Kordian*, Jahołowski played the Caretaker, the Doctor's assistant and at times also the Doctor's replacement.

One can of course assume—and this is what I am doing—that the small number and the incompleteness of these testimonies also proves that the response was rather weak. In any case, all that we can say about *Kordian* today is an approximation based on the testimonies that survive and on our interpretations of these testimonies.

The first impression I had was the clarity of the essential concepts articulated fully in comments made by Grotowski and Flaszen at the time of *Kordian*'s premiere. The starting points for reviewers are themes and formulas provided by the creators: the insane asylum, archetype, dialectics of derision and apotheosis, stage-auditorium conflation. One could of course complain that this dynamic led to a 'programmed reception', but we can also assume that the creators' comments represent part of the work. At the very start of the 1960s, Grotowski and Flaszen in effect performed their commentaries on the page in the same way that they enacted them on stage. The ritual in *Forefathers' Eve*, the insane asylum in *Kordian* and soon the concentration camp in *Acropolis* existed in the audiences' perceptions, and were mounted within them before they even entered the theatre.

Critics (at least some of them) were aware of this and though they were of course intelligent people, they did not report that some sort of manipulation was going on. They rather assumed that commentary was a means for directing both 'ensembles', serving to show the spectators what roles they were to play. In the majority of cases, critics did not limit themselves to reiterating interpretations provided by Flaszen or Grotowski; they crafted reports of their own unique experiences. They tried to interpret ideas presented in the creators' commentaries in their own ways, and in so doing they maintained the importance of the themes the creators indicated. Critics really experienced some of the themes suggested by the creators as most important in the performance regardless of Grotowski's and Flaszen's commentaries. If this were not the case, critics would likely have reacted against the creators' suggestions.

This means that the essential idea of the whole performance was received more or less without question by audiences; the public really did experience in a range of ways the feeling of being locked up with

Kordian in an insane asylum. Moreover, this foundational proposition-seen as more than a director's 'concept'—was generally well received. Kwiatkowski wrote that

> what seemed like a risky conception turned out to be remarkably fruitful both intellectually and aesthetically. As a polemical device in discussions about the problems of *Kordian*, and not only *Kordian*. As a transistor, an amplifier of the massive power of expression contained in this performance. As a starting point for the creation of a theatre structure. As a closing point for modern dramas.
> (Kwiatkowski 1962: 4)

Kwiatkowski not only flawlessly reads and confirms Flaszen's suggestions, but also points to aspects of the essential idea that was missed by the literary advisor of the Theatre of 13 Rows. In Kwiatkowski's opinion, the decision to set *Kordian* in a hospital for the insane is a cohesive act of great power that serves artistic, ideological and performative functions that cannot be separated from one another. Grotowski created a theatrical solution that emerged out of a deep reading of the source text—something Kwiatkowski stressed—destined to be used only in defined circumstances, namely for the purposes of this very performance. I stress it here because it seems to be a key factor. Grotowski's greatness as a director was based on his ability to create more than just a 'concept' for each new performance. He created unrepeatable theatrical micro-worlds that could not be transferred into other circumstances or used for the needs of other performances. This is something the majority of those copying him could not understand.

Marta Piwińska and Jerzy Kwiatkowski—both being acclaimed critics and respected academics—authored two key reviews of *Kordian*. They tried to describe the basic principles of the production as rationalizations of Romantic visions stripped of their 'metaphysical' autonomies and located in a staged 'inner theatre' found in a hospital. In *Kordian* all the visions and other metaphysical and transcendental elements found in the Słowacki original—along with devils and angels—turn out in the

Opole version to be delusions of the central protagonist which the 13 Rows staged as emerging out of a therapeutic process involving all those in the theatre. Grotowski gives a singular answer to the metaphysical puzzle of *Kordian*: What you see is all that there is, and all things supposed to be 'from another world' are hallucinations of a crazed mind. No critic doubted that there is no 'other worldly phenomena' in *Kordian*. Grotowski showed—and audiences and critics experienced—the death of national myths and the patriotic religion. No descending angels, no visions, no prophecies waited in the wings. The Doctor is completely victorious, and Kordian cannot offer any resistance, either through metaphysical truths or through messianic beliefs that both Słowacki and Mickiewicz used to resist the world's cruel logic. If a point of resistance was to be found then it had to be immanent not transcendental.

The easiest way towards a point of resistance might have seemed to be through empathy—which Grotowski used to construct an ethical connection between audiences and the suffering hero. Indeed, it was easy to identify with Opole's Kordian, if not through the process of accepting his mythic character as a 'national hero' then through empathizing with a martyred and battered human being whose youth, and the beauty of his nobility, likely aroused feelings of 'tenderness'.[22] It seems that Grotowski wanted to defend himself and his audiences against this easy emotional identification, and thus sought to oppose the force of cultural and emotional memory connected with the classic, well-known text. And yet unlike in *Forefathers' Eve*, he did not rid Słowacki's play of its best-known fragments. Instead, he placed the responsibility for this aspect of *Kordian*'s performative impact on the shoulders of his actors. This marks the first time at the Theatre of 13 Rows that Grotowski trusted his actors with a responsibility of this magnitude.

If we look at all that what we know about the acting in *Kordian*, on the one hand we can note a very strong vocal stylization based on a liturgical melopeia, and on the other hand we can see an equally strong,

---

22 This word was used by Eugenio Barba to describe the emotional impact elicited by Cynkutis (see Barba 1999: 27).

biomechanical stylization of physical actions that occasionally became highly acrobatic. In addition, there was no logical connection between the two means of acting. Two components of the performance served to give these strange, stylized vocals and actions a relative cohesion. First, there was the general frame of the insane asylum where dissonant fits and starts would have easily been seen as standard symptoms of the environment's 'madness'. And second, there was the quality of the whole formal composition. In the apparent 'madness' of the performance we find method but also precision, and this precision ensured that the actors' 'madhouse' did not descend into chaos. Kwiatkowski truly valued this and noted that in *Kordian* 'some kind of new style of playing is coming into focus [. . .], certainly not limited to the negation of traditional acting methods' (1962: 4). He described this new acting style in terms of what he called a 'principle of negatives', and he defined this principle by referencing examples from *Kordian*.

> Kordian's opening monologue is uttered in the tone of a miserable complaint—a 'yurodivy' upstart's song; [. . .] the more pathos-laden sequences are here pronounced in a nonchalant fashion, and words meant to arouse terror are delivered as to make fun of them (such as in the scene with Fear and Imagination). Those actors not only jump gracefully all over the beds, they also balance between fun and hysteria, between scandal (the performance takes place among a crowd of 'normal', calm people) and pathos. And the physical acrobatics had to be echoed by a very odd sort of acrobatics of inner experience.
>
> Thus, thanks to the confidence in the way the actors performed, the performance develops from surprise to surprise, from shock to shock. *A rugged texture of the performance is created, its antithetical structure evolving.* (Kwiatkowski 1962: 4)

I highlighted the last sentence because it seems to me very important for attempting to understand how Kwiatkowski uses 'negativity' to describe this new style of acting. This is an approach to acting that thoroughly countered the stereotypical expectations audiences brought to the theatre. This 'negation' is affirmed by both the text itself and Grotowski's emergent theatrical practice. Nothing was the way audiences expected it to be, nothing fit their pre-existing tastes. Why? I think Grotowski was looking for his own version of the estrangement-effect— which he found in what Kwiatkowski called his 'rugged, [. . .] antithetical structure'. We can observe here something obvious yet seemingly disappearing in a ritualistic fog: Grotowski's determined resistance of that which is easy and smooth, his insistence on shocking audiences, his love of distance and disharmony and his constant attempts to make it harder for typically theatrical mechanisms to function in terms of audience identification and shared experiences between actors and audiences. Like Brecht, Grotowski did not trust theatre as a fiction that unites actors and audiences in a shared illusion of a common experience. He manifested his distrust by placing distance and estrangement at the very centre of his theatre, right between actors and audiences. He thereby strengthened the effect of his performative processes, directed its power towards provoking audiences and also focused his work with actors on the actors themselves.

From the very beginning of his work, Grotowski looked for ways to resolve the apparent paradox between the unity and cohesion of staged action and its separation from the illusory unity of theatrical experience. In *Kordian* he explored this paradox in the reality of theatre and the hospital by emphasizing the distance between the two as a 'negative' justification for the strange form of performance used in the 'inner theatre' of *Kordian*. The multi-layered nature of this performance decidedly facilitated his antithetical approach. This approach also strengthened the collective experience of simultaneously being in a theatre and in a hospital, and thereby gave rise to shocking and unique effects.

The 'antithetical' acting style was largely responsible for the successful functioning of the multitude of layers of fiction and reality which as I have already mentioned had a huge impact on the way *Kordian* functioned as a dialectical process. At the start of the 1960s, Grotowski did not assign any strictly philosophical meaning to his use of the concept of 'dialectics'-either Hegelian or Marxist-in relation to his theatre sense.

For Grotowski, 'dialectics' only meant that in his creative process and performance itself there was no drive to blend or soften contradictions, and no pointing to some 'correct' choice between them. Rather, he aimed to emphasize, and allow audiences to experience, such opposing values as elements and as forces equally important for creating a 'complete' whole.

Grotowski's approach to supporting a dialectical experience functioned in *Kordian* without being limited to Kudliński's often-repeated formula of 'derision and apotheosis'. In fact, Kwiatkowski wrote that the 'dialectics of derision and apotheosis isn't really applied [. . .] to *Kordian*. Here we are rather dealing with dialectics of opposition and empathy, or grotesque and tragedy' (Kwiatkowski 1962: 4). Kwiatkowski presents oppositions that do not refer to aspects of performance—as they do in Kudliński's formula—rather his dialectics of opposition and empathy refer to the experience of the spectators, and are related to aesthetic categories of grotesque and tragedy. In his review of the Opole *Kordian*, Kwiatkowski firmly accentuated elements of the performance such as its antithetical structure, its shocking tactics and its elements of contemporary aesthetics which involved both the beauty of the 'convulsive' and art 'based on contrasts, grinding opposites' (1962: 4). His emphasis on these elements plainly suggests that the dialectics of opposites at play in *Kordian* were really grounded in the experience of the viewer.

This seems to be confirmed by Eugenio Barba, a significant and trustworthy witness who was disappointed by *Forefathers' Eve*, but after seeing *Kordian* believed in Grotowski's potential.

> Kordian's patriotic tirades became the outbursts of a sick mind. The spectators were the patients, scattered around the room between beds on which the actors moved about giving life to visions of madness. Zbigniew Cynkutis was Kordian. The tenderness aroused by his youthfulness and the melodious quality of his voice clashed constantly and surprisingly with his acrobatic vitality. [. . .] This physical intensity gave the performance a suggestive force, that I did not remember from *Forefathers' Eve*. [. . .]

In *Kordian* I saw abstract theory become flesh and blood: archetypes, the dialectics of apotheosis and derision, the direction of the two *ensembles*, all gave rise to a situation of heroism and abnegation, with which I could identify. At the same time, a mocking irony was thrown in my face like a bucket of cold water freezing my reactions. [...]

In *Kordian* there was no longer this arbitrariness, which has seemed to me to characterise the actions of the actors in *Forefathers' Eve*. I perceived a paradoxical logic which emphasised the text as though it was speaking of me and of the present. [...]
(Barba 1999: 27–28)

Barba's recollection of *Kordian* many years later constitutes an experience of antithetical singularity and dialectically opposed reactions. These led Barba towards a complete confrontation with the layered and irresolvable spirit of the events and the choices from which his experience was derived. He wrote this report as a young Italian after he had traveled from Norway to Poland under the influence of Andrzej Wajda's film *Ashes and Diamonds*. His observations are representative of the reception expected by the Opole theatre company; they are modern and based in personal perceptions, they exemplify an ironic questioning of simple identification and they showed how the performance led Barba to a sharpened experience of the relevance of 'heroism and denial'.

It also seems important to pay attention to the lack of arbitrariness in the actors' actions; the dialectical aspect inherent not only in their actions but also in the very ways the actors' identities were shaped and delivered. Barba found in *Kordian* this dynamic plurality of motivations which until today still characterizes his Odin Teatret, and causes endless problems for audiences keen on demanding 'messages'. If we consider how much Barba and his work owe Grotowski—and that in some way the beginning of Barba's path was shaped by the Opole *Kordian*—then at the very least we can say that *Kordian* was successful and seminal. It changed the life of young Italian theatre maker, and hence influenced the way global theatre evolved.

From this elated and triumphant mood let us now come back to earth. It is not possible to claim that the production of *Kordian* was a historical success that changed the way the Theatre of 13 Rows was received, that it decidedly influenced Polish theatrical life, or that it changed the attitudes of many Poles. That we know nothing about such consequences best proves that it was not so. Such a notable influence in political and ideological realities comes across in action, and hence cannot remain hidden for long. If—as I tried to prove at the outset of this chapter—one of the motivations for using Słowacki's drama was to offer an experience connected with the current political reality, and to develop a defined strategy of political involvement through profanity, then these aims were mostly not achieved. This is more or less proven by the lack of such recognition in reviews and criticisms; furthermore proved by *Kordian* not becoming an important, recognized performance in the Polish cultural and social life of the time. We could of course argue that the Theatre of 13 Rows in Opole is not the National Theatre in Warsaw, and that Grotowski had no chance of achieving this scope of influence. Agreed. However, this is not the scope we are talking about—we are talking about power. Aside from Barba's report, no other report speaks of a real change in attitudes towards Romantic visions and national myths. Even Kwiatkowski's and Piwińska's deeply moving and laudatory reviews focus more on the accuracy with which Grotowski followed the Słowacki original, on the Opole staging processes, and on the new theatrical model that emerged in the performance.

Paradoxically, this failure can be seen as a 'success' in the sense that *Kordian* unmasked the falsity of the belief that national myths were really present in the collective identity and existence of the nation. The lack of response to such a drastic attack on the avatar of Polish Heroism and his sacrifice shows that Poles did not care much about this hero, his sacrifice, or his devotions. Perhaps Poles did not react because they were indeed already asleep, and were happy to stay slumbering while their supposedly 'national' ideals of sacrifice and poverty were only held dear by Barba— an Italian theatre practitioner who happened upon Poland and Grotowski, and years later—having become a world figure himself—would write a surprisingly positive book about the 'land of ashes and diamonds'. In reality, Poland was a land governed by the Doctor, 'a stain on infinite heaven' (Słowacki 2010: 24).

Grotowski himself did not have a negative view of his audiences. He assessed the impact of *Kordian* from a historical perspective, from a point of view relative to his subsequent theatrical endeavours. He chalked up audiences' lack of reaction to *Kordian* to his own mistakes and errors. In a 1967 interview conducted by Richard Schechner and Theodore Hoffman, the editor and associate editor of *TDR*, Grotowski analysed *Kordian* in terms of his attempts to construct novel relations between actors and audiences. Grotowski referred to *Kordian* as an example of his most advanced attempt to integrate stage and auditorium, and he also synthesized his own conception of the performance with a summary of spectators' reactions.

> For example, in *Kordian*, a play full of glory, individuality and romanticism we transformed our space into an insane asylum (this was before *Marat/Sade*, in 1960).[23] In the original play— written in the time of Russian domination in the 19th century—one scene was set in a mental hospital, where Kordian was put because he had made an attempt against the Tsar (afterwards he was condemned to death). We made this scene the frame for the totality of Kordian's story, and the entire space became a big room in a mental hospital, with hospital beds and so on. The actors were on the beds along with the spectators. The actors were either doctors or patients, the most interesting cases. The Chief Doctor sometimes provoked patients, pretending to be the Pope or Satan. He treated some of the spectators also as patients. Those spectators who were treated as patients were sometimes furious; it happened also that others were proud because they had been judged 'normal'.

---

23 *Kordian* premiered not in 1960 but in 1962. This obvious mistake made by Grotowski that was neither corrected by the author nor the editors and was also included in the reprint of *The Grotowski Sourcebook*. It is strange that Grotowski gives a wrong date for *Marat/Sade*: written by Peter Weiss, directed by Peter Brook and premiering in 1964. Hence *Kordian* was still two years earlier. Maybe Grotowski wanted to emphasize the pioneering aspect of his concept? Or maybe it was just a simple mistake.

After a few minutes the audience understood that this was no joke: the greatest myths of Poland were analysed the myths of craziness. Kordian resolves to sacrifice his blood for the motherland. In the original play he decides this on Mont Blanc, before God and all Europe. But in our performance the related text was said by a man in a straitjacket with doctors bleeding him as they did in the 18th century. Kordian's motivation—to give his blood for the nation—was the kind of motivation that was real to everyone. At the moment there happened hysterical cries among the spectators—certain very deeply rooted national values were attacked in order to revalue them.

I think that it might be difficult for a foreigner to understand the associative mechanism which operated in *Kordian*. My nation has been faced for centuries with the question of heroism and sacrifice. Our production of *Kordian* was a perverse counter-case to the arguments about the uselessness of sacrifice. Kordian gives blood for the motherland—literally—but his act is alienated and without collective backing. A cynic would say in such a situation: 'This must undoubtedly be a madman', therefore the whole action was located where Kordian really is a madman: in a madhouse. We were emphasizing that Kordian's attitude is crazy to the extent that he is out of a realistic perspective. At the same time, we believed that Kordian's action was obviously and deeply human—not his alienation, but his capacity for sacrifice. So we thought: Let us confront Kordian with the Chief Doctor, who will represent common sense in its cynical, egoistic form—i.e. an individual is 'normal', when he gives his whole mind to his own narrow interests. The doctor was a 'normal' man, but his 'normality' was vulgar and dirty' it was lower-minded that Kordian's craziness and this was the second plane of the performance. For, in the final settlement, Kordian was wrong because he wanted to act in alienation, or isolation, if you prefer, but he was right in wanting to do something of a higher value, to sacrifice his life and blood. When the spectators left the theatre, they judged Kordian morally right, even though his act took place in a madhouse. They expressed this opinion in an unambiguous way. The contradictions in Kordian's attitude were brought to light and the performance, through apparent negation of Kordian's behaviour, aimed to affirm it.

When I talk of unity of action that is the kind of unity I am thinking of. But the action must go beyond this. It must open into life, the unexpected in life. It is cruel, because it is true. We did a lot of experiments like that: plays where the actors encircled the spectators, where they asked the spectators questions, where they touched the spectators. But we saw there was always cheating and trickery on our side. And at the same time we were looking for a kind of spontaneity from the audience that is impossible in our society. We looked for common reactions which are possible only if people all have the same faith-references, if they "know the liturgy' well. Today there are many half-faiths—a real Tower of Babel—so it is impossible to find this kind of ritual. One can stimulate external phenomena and make the audience to sing with the actors—often out of tune, and sometimes feeling a certain rhythm as when they are listening to jazz—but it's not a deep, authentic participation. It is participation of the common mask.

On the other hand, we ignored the obvious fact that the spectators are anyway playing the role of spectators—they are observers! And when we put them in the role of madmen, we simply disturb their natural function as observers—or, in the best case—as witnesses, in consequence their reactions were not natural. The unity of place, time and action was not accomplished.

(Grotowski 1968b; Schechner and Wolford 1997: 48–50)

This quote is very long but it seems important for several reasons. First, because of the synthetic presentation of the spectators' reactions. Grotowski recalls how diverse they were—from hysterical tears to anger at being cast as 'lunatics', and even pride at being judged 'normal' and therefore, let us add, the Doctor's allies. And yet it seems the final reaction is the most important, and according to Grotowski it is expressed in 'an unambiguous way' by audiences upon exiting the theatre: a sense of solidarity with Kordian, and the realization that he was morally correct in the face of the Doctor's pragmatism. This seems to me to be most important, not only because of the importance it holds for Grotowski but also because the sentiment is confirmed in Polish reviews. I have already quoted Szczawiński in his comments about audiences as 'brethren' and 'co-actors' who can grasp the shocking meaning of the sacrifice made by Kordian. Kwiatkowski describes this sense of solidarity in an even more straightforward way. At the time, he wrote that in *Kordian*

> a certain closed loop is created [. . .]. The audience finds itself inside some sort of action. In spite of their sovereign psychological position, in spite of their scepticism—the sort modern audiences exemplify—they begin, whether they like it or not, to feel part of a certain community, to feel a sense of solidarity with the actors. It is for those two hours with them 'against' the whole world. The division, barrier, which vanishes between the auditorium and the stage did not disappear completely. It now circles the whole space, creating from it a unique 'unity', a unique 'organism'.
> (Kwiatkowski 1962: 4)

This is not only a confirmation of the audience experience Grotowski mentioned in the interview cited above, this is also an opinion that insists more questions be asked of *Kordian* and its creator. If the audience felt inclined towards solidarity with the actors 'against the whole world' then what happened to 'dialectics'? How can we talk about the multi-layered and antithetical reality of the theatre event when we have a simple alternative possibility: on one side the actor-martyr and the community supporting him, and on the other side the evil world against which we act in concert? Kwiatkowski evidently does not see any contradiction between this experience and what he mentions later, the antithetical aspect of the performance and its dominant 'convulsive aesthetics'. He also did not notice the emerging danger—which in light of my own experiences of a 'Mass for the Fatherland' is obvious—that this community will turn into a 'holy' union, exalt itself and at the same time lose the chance to think critically and act effectively. The union being established here represents a denial of the 'dialectics of derision and apotheosis' which as a theatrical approach is aimed against this sort of 'sacred community'. After all, this is the point of *Kordian* and later, the point of *The Constant Prince* and *Apocalypsis*. In rational, earthy, historical categories the hero fails. And there are no supernatural interventions that justify his 'victory beyond the grave'. Real solidarity with such a hero means that even when he becomes laughable, rejected, pitiful and powerless, one remains faithful to the attitude he embodied. Casting audiences as Kordian's co-actors was meant to encourage this very experience, to make them a laughing-stock as insane folks, and eventually save them from their otherwise imminent fate of becoming allied with the Doctor. Meanwhile, Kwiatkowski's report indicates a very different sort of experience paradoxically rooted in the reality of theatre, and so, also rooted in the level of the performance that was always so important for Grotowski. The spectators felt they were a part of the event that— thanks to its experimental and seemingly special, 'exclusive' character, and right in line with its creators' comments—was recognized as set firmly against compromise, vulgarity and philistinism. Invited to become its participants and co-creators, the audiences might feel to be on the same level as the actors and the director, and consider themselves nonconformists who use the theatre as an act of resistance or critical commentary towards 'external' sociopolitical realities. This is a well-known mechanism working in political theatre even today: hard attacks against defined phenomena or groups almost instantly leads to the formation of cliquish, 'elite' groups of 'initiated ones' that elevate the status of their members by separating themselves from 'profane crowds'. The guilty and diseased are always 'them', while 'we' are those who recognize and expose this disease, thus having right to feel superior.

This attitude is certainly far from honest and sincere, and is far afield from the shock of critical self-recognition. It works in an exact opposite way blocking such self-analysis. Grotowski probably understood this, and that is why in the interview quoted above he said that the experience of *Kordian* was not authentic, the 'action' involved was not transgressed. It did not 'open into life, the unexpected in life'. The audience played out the very version of themselves in which they felt most comfortable in the given situation. As a result of the work on this performative mechanism, the assumed 'dialectic' slipped into a staged solidarity with the hero set against the world while remaining isolated or alienated from that very world. A unique and risky situation became comprehensible and safe.

In his interview with *TDR*, Grotowski contended that he solved the problem of his audiences artificially enacting their given role in his *Tragical History of Doctor Faustus* by creating a situation that allowed audiences to retain their status while simultaneously placing them within the unfolding structure of the performance. I agree. But perhaps this solution also avoided the problem Grotowski tried to tackle in *Kordian* and earlier in *Forefathers' Eve*, namely the problem of the ineffectiveness of theatre as a mechanism of profanation. Grotowski's 'grand' aim was to prepare structured experiences that can replace religious rituals as a means for challenging death and the sense of the absurd with which death is associated. The audience sliding into a unique, conciliatory experience that simultaneously exalted the actor-martyr—soon to be referred to as 'holy'—meant that in reality the performance created something that simply resembled rituals, and thus remained mere simulacra. It had a certain power but it still did not bring lasting consequences for people's lives. If we use terms coined by Richard Schechner (1981: 83–113; later used by Auslander 2003: 263–90) we could say that that these experiences were 'transportations' not 'transformations'. This seems paradoxical because according to Schechner transformations—the permanent change of status that is most often the result of initiation—are enacted by specialists who perform serial transportations, repeatedly experiencing strengthening and renewal. If we assume that Grotowski in his later achievements managed to create a performance of actors' transformation—the 'total act', Action—then in relation to audiences—or 'witnesses' as he preferred to call them—at best he managed to create a performance of transportation mediated by observed transformation. In effect his attainments are subjected to such criticisms as were levied by Grzegorz Niziołek who wrote about the 'kitsch effect', and put forward the thesis that the impact of the most important performances by Grotowski and Konrad Swinarski stripped Polish theatre of critical tools,[24] 'disabled' and 'drugged' it. Niziołek accused Grotowski of

> creating a realm of exaltation related to the experience of myth-ical totality, combined into one whole historical visions and religious ideas. […]
>
> After years of post–Second World War revisions, analytical criticism and sneering provocations in later performances by Grotowski and Swinarski the community and religious myths not only returned in a tragic aura of indefatigability but—more importantly—theatre served them also as a medium for incar-nating, actualizing and ritualizing, and at the same time opened a perspective of a new beginning, hence the perspective of good news.
> (Niziołek 2012: 130–31)

It is hard to disagree with this perspective on the 'illusion of salvation'—something at least some of the audiences received from watching Grotowski's performances. I am not sure if the case of *Apocalypsis cum figuris* fully belongs to the mechanisms described by Niziołek, especially in the local Polish context where its impact was a lot more complex. And yet an application of this analysis to *The Constant Prince* seems to me particularly accurate. What is more pressing here is that it also applies

---

24 Konrad Swinarski (1929–1975), one of the most important Polish directors of the second part of twentieth century. He studied art and theatre before becoming one of the assistants of Bertold Brecht at the Berliner Ensamble (1955–57). As the director he worked both in Poland and Germany (he successfully directed the world premiere of Peter Weiss' *Marat/Sade*, 1964). He was especially acclaimed for his innovative and provocative stagings of Shakespeare and Polish romantic drama. For more information, see: https://rebrand.ly/bphe9r9

to the Opole *Kordian* where the 'kitsch effect' manifested itself fully for the first time and nullified the performance's intended profanation. Although Grotowski recognized its symptoms, he did not mitigate the strength with which it functioned, and thus it eventually meant that instead of a dialectical and singular experience that might have become a 'truth-procedure'[25] he created a series of illusions of salvation. He would come to abandon them soon enough, and he aptly noted their ineffectiveness just as he recognized the ineffectiveness of other performative mechanisms within *Kordian*.

In spite of all the critical comments I quote above—and have formulated myself—I am still very much opposed to completely negating the effects of Grotowski's practice. Even if he holds a share of responsibility for the 'drugging' of Polish theatre, even if he was well aware of how his performances worked along the lines of visibility and invisibility by manipulating the audience's perceptions, and even if from today's perspective he may be accused of many things—including an unjustified sense of missionary zeal and confidence—he still is 'unique'[26] in his relentless, 'mad' refusal to get bogged down in discoveries, definitions, positions and ideologies. He also refuses to give in to the comforts of unstoppable 'critical' thinking that never arrives at any 'positive' programme.

In Paris just a few years after the premiere of *Kordian* Grotowski, who was by then a world-famous artist, explained his basic attitude by way of a negative example, the well-known history of Percival who did not ask questions. In his comments on the myth, he surprisingly made reference to *Kordian*.

> I think that when we ask key questions, or even just the one key question, because in fact there seems to be just the one, it is easy to end like this, that we will be seen as crazy, just as happened to Kordian in our performance. And maybe we really

---

25 One of the crucial terms of Alain Badiou's philosophy of Event (2005).

26 'Grotowski is unique', the very first words of Peter's Brook preface to *Towards a Poor Theatre* (see Grotowski 1968a: 11).

will become crazy as Kordian did in spite of all his sublimity. But not posing questions, which is what the Doctor does in *Kordian*, step by step our lives will be transformed, to follow certain lines, a quality totally different than the one we desired, and we will be full of suffering, sad, and deeply alone. This is why I think we should not repeat Percival's mistake. (Grotowski 2012: 372–73)

Grotowski may be accused of many things. But he did not make the same mistake as Percival.

Dariusz Kosiński

CHAPTER SEVEN

Our Acropolis

Acropolis after Stanisław Wyspiański

On 1 March 1962, the Theatre of 13 Rows changed its name and became the Laboratory Theatre of 13 Rows. That very year, on 10 October, the newly named Laboratory Theatre premiered *Acropolis*. This performance based on the work of Stanisław Wyspiański is now part of the canon of the most important performances of twentieth-century theatre. Previously, the Theatre of 13 Rows presented their productions only in Poland, their international presence resulting entirely from reports made by 13 Rows artists, critics and historical accounts. However, as the Laboratory Theatre of 13 Rows, they staged *Acropolis* outside of Poland in great cultural centres—Amsterdam, Brussels, Paris, New York. Internationals witnessed, described and commented on the performance. The performance's place in the Western canon, the multivalent history of its reception and inter-pretation and the value and meaning critics, historians and theorists ascribe to it all demand a special effort to cut through all this content and escape what is already 'well-known'. To further complicate the critical interpretation of *Acropolis*, it can be seen on film officially accepted by Grotowski.[1] Not only did Grotowski himself 'accept' the film version as valid, *but* he also carefully controlled the edition of the film. Therefore, writing about *Acropolis* means entering a completely different archive than that of the 13 Rows' previous productions.

---

1 *Acropolis* was filmed between 27 October and 2 November 1968 in England for Public Broadcast Laboratory from New York. The film was directed for TV by James McTaggart and produced by Lewis Freedman. It was aired in 1969 and in 1980s published also on VHS tape. Because of copyright problems it was not officially published later but the copy of VHS version can be seen today on YouTube.

That is why—departing from my approach to previous chapters—I will not present a detailed description of the performance. The reader can see the film version of the performance. Instead, I focus on aspects that are unknown especially to the international reader, and on my own interpretation of the performance in the context of Grotowski's relation to Polish culture and Christianity. In doing so, I assume that the reader has a basic knowledge about the performance.

Acropolis 1962

Acropolis was the first performance Grotowski and his actors consistently presented even after they premiered their next production. Prior to *Acropolis*, his company did have occasion to present subsequent productions alongside one another.[2] However, *Acropolis* was the first that they performed for several years with changes in the cast. This unique situation presents a whole host of problems. The performance presented between 1962 and 1969 is generally considered to be 'the same production'. Of course, one can also find information about subsequent versions with separate premieres reported in documents and calendars.[3] Until now—as far as I know—no one has asked if there were any deeper and more serious differences between the various iterations of *Acropolis*. It is even possible to entertain the possibility that each premiere can be differentiated solely due to changes in the cast, and that Grotowski's differentiation of these versions of *Acropolis* showed how much Grotowski respected his actors' individual contributions. While I do not disagree with this argument per se, I take a closer look at the various premieres of *Acropolis* in their historical contexts in order to question the commonalities and differences across the iterations.

---

2 This was the case with *Orpheus* and *Cain* which were performed together on tour in Katowice, Krakow and Warsaw in 1960; with *Mystery-Bouffe* and *Shakuntala* performed together in Wrocław in 1961; and finally with *Forefathers' Eve* and *Kordian* performed together in 1962 in Kraków and Białystok.

3 The easiest to access is the entry in the online Grotowski Encyclopaedia that I co-created for the Grotowski Institute: https://rebrand.ly/ok18okx

In Grotowski's important lecture, 'Theatre and Ritual', delivered in Paris on 15 October 1968, he listed the Laboratory Theatre's productions in chronological order.

> We did *Acropolis, Doctor Faustus* by Marlowe, *The Constant Prince*, and then another version of *Acropolis*, and finally *Apocalypsis cum figuris*.
> (Grotowski 2012: 364)

Grotowski clearly separated and differentiated two versions of *Acropolis*. He placed the first version before *Faustus* (1963), thus directly after *Kordian*. He placed the second premiere of *Acropolis* after *The Constant Prince* (1965) and before *Apocalypsis cum figuris* (1969). If we remind ourselves what sort of breakthroughs and turns took place in Grotowski's practice and thinking between 1963 and 1968 it then becomes clear that the first *Acropolis* was likely quite different than the one we know from the film and numerous descriptions. I say it was 'likely quite different' not because I believe that Grotowski changed the script to any serious degree, or because I believe he drastically altered the action on stage, but because the actor's skills and potential expanded immensely in the intervening period. By this 'expansion' I mean the actors of the Laboratory Theatre reached a greater level of mastery of voice and body.

Between 1966 and 1969 Grotowski worked out these crucial achievements first with Ryszard Cieślak, and then with other company members. This work culminated in the 'total act', a discovery essential to Grotowski's research. One of the consequences of this discovery was a total change in the way the actors existed, a transformation in the quality of both their human and artistic presence. At this point I do not want to engage in debates about what the total act might have been or what meaning Grotowski may have assigned to it. A discussion of these issues is beyond the scope of this chapter, and I have already written about it elsewhere (see Kosiński 2007: 438–53). The important point is that after the first full appearance of the total act in *The Constant Prince*, Grotowski contrasted all 'derisions' and 'apotheoses'—the dramaturgy of sacrifice and rebellion, and of transgression and transformation—

with circumstances that negate such experiences. Thus, subsequent dialectics had to be fundamentally different. This especially applies to *Acropolis* and its versions. Grotowski indicated that the finale of *Acropolis* was one of two examples of the total act alongside Cieślak's role in *The Constant Prince* (2012: 370). It seems to me that Grotowski could only be referring to the final version of *Acropolis* which was created after the discovery of the total act in *The Constant Prince*. I argue that this version of *Acropolis* is the 'other version' to which Grotowski referred in his Paris lecture. This clearly suggests that the new version differs from the earlier iterations of *Acropolis*. I need to use plural—'earlier iterations'—because before 1965 there were four versions of *Acropolis*. In 'Theatre and Ritual' Grotowski simplified the complex history of the production, which is a good thing because it extracts key differences related to his breakthrough creation of the total act. But it is also wrong because it obscures and dismisses the differences among earlier versions.

Acropolis was staged in public for the first time on 10 October 1962; this date is considered the official premiere. One important aspect of this version of *Acropolis* is that it was the only version in which two actresses participated: Rena Mirecka who performed in all versions of *Acropolis* and Maja Komorowska who was part of the cast only for the 1962 version. In this version, Komorowska performed the roles of Clio, Rachel and Helena. This means that in the 1962 version some of the most famous scenes of the filmed *Acropolis*—which also received the most attention in reviews and reports—were absent. For example, there was no homosexual love scene between Paris and Helen.[4] It is also likely that in subsequent versions there was no wedding scene involving Rachel, and thus no oven pipe that 'replaced' Rachel in that scene. Instead, the first version included a scene of her meeting Jacob.[5]

For the most part, the first version of *Acropolis* remains unknown to us. It likely did not include elements that its creators later emphasized as important. Instead, it contained scenes that no one took the time to

---

4 A male actor performed the role of Helen in later versions of *Acropolis*.

5 This scene was witnessed during rehearsals by the journalist Stefan Bratkowski (1965: 157).

record, and which we therefore cannot fully reconstruct. In fact, all we know about the first version of the performance is that it probably was the most different from those that followed.

The female roles are the most mysterious and unclear aspect of *Acropolis*. We do know that Ewa Lubowiecka took part in the first *Acropolis* rehearsals alongside Mirecka and Komorowska. However, the fact that she 'took part' is not necessarily saying much. In order to uncover her role—and the *Acropolis*-in-progress in which she performed—I will quote the actress at length. Lubowiecka spoke about her experience participating in *Acropolis* in a previously unpublished statement she made during a 1993 meeting with actors of the Laboratory Theatre of 13 Rows.[6]

> [Zbigniew] OSIŃSKI (*to Lubowiecka*): You mentioned that work on *Acropolis* was simply very challenging physically.
>
> LUBOWIECKA: Of course it was. [. . .] Not only physically! Psychologically! Now do imagine sir that there is a love scene between two women in a bath, and I am supposed to be in it—the Clio-Maiden scene in *Acropolis*—and I am supposed to perform this love scene, my God, love . . . Erotic even! Yes! I would dare to say—sexual. And I am supposed to act it with a woman I hate (*laughter*), someone who repulses me physically and if I was a man after twenty five vodkas I would sooner kill her than touch her . . . And I am to be with her in this bath (*laughter from others*) . . . This is one of the more horrific memories in my life! [. . .]
>
> In early 1960s there was no question of getting undressed. Of course, these were the years of mini-skirts and plunging necklines. But this was something completely different, for it was private. But here we have *Acropolis* and Szajna's scenography, so we know what it was like . . .

---

6 The meeting took place on 12 March 1993 in Wrocław at what is now called the Grotowski Institute. At the time of the meeting the institution was known as the Centre for the Study of Jerzy Grotowski's Work and for Cultural and Theatrical Research. The recording from this meeting and its transcription can be found in the GIA.

Besides, his whole work was somehow filtered through Auschwitz and his very personally challenging experiences. And he's designing the costumes. [. . .] I put onto my naked body a patched-up sack, and somehow I get used to it during the rehearsals . . . Because a sack . . . makes sense in the context. So it doesn't matter if it scratched here and there . . . And then all of a sudden during dress rehearsals there comes the decision that such a Beautiful Helen—for that's how I was to be—had to wear something feminine . . . Because I had stopped being a woman . . . I had this beret with an antenna on my head, yellow clogs and that sack . . . and so we had to cut out holes . . . where could those holes be cut? (*laughter*) You could pardon the phrase—on the ass, but who knows—man, woman?—no way of knowing. So on we go. Up front—then the holes have to be cut at the breasts . . . And so do imagine how one feels—I repeat, please try to imagine that now you're laughing and so am I—but at the time this was no laughing matter, when they cut those holes and I knew that I will be running around that hall, rubbing up against people, right? These might be pleasant circumstances *en deux*, but not *en masse* . . . And so it wasn't very nice wearing that, and yet one had to submit . . . Later on, thankfully, Maciej Prus played the Beautiful Helen (*laughter*) . . .

Lubowiecka's story is a clear example of violence within the company, and the authoritarian position of the male director over an actress. Grotowski's destruction of the boundaries of intimacy is relevant to contemporary issues being intensively discussed today within the conceptual framework of the #MeToo movement. It is a serious problem in relation to Grotowski's work, and the whole tradition of the Laboratory Theatre but of course it needs a far more detailed examination and deeper study than I can provide now, so I will leave it aside.

In the context of *Acropolis'* complicated history, Lubowiecka's recollection is revelatory in that it forces us to question the historical assumptions about her 'taking part in rehearsals', and to ask about the shape of the 'first version'. Lubowiecka clearly states that she participated in 'dress rehearsals.' Her report also clearly shows that the costume with cut-out holes for her breasts was truly shocking for her. This allows us to imagine that her decision to leave the company was related to these instances.

Maciej Prus was a young actor who arrived in Opole in September 1962 to work with the Laboratory Theatre. In an interview with Agnieszka Wójtowicz, he reported that when he started work with the company he was immediately included in the cast of *Acropolis* which in his account was already missing Lubowiecka. According to Prus' report he 'joined a ready-made performance', and played in the premiere that was 'set for 14 October 1962' (Prus quoted in Wójtowicz 2004: 241). Prus supplies dates that seem wrong. The first *Acropolis* premiere was on 10 October, and not on the 14th. Furthermore, Osiński reports that the version that featured Prus was first shown on 2 November (1998: 100). And so, it is possible that the former actor of 13 Rows incorrectly recalled how he got the role of the 'beautiful Helen', and that he actually first entered the version of *Acropolis* the 13 Rows staged starting on 2 November.

To put some order to the complicated history of *Acropolis* we have to add one more version of the performance that I call 'version zero'. This first version was rehearsed right up until the final weeks prior to the premiere, and included three actresses—Maja Komorowska, Ewa Lubowiecka and Rena Mirecka. We can assume that Mirecka appeared in this version, as she did in subsequent versions, in the roles of the Maiden, Rebecca and Cassandra. Lubowiecka reports that she played Clio and Helen—roles that were later played by Maciej Prus. The remaining female characters are Rachel and Hecuba who did not appear fully in later versions, and instead were present only as voices or objects. It seems logical that these were the characters rehearsed and performed— albiet briefly—by Komorowska.

If this attribution of roles is correct then 'version zero' included a lesbian love scene that later became a heterosexual rape scene in which a woman perpetrated the rape on a man. Of course, the scene between Paris and Helen would have meant something else entirely with Helen being an attractive, full-bodied woman with her bust on show. Speaking plainly, Helen in 'version zero' would have been depicted as a prisoner turned into a camp prostitute, and the jeers and laughter that accompanied her love dialogues with her 'beloved' would have had a very different tone and meaning than the laughter aimed at the homosexual couple from later versions of the same scene.

Komorowska's presence involved other important differences, most of all in the role of Rachel. Komorowska in the role of Rachel must have had a completely different effect and meaning than later versions in which the actress was replaced by an object. If we are to believe Bratkowski, and assume that Rachel's meeting with Jacob near the well was played as Jacob discovering the lifeless body of his dead beloved, then the wedding scene that followed might have been a scene involving betrothal to a dead woman. After such a wedding Jacob would have awakened in the arms of the camp prostitute performed by Lubowiecka. This sequence of action seems logical, and betrothing an undead would have had more power than Jacob marrying a pipe. Komorowska playing the role of Hecuba would have also given more power and a different meaning to the sequences featuring Priam and Hecuba. In these scenes Priam's wife who lives in the past was present in the flesh and not just as a voice. This scene performed by the couple could be easily seen as analogous to the scene of the ageing lovers from the finale of *Shakuntala*. 'Version zero' as reconstructed here is likely to have existed only in rehearsals. The premiere—the first official *Acropolis*—probably included Mirecka and Komorowska, and not Lubowiecka.

The premiere was thus very different than 'version zero'. However, my characterizing the premiere as 'very different' is not specific, it is indeed a generalized conclusion. Unfortunately, we do not have the necessary information, and therefore cannot specify the premiere's differences or similarities to 'version zero' with certainty. Lubowiecka's unexplained departure shortly before the premiere forced changes to the ready and tested structure of the performance. Someone had to assume her roles quickly. It seems that at first Barbara Barska took this on. Barska can be seen doing so in surviving photographs,[7] but it is almost impossible to date them precisely or to explain her participation in the work, especially because Barska officially left the company on 1 October 1961. Perhaps the former actress of the Theatre of 13 Rows agreed to help her former colleagues after Lubowiecka's sudden departure, and as a result she rehearsed Lubowiecka's part for some time. This is currently beyond our ability to confirm. But because there is no mention of Barska in the cast listing from the premiere of *Acropolis* it seems likely that she only took part in some rehearsals.

The first official version featuring Mirecka and Komorowska—the latter performing Clio, Rachel, Helen and Hecuba—was shown on 10 October 1962. After a mere six presentations the pregnant Komorowska had to stop working, and thus the performance had to be substantially re-organized and re-structured. This shift resulted in the second version of *Acropolis* which premiered on 2 November 1962[8] when the play was 'revived' as the newspaper *Trybuna Opolska* wrote (see Osiński 1998: 100). This version is the most well documented version from the early 1960s probably because it was presented both in Opole and in guest performances in various Polish cities including Wrocław, Poznan, Katowice, Łódź and Krakow between the autumn of 1962 and the spring of 1963. Most Polish reports on *Acropolis* refer to this version, including the comment Flaszen published in the prestigious Polish theatre journal *Pamiętnik Teatralny* [The theatre memoir]. Additionally, fragments from this version were recorded for a radio programme *Acropolis of Our Times* (*Akropolis naszych czasów*) produced by Polish Radio in Opole and likely aired in late autumn or early winter of 1962.

---

7 See the first three photos from the 'Akropolis' gallery accessible online: https://rebrand.ly/jrvlkOy

8 Most sources cite 24 November as the date of the first presentation of the second version of *Acropolis* but I accept Osiński's argument from 1998 not only because he was a trustful researcher and an expert in Grotowski but also because it seems unlikely that the pregnant Komorowska would tour with the company in November-especially since she officially left the Theatre on 1 November 1962.

After a series of presentations of this version in Opole and on tour in November and December of 1962, the company began working on *The Tragical History of Doctor Faustus* which premiered on 23 March 1963. The last presentations of the second version of *Acropolis* took place in May 1963 in Kraków alongside *Faustus*. Up until this point the company's work on *Acropolis* had progressed like others had in the past, and it must have seemed like the run of *Acropolis* had reached its end. But suddenly the Laboratory Theatre broke their own pattern, and after a year's break they suddenly returned to *Acropolis*, premiering its third version on 10 June 1964. In the intervening year, Cynkutis and Maciej had both left the company, albeit for different reasons, and Cynkutis only left temporarily. Mieczysław Janowski and Andrzej 'Gaston' Kulig took on Cynkutis' and Prus' roles respectively. The Laboratory Theatre not only premiered their third *Acropolis* after the premiere of *Faustus*, they also premiered it almost two months after their first performances of *Hamlet Study*.[9] The second revival of *Acropolis* would not have raised any eyebrows if *Acropolis* had simply remained an ongoing fixture of the Laboratory Theatre's repertoire as did *The Constant Prince* and *Apocalypsis cum figuris*. But that is not what happened. The Laboratory Theatre had not presented *Acropolis* since the late spring of 1963. A year later they suddenly revived the production. Why?

Thanks to detailed research by Osiński the answer is simple. A Commission formed by the Theatre Department at the Ministry of Culture visited the increasingly struggling Laboratory Theatre on 7 and 8 April 1964. In their report to the Ministry, they proposed a revival of *Acropolis* (Osiński 1998: 154). Following this proposition Grotowski— who probably discussed the idea with the members of the Commission, and maybe even suggested it—wrote a letter dated 21 May 1964 to the Department of Culture at the Presidium of the Regional National Council in Opole.

---

9 *Hamlet Study* premiered 17 March 1964. See Chapter 9 for Wanda Świątkowska's treatment of *Hamlet Study*.

In line with the suggestion made by the Ministerial Commission in May of 1964 we are working on restoring *Acropolis* after Wyspiański, which the Commission considers a decisive performance—shall we say—for export.
(Grotowski quoted in Osiński 1998: 154)

This letter clearly posits that the Commission's recommendation was the reason the Laboratory Theatre began working on an *Acropolis* revival. We would also do well to keep in mind that this was a time of increasing efforts to raise international awareness of the Laboratory Theatre. Eugenio Barba played a key role in these efforts. Not long before the premiere of the third version of *Acropolis*, Barba wrote and published a brochure titled *Le Théâtre-Laboratoire '13 Rzędów' d'Opole ou le théâtre comme auto—penetration collective* [The Laboratory Theatre of 13 Rows in Opole, or the theatre as a collective self-penetration]. The pamphlet contained an important text on *Acropolis* written by Flaszen that presented the first explicit formulation of what would soon be called 'poor theatre' (see below). *Acropolis* was particularly well suited to garner international recognition in the sense that the performance combined universally recognizable myths with theatrical re-enactments of concentration camp trauma.

The Laboratory Theatre presented the third version of *Acropolis* in Opole, and three times as guest performances in Wrocław—to increasingly disengaged audiences. Osiński concluded that two performances (14 June 1964 and 16 September 1964) were cancelled due to poor ticket sales (1998: 160). And yet Grotowski continued to perform *Acropolis* as if he felt that he had to perfect it in hopes that one day it would become a triumph.

In the beginning of 1965, in search of better working conditions the Laboratory Theatre moved from provincial Opole to Wrocław where it worked until its official dissolution in 1984. To inaugurate the company's move to their new space the Laboratory Theatre performed *Acropolis* in Wrocław on 16 January 1965. This presentation was the premiere of the fourth version of *Acropolis*. The fact that they billed this performance as the premiere of a new version seems to prove that the differences between versions was not limited to changes in the cast—and there was no change to the cast from the third to this fourth version. The fourth version was most probably novel because the performance had been moved to a different space which would have resulted in changes to the staging. Yet we know very little about this new version because it was relatively rarely performed. In June 1965 Molik left the company for some time for personal reasons, and the Laboratory Theatre stopped performing this version at that time.

Nearly two years later Molik returned, and half way through April 1967 the Laboratory began to work on *Acropolis* again. Their efforts resulted in the fifth and the best-known version. This version featured Zygmunt Molik (Jacob, Harpist), Rena Mirecka (Rebecca, Cassandra), Antoni Jahołkowski (Isaac, Guard), Ryszard Cieślak (Esau, Hector), Zbigniew Cynkutis (Laban, Paris), Stanisław Scierski (Clio, Helen) and Andrzej Paluchiewicz (who voiced Rachel and Hecuba). The Laboratory Theatre presented this version for the first time on 17 May 1967 in Wrocław, and then showed it abroad in Holland and Belgium (June 1967), Edinburgh (22–30 August 1968), Paris (24 September–26 October 1968), Aix-en-Provence (4–26 November 1968), and finally New York (4–15 November 1969). This is this version that was filmed between 27 October 1968 and 2 November 1968 in a studio near London for US television.

My abbreviated narration of the complicated history of *Acropolis* and its various versions shows that in the case of this performance it is very hard to talk about a singular 'theatre work'. Differences between the versions cannot be reduced to changes to the cast, to the script, or to the course of action, even if such changes were important. Perhaps the most important differences for us to keep in mind were the radical changes in the context and function of the different *Acropolis* versions created between 1962 and 1967. I argue that it is important to differentiate between early versions of *Acropolis* and later versions developed in connection with work on the 'total act' between 1964 and 1965. But I will begin by focusing on the *Acropolis* that premiered on 2 November 1962, the best known of the earlier versions.

Here in Our Auschwitz

Of the many questions one might ask about *Acropolis* perhaps the simplest and most naive is related to its source text. How did Grotowski conceive the idea to tackle a poetic drama written by Wyspiański in 1903–4? As opposed to *Forefathers' Eve* and *Kordian*, Wyspiański's *Acropolis* did not—nor does it now—form part of the core, canonical Polish repertoire. Although Wyspiański's *Acropolis* is highly respected and valued among academics, it is not a play that first comes to mind when one thinks of a 'great work', and it certainly does not belong to those works that every self-respecting Polish theatre director should stage at least once in their life. So why did Grotowski take on this particular drama, and why did he choose to do so at the particular time that he did?

Jerzy Falkowski asked Grotowski this very question during a conversation that Falkowski included in the first part of the radio programme *Acropolis of Our Times* (*Akropolis naszych czasów*).

FALKOWSKI: Why out of all the dramas by Wyspiański did you choose *Acropolis*?

GROTOWSKI: This particular play is set in Acropolis but also at the same time at Wawel Castle, by which we mean the Polish equivalent of the original Acropolis, where the whole of our European tradition, all the narrative threads, both biblical histories as well as those from days of antiquity somehow meet. The play is set upon a 'cemetery of tribes'. And this is where we come to cast judgement upon the values of European culture, to judge that which is viable and that which is tragic within it. It seemed to us that *Acropolis* was a wonderful excuse, or even something more than an excuse—material—to reconstruct, to organize a new judgement on values, this time from the point of view of our most recent historical experiences.
(Falkowski 1962b)

According to this response it was not the text that caught the director's attention, but more so the confluence of important ideas that the text enabled him to put into action.. The key factor leading Grotowski to work on Wyspiański's drama was the possibility of setting the myths that represent European civilization in a concentration camp. He was not interested in juxtaposing the relation between Wawel and the Acropolis—the relation between the national and the universal. Instead, he was concerned with exploring Acropolis-Auschwitz as a place of 'final judgement' for European civilizations.

In commentaries on the performance published thus far, authors often repeat the notion that this 'judgement' involved stripping the values of European civilization of all their beauty and sublimity.. Another equally important but less emphasized factor—one that was important to the creators of *Acropolis*—was the removal of strict oppositions between victims and executioners. Flaszen wrote that

> there is a sick confidentiality, an ambiguous kinship between the role of executioner and the role of victim. In this picture, there is no one who can be associated with the executioner, with the spontaneous power that is separated from the community of prisoners. [. . .].
>
> The prisoners are convicts and at the same time—as if fulfilling a higher unwritten law—their own oppressors.
> (Flaszen 2010[1964]: 89, 90)

Many critics and commentators parroted the notion that in *Acropolis* the Laboratory Theatre represented the experience of life in a concentration camp. But this could not have been the case because of the simple and important fact that the performance did not include any guards or executioners. Many years later Grotowski addressed the tendency to represent concentration camp life using the opposition between the prisoners and oppressors.

> It would have been quite easy to create a rather moving story about Auschwitz with various contrasts. Of course the executioners were diabolical, the victims saints who happened to be dehumanized at times. In general the prisoners at Auschwitz were people surviving terrible oppressions. Their ranks included

heroes and saints, but when we—in 1962—worked on our version of *Acropolis*, literature and film had already shown that side of it, and at times even made it more easy on the eye, reducing the dehumanizing realities. Meanwhile we wanted to highlight the automatism of the historical setting. We wanted to show how the prisoners were building crematoriums—for themselves.

(Grotowski 2012: 655)

'Automatism of the historical setting' is an evocative phrase, but it also concealed questions and problems that when put another way show the terrible implications of this idea. Because in the Laboratory's *Acropolis* there are no perpetrators—the prisoners are building crematoriums 'for themselves'—would we not be justified in levelling accusations of historical revisionism, or even 'Holocaust denial' at Grotowski and his company? Highlighting the absurdity of this apparent Catch-22 may help lift *Acropolis* out of the perhaps paralysing reading of the creators' intentions. This means reappraising the well-worn idea that the Laboratory Theatre's *Acropolis* is an attempt to stage the realities of concentration camp life in a theatrical setting. With due respect to those who describe Grotowski's *Acropolis* as an attempt to do just that, this was not the goal of the performance. Grotowski created *Acropolis* to confront us directly with the accusation that Auschwitz represents the culmination of what we call 'our civilizations'—not their corruption but their final conclusion.

Grotowski supplied retrospective comments on the motivations that led him to stage *Acropolis* in an interview with Margaret Croyden in January 1969.

Acropolis is based on a classical Polish play. [. . .] It dramatized the past from the perspective of heroic values. Since the Second World War, we have noticed that the great, lofty values of Western civilizations remain abstract. We mouth heroic values, but real life proves to be different. We must confront the great values of the past and ask some questions. Do these values remain abstract or do they really exist for us? To discover the answer, we must confront the most bitter and ultimate trial: Auschwitz. Auschwitz is the darkest reality of our contemporary history. Auschwitz is the trial for humankind. What has been our goal in this play? To put two opposite views on the stage, to create brutal confrontation in order to see if these past dreams are concrete and strong, or only abstractions. In other words we wanted to confront our ancestral experiences in a situation when all values were destroyed, and this is why we chose Auschwitz. What was the reaction to the play? The audience watches the confrontation; they observe the dreams of the prisoners, and the dreams of the great people of our past. Past dreams appear annihilated by the reality of Auschwitz. But in another sense the dreams survive, because they give weight and depth to the prisoners, for they feel themselves part of the collective past. Man in that situation is being tested, pitted against past ideals. Does he survive the test? The audience will decide.

> [. . .] It is impossible to create if we destroy the bridge to the past. Myth or archetype links us to the past. The past is a source of our creative efforts. To be sure, our life is individual and personal; we live in the present, but we are the result of something larger—a greater history then our own personal one—an interindividual and interpersonal history. When we produced *Acropolis* I was forced to confront my own roots and, at first, I discovered that I wanted to crush the mirror of the past. I knew it was impossible—my image was reflected in that mirror. Consciously I said 'yes' to the past and realized that the past was not annihilated, but reinforced.
>
> (Grotowski 1969b; quoted in Schechner and Wolford 1997: 84–85)

Although we know a lot about the terrors of concentration camps, realize what they represent and what consequences they brought, for us they yet remain historical, something distant and closed in the past. So our 'knowledge' of them is only historical, theoretical and therefore also somehow theatrical—it is the knowledge of those who watch from a safe distance—the knowledge of spectators. To know in another way, to find a new vantage, to become a witness we need to gain some direct experience.[10] How? By taking a day trip from Krakow to Auschwitz, as have millions of tourists? Maybe. But no trip, no visit to a museum, no film, no reading and no performance—no work of art will get us any closer to the knowledge of a 'witness' until we acknowledge that concentration camps were the fruits of the same culture of which we are a part. And this is far from easy. It is much easier to claim that Auschwitz was a product of historical circumstances—that it happened 'once upon a time' and that it will happen 'never again'. The Shoah is exceptional, and that thankfully we will not need to confront what it represents; we are thus practically permitted to forget it.

Grotowski decidedly rejects these sorts of avoidance strategies and engages in a radically acute confrontation—not with the camp as a historical construct produced by a specific ideology and specific individuals, but rather with the camp's mechanisms that led to an extreme reduction of human beings and their needs to the level of a basic and irreducible struggle for survival. Grotowski saw this mechanism as originating in the culture and civilization of which he himself was a product. Out of a necessity to ask about Auschwitz he asked about his own self, about that which created him, and about what—in a simplified sense—can be called a tradition of the past. Cultural models, sets of values, patterns of behaviour and ways of ordering life accepted so deeply, and for so long that they became treated as 'natural'. He said 'yes' to his past, and thus accepted both the image of mankind as dehumanized prisoners and a vision of the past as a dream played out by what remains. This acceptance led Grotowski to what he described as a strengthened image of the past— one that surprised him. For Grotowski the sheltering construct of culture—when confronted with the reality of Auschwitz—turned out to be

---

10 In Polish, the two words 'witness' and 'experience' are close to one another. They belong to the same group—*świadek* (a witness) is someone who experienced *doświadczenie* (an experience) meaning literally 'something to witness about'. I am sure that when Grotowski speaks about the difference between the spectator and the witness (2012: 359–360), he has the Polish words in mind. I analyse these nuances further in the next chapter.

effective. In other words, the 'Western civilizations' that he referred to in the interview cited above have survived this extreme test of concentration camps. They survived it in a strict sense—by rediscovering the sorts of values that retain their power even when confronted with the realities of Auschwitz. This discovery is not the result of some 'objective' process. By saying 'yes' to his own—and our own pasts—Grotowski made a personal decision that was key to his creative and personal journey through life. He did so on the 'cemetery of tribes' as a way to confront the memory and the remnants of humanity that he summoned to the stage for him—and for others—to experience.

What Grotowski and the Laboratory Theatre achieved in Opole in the autumn of 1962 represented the next step of a logical and artistic continuum after they had explored the suffering and self-sacrifices of Konrad and Kordian subjecting them to dialectical tests. If the *Passion of Christ* may be seen as a model for previous performances, then according to the logic of the Gospels' narrative—which serves as the foundation of Polish, and therefore Grotowski's home culture—the next step is the Resurrection. And Wyspiański's *Acropolis* is one of only a few Polish dramas that emerged from Romanticism that did not centre on martyrdom and suffering but rather on resurrection. And if Grotowski wanted to run a complete dialectical test of the drama of Jesus as a model for human actions—and I am convinced that by this time this is what he really wanted to do, and not only as a model for Polish theatre or culture—then the most difficult challenge in that process was to not perform another *Passion*, but rather to confront the concept of Resurrection. Apart from *Acropolis*, the Polish theatre repertoire offers similar possibilities in late 'mystical' texts by Juliusz Słowacki. This is especially true of *The Constant Prince* and *Samuel Zborowski*,[11] and Grotowski—again,

---

11 Grotowski planned to stage *Samuel Zborowski* after *The Constant Prince*. He created the script for the performance, Gurawski proposed some space designs and the company started the rehearsals. But in the course of the work Grotowski realized that he is repeating himself and stopped the work on Słowacki's drama. But some improvisations that the actors did inspired him to develop another creative process that led finally to *Apocalypsis cum figuris*. Grotowski told this story in his speech *On the Genesis of 'Apocalypsis'*, published many years later (Grotowski 2008[1969]).

logically and consequently—went on to create performances based on both these works. Among these performances, only *Acropolis* lacks a leading 'Christ-like' protagonist thus allowing Grotowski to run his most radical and simultaneously his most vividly political test. He sought the possibility of saving the collective rather than an isolated individual—a 'sage', a 'saint' or . . . 'Performer'. *Acropolis* helped him pursue this possibility, and provided a firm foundation from which he sought to attain it.

In this struggle Grotowski remained deeply faithful to Wyspiański. Professor Ewa Miodońska-Brookes—my wonderful teacher in Kraków and the most insightful analyst of Wyspiański's work—wrote that the resurrection at the heart of Wyspiański's *Acropolis* should be understood not as an eschatological event foretold by Christianity, and even less so as an allegory representing Poland regaining its independence. Rather, she argues that it should be understood in relation to a basic human duty, an ethical and existential obligation to

> the eternal, painful effort of breaking free of that which one is, in order to strive towards that which one can be, that which one should be, which one desires to be; this rejection of the self in that which is accidental and temporary, in order to become more oneself in that which is essential, which emerges out of the discovery of a calling.
> (Miodońska-Brookes 1980: 64)

Miodońska-Brookes identifies an obligation to the self-determination of individuals and communities as 'the most common and natural law of self-aware beings'. Meanwhile, in Wyspiański's *Acropolis*, this law is revealed 'not merely in categories of privilege, but also duty, obligation and calling', and it also refers to 'all that exists on the level of human individuals, the level of nations and the level of human civilizations' (Miodońska-Brookes 1980: 125). This sort of analysis allows the researcher to formulate a key interpretation of the whole drama.

> The purpose of constant activity, alert readiness, inner strength always being at the ready, creative energy, and the postulate of eternally recreating the self in relation both to God and the

world, demands here that the human being or humanity will judge itself permanently, will perceive its own existence mainly in terms of responsibility for the self and before the self, and will treat human conscience as a sign of an eschatology eternally present.

(Miodońska-Brookes 1985: *xlix–l*)

The formula Miodońska-Brookes reads into Wyspiański's drama means that resurrection is not an eschatological fact happening in some predicted future, but rather a duty of each individual and collective regardless of their relations with God. Her interpretation perfectly complements Grotowski's thought and practice—the drive to live so as not to 'rot with the body' as he used to name it using the expression by Master Eckhart. Grotowski also strove towards a salvation that he believed to be possible 'here on earth', a declaration of faith that he expressed with clearly 'glowing eyes', shocking Zbigniew Raszewski (Raszewski 1997: 50). I often mention that the fundamental moral imperative to which Grotowski remained true his entire life involved a relentless drive to fulfil one's potential—to strive to become a human being 'who lives' (Grotowski 2012: 957).[12] This imperative seems to me to be very close to that which Miodońska-Brookes read so well into Wyspiański's *Acropolis*. And it is in reference to this invocation and relevant conceptions of resurrection and salvation—as a challenge and not as a reward—that Grotowski remained most deeply faithful to Wyspiański.

This real, deep loyalty led him to suggest that this demand, and the very real possibility of triumphing over death and achieving salvation right here on earth had to be questioned in the most painful and radical way. Grotowski did so by confronting the crematoriums of Auschwitz.

---

12 This phrase appears exclusively in the first version of the text '*Holiday*' published in English in 1973. Grotowski removed the entire final section of the original in subsequent English versions. Grotowski later composed a single text from three separate texts—including '*Holiday*' and published it in the *Grotowski Sourcebook* (Schechner and Wolford 1997: 215–25). In this version the sentence to which I refer here vanished. I quote it here because it seems to me to be a crucial phrase for understanding Grotowski's way of thinking. In the English translation it says 'Man as he is, whole, so that he would not hide himself; and who lives and that means—not everyone' (1973: 119; emphasis in the original).

He transplanted Wyspiański's text, a text that writes moral obligations as matters of faith into his understanding of resurrection, to Auschwitz. The characters presented in 'our *Acropolis*' were confronted with the most painful 'dialectics'—an apotheosis of ethical challenges and a cruel derision of the Shoah's mass extinction.

This is the essence of the trial and judgement to which Grotowski subjected 'civilized values'. He especially called Christianity and its fundamental doctrine of Resurrection to task. If 'in Auschwitz the saviour never came for those who were killed', then it is in Auschwitz that one who was raised in the context of Christian eschatological hope must ask questions about the possibility of salvation, and the chance for resurrection (Grotowski 1969b; quoted in Schechner and Wolford 1997: 50). These questions were (and still are) a radical challenge to Christianity, and its ideals of love, mercy and salvation through sacrifice. And yet Christianity—especially Catholicism, and especially in Poland—very rarely dares look into this void, being afraid of what it might find. Grotowski sought 'secular' holiness in his own cultural context which was Christian, Catholic and Polish. He had to summon the courage to peer into the void and seek truth there.

Reading out the Scenes from *Acropolis*

One of the most frequently falsified aspects of the work of Grotowski's theatre—especially by international commentators—is the 13 Rows' attitude towards poetry and literature. There is an almost axiomatic belief that Grotowski and his actors did not care for the words they uttered on stage; that they created a 'physical theatre' hunting after 'inner impulses' without paying attention to diction. It is foreign reviewers and commentators who are responsible for this global stereotype. They focused on other aspects of the performance perhaps because they did not know Polish, and so, lacked an understanding of Polish texts. Some of them expressed sadness that they could not understand what the actors said while others were irritated, their irritation leading them to reject the performances. Still others—among them Grotowski's greatest admirers and supporters—thought that they did not *need* to understand the words because they were versed in the 'universal language of theatre', a language they worshipped. According to a convincing analysis by Magda Romanska, this mechanism was imbued with postcolonial attitudes that were especially hard at work in the case of *Acropolis* (2012). This resulted in a widespread, international stereotype that in order to understand the meaning of this performance any sort of familiarity with the text— be it the Wyspiański original or Grotowski's script—did not matter. The concept of 'physical theatre' and the rule of aesthetic distance, or even isolation, between the actors and viewers seemed to perfectly accommodate the foreigners' ignorance of Polish. This perfect storm led to an illusory justification of foreigners' incomprehension of the composition of the whole, and thus Wyspiański's great poetry became little more than musical noise, an exotic or ancient song from the edges of the world, 'magical' and 'ritualistic', without literary meaning.

It is not clear to what extent Grotowski consciously intended for his works to be received this way by foreigners keen on seeing his 'export' performances. Yet perhaps their lack of understanding worked to Grotowski's benefit; somehow he made it part of his strategy, if not his artistic approach then at least a helpful marketing tactic. Regardless, this lack of caring what the characters said on stage led to a general disregard for Polish drama. This disregard was soon accepted both abroad and in Poland as something obvious. It is a clear example of cultural colonialism operating in the very heart of 'liberal', mostly French and American theatre culture. As a result, we see an increasingly one-sided perception of the Laboratory Theatre and its founder as 'word cannibals', exemplars of 'physical theatre'—whatever that might be. Great Polish drama was simultaneously sidelined and unfairly marginalized. I mention this with great sadness not as a 'local patriot' but rather as a theatre enthusiast lamenting that the majority of my Western peers immerse themselves in Shakespeare and Beckett until they are sick to their stomachs, while neglecting Wyspiański and Słowacki.

This whole situation was disastrous for *Acropolis*. Its powerful text and the ways it deployed language were of crucial importance to the Opole *Acropolis*. It seems all too clear that if the most important aspect of the performance was to test the myths of European culture in a concentration camp, then these myths—which exist powerfully in Wyspiański's carefully chosen and purposeful, poetic words—would have to appear in ways that allowed the audience to receive them through the text. And this need for accessibility in the performance could not be substituted even by the most suggestive commentary from Flaszen because if the audience did not understand what the actors were saying, it would not fully engage the European myths that the Laboratory Theatre confronted with the horrors of Auschwitz.

An interesting aspect of early versions presented in Poland, not meant for export, was that Grotowski was very careful to ensure that the text was audible. Polish reviewers frequently noted that the Laboratory Theatre of 13 Rows worked very hard on the pronunciation and recitation of the text. Zbigniew Raszewski—a great theatre historian—was particularly demanding regarding language, diction and clarity. In his review of the 1962 *Acropolis* he wrote that 'it has been a long, long while since Wyspiański's words have been uttered with such expression [. . .]. Wyspiański's poem, a reef that so many "standard" productions came crashing against, is unreservedly a discovery within this theatre' (Raszewski 2006[1964]: 233). When listening to fragments of the performance recorded for radio, I had the immediate impression that the actors of the 13 Rows recited Wyspiański's words with particular care, even more so than in *Kordian* which the company also recorded for the radio. This seems to confirm the importance and gravitas of Wyspiański's text in a performance that was billed as being based on Grotowski's script, and composed 'to the words'[13] of the poet.

---

13 The literal translation of the Polish on the poster of the production. This phrase resembles the one used for the Opole *Forefathers' Eve* which reads 'the words by Adam Mickiewicz'. The *Acropolis* poster goes a step further indicating not only that Grotowski used the text by Wyspiański but that he built his own creation as something added to Wyspiański's work—or even as an autonomous work accompanying the words of the poet.

But this respect towards the text did not solve the problem. Quite the opposite! The drama by Wyspiański is difficult, complex and challenging. It lacks a linear narrative and, in fact, has no human characters. All the actions are carried out by animated works of art from the Wawel cathedral in Kraków—the most important Polish shrine, a place where kings were crowned and buried. The drama is made up of four relatively autonomous parts. In the first part, monuments placed upon the graves of great Poles from bygone times come to life, and go looking for love on the 'magical' night of Easter Sunday Eve.[14] Part two, inspired by the tapestries hanging up inside the Wawel cathedral, featured scenes from the siege of Troy the night before the decisive fight between Hector and Achilles. The images on those tapestries also provided the narrative for part three which tells the biblical story of Jacob, detailing his treacherous theft of fatherly blessings from his elder brother Esau to their final reconciliation. Finally, the fourth part taking place just before dawn is almost entirely comprised of the great hymn sung by the harpist David, accompanied by the Chorus, announcing the coming Resurrection. The drama culminates and ends with a vision of Apollo-Christ who rides into the cathedral on a golden chariot smashing the cathedral's roof and crushing its golden coffin containing the remains of St Stanisłav—Poland's Patron Saint—whose body lies in the heart of the cathedral. The multilayered meanings of Wyspiański's drama, its complex symbolism, and its intricate structure are among the reasons it was rarely staged.

Grotowski made many cuts and changes to the text.[15] Some were subtle, apparently insignificant, and yet they profoundly altered the meaning of the story. For instance, Grotowski removed most of the original drama's references to Wawel Castle and references to God and his power. The scale and impact of some changes were obvious. One changed the order of the acts. Grotowski put the 'ancient history of Jacob'—

---

14 This represents a sort of blasphemous take on the Polish tradition of Saint John's Eve. Prior to Christianity's 'sanitizing' effect, Poles celebrated the night before 24 June as a night of sexual orgies, bathing, bonfires and magic connected with a fertility cult. It was generally led by women (see Kosiński 2019: 63, 65).

15 For the detailed report, analysis and interpretation of the changes see Masternak 2013.

Wyspiański's Act 3—before the Trojan sequence—Wyspiański's Act 2. This change went largely unnoticed—partly because the creators of the performance did not draw attention to it. But according to Agnieszka Masternak (2013) who refers to Jan Błoński's (2007) interpretation of Wyspiański's drama this alteration is very important. Błoński read the original drama's sequence of acts as a conscious composition reflecting the order of how human life evolves from a pessimistic world of necessities manifested in the fatal nature of Greek tragedy towards a freedom of choice represented by the biblical Jacob, especially in the moment when he alters his own fate by breaking the curse between him and his brother. Though Jacob fears Esau's vengeance, he heads back to his homeland to make amends. Grotowski decided to erase the possibility of this interpretation—which centred on the self-development of humankind by altering the order of acts and by removing most of Wyspiański's Act Three including Scenes 14 to 21 and Scene 23. Especially noteworthy is his removal of the scene of reconciliation of Jacob and Esau, Scene 25. Grotowski effectively concludes Jacob's story on the night he weds Rachel. Grotowski reconstructs the later scene of Jacob wrestling an Angel by combining Wyspiański's Scene 24 with Scene 22. While in Wyspiański the scene simply narrated the history of Jacob, Grotowski makes it integral to the structure of the 13 Rows' performance.

Grotowski altering the order of acts and putting the story of Jacob before the fall of Troy also meant that the performance started with the story from Genesis making the 'people Israel' the heroes of the performance. For Grzegorz Niziołek, this was proof that the Theatre of 13 Rows intended their *Acropolis* to be a performance about Jews and the Shoah (2013: 290).[16] There is certainly plenty of truth in this. The shift towards, and sharpening of questions related to the Shoah—evidenced in juxtapositions between the concentration camp setting and heroic tales of Polish martyrdom—could only amplify the provocative character of the performance. If an aim of the shift was to pose questions about the possibility of salvation through the Christian understanding of

---

16 His chapter on *Acropolis* was not included in the much-abbreviated version published in English (see Niziołek 2019).

Resurrection, then formulating it with a reference to the 'people Israel' was a twin provocation, directed both towards Jewish monotheism and the sorts of Christian anti-Semitism that while not reflecting the teachings of Jesus had become conventional in European Christianity up until and even after the Shoah.

Among the key changes made by Grotowski noticed by Masternak is that he severely cut Wyspiański's Act One retaining only four of its nine scenes, and even these were noticeably shortened mostly through the removal of verses referring to the growth in strength, power and will experienced by the awakening figures. These cuts also led to the reduction of the number of characters.

Similarly, in the Trojan act—which Grotowski placed third in his reordered sequence—the most influential change involved the near-complete erasure of Hector, Wyspiański's most important character. Grotowski cut the prologue, a sequence that signified the exceptional status of Hector's character. He cut numerous lines spoken by Hector and entire scenes related to him including his dialogue with Paris, the scene when Hector parts from Andromache and his conversation with Priam. What was left Grotowski condensed into almost gnomic fragments such as the phrase 'Ilium—Living, and ageless' (Wyspiański 2019: 406), and Hector's last words—'Look, father, how deep is the night;/ Look, father, thus I go to die' (428). These words like stones—hermetic and apparent—completely erase the creative aspect of Hector's suffering and the heroic dimension of his choice to die, characteristics in which Ewa Miodońska-Brookes saw his 'soul's imperative manifested' (1985: *lxviii*). In Grotowski's script and in the 13 Rows' performance Hector is essentially already dead, as rock-hard as his own tombstone; his attitude and his readiness to die seem completely incomprehensible.

Finally, Grotowski made very important changes to the fourth act by severely shortening the Harpist's grand monologue from 240 lines to 49. He removed lines that confirmed the fulfilment of God's promise, that affirmed the coming of the Saviour (v. 201–48). Grotowski ended the monologue-prayer with a chord of disappointment about God's unkept promise. In Grotowski's script, the final scenes of his performance immediately following the end of the monologue-prayer, a flood of simultaneous voices arose culminating with the farewell line 'Be well'. Grotowski moved this line from Hector's farewell in Act 2 of Wyspiański's original. Grotowski then scripted a final song for the Chorus and the Harpist intertwining into it two strophes from the Harpist's final song (v. 384–87, 391–95) with a third one (v. 401–4) to create the ecstatic song that finished the performance.

Despite Grotowski removing a large number of lines and making notable changes, he retained all key composition points, and respected the essential meanings of Wyspiański's drama: a journey through myths fundamental to Judeo-Christian civilization all the way up to its foretold culmination in the coming of the Messiah.

A Beverage with a Rather Mysterious Yet Strong Aroma

I borrow this section title from a title formulated by Jan Paweł Gawlik (2006: 169). I do so because Gawlik's title refers to something that is still missing from the discourse on *Acropolis*—as well as most other theatre works—aroma. The mere thought of 'aroma' connects us to senses other than seeing and hearing, and therefore to experiences that are very tricky to verbalize and yet have an unquestionable direct power. Gawlik describes *Acropolis* using words that suggest a connection with wine. This move seems apt not only because the performance 'went to one's head', and stunned witnesses like wine but also because describing the performance represents a real challenge. One can only meet the challenge of describing the experience of *Acropolis* by analogy, by referencing other evanescent experiences such as Gawlik's referencing the taste and aroma of wine. The wine metaphor leads towards a method that could be called 'poetic exactitude'. I try to use this method in what follows. Thus, what comes next is not a reconstruction of the performance but an attempt to go beyond images and their arrangement in pursuit of something more direct.

The performance began with an entrance into the auditorium and a view of a unique installation created mostly by Józef Szajna.[17]

> The centre of the auditorium was occupied by a black chest that looked like a catafalque [...]. Set upon it—a pile of ordinary plumbing parts (pipes)—on the very surface a rusty bathtub, reminiscent of a metal coffin.
> (Chodzieski 1962: 4)

The rest of the installation was made up of found objects including some wheelbarrows. The used and marred objects gave audiences who did not have access to Flaszen's commentary an odd or even comical impression.

> Sitting down upon chairs that seemed to be set out randomly, around a pile of pipes, authentic bits of iron stoves, alongside a real, battered, iron bathtub, people supposed that they had by chance stumbled into a scrap yard. This mistrust vanishes with the appearance of actors.
> (Sławińska 1963: 3)

---

17 Józef Szajna (1922-2008) was a Polish painter, visual artist, stage designer and theatre director invited by Grotowski to work with him on *Acropolis*. At that time Jerzy Gurawski—who was a permanent collaborator of the Theatre of 13 Rows—had been called for military service. Szajna designed props and costumes for the performance and was also named the co-creator of the staging (not the co-director!). When the Laboratory Theatre and *Acropolis* became internationally famous, Szajna started to accuse Grotowski of diminishing his role in the creative process. It is not the aim of this text to present in a detailed way Szajna's involvement and contribution to *Acropolis*. In spite of the artist's own complaints, Grotowski and Flaszen repeatedly stressed the value of his involvement, including his input as a former inmate of Auschwitz. Even so, *Acropolis* has been entered into the canon of world theatre as Grotowski's creation. With all due respect to Szajna and his contributions to the shape the performance, I think this is justified. It was Grotowski who for a range of reasons took on the challenge of creating this performance, and it was he again for a range of reasons who invited Szajna to assist him. *Acropolis* was—to use a military metaphor—Grotowski's battle. In this 'battle' Grotowski sought out a mighty ally and found it in Szajna who ably assisted Grotowski in achieving artistic victory. Later Szajna in his own important work dealt with his personal experiences creating from 1971 subsequent versions of his own important and innovative performance *Replika* ("Replica").

314 · DARIUSZ KOSIŃSKI

The actors' entrance was composed, choreographed and directed with a precision that helped Grotowski reconstruct the work on this sequence many years later.

> The auditorium is empty, the audience spread out, the centre of the hall occupied by the black chest covered with iron pipes. Noises can be heard off-stage, actors who are like Auschwitz prisoners carrying heavy work tools enter and direct themselves towards the centre, standing either side of the chest and recite the classic drama text as a prisoners' complaint. One of them climbs upon the chest and the iron pipes and begins to play upon his violin a well-known, jolly tune that had been played by the prisoners' orchestra in Auschwitz.[18]

> When I was doing this as a theatre director, I was very precise in referencing that which helped me direct the audience's attentions. The audience would sit around the whole space, which was not divided into stage and auditorium; and it was in the centre of this space that the large wooden chest had been set up, covered with a range of iron stove pipes. Next, the audience would turn their heads outwards, because they heard the footsteps of actors approaching, wearing wooden clogs. The audience saw them as they entered the space, and could follow their progress across the whole hall to reach the wooden chest. At first everyone could see the whole group, though in time they would focus on a single actor in order to see what he might have been carrying, what that could be.

> Once they focused on this it was necessary to capture their attention in order to fix it on the actor with the violin, because he was the one to speak the first line of dialogue, the first bit of information. Hence this was necessary.
> (Grotowski 2012: 825)

---

18 Here Grotowski mentions a very popular song—*Tango Milonga*, written by the Polish-Jewish composer Jerzy Petersburski and known to the world as *Oh, Donna Clara*. I don't know why Grotowski called this tune 'jolly'. One can use many words to describe the song but 'jolly' does not seem appropriate.

Grotowski's description is interesting in that it differs from the sequence of scenes known from the film in which Zygmunt Molik enters holding a violin, stands on the chest in the centre, starts his monologue, and only then—once he has said the first sentence—do the prisoners enter the space. Perhaps Grotowski had forgotten—or perhaps not—but nevertheless he precisely described a beginning of a performance that differed from that of the filmed version. Polish critics from the early 1960s tended to comment on how *Acropolis* actors entered the space, leading many to wrote about the appearance of a 'procession of characters dressed in costumes sewn from sacks, wearing camp berets and wooden clogs' (Kłossowicz 1964: 7).

This all may seem a trifling matter but it touches upon a key element of *Acropolis*—its actual hero. In earlier commentaries and reviews we tend to find the conviction that the performance—unlike those that came before and after—perhaps with the exception of *Apocalypsis cum figuris*—lacked a central character. The 'hero' thus became a collective hero, the group of prisoners. The creators meant this to be clear at first glance thanks to the uniform costumes worn by all actors:

> Bags with holes in them on naked bodies. The holes are lined with colourful layers and cut as if they were not only defects in the clothes but also tattered organic matter, the body's pulp torn apart and showing its insides. The actors wear heavy wooden boots on their feet, and dark berets on their heads—a poetic version of concentration camp prisoners' uniforms. The garments are identical, depriving people of their individual features; they cover up any attributes of social status, gender, or age. They transform the actors into identical, tormented, organic creatures.
> (Flaszen 2010[1964]: 90)

For Flaszen, the result of this and other decisions was as follows:

> There are no characters, or individually differentiated figures. There is only an image of society; a metaphoric representation of a species in a critical situation. In fact the actors create a

single creature pulsating with a changeable rhythm, talking, singing, making noises with objects. A plasmatic, polymorphic and shapeless creature, separating for a while only to return and become one throbbing body. Something a bit like the image of a drop of water under a microscope.
(Flaszen 2010[1964]: 90)

This sort of collective hero appears straight away as a relatively coherent whole acting as a collective. Meanwhile, in the film and in the programs printed for the last internationally presented version, the character played by Zygmunt Molik really does seem to stand out. He is the one who initiates the staged proceedings, and he was the one Grotowski confirmed as a real co-creator of the performance in a letter to the public (Grotowski 1969a). Despite how the entrance looked, starting with the first words of the performance and continuing throughout until the finale, the character performed by Molik functioned as the one who led and dominated the performance in all its versions. He is the one who regulated the course of events and made the most important decisions. So even if there was an intention to create a collective hero, Grotowski's imagination and stage practice led to the creation of a leader and the staging of his ambivalent power which serves as a telling analogy to the position and authority of the creator of the performance, Grotowski himself.

His position and role are clearly presented by the Prologue that opens the performance. This is the only sizeable fragment of text that does not come from Wyspiański's *Acropolis*, and is also not composed using Wyspiański's words. It was built from fragments of a note written by the poet's friend Adam Chmiel after a conversation with Wyspiański on 28 January 1904, and a text written the same year by literary critic Zenon Parvi. Grotowski likely took these fragments directly from the appendix to the critical edition of Wyspiański's *Acropolis* in which the editor Leon Płoszewski printed both fragments on subsequent pages (Płoszewski 1959: 390–91).

We already know well that Grotowski often used prologues as theatrical devices. Faithful to the basic, traditional functions of theatrical prologues, he used them to inform audiences about what they were about to see in order to help them follow and understand the performance. This is precisely what he does in his Prologue to *Acropolis*. Grotowski created a word collage for the prologue that presents the upcoming sequence of scenes according to Grotowski's own personal composition.

> I am reading out the scenes from *Acropolis*, happy with them, and I feel like each scene has behind it the perspective of the air.
>
> Action: resurrection night in the cathedral at Wawel hill—our own Acropolis.
>
> It begins with angels carrying St Stanisłav's coffin, and having descended to the tiled floor, figures come alive along with the monuments in the cathedral. Jacob's dream—Judaic. Heroes descend from the tapestries upon the walls of the cathedral nave. Helen and Paris—the heroes from Troy descend from the second tapestry. The end—Christ Resurrected, the Saviour descends to the earth from the central altar.
>
> This drama, which fantastically and symbolically exceeded all those before, is in some way an image of developing humanity, with the elements of its military and pastoral lives, over which however the power of song dominates.
>
> (Chojak 1968: 1)

Grotowski presented the condensed action of *Acropolis* using words borrowed from Chmiel but arranged them in such a way as to tell the order of events as modified by the director. Grotowski took the last paragraph from Parvi, and used it to capture the theme of the synthesis of civilizations, while also ironically present it in archaic language.

And yet Molik's delivery of the Prologue also has a different meaning related to a different theatrical device also very much favoured by Grotowski: as a meta-theatrical frame by revealing that all that was to follow was a prepared performance. If it is so, the question remains: what kind of a performance would it be?

Flaszen wrote:

During breaks in their work, this peculiar society spins its species' own kind of dreams. The pathetic convicts take the names of Old Testament and Homeric heroes, identify with them and perform, within their limits, their own versions of these famous stories. There is something in this of collective daydreaming and of imagining another reality (not unfamiliar to prison societies); and there is something in these materially-incarnated fantasies of grandeur, dignity, and happiness. But the game might be cruel and bitter; including mockery of one's own lofty aspirations undermined by reality.
(Flaszen 2010[1964]: 90–91)

During the Second World War, prisoners occasionally staged theatre performances. There were even some stable and professional companies working in camps for prisoners of war. Although in concentration camps and gulags this type of enterprise tended to be rare—due to the terrible conditions and exhaustion suffered by the inmates—prisoners put on performances. What Flaszen's comment suggests is that the prisoners in *Acropolis* are presenting such a performance. Accordingly, the Prologue presents a frame that is probable—that of a concentration camp amateur theatre that performs a varied repertoire, and tonight they happen to be performing 'scenes from Wyspiański's *Acropolis*'.

The Prologue also has a more literal meaning serving to reveal the theatricality of the performance taking place 'here and now'—in Opole, Łódź, or Kraków. Grotowski often used this device, never hiding the nature of the event in which audiences were to take part. At the beginning of *Acropolis*, Coryphaeus (Molik)[19] presented the Prologue as if to represent a director announcing the beginning of his show. This is the core of his 'leading role': it is he who prepares, initiates and leads this game.

---

19 In the course of the performance Molik (like the other actors) performed several characters: Jacob. Priam, Harpist. But generally his role was to lead the performance as the main voice and at the same time someone who organizes it. The term Coryphaeus seems to be the best name for the character though on the official cast list it appears as Jacob-Priamus.

When Molik entered the *Acropolis* performance space with an even gait, turned to the audience, presented basic information and continued to steer the action throughout the performance, it reflected a direct continuation of the Doctor in *Kordian*.

Upon Molik's entrance, audiences found themselves in a theatre where a performance was about to begin. Much as in the case of *Kordian*, this explicit theatricality was complemented by a painful 'reality' that provided dramatic contrast with the 'illusion' the 13 Rows staged. This contrast in *Acropolis* was stark. Zbigniew Raszewski aptly encapsulated this contrast—'actors reciting *Acropolis* while building a concentration camp' (2006[1964]: 236). The fundamental arc of physical actions in *Acropolis* was building the extermination incinerator; these actions showed the actors 'really' performing construction work. They used pipes, steel cables and iron to literally build the performance environment around the spectators. They used hammers and nails to fasten pipes to the wooden floor, and at the same time fastened the reality of their physical actions to their representation of a concentration camp, and to the narrative of *Acropolis*.

There were four overlapping and permeating layers of performance action: (1) the theatrical presentation of (2) prisoners working in, and building a concentration camp who also (3) performed the heroes of (4) *Acropolis*. But there is one more level that resounds so powerfully in the first song of the Chorus of prisoners, one that defines their own situation. Let us read this self-definition.

> Singers—
> On the cemetery of tribes—
> Come here on this day of Sacrifice—
> On the cemetery of tribes—
> Our Acropolis!
> Only once a year.
> Our Acropolis!
> They come here but once a year,
> On the cemetery of tribes—

The sentence of the Word is read.
Our Acropolis!
They have gone—and the rings of smoke still float aloft.
(Chojak 1968: 1–2)[20]

Grotowski composed this text using fragments from Wyspiański's poetic introduction to his drama. Grotowski's composition informs audiences about a unique ritual gathering that only happens once a year, taking place on a tribal cemetery representing 'Our Acropolis'. The Chorus informs the audience of the deeper meaning behind what the actors recite as they build the camp itself. The words of *Acropolis* become 'words of judgement', and the actors' actions become a sacrifice. Hence what the actors do throughout the performance is not only a recitation of Wyspiański, and not only a depiction of 'an image of evolving humanity'. They also cast judgement upon our civilization. So yet another layer of the performance simultaneously serves as an encompassing frame, the enactment of a judgement day.

This does not mean that the context of the concentration camp is neglected. It is in these scenes of exposition that we find the subtle insinuations that make Wyspiański's words suddenly sound remarkably apropos in the context of Auschwitz. For example, this is true with regard to the verse from Wyspiański's text that Grotowski used to compose the Chorus's explanation of 'our Acropolis'. It is also repeated at the end of the performance 'They have gone—and the rings of smoke still float aloft'.[21] This phrase is derived from the words of one of Wyspiański's Angel's. Angel 4 in the original text says:

D'you smell that——still the fragrant mist
Of incense rises like a cloud
And spins like cobwebs [. . .]
(Wyspiański 2019: 355)

---

20 This translation is direct from the Polish script not from the translation of *Acropolis* by Charles Kraszewski.

21 In the English translation by Charles Kraszewski—'They've gone [. . .]. Behind them, puffs of incense wrap around' (Wyspiański 2019: 349).

In the original, Wyspiański's Angel referred to the incense and candle smoke that drifted up from the altar and floated by the face of the Angel. In the performance set in Auschwitz such fragments were used to introduce this new context and to construct a web of references to the death camp. Another example of this strategy may be the repeated words chanted by a character performed by Rena Mirecka—'Hair, hair . . . / . . . Hair . . . / . . . hair . . . / . . . hair' (Chojak 1968: 5). It originated from verse 214 in the original drama—'it is my hair which is ringing'.[22] In his edits, Grotowski established a clear connection to one of the most horrific images associated with Auschwitz, piles of hair shorn from the heads of concentration camp inmates.

The whole opening sequence—'Prologue', first song of the Chorus, and first actions of the individual characters—was grounded on the tension between the expected coming of new life announced in 'Prologue', and all-encompassing death. Thus, the central conflict of the performance was presented and played out at the very beginning as a dramatic question of how to find hope for a new life in the factory of mass extinction.

The search for an answer seems to be started by Coryphaeus who presents the 'Old Testament History of Jacob' to his 'team' retelling it in shortened form as a second prologue. Taken directly from Wyspiański, the 13 Rows version retains only fragments from the original. Both dramatize sequences in which Jacob cheats Esau and steals their father Isaac's blessing, angels descend with a message from God and Jacob meets Rachel—who is presented as a kind of a 'prize' for honoring God's will. While Wyspiański dramatized the entire story of Jacob until his final meeting and reconciliation with his brother, Grotowski cut the story after Jacob's fight with the Angel. In a sort of prologue to this part of Jacob's story both Wyspiański and Grotowski told a tale of sin, and of reunion with God by submission to his will. Hence, in both versions Jacob's story is a story of salvation, a story of human triumph in the struggle for happiness.

---

22 In the English translation by Charles Kraszewski the verse reads differently: 'it's my locks that sigh' (Wyspiański 2019: 360). In this translation, the 'hair' used by Grotowski is lost.

322 · DARIUSZ KOSIŃSKI

'Jacob's History' is a performance within a performance—the camp theatre presents it to enliven a dying human being, and to strengthen one another's weakening hope. Coryphaeus himself takes on the role of the main hero, and continues to do so in subsequent scenes. Jacob's history evolves in line with Molik's prologue to this part and culminates at the point when the hero runs away from home. A pivotal breakdown takes place in the pre-announced scene of the dream at Bethel. Grotowski substantially shortened and then rebuilt this dream. In a sense he removed its core. In Wyspiański's original, the story featured a long fragment narrativizing the biblical story of a long procession of angels descending and ascending—Jacob's ladder—with God positioned above it all. Grotowski crafted Wyspiański's latter verses transforming this story into a hymn of despair (v. 221–28 and 233–45). Or put another way, Grotowski's version proceeds in line with the description that appears in Flaszen's commentary.

> The passive despair of a people who are irreversibly condemned: trusting in divine help, the angels' words from Jacob's dream are recited by four prisoners who are standing in tormented poses against the walls in different parts of the room; their recitation sounds like a ritual complaint, a melody from the Jews' biblical lamentation at the Wailing Wall.
> (Flaszen 2010: 91)

This becomes one of the most powerful moments in the performance, a scene of darkness and hopelessness. This moment was all the more overwhelming because the 13 Rows' production placed it at the point where according to the biblical account—as well as Wyspiański's drama—Jacob recognized the necessity of trusting in God's providence and blessing. In Wyspiański's drama, Jacob spoke these words. In the Opole performance, this was delivered by the individual voices of all the actors speaking in turn:

> Thus dost Thou each day freshly make
> Thus dost each back with labour break.
> Thus leadest Thou all out from the night.
> Thus temptest Thou all with false delight.
> (Wyspiański 2019: 448)

In this we see what may be the most important theme in Grotowski's difficult theatrical endeavour, the motif of illusory beliefs and deception. Grotowski's key question becomes. 'Is everything that civilizations offer us in terms of values not in fact illusory when humanity is brought to its very knees—to the level of ruthless and also hopeless struggle for survival?'

Subsequent scenes sharpen this question, and accentuate the contrast between illusory values and the methods employed to fight for them. In a surviving 13 Rows script from 2 November 1962, the sequence of scenes differs from the one popularised in the film version. In the 1962 script, Grotowski retained their original order—Jacob first meets Rachel, then arranges to meet Laban, and the wedding follows. In the film version of 1968, the sequence of scenes seems a lot more logical and coheres better with the whole composition of this part of the play. After the end of Jacob's dream, the hero meets Laban—not shepherds—and starts to battle him over Rachel. Jacob wins, kills Laban and then initiates a lyrical wedding scene.

Perhaps when Komorowska was still in the cast of the first version—which premiered in October 1962—this sequence was longer, and performed with a special score of actions. I suppose that Stefan Bratkowski—an important journalist and reporter who visited Grotowski's theatre in 1962—witnessed some of these scenes, and described the visit in his reportage (1965: 156–57). Bratkowski describes a sequence featuring a man and woman chasing and romancing, which in the context of Auschwitz was interpreted as 'a demented vision of people [. . .] condemned to death'. Grotowski informed Bratkowski that what Jacob 'picked from the earth represented the stiffened cadaver of a girl "escaping" from him'. Based on this report, I conclude that Jacob first met Rachel, 'chased' and 'romanced' her, only to discover she was dead. So this was a scene that might serve as an introduction to the sequences connected to the negotiation with Laban and Jacob's subsequent wedding to Rachel. Bratkowski's report does not mention Laban, but we already know that Grotowski often worked on sequences separately and only met with those actors involved in the scene at hand. So it is not hard to imagine that—if my reconstruction is correct—in the

324 · DARIUSZ KOSIŃSKI

Acropolis rehearsed in Spring and Autumn of 1962 Jacob married a dead girl not a pipe, thereby awakening the ancient phantasm of an uncanny, beautiful, undead demon bride who uses love and desire to tempt him and imprison him in the domain of the dead.[23]

When Komorowska left the company, they had to change the scene. They replaced the dead bride with a simple object, a pipe. But what remained was an illusion Coryphaeus (Molik) performed with all his acting powers and directorial talents. The scene was performed in this way beginning with the 2 November 1962 version.

> A prisoner takes a piece of pipe, there's nothing else, and begins to look for the woman. He touches the pipe as if it were a woman. For other inmates this becomes reality and some of them answer with actual texts, as if the pipe was a woman. To the other prisoners it becomes reality and some of them answer, with proper text, as if the pipe were a woman. For the first prisoner it is the pipe that has answered. The marriage procession is that of tragic farce. A man and a woman—a man and a pipe—and they begin to sing songs of marriage that are very well known in Poland. At that moment an authentic process begins in the actor, a return to memory of life—no more buffoonery. Then the marriage procession, laughter and songs, and the rhythm of the wooden shoes.
> (Grotowski 1969b in Schechner, Wolford 1997: 51–52]

Grotowski's description of this scene essentially reflects the way the 'Grotowski method' works. With specific and precise physical actions, the actor 'magically'—as Grotowski liked to say back then—transforms reality. In this scene it takes the form of Jacob changing a grotesque and pitiful 'surrogate object' into a bride. One way to understand the mechanics of this transformation is to juxtapose it to the 'unrealistic' transformation of bread and wine during the Eucharist. This juxtaposition is in fact introduced into the scene by the sound of a ministrant's bell. At

---

23 Let me also add that a similar phantasm appears in Tadeusz Kantor's *Theatre of Death* performances. A very similar scene of marrying the dead bride appears for example in his *I Shall Never Return* (1988).

the end of *Acropolis'* uncanny wedding scene, Mirecka struck two iron nails together, producing a sound reminiscent of a small bell.. The sound is similar to the sound of the small bell that a ministrant rings to celebrate the Elevation in the Holy Mass, a key moment of the Eucharistic Sacrifice in which the bread and wine are transformed into the body and blood of Christ. With all he has at his disposal, Coryphaeus performs a sequence that culminates in a 'transubstantiation' that is apparent to those looking through 'eyes of faith' though it remains invisible in the physical dimension. It seems that this is a way he tries to renew hope among his fellow actor-prisoners. In order to discover another dimension of reality, and thus escape the suffering and terror of the cemetery of tribes, one must look with 'eyes of faith' beyond the material world.

But when the ministrant's bell resounds everything vanishes. Jacob discovers a man in his bed instead of Rachel. Jacob—and everyone present—realizes hat the previous scene, with all its signs of salvation and redemption, was illusory. Coryphaeus's performance ends with a return to the harsh reality of feverish work, a world full of death.

The scene of the struggle between Jacob and the Angel presents a similar sort of defeat. Though the story belongs to the biblical history of Jacob, in Grotowski's *Acropolis* it is no longer a part of the performance initiated and led by Coryphaeus. This is how Flaszen described it:

> Jacob's struggling with the Angel is a fight between two prisoners; one of them kneels down supporting a wheelbarrow on his back, while the other lies in it with his head hanging down. A dramatic skirmish follows; a kneeling Jacob, trying to free himself of the burden of his opponent, flexes himself to get up but falls down, while the prone Angel bangs his head on the floor; when the Angel wants to crush Jacob, he smashes his head on the wheelbarrow edge and Jacob, with the greatest effort, stays underneath his burden. The fighting men cannot free themselves from each other because they are chained to their work tools; to make their torture worse, they cannot properly give vent to their mutual anger. Here is that great Old Testament scene: two victims torturing each other under the

326 · DARIUSZ KOSIŃSKI

> pressure of Necessity, the anonymous power of which is at the
> heart of their conflict.
> (Flaszen 2010[1964]: 91)

Necessity is also another name for the depersonalized power that rules over the reality of the camp, and leads to the inevitable atrocity prepared by the inmates for themselves by themselves. The scene of Jacob's fight with the Angel represents a counterpoint and end to Jacob and Rachel's theatre, while also leading towards the 'Trojan act'. The sequence of wedding and love was only a dream about an escape from necessity. The dream is over.

The centrepiece of the 'Trojan act' features Paris and Helen enacting a derision of a dream of mystical love modelled on the *Song of Songs*.

> Paris and Helen of Troy present the charm of sensual infatuation; however, Helen is also a man. The lyrics of their courtship are accompanied by the other prisoners' lecherous laughter: in their world, eroticism is degraded and deprived of any intimacy; it is replaced by the unisex groups' coarse barrack-room lust.
> (Flaszen 2010[1964]: 91)

At the start of the 1960s Poland was ruled by prudish and homophobic Catholic and Communist authorities. The very act of staging a homosexual encounter would have been perceived as degeneration and degradation (as it is already in the quoted comment). We should also note here that in *Acropolis* love and desire function as possible means for escaping the inevitability of death. In this scene we have an example of a movement from longing for, and believing in the possibilities of, erotic fulfilment towards another road to resurrection by recognizing the illusory nature of love and desire. This thread culminates in Mirecka singing the lyrical Maiden's song taken directly from Wyspiański. This song began in the midst of Helen and Paris' dialogue, weaved through it, and emphatically denied any sort of erotic or romantic longing: 'I shall remain a maid,/ Safe with shuttle and loom' (Wyspiański 2019: 424).

In Grotowski's script the second part of the Trojan scene—the dialogues between Priam, Hector and Hecuba-is even more static and submerged in death and in an incapacity for any sort of change than the corresponding conversations in Wyspiański's original. Coryphaeus—who is so dynamic until this point—takes the role of the old king Priam who seems to acknowledge the rules of necessity, submit to the inevitability of death and therefore gives up on action. His wife Hecuba—who audiences heard only as a voice—seems to already be dead, as is the case with their son Hector. All of them are finally called to a prisoner's appeal where it seems that nothing can be changed. The only thing left among those who submitted to death was 'the aggressive despair of the condemned who rebel against their destiny'. This 'aggressive despair' is the tone that dominates Cassandra's monologue performed by Mirecka as described by Flaszen.

> A woman breaks loose from the rows of prisoners at the roll call. Writhing hysterically and fainting almost lyrically, she prophesies her society's extermination. She sings hoarsely with vulgar, self-destructive satisfaction, suddenly moving into a quiet cantilena of sorrow. Instead of the cawing of crows suggested in the original text, her monologue is stopped short by the quick guttural voices of the prisoners standing in a row as if responding to the command: 'Be counted!'
> (Flaszen 2010[1964]: 91–92)

Cassandra's curse leaves no hope, and the cruel, derisive tone in her voice is supported by the same lyrical melody Mirecka sung only moments ago when she rejected love-play.

Cassandra's prophesy reinforces the performance's decidedly dark direction, heading down this deathly path without any chance of return. Coryphaeus responds to Cassandra's despairing lament with a prayer, a great accusation depicting hope's betrayal and the end of trust. Coryphaeus climbs on the shoulders of the inmates who are lined up for counting. But even this gesture goes unanswered. The inmates bid each other farewell using Hector's words from Wyspiański's original—'Be well'—which Hector utters as he goes to his own death. The performance seems close to the end at the edge of dark and desperate night.

At this point a call was heard, 'Harpist! Thou singer of the Lord . . . [. . .] A growing crowd/ Awaits your song, awaits your harp' (Wyspiański 2019: 487). The voice seemed to come 'out of nowhere' but in fact—as with the voices of Rachel and Hecuba—it was a theatrical voice so the voice comes 'out of the theatre'.[24] This voice did not deliver a transcendent message. It did not enlighten the Harpist but rather reminded him of his most basic duties. Coryphaeus is after all an artist, the one who directs the creation of 'Acropolis' and manages it as his own. The voice called Coryphaeus to fulfil his ethical obligation as a craftsman which in essence is very simple: to fulfil his professional duty. At first Coryphaeus is filled with doubt. However, one of his co-inmates (Ryszard Cieślak) heeds the voice's call, and transforms it into a call from one of Coryphaeus' fellow brothers. Such a call cannot be rejected.

Coryphaeus begins his final performance. Flaszen recounts it as follows:

> And finally, hope. The exhausted gathering led by the Singer finds its Saviour. Who is this one for whom they are so desperately looking? It's a corpse. A blue, shattered headless dummy that looks like a skinny, dead prisoner. With both hands, the Singer lifts up this pathetic form in a solemn gesture, like the priest lifting the holy chalice. The crowd, staring at him with a religious impulse, follows the leader in single file. They start singing a welcoming song to praise the Saviour with a melody like a Christmas carol. Their song becomes louder, turns into ecstatic howling, shrill voices, wailing, and hysterical laughter. The procession circles around the big box in the middle of the room with their arms outstretched towards the Saviour, their eyes rapturously focused on him. Some prisoners stumble, fall down, crawl, and then pick themselves up to swarm around the Singer, chaotically. It looks like a medieval religious event, a procession of flagellants, church beggars, dancers entranced by religious ecstasy. They calm down and sometimes stop. The

---

24 In the film, it is the voice of hidden actor Andrzej Paluchiewicz who earlier voiced Hecuba.

silent stillness is filled with the Singer's song of prayer, answered by the others in the beginnings of the litany. Finally, at the peak of ecstasy, the crowd reaches the end of its wandering. Amidst the silence, the Singer cries out in prayer, opens a lid in the box and goes in with the Saviour dummy. Singing hysterically, the others follow him in, one by one, in a trance. All the convicts disappear into the hole, and the lid slams shut. Sudden silence. After a short pause, a sober, matter-of-fact voice is heard from inside the box: 'They are gone—and the smoke spirals upwards'. The joyful madness found its ending in the crematorium oven. (Flaszen 2010[1964]: 92)

Coryphaeus 'animated' the lifeless rag doll. He performed a literal 'reanimation', the same as actors in doll and puppet theatre. Thus, he reanimated this doll of old stockings he initially treated as if dead. He gave the doll a name taken from Wyspiański, and chanted it, 'Salvator!' thus Christening the doll 'Saviour!' Others joined in and cried out 'There he is!/ Power, might' (Chojak 1968: 54). Inmates join in Coryphaeus' performance as if they had been waiting for him to start. Coryphaeus leads them in a procession as they start to sing.

In the musical composition of the final chorus, Grotowski used several well-known, traditional Polish melodies. The first part of the chorus is sung to a traditional melody of a lullaby known to all Polish children: '*Był sobie król*' (There was a king). This lullaby is strongly associated with childhood and evokes idealized images of home, warmth and safety—all of which are so clearly absent in the concentration camp. And yet it is worth recalling that the lullaby is not entirely innocent. Its text written by Janina Porazińska (1882–1971) relates a 'harsh fate' and 'cruel death' suffered by protagonists of the story told by the lullaby—all of whom loved one another. At the end of the lullaby, all three heroes are eaten. 'The dog ate the King,/ The cat ate the Page,/ the mouse ate the Princess'. And yet, just when a child listening to this terrifying story is ready to burst into tears a twist in the tale brings cheer by revealing that all the characters were actually sweets. The King was made of sugar, the Page made of gingerbread and the Queen made of marzipan. I do not know if anyone sang this lullaby to Grotowski when he was a child. But I heard it as a child, and I remember it well—especially the twist in the tale that was not cheery at all. It rather seemed to me at the time to be a sort of sad joke that revealed the cruelty of our world by barely masking it with a silly trick. In fact, it is hard to imagine a more apt choice of song to start the finale of *Acropolis*. All the associations it inspires with childhood would bring to audiences' minds the essential cruelty of the world as it really is. along with its inherent sadness. Singing Wyspiański's words 'All pain and tears will fade away' (Wyspiański 2019: 490) to the tune of this melody constituted a very subtle and powerful dialectic of derision and apotheosis.

In the second part of the final chorus Coryphaeus sets a similarly powerful cultural play in motion when he sings his hymn to the tune of a traditional Polish Christmas carol about Christ's second coming.[25] The tune is typically used to sing about his birth. Critics and commentators overlooked the fact that this chorus was built from Wyspiański's poetic stage directions. The choral singing and the procession of prisoners states that which the poet left as a mere sketch in stage directions, a vision of a possible future. When Coryphaeus-Harpist and his team entered the crematorium they embodied the second coming, the Salvation that Wyspiański scripted but never actualized.

This salvation—much like the earlier wedding—is staged using meagre props and found objects, and therefore the props themselves visibly resist being 'real'. Yet the actors' powers and non-verbal acumen especially with music enabled genuine identifications and feelings. The ambivalence during the finale of *Acropolis* played out a self-aware, theatrical ambivalence that refused the resolution implied by undertones that intentionally evoked salvation. In this scene, salvation functioned

---

25 The melody is similar to two carols: 'Lulajże Jezuniu' [Sleep little Jesus] and 'Wesołą nowinę, bracia, słuchajcie' [Listen, o brothers, to the joyful news]. In Poland these carols are very well-known. For the international reader the melody may be associated with Fryderyk Chopin's Scherzo h-moll, op. 20 in which the composer used 'Lulajże Jezuniu'. Maybe it is worthwhile to note that the same melody was much later used by Tadeusz Kantor in his *Wielopole, Wielopole* (1980).

more as a lie told to those tortured to death, a consolation fabricated by those perishing to comfort themselves. What seems certain and unquestionable is the need to perform this play because it represents a fundamental human duty regardless of whether God will ever answer the call from the depths. This duty relates to each and every human being, but in a specific way touches upon artists, not as 'sages' or 'prophets' but as craftspeople and specialists. Atop the 'cemetery of tribes' and amid a moment of trial and tribulation, the Harpist has to answer the call.

The Reality Effect

In comparison to the two previous 13 Rows performances which presented powerful explorations of collaborations, co-habitations, compresences and other modes of relationality, *Acropolis* marked a radical development. Grotowski himself took note of this change.

> In the case of *Acropolis*, audiences mingled with actors; as a result, a chasm opened up. Actors wove in and out of the audience, mingling among them through space, but not noticing them at all. Even if they noticed them in certain moments this happened without follow-up, no chance of contact here, these being two separate worlds. In *Acropolis* these really were two worlds, because actors were in a way shreds of human beings, the people of Auschwitz, fallen, extinguished, while the audiences—they were the living ones who had a fine supper and went to the theatre in order to take part in a certain sort of cultural ceremony. Emotive transference was not possible—and in order to dig this chasm between two worlds, two realities, two kinds of human reactions, we needed—opposite to what one might expect—to mix the two groups. This conclusion is very important.
> (Grotowski 2012: 360)

In *Acropolis* this closeness between audiences and actors—achieved by simultaneously mixing them together and emphasizing their separation—had a fundamental meaning.

The spectators sat throughout the room. They were treated as people of another world, either as ghosts which only got in the way, or as air. The actors spoke through them. The personal situation of the spectators was totally different from that of the characters. The spectators functioned both as spectators and within the context of the play. They are in the middle, and at the same time they are totally irrelevant, incomprehensible to the actors—as the living cannot understand the dead.
(Grotowski 1968b; quoted in Schechner and Wolford 1997: 52)

Grotowski's analysis begs a question: what does it mean that the spectators were also meant to function 'within the context of the play'? I think it means that they were to perform the living that cannot understand the dead. This is exactly what Grotowski told Margaret Croyden.

In *Acropolis* the public represents the living watching 'the dead' inmates in their nightmare dreams. Ultimately the audience must give its own answers. Will humanity retrieve its past dreams? Can they [sic] survive the greatest brutality of the century? Is there hope? The answers are left to the audience.
(Grotowski 1969b; quoted in Schechner and Wolford 1997: 87)

Thus we are not dealing with knowledge about the historical context of the concentration camps but rather with a deeper awareness related to the possibilities of human becoming, and how ineffective the existing 'respected' values of our culture are in saving us from ourselves. *Acropolis* as staged by Grotowski encourages us to concern ourselves with the need or even a necessity of making our own decisions. We must do so while confronting an incomprehensible and inexplicable yet real experience, the one the 13 Rows presented to us in *Acropolis*.

Flaszen formulated an appeal, a question aimed at audiences:

The performance can be understood as an appeal to the spectator's moral memory and moral subconscious. Who would you be at the hour of the ultimate test? Just a wreck of a man? Or a victim of the collective delusions of self-consolation?
(Flazen 2010[1964]: 89)

One could justifiably respond with another question: At such an hour who else *could* I be?! After all, the performance presented no other possibility. And yet posing this question—indeed the very act of ordering the audience who are alive and therefore cannot understand the dead to understand the performance on their own—allowed the audience a chance to answer an analogous question to the one Coryphaeus answered in the finale of *Acropolis*.

Polish critics and commentators writing about *Acropolis* between 1962 and 1963 often discussed the question of the performance's impact on the audience and the overall effect of the performance.[26] The authors made it clear that for them such impact was the most important aspect of the experience of *Acropolis*. Many reviewers and critics point to the most important elements linking the reality of the performance and the reality of audiences, namely, namely, the musicality, the materiality of objects, and the actors' performances. They also mentioned effect of the performance space on audiences' experience. The space was claustrophobic and stuffy, imbued with the smell of sweat, evoking a pervasive sense of physical discomfort.

There is no need to reiterate this discussion here. Instead, I want to use a handful of bullet points to show that all of the elements mentioned above helped audiences situate themselves in the world of the performance breaking through the barriers separating the reality of the concentration camps from the experience of 'ordinary' reality. Those who are living are unable to understand the dead. This is true. But they are able to experience the same sounds, materials, smells; the same cramped spaces that the 13 Rows used to represent the world of the camp. This seems to be the key major contribution of Józef Szajna to *Acropolis*. Part of this contribution consisted of introducing ready-made and already-used objects.

---

26 The full bibliography of the texts can be accessed online at https://rebrand.ly/7vzaq2p . In the Polish version of this book I analysed the reviews in detail (Kosiński 2015: 251–57). Because of limited space, I cannot repeat this analysis here.

The scenic elements of *Acropolis* were not abstract, but neither were they realistic. These elements were concrete objects, things from bad dreams, but all completely 'untheatrical'. Szajna found these objects in flea markets and junk shops.

(Grotowski 1968b; quoted in Schechner and Wolford 1997: 52)

Szajna knew the traditions of the avant-garde well. He also knew that by using such devices he would be following very specific precepts. Was he aware that, in this way, he was perhaps repeating the wartime 'discoveries' made by Tadeusz Kantor who utilized found and second-hand items as elements of a 'lowest rank reality' in his underground staging of *Powrót Odysa* [The return of Odysseus] also by Wyspiański? I do not know. I am not interested in the argument which has been going on for years over 'who was first'. If I refer to Kantor it is only because his description of these items as representing 'a lowest rank reality' seems apt for such items in *Acropolis*. Szajna introduced cheap, shoddy, used-up stuff that played a very important role in establishing an effect of realism in the performance. They contributed to the realism of the performance by conveying their material and physical presence through sensory effects. They also evaded literary symbolism; their banality ridiculed this sort of theatricality. Finally, they contributed to the realism of *Acropolis* through their histories, the mere fact that they had already been used. They represented items both unique and irreplaceable. In all these dimensions, the objects used in *Acropolis* represented the unquestionable here-and-now effect of what took place during the performance.

And yet Grotowski went even further in establishing a realism in his *Acropolis* apart from Szajna. I mean the performance's two inter-related uses of music. The first was commented upon by Grotowski in the radio interview with Falkowski:

In this performance we are trying to create a musical score, based on concrete music, emitted as the actors perform their roles, using the tools provided for us by our friend Szajna, all that scrap metal, which knocked or rubbed together, smashed up and so on—allowed us to compose some forms of music.

(Falkowski 1962b)

Also Flaszen stressed creating a soundscape resembled a composition of 'concrete music'[27] using objects, tools and the wooden clogs worn by the actors (2010: 93).

The use of raw, realistic elements constituted yet another avant-garde-ish strategy in *Acropolis*. The performance's creators used concrete music to make compositions with direct, physical impact—not just the aesthetic impact from standard musical instruments. Using the scratching of metal nails against a ribbed boiler pipe, the knocking of hammers and wooden clogs, the performers caused very powerful, affective sensory reactions in the audience drawing them in to the action on the level of sound and touch rather than relying on symbolic musical artifice.

The second aspect of musicality in *Acropolis*—songs and chants—is something Grotowski only seemed to notice very late in his career towards the end of his life. Grotowski told Jean-Paul Thibaudat as much in the last interview he gave published during his lifetime:

> Today for example I use the processes connected with ancient song as a vehicle. And yet when I watch archive footage of the Laboratory Theatre, including *Acropolis*, I see that these performances were sung. At the time I didn't know this, didn't think of it. This performance was filmed, and I didn't want to see the footage for a long while. In the end I finally allowed myself to watch it—in fact it's not that bad—and then I realized that it had been sung.
> (Grotowski 2012: 904)

This is odd—especially considering the large number of songs and melodies used in the performance. Grotowski always tended to use well-known songs and various musical stylizations—especially liturgical ones—but in *Acropolis* he really outdid himself. Perhaps he used music intuitively and not necessarily consciously. Most of the songs and

---

27 Concrete music (*musique concrète* in French) is a type of avant-garde musical composition using not only the sounds of instruments and voices but also natural elements and technical environments (animals, machines, everyday sound etc.). *Musique concrète* was developed by the French composer Pierre Schaffer in 1940s. In the 1950s, concrete music attracted such composers as Olivier Messiaen, Pierre Boulez, Jean Barraqué, Karlheinz Stockhausen, Edgard Varèse, Iannis Xenakis, Michel Philippot and Arthur Honegger.

melodies were deeply rooted in the personal and collective cultural memory of the Polish audiences. They instantly aroused specific associations, and also—as Grotowski would say later—a series of internal impulses. Grotowski likely had this effect in mind with regard to his use of song during his later work on *Action* (from *c.*1989) where certain traditional songs were 'vehicles of verticality'.

All the elements of *Acropolis* that I mention in this chapter created an arsenal of devices that worked on a subconscious level upon audiences who 'could not understand the dead'. In a book written from a cognitive psychology perspective, Teemu Paavolainen described this whole mechanism thus:

> the *Acropolis* audience was scattered around the scenic architecture, subject to multiple levels of emerging CONTAINMENT. At the start they were already in an enclosed 'network without exit', as Szajna had the whole room wired up with a crisscross structure of ropes (evoking not only the barbed wire of the concentration camp but also a spider's web that entwines the cathedral pillars in Wyspiański opening poem). At the end 'the entire room was oppressed by the metal': distributing the central pile of stovepipes among the spectators—hung on the ropes, nailed to the floor—the actors 'include[d] them in the architecture of action'. Sensitizing them to 'the pressure of congestion and limitation of space'. Finally, apart from 'threatening ubiquity' of the actors' bodies—moving in on them from all sides yet leaving them physically intact [. . .]—the audience was also engulfed in 'a concentration camp of sound'. In Flaszen's description they were 'penetrated' by everything, 'from inarticulate groans' to 'the most sophisticated oratorical recitation' mixed 'in a new Tower of Babel—in a clash of foreign peoples and foreign languages meeting just before their extermination'.
> (Paavolainen 2012: 145)

All sensual, physical, dynamic experiences in the performance were supposed to lead audiences beyond representation to a very tangible level beyond 'history' and even beyond 'shock' or 'restaged trauma'. The use of these dynamics reflected the creators' desire to complexly affect the audience, to enact a disturbance—a consciously instigated dissonance—to break through the totality and thickness of the montage achieving a heightened sense of reality in the audience's experience. The Laboratory Theatre evidently strained to draw audiences into the reality of the performance rather than losing them within it. The 13 Rows maintained audiences in their role as spectators so spectators could find and formulate their own responses to *Acropolis*. Grotowski wanted these responses to emerge from something other than sympathy; he did not want sentimentality, being 'overcome with sympathy' for the terrible fate faced by the prisoners.

A grotesque manifestation of this drive—almost funny and yet very realistic in its awkward effect—was the final 'accord' of the audiences' presence in the auditorium. This moment was not a deep silence, with echoes of a moving song, or graceful gestures in slow motion—as the 13 Rows ended the performance in the film. In the 1962 performance after the last words of the performance were spoken—'They have gone—and the rings of smoke still float aloft'—the cloakroom attendant entered the performance space and requested that everyone leave the auditorium quickly in order to allow the actors crammed into the wooden chest to get out. This choice made a grotesque dissonance the grand finale. Zofia Senwtowa—an Opole journalist writing under the pseudonym 'Aunt Agnes'—perhaps best described this moment in a derisive report ridiculing the performance.

> And that was when the cloakroom attendant ran on stage and began politely encouraging the audience to file out quickly, because the actors would suffocate inside that chest. That was when I learned that in a self-respecting theatre a mortal does not present themselves to the audience, no matter what sorts of applause they would attract. And it was they who seemingly had said goodbye to this world and had to suffocate until the auditorium emptied. Thankfully there were no crowds, yet still just in case some holes should have been drilled in the chest to let air in, because it's easy to come to a tragic end.
> (Senwtowa 1962: 6)

Of course, in retrospect it is hard to say if this dissonance was intentional—or simply the result of a failure on the part of the 13 Rows to find a more elegant way to end the performance. I believe Grotowski would have found a different solution if he desired to do so. Furthermore, this comical disruption to the shocking and disturbing finale seems to me to be very much in line with what Grotowski was trying to achieve in the early 1960s, and also in line with his penchant for irony. Only Grotowski could have come up with this sort of idea, and have the gall to put it into action—to stage a 'Bacchae dance' and procession floating through the air to the sound of Christmas carols, and leading the audience to experience profound shock—all in order to then knock it all down by drawing the audience's attention to the artifice and theatricality of the proceedings, packing actors into the box and implying to the audience that the actors might experience asphyxiation, mirroring the suffering of camp inmates. Indeed, the actors might have said of Grotowski 'he's not been stingy with our chore,/ Our LORD/ Our maker and tormentor' (Wyspiański 2019: 353). One can only imagine the impact on audiences who were amazed—or maybe outraged that they had been 'fooled'—ultimately and finally reminded that the performance and the actors were all too real, and that this unexpected moment potentially positioned the spectators as perpetrators. Did they not—by leaving the hall calmly and quickly—prove their own humanity? Did they not choose to return back to themselves in spite of their evident shock, their upset fidgeting and askance glances into the void of *Acropolis* as they left the theatre? Was this not a gesture through which culture and good manners returned to the theatre, evidencing the reality of the lowest rank the decision played out by Coryphaeus and his chorus?

What Is Truth?

Having sifted through a mountain of materials and putting forward several (perhaps premature) interpretations of the performance from 1962, I now return to the fundamental question of meaning and truth in Grotowski's *Acropolis*.

Zbigniew Osiński presented his understanding thus:

In its whole structure the performance resembles a Passion Oratorio. But the Passion is treated with irony. *Acropolis* moves between an apotheosis and a heresy. The performance is driven by the ambivalence of the resurrection and death of camp prisoner—Christ, and the agony and the annihilation of our civilization and its traditional values.
(Osiński 1972: 201)

It is hard to contend that such a precise author would make a mistake amid such an important claim—hence we are justified in assuming that he consciously took on this altered, and in some way illogical sequence of 'resurrection and death of camp prisoner—Christ'. Was Osiński trying to suggest that *Acropolis* was a way of acting out the Second Coming of Christ who reveals himself in Auschwitz only to be killed there again— this time once and for all? Such an interpretation seems compatible with the sequences involving the doll as a representation of the Saviour brought in during the 'Prologue' by Coryphaeus and tossed on the ground at the point when he speaks about the coming of Christ-Salvator. It is then hung upon barbed wire in a mirror image of iconic photographs of inmates' dead bodies and hence taken up in the finale. This account suggests that the camp-wide 'Passion Oratory' on the one hand served as the staging of a rejected Second Coming, the (imposter) Saviour is killed again, and on the other hand presents a radically derisive, brutal levelling of Polish messianism brought down from its lofty perch to a bloody earth.

Following Osiński's interpretation one could say that after *Forefathers' Eve* and *Kordian*—with their staged attempts of derision using madness and jest—in *Acropolis* the Polish Messiah would undergo the harshest confrontation, a confrontation with the Shoah. And in this confrontation, no dialectical reasoning could save him from death, which occurs after his resurrection. Christ returned to Auschwitz only to be murdered there. It may have been an act of solidarity but it brought no hope for salvation.

Zbigniew Raszewski seemed to understand the performance in a similar way.

> Wyspiański's *Acropolis* is considered to be an expression of faith in the indestructible power of life, in its meaning and justice. In the Laboratory Theatre of 13 Rows, prisoners proclaim this faith, and forcefully enough to experience hallucination. In reality they are so debased they abuse one another. In Wyspiański's original there is no shortage of cruelty. And yet all dissonances are resolved as if in a classic harmony. In the Opole staging every word of hope is a judgement passed upon the self. Every hammer blow brings the moment of execution closer. Once the camp is ready the prisoners form a procession, and then Wyspiański's poems become a scream [...]. Thanks to remarkable technical skill the procession seems to float in mid-air, until it is eventually sucked into a trash can.
> (Raszewski 2006[1964]: 237)

Reading this fragment it is hard to doubt that, according to Raszewski, *Acropolis* signified a negation of salvation and rejected the hope that, in the finale, all would be revealed as mere hallucination. There is no talk here of anything sacred—only the image of people poisoned with the illusion of salvation while they organize their world as a collective form of hell.

But in light of this interpretation, the words that follow in Raszewski's report are surprising and mysterious.

> In the Opole *Acropolis* there is much truth. The quicker we learn and understand it, the better. The opposite of truth is falsehood, which harms life, for it impoverishes it.
> (Raszewski 2006[1964]: 237)

What is this 'truth'? Is it merely the truth of an anti-aesthetic chaos, and finally the shock that comes with unmasking illusions of salvation? Raszewski is somehow enigmatic in his statements, and there seems to be no use in trying to work out what it was he was really trying to say.

Reoccurring questions about truth in the context of *Acropolis* seem to me—though perhaps also for Grotowski who was a careful reader of the Gospels—as if emerging straight out of an evangelical understanding of truth and resurrection. In this view, resurrection is not a mere concept, project or idea but is something manifested by the Son of Man. When Jesus spoke about the truth he usually pointed at himself and said 'I am the way and the truth and the life' (John 14: 6), and 'I am the resurrection and the life. The one who believes in me will live, even though they die' (John 11: 25–26). In this context, *Acropolis* seems to be a performance that begs the question Pontius Pilate asked Jesus: 'What is truth?' (John 18: 38). The performance did not pose this as a philosophical question but rather as a practical question in terms of action by performing a drama on resurrection in a death camp, and by deciding to speak on behalf of a truth other than the one created by the staging of concentration camp trauma.

Grzegorz Niziołek asked what 'resurrection' might mean in the context of a death camp, and juxtaposed an analysis of camp trauma produced by Antoni Kępiński with Grotowski's descriptions of the total act. His comparison led him to conclude that 'One thing seems almost certain to me: Grotowski's aim was to repeat in a changed life circumstance that concentration camp experience of having one's life mask destroyed' (Niziołek 2013: 293). Niziołek writes mainly about the film version of *Acropolis* with the aid of *Towards a Poor Theatre*. He places the filmed *Acropolis* it in its 1968 context, and in relation to Grotowski's battle at the time to establish his 'method'. The essence of his method was to smash apart the 'life mask' and strive to discover the self in earnest. I also believe that—as Niziołek writes—it is in this context that Grotowski radically, and provocatively used 'shocking historical experiences to ensure effectiveness (or maybe in other words—the force of conviction) of his own strategies' (Niziołek 2013: 293). Yet, in 1962 Grotowski did not have any ready-made strategies nor a 'method' and thus Niziołek's claims are hard to apply to the version of the performance that is the focus of this chapter.

However, I propose that we place *Acropolis* in the context of Grotowski's earlier work on Polish Romantic drama. In this context, one could argue that in *Acropolis* Grotowski conducted a certain personal and social process that reduced everything to ground level—the level of a concentration camp—in order to test the 'myth' of Christ both as a Christian and as a Pole. In the context of Auschwitz, he questioned all forms of messianism understood here as a waiting for the Saviour to come. And simultaneously though perhaps paradoxically he confirmed the necessity of fighting for redemption. What then can we extrapolate from the *Acropolis* finale in which Coryphaeus—the leader of a community doomed to annihilation—creates a saviour by staging a Second Coming with the hymn sung to praise a dilapidated doll? If we now transfer the devices used in earlier performances of the 13 Rows to this scene—and think of Coryphaeus as someone who like Kordian is clearly mad but without whose madness life collapses into the emptiness of the Doctor's rational void—then the finale of *Acropolis* should be understood as the image of the Saviour who may be a creation of deceit, an illusion, maybe even a lie but is at the same time necessary. For without this deceit and this illusion we are left with nothing but the camp, the result of the Doctor's rational logic stripped of cultural fictions. In deep disagreement with this—and in search of an opportunity to build a point of resistance—Grotowski worked on his *Acropolis* in 1962 without finding any possible foundation of truth other than an act of creative will, an act of making a decision and an act of saying 'yes' to the past and pointing to the self alone just as Jesus did.

This decision fulfils the criteria of the ethics of being a human as formulated by Alain Badiou in his *Ethics*. Badiou rejects the definition of a human being as someone who 'is able to see the self as a sacrifice', and does so specifically in relation to scenarios involving torture and concentration camps.

> In his role as the executioner man is an animal abjection,
> but we must have the courage to add that in his role as victim,
> he is generally worth little more. The stories told by survivors

of torture, forcefully underline this point: if the torturers and bureaucrats of the dungeons and the camps are able to treat their victims like animals destined for the slaughterhouse, with whom they themselves, the well-nourished criminals, have nothing in common, it is because the victims have indeed become such animals. What had to be done for this to happen has indeed been done. That some nevertheless remained human beings and testify to this effect, is a confirmed fact. But this is always achieved precisely through enormous effort, an effort acknowledged by witnesses (in whom it excites a radiant recognition) as an almost incomprehensible resistance on the part of that which, in them, does not coincide with the identity of victim. This is where we are to find Man, if we are determined to think him [*la penser*]: in what ensures, as Varlam Shalamov puts in his *Stories of Life in the Camps*, that we are dealing with an animal whose resistance, unlike that of a horse, lies not in his fragile body, but in his stubborn determination to remain what he is—that is to say precisely something other than a victim, other than being-for-death, and thus: something other than a mortal being.

An immortal: this is what the worst situations that can be inflicted upon Man show him to be, in so far as he distinguished himself within the varied and rapacious flux of life. [. . .] The fact that in the end we all die, that only dust remains in no way alters Man's identity as immortal at the instant in which he affirms himself as someone who runs counter to the temptation of wanting-to-be-an-animal to which circumstances may expose him. [. . .].
(Badiou 2013: 11–12)

Grotowski and his actors without making their task any easier used *Acropolis* to conduct a dramatic process of revealing immortality understood as a radically non-religious, secular version of salvation: the resurrection of humanity in Auschwitz.

It is only later on—and was it not as a result of this fundamental choice?—that they created a method for reaching a para-religious experience of non-confessional holiness. Even if we are to consider this experience to be an illusion or a trick—and I have no right to convince anyone otherwise—then still the very decision to create it seems to be necessary. Without it we remain powerless in the face of the ever-present threat of camp life. It is precisely here in the experience of how the only thing we craft ourselves, and uniquely within ourselves is the camp that I see the anti-systemic aspect and burning relevance of Grotowski's work. Work that is especially relevant today when systems drive towards us to feel at home in 'our Auschwitz'. *Acropolis* and its stifling atmosphere of calculated shock can be interpreted quite differently from Niziołek's proposal—not as a re-staging of the traumatizing experience of the camp, but as a pre-staging of the trauma of meeting human beings stripped of all 'illusions'. Perhaps Grotowski foresaw this encounter by looking into his country's past—and into himself. In staring into the void, Grotowski made a decisive choice.

Dariusz Kosiński

CHAPTER EIGHT

'To heaven? You blaspheme in vain'
The Tragical History of Doctor Faustus
after Christopher Marlowe

Turning the Table

The Laboratory Theatre of 13 Rows' premiere in Opole of *The Tragical History of Doctor Faustus* on 23 April 1963 marked a milestone in the history of Grotowski's theatre. First, this marked the final performance where he emphasized the archetypes and the dialectics of derision and apotheosis. Second, *Doctor Faustus* paved the way 'towards a poor theatre' defined not by poverty but by the total act. Grotowski worked on the total act, achieving his first—albeit preliminary—success during individual rehearsals with Zbigniew Cynkutis for *Doctor Faustus* (Cynkutis 2000 and Wójtowicz 2004: 239–47). Third, *Doctor Faustus* was the first premiere of the Laboratory Theatre of 13 Rows that received international attention as the company began to seek international recognition in earnest[1]—a search that succeeded largely due to Eugenio Barba.[2] Most importantly, *Doctor Faustus* marked the company's final work on practices of profanation, as they transitioned towards the creation of their own alternative liturgy.

---

1 As I proved in the previous chapter, the 13 Rows created the internationally renowned version of *Acropolis* after the premiere of *Doctor Faustus*.

2 One of his most important and brave 'actions' in this respect was an excursion to Łódź that Barba organized for a group of international theatre critics and researchers taking part in the World Congress of the International Theatre Institute in Warsaw in June 1963. Barba hired a bus and without informing the Congress organizers took this group to Łódź where the Laboratory Theatre was presenting *Doctor Faustus* on tour. Some of the critics considered this visit the most important experience of the Congress.

345

In the first half of the 1960s—up until the company's staging of *The Constant Prince* which premiered on 25 April 1965—one of Grotowski's main concerns was related to audience response. As a result of this concern, he sought a special, situational approach to audience engagement that supported, and in fact enhanced the effects of the performance. Jerzy Gurawski was a remarkable and revolutionary agent in this process. His innovations generated new results with each performance. In all of his work for Grotowski he linked the general situation designed by the director with the shape of the performance space, and with the tools with which the actors worked. In comparison to prior 13 Rows performances, the spatial concept for *The Tragical History of Doctor Faustus* most closely resembled that of *Kordian*. In both cases the entirety of the performance was set in a frame that was extrapolated from one scene of the original text on which the 13 Rows production was based. In *Doctor Faustus*, Gurawski based the spatial arrangement on the finale of the whole drama, Faustus' 'last supper' on earth.

> The text was adapted in such a way as to have the final scene—a feast with students during which Faustus, moments before death, settles his moral accounts—frame the performance. It was presented as a feast during which Faustus offers the audience dishes made of the key events in his life.
> (Flaszen 2010[1964]: 97)

The space crafted by Gurawski was based on a monastic refectory, and the audience played many roles at once—Faustus' invited friends and students. For the performance, the 13 Rows entirely covered up the small performance space with unvarnished, wooden planks, and created three rectangular, wooden tables, two longer tables and one shorter table made of the same unvarnished wood. The two longer tables featured benches for audience members that ran the length of their longer sides. These benches had tall backs—1.7 meters high. The company set these two larger tables parallel to each other with a small gap between them through which the actors moved during the performance. The gap between the tables provided more than just a passageway for actors. For example, at one point it served as a river in which Faustus was submerged and baptized. The third, slightly smaller table stood at the end of the hall perpendicular to the two other tables. Together the three tables created a horseshoe shape with very long sides.

The tables were key elements in the performance. They served as stages on which Faustus acted out retrospective scenes as well as scenes in the 'present' like the farewell final feast. Generally, the two longer tables served as stages for past events while the smaller table was a stage for 'the present'. During the performance, Laboratory Theatre actors filled the auditorium and surrounded the audience with sounds, movements and actions that intervened in audiences' experiences from completely unexpected angles. A fragment of the performance recorded by Michael Elster in his 1963 film *The Letter from Opole* (*List z Opola*)[3] shows that this performance aroused unease in audiences—a stark contrast to the solidity of the set design. Indeed, the set design's initial appearance of solidity quickly turned out to be misleading. In the performance, actors lifted the heavy-looking tables into the air, disassembled them, and moved them around the space with ease. For Grotowski, the surprising facility with which actors could transform the space by manipulating these solid objects represented a key means of constructing the performative event. Over 20 years after the premiere of *Doctor Faustus*, Grotowski recalled the company's transformative discovery of the versatility of simple, wooden tables.

> Let us take for an example the table—I am thinking here about the table in *Dr Faustus* after Marlowe, which we staged back in Opole. All the audience were seated at two long tables. This was Faustus' last supper, at which he presents the events from his own life as if they were dishes served at the feast, before he falls into the hands of the one who rules the Earth. And so, we have a table. I look at the table, look at the hooded monk asking

---

3 *The Letter from Opole* (*List z Opola*) is a short, 28-minute documentary film made by British director Michael Elster as his diploma work at the State Higher Film, Television and Theatre School in Łódź. The film is about the people and work of the Laboratory Theatre, and includes some scenes from the company's training, an interview with Grotowski, Flaszen and Gurawski, and a six-minute fragment of *The Tragical History of Doctor Faustus* featuring footage from a rehearsal and a public performance. The whole film can be seen online on YouTube.

Faustus to confess. There is no confession box, while I, with the way I was raised and with my cultural context, feel that the real confession should take place in a confessional, otherwise it is in part improper. We have no confession box, but we can move a table, turning it on its side. The monk is on one side of it, Faustus on the other. And so, the table becomes a confessional, to then become a ship, a forest path, and many other things. It was not possible to invent this earlier.
(Grotowski 2012: 789)

Given the significance of this discovery, it is no surprise that Grotowski remembered it vividly. This relatively simple device—a wooden table— was thoroughly developed and transformed, turning the entire perform-ance space into a playground for the creators' use of the tables.

These movable tables became a starting point for Faustus' farewell feast. In the commentaries and reports from Grotowski and his colleagues that I quote and analyse below, this feast is consistently referred to as the 'last supper'. In a now well-known article, Eugenio Barba, who was the director's assistant for *Doctor Faustus*, articulates the company's pro-fane appropriation of religious imagery.

Faustus has one hour to live before his martyrdom of hell and eternal damnation. He invites his friends to a last supper, a public confession where he offers them episodes from his life as Christ offered his body and blood.
(Barba 1968: 79)

The 13 Rows presents this juxtaposition of Faustus and Christ's Last Supper directly; scenes from throughout the performance are treated as offerings, just like the bread and wine that are turned into the Lord's Flesh and Blood in the Eucharist. *Doctor Faustus'* creators carefully planned this act of theatrical profanation, directing it at the Catholic lit-urgy. In contrast with the company's previous profanations, this one lacks any playfulness. Instead, the Laboratory Theatre clearly staged the per-formance as a substitute Eucharist. One could of course suggest that this substitution remained in the realm of the theatrical 'as if', and that the 13

'TO HEAVEN? YOU BLASPHEME IN VAIN' · 349

Rows merely plays with a taboo analogy. However, I argue that Grotowski took this substitution seriously, that this conscious act of profanation was in fact thoroughly intertwined into the entire performance.

Based on Barba's description of the basic performance situation— the audience are Faustus' friends and students who he invited to a feast— we can see that the concept of *Doctor Faustus* was not far from the situation of *Forefathers' Eve*. In the 13 Rows' performance based on Mickiewicz's drama, the audience also took part in a 'social gathering'. However, a key difference emerges. In *Forefathers' Eve*—as in *Kordian*— there was an effort to give the audience an elevated status akin to that of an actor. Years later, Grotowski, critical of these strategies, pointed to alternative tactics the 13 Rows employed in *Doctor Faustus*.

> In Kordian we ignored the obvious fact that the spectators are anyway playing the role of spectators—they are observers! And when we put them in the role of madmen, we simply disturbed their natural function as observers—or in the best case—as witnesses; in consequence their reactions were not natural. The union of place, time and action was not accomplished.
>
> We solved this problem when we did Marlowe's *Doctor Faustus*. For the first time we found a direct word-for-word situation. The dramatic function of the spectators and the function of the spectator as spectator were the same. For the first time we saw authentic spontaneity. The audience was treated as Faustus' invited guests, people whom Faustus seeks so that he can make an analysis of his own life. The spectators are around a long table and Faustus, with other people from his life, arranges for them a flashback. It was absolutely tangible. If, for example, he were to say, 'now you will see the scene of when I first met the Devil. I was sitting in a chair like this, and I was listening to a song'. Then there is a song and in the front of the spectators someone comes in. The confession was authentic because the actor really mobilized the associations of his life. At the same time, he made Faustus' confession with the text, he accomplished his own very drastic but disciplined confession.

There were waves of movement in the room. Faustus never waited for answers from the spectators, but he observed their eyes and we saw in them some physical symptoms of the impact, and also one could hear their breathing; something real was happening.

(Grotowski 1968b; quoted in Schechner and Wolford 1997: 49–50)

Grotowski and his team thus found in *Doctor Faustus* that which they had tried to discover through repeated attempts to involve audiences in previous performances. In *Doctor Faustus*, spectators became the characters, and each of them in their own way played out within themselves the conflicts and dilemmas of the protagonist. The Laboratory Theatre achieved this feat by giving the audience a whole new role, that of witnesses. Beginning with *Doctor Faustus*, the company no longer prepared for their audience's experiences of taking part in performances; now the director and the actors prepared performances that the audiences were to experience as witnesses.

The Polish word for 'experience' is more precise than in languages that use words derived from the Latin *experientia* which refers to the process of gaining or extracting knowledge directly: *ex*—from, and *peritus* that which is verified, lived through. Alternately, the Polish word *doświadczenie* points to an event as something destined to be confirmed and conveyed—*do-świadczenia* (to-witness) instead of something from which to 'extract' knowledge. *Doctor Faustus*' creators invited audiences to inhabit the role implied by this Polish alternative. For Grotowski this was a very important discovery.

We had many discussions within our team which might have led to a change of attitudes between *Kordian* and *Acropolis* (first version) and then between *Acropolis* and *Doctor Faustus*. What did we notice? When for an example we want to give the audience the chance to take part emotively, directly yet emotively— meaning the chance to identify with someone who carries the responsibility for the tragedy taking place-then we should distance audiences from the actors, in spite of what one might think. The audience, separated by space, put into the position of someone who as an observer is not even accepted, who remains solely in the position of observer, is in fact capable of interacting emotively, because as a result they can rediscover in themselves the ancient calling of the audience. We should ask the question as to what this calling might be, just as we might ask about the calling of the actor. The audience's calling is to be an observer, but what is more, to be a witness. The witness is not someone who pokes their nose into everything, who tries to be as close as possible, to interfere with the actions of others. The witness remains slightly off to the side, not wanting to interfere, desiring to remain aware, to see what is happening from start to finish, and to retain in memory the image of events preserved in him.

(Grotowski 2012: 359)

And yet in *Doctor Faustus*, the audience was asked to do more than witness. The 13 Rows provocatively placed them within another, self-referential frame. They did so through two folk characters, Bartek and Kuba played by Zygmunt Molik and Maciej Prus.[4] Grotowski turned these clownish minor characters who appear only in interludes within Marlowe's 'tragical history' into commentators who sat on benches among the audience throughout the performance. Grotowski's choice to cast Molik was provocative. At the time, it was widely believed that Molik was the best actor in the company. Grotowski himself must have thought highly of Molik's acting, casting him in the roles of Gustav-Conrad in *Forefathers' Eve*, the Doctor in *Kordian*, and Coryphaeus in *Acropolis*. And yet in *Doctor Faustus*, Grotowski cast Molik as an interlude character alongside a less experienced and much less renowned member of the company. Perhaps Molik himself wanted to take a break? Or did Grotowski's decision arise out of some sort of conflict? After all, Molik would leave the Laboratory Theatre within the next three years. Or maybe Grotowski cast Molik in this role because of the actor's personal proclivities which Flaszen mentioned in the context of *Faustus*.

---

4 When Prus left the company in the autumn of 1963 he was replaced in the role by Mieczysław Janowski.

352 · DARIUSZ KOSIŃSKI

> Zygmunt Molik, an excellent actor with the sceptical nature of
> a skilful craftsman, sat in the audience, among Faust's invited
> banqueters, making a reckoning of his life—and was supposed
> to interject stupid remarks as though a simple spectator.
> (Flaszen 2010: 286)

Flaszen's characterization of Molik's assignment—'to interject stupid remarks as though a simple spectator'—seems to me to be of particular importance. The two 'commentator' characters played 'simple spectators', and thus their trivial comments and observations were somehow offered on the behalf of the audience of which they were a part. British critic Michael Kustow acutely later reported:

> Two of them sit on the benches with us, and speak low-comic
> lines [. . .] sceptical of Faustus, cutting him down to our size.
> (Kustow 1963: 14)

Bartek and Kuba therefore created a second role for audience members to play, a role far more lowbrow than that of friends invited to attend a 'last supper'. Bartek and Kuba invited spectators to become trivial, 'stupid' observers, interrupting the solemn tragedy with absurd anecdotes and folk songs. The short interruptions Bartek and Kuba initiated were very important for the performance. Kustow wrote that Bartek and Kuba's interjections led the audience to feel as if they were also becoming cynical and vulgar. This shows that through the two folk characters audiences became aware of their own distance from the drama unfolding before them, and felt this distance as a barrier, an uncomfortable separation. This led audiences to question who they were, confronting them with actors who stripped themselves of their dignity, baring themselves down to the bone. This discomfort pointed audiences beyond the role of ironic spectators, pushing them towards becoming witnesses. In other words, presenting audiences with these caricatures of spectatorship aimed to prevent them from adopting such roles themselves.

Saint Sebastian and the Duality of Desire

After the malleability of the set, Grotowski's second key idea for the Laboratory Theatre's work on Marlowe's drama was to portray Faustus as a saint. Flaszen spoke about this plainly.

> The director found some similarities between Faustus' story and saints' biographies. If sanctity is understood to be an uncompromising striving for the truth and a fondness for extreme attitudes that absorb human beings in their entirety, then Faustus is a saint. The director models Faustus' life after medieval hagiographic clichés. Through his baptism, mortifications, fighting against desire, performing miracles, and finally his martyrdom, Faustus heads towards the ultimate ambiguously cruel apotheosis.
> (Flaszen 2010[1964]: 97)

In this way, Grotowski constructed the performance to tell Faustus' story retrospectively as a miracle play, a drama about a saint.[5] Following the tradition of such plays, Faustus' self-staged hagiography began with a transformation: abandoning his old life and turning towards a new one. As a result, it became possible to perform further miracles, thus confirming the saint's power to transform his surroundings and the world. The performance was crowned by a martyrdom sequence, just as it would be in a conventional, hagiographic miracle play.

Critics writing about the Opole *Doctor Faustus* often mentioned the main character's youth, physical beauty, grace and innocence. Zbigniew Cynkutis' youthful, handsome appearance played a key role in this perception. He did not play Faustus as an old man. Instead, he portrayed Faustus as a delicate and sensitive soul ensnared by the world's cruel mechanisms. Barba wrote about the way Cynkutis played his role as it related to the performance's frame as a miracle play.

---

5 Marlowe also used the miracle play to construct the story of Faustus drawing on Catholic conventions from plays about the saints—which at the time were banned in England—in order to show the life of a man who was condemned. However, Marlowe's drama opposed the miracle play's original aims.

> The role [of Faustus] is played by an actor who looks young
> and innocent—his psycho-physical characteristics resemble St.
> Sebastian's. But this St. Sebastian is anti-religious, fighting God.
> (Barba 1968: 80)

This resemblance brings to mind legends of St Sebastian's martyrdom: the story of a converted Roman soldier shot with arrows for his Christian belief. It also recalls the iconographic tradition related to St Sebastian, once among the most popular and complex representations of a Catholic saint. Paintings of St Sebastian's martyrdom often emphasize his beauty, depicting a young, male body rather than his piety. In addition, St Sebastian was often depicted especially during the baroque period in ecstasies that combined suffering and erotic delight. In this respect, St Sebastian is considered to be an icon of homoeroticism. For these reasons, St Sebastian made an ideal figure upon which to project the 'saint rebel' dreamt up by Grotowski and Cynkutis—especially in the context of the many auto-erotic and other sexual scenes and allusions in Grotowski's *Doctor Faustus*. Cynkutis' Faustus does not engage in overtly homosexual acts, though such portrayals would appear in *Apocalypsis cum figuris*. In *Doctor Faustus*, he directs his sexual activity towards women, and towards himself. The creators of the Opole *Doctor Faustus* depict Faustus' relations with women as unfulfilling, disturbing, maybe even repulsive while relating his auto-eroticism to notions of excess and the release of repressed drives. Based on the qualities the 13 Rows associates with Faustus' sexuality, I argue that this Faustus—just like St Sebastian—represents at the very least a strong commentary on homoerotic desire.

There is little doubt that Grotowski and Cynkutis' Faustus has masochistic tendencies. Faustus seeks pain and debasement and at times he harms himself as in the scene when he is reading his pact with the Devil. This scene can be seen on Elster's film, but it is something neither Grotowski nor Cynkutis spoke about. But it is also not hard to imagine audiences feeling shock and shame. This was not only due to the audiences' proximity to the actors but also to the creators' transgression of historical boundaries of intimacy in 1964 Communist–Catholic Poland.

Above all, Cynkutis' impact on audiences was related to confronting them with an uncomfortable heteronomy.

Through the figure of their St Sebastian/Faustus, the Laboratory Theatre tethered 'innocence' to non-normative sexuality, which was defined in those days as 'perversion' or 'aberration'. In 1964, there appears not to have been a normative cultural language with which Poles could connect 'innocence' and 'aberration', and therefore the creators of *Doctor Faustus* found recourse to metaphors and cultural icons. So, when the Laboratory Theatre presented an unnamed yet clearly homosexual-masochistic action, the limitations of their cultural surroundings likely increased their efforts' effectiveness and affective powers. In addition, *Doctor Faustus'* creators connected these forces to images, gestures, actions, songs, costumes and prayers that they derived from Catholic liturgy and performative tradition. St Sebastian—an ambivalent icon experiencing the solitary delight of becoming a martyr—thereby became the patron saint of this performance.

In this context, I would like to ask a question that has not been posed: Why did Mephistopheles appear as both a woman and a man, Rena Mirecka and Antoni Jahołkowski? Reviewers mostly accepted and praised this choice as a directorial decision, something interesting and inspiring. Yet, interestingly enough, no one considered the motives behind it, nor asked how effective it was. We could of course say that Grotowski splitting Mephistopheles into two characters gave him the chance to introduce complex, inter-textual games, to spin a web of cultural associations and connections—at times mean and misogynistic—a topic to which I will return. But I think these outcomes were merely side effects, that having the Tempter appear as both a man and a woman was connected to the subtext of bisexuality also inhabiting the protagonist. Between Faustus and Mephistopheles there of course exists an erotic tension—and in some of Grotowski's scenes this subtext was strong—for example, in the alternating breathing of the two Mephistopheles who lie stretched out on the ground while Faustus masochistically prostrates himself and signs away his soul to the Devil. Mephistopheles' duality allows the bisexual hero to play within this tension.

It is also possible that splitting Mephistopheles in two is a way to mask the hidden topic—homosexual desire—by balancing it with a female Mephistopheles. However, this is merely a hypothesis the confirmation of which would require further detailed analyses of the economy of desire and the ways in which Grotowski manages it in his performances. This analysis is especially relevant for Grotowski's last four productions—from *Doctor Faustus* to *Apocalypsis cum figuris*, culminating in the homoerotic and masochistic figures in *The Constant Prince*, where Grotowski depicts another holy martyr in a way that approximates St Sebastian. These performances all seem to be constructed of complicated webs of desires related to taboo sexuality. Grotowski staged such webs as early as *Cain* (1960), but in *Doctor Faustus*, he made them central to the theatrical event, adding an extra layer of meaning to enhance the performance's impact on witnesses.

Pact with the Devil

In the historical record, we have two more or less congruent accounts of the sequence of action Grotowski derived from Marlowe's original drama. Flaszen composed the first, shorter list, which the company printed and distributed to audiences. Eugenio Barba included the second, longer list, along with descriptions of individual scenes, published first in Italian, later translated into English, and finally included in *Towards a Poor Theatre*.

To present an immediate outline of the entire performance, I will quote Flaszen's shorter list of scenes in full.

> The start of the feast: an announcement about the public confession.—The action moves back to the past.—Faustus struggles with himself in his laboratory.—Confession before ordination. Cornelius and Valdes teach Faustus how to cast a spell on the spirits.—Through the forest, to the place for sorcery.—Evoking Mephistopheles: the Annunciation.—Mortification.—A walk and a spiritual conversation with Mephistopheles.—The baptism.—Signing the pact with the Devil: complete destitution.—

Getting dressed in sanctified robes.—Reading a holy book—a woman?—Temptation of the saint.—Discussion about the universe: Mephistopheles praises the music of the spheres.—Ralph and Robin:[6] how trivial is this creature.—The seven deadly sins.—A trip to Rome on dragons' backs.—Faustus, motivated by love, slaps the Pope's face, to heal his pride.—At the emperor's court: Faustus summons the spirit of Alexander the Great and his lover.—Scene with Benvolio: Faustus heals this man possessed by rage, restoring the inner child in him (a miracle).—The action returns to the present.—Faustus summons Helen of Troy's spirit, alluding to the reproductive functions of love.—Mephistopheles shows Faustus the paradise that he would gain if he obeys God (a good death), and the hell for disobedience (a bad death).—Faustus reveals to the audience the inhumanity and indifference of God who does not care about the human soul's salvation: the ecstasy of the highest protest, the start of eternal suffering.—Mephistopheles elevates Faustus for the eternal agony, *Ite, missa est*: those who played the role of executioners perform it solemnly and amicably.
(Flaszen 2010[1964]: 98)

In his report, Flaszen clearly introduces his own division of the performance into four distinct parts with different themes and separate constructions. The first of these is a typical feature of Grotowski's scripts and performances: a Prologue in which the company sets up a frame for the performance and establishes the starting points of the action. Part two encompasses the first half of retrospective scenes, including Faustus preparing to summon the Devil, meeting with Mephistopheles and all that is connected with Faustus signing his pact with the Devil. Part three shows subsequent lessons, those Mephistopheles gives to Faustus as well as the miracles performed by the Doctor. Part four is the finale returning the performance to the 'present', to Faustus' last supper.

---

6 The English translator and editor of Flaszen's texts reintroduced Marlowe's original names. However, in the performance the company used the Polish names Bartek and Kuba.

The Prologue was relatively short. Flaszen renders the Prologue in a single phrase, 'the start of the feast: an announcement about the public confession'. In Barba's report he details the specifics Flaszen glosses over by dividing the Prologue into three scenes:

Scene 1. Faustus greets his guests.
Scene 2. Wagner announces that his master is soon to die.
Scene 3. A monologue in which Faustus publicly confesses as sins his studies and exalts as a virtue his pact with the Devil.
(Barba 1968: 81)

The script archived at the GIA confirms Barba's list (Grotowski 1963b).

At the start of the show 'Faustus, full of humility, his eyes empty, lost in the imminence of his martyrdom, greets his guests while seated at his small table, his arms open as on the Cross. Then he begins his confession' (Barba 1968: 81). His assistant Wagner, wearing a hood, interrupts Faustus in a surprise entrance from beneath one of the table tops, lifting it up and revealing himself to what must have been a shocked audience. An 'audience member'—actor Maciej Prus—suddenly interrupted Wagner. Prus hit the table top with his hand and exclaimed 'What is happening to Faustus?' (Wójtowicz 2004: 99).

Prus' interruption signalled the beginning of Scene 3. Elster filmed fragments of this scene (1963: 19 min 33 sec). After another interruption by a second 'audience member' (Molik), Faustus began his public confession. Barba reports that 'what we usually call virtues, [Faustus] calls sin—his theological and scientific studies; and what we call sin, he calls virtue—his pact with the Devil. During this confession, Faustus' face glows with an inner light' (Barba 1968: 81). Thus, in the Prologue, audiences encountered the fundamental framework for the ensuing drama—including the protagonist's attitude and key staging elements—the illusory stability of the set construction, and the presence of 'trivial commentators' in the form of actors placed among the spectators.

In the first part of the actual 'tragical history' audiences witnessed Faustus summoning Mephistopheles and signing a pact with the Devil. This sequence opened with a moving, retrospective scene.

> Faustus stepped from the top-table (the present tense) onto the
> long, trestle-tables (flashback) to tell us how he had arrived at
> this stage of imminent death and damnation
> (Kustow 1963: 13)

This description matches the film recording of the scene (Elster 1963: 19 min 50 sec–20 min 40 sec). Faustus stands on the shorter table and melodically recites a fragment of the first song of the Chorus that in the Marlowe's tragedy depicted the hero in his study. Cynkutis makes gestures signifying the outline of a square room, and his demeanour is reminiscent of an academic giving a lecture or a presentation. The situation changes dramatically when he climbs atop one of the longer tables for a flashback. He expressively alters his attitude and tone of voice, and delivers a shortened version of a monologue from the beginning of Marlowe's drama in which the hero expressed his disappointment with the knowledge he gathered in his studies.

Faustus ends his monologue with extended cries of 'Physics, farewell! / Divinity, adieu!' The first appearance of Mirecka-Jahołkowski's Mephistopheles interrupts Faustus' monologue (Elster 1963: 20 min 40 sec). Audiences do not immediately know what this strange creature will be. It emerged from one of the wooden walls behind the seats for the public, and slowly arose from an initial, deep bow to the rhythm of slowly recited words. Once the monstrous couple was fully erect they bowed again at the same, slow pace thus disappearing from the audiences' sight. Jahołkowski recited lines from the original drama that belonged to the Good Angel, 'O, Faustus, lay that damned book aside', and Mirecka recited those of the Evil Angel, 'Go forward, Faustus, in that famous art'. But they both acted together as one, and thus signalled the united duality of apparent opposites familiar to us from *Cain* (Alfa-Omega).

Barba describes the following scene.

> Faustus talks to Cornelius and Valdes, who come to initiate
> him in magic. Cornelius turns a table into a confessional booth.
> As he confesses Faustus, granting him absolution, Faustus begins
> his new life. The spoken text often contradicts its interpretation;

for example, these lines describe the pleasures of magic. Then Cornelius[7] reveals the magic ceremonies to Faustus and teaches him an occult formula—which is nothing other than a well-known Polish religious hymn.

(Barba 1968: 81–82)

In visual terms Cornelius (Andrzej Bielski) and Valdes (Ryszard Cieślak) were monks. Their conversation with Faustus about the sin of practicing magic was akin to a confession, and hence it was a sacrament. Furthermore, it involved the speaking of specific words—just like the magical practices Valdes and Cornelius taught to Faustus. This scenario fits familiar Grotowskian patterns. Grotowski resolutely used sacramental gestures, words and forms of behaviour to achieve aims directly opposed to the ones for which they were designed.

Flaszen dubbed the next scene 'Through the forest, to the place for sorcery' (2010[1964]: 98). Elster filmed the scene; it is one of those sections of his film that show the diversity of the Cynkutis' acting tools (Elster 1963: 21 min 17 sec–22 min 40 sec). 'By imitating a gust of wind, the tumbling of leaves, the noises of the night, the cries of nocturnal animals, Faustus finds himself singing the same religious hymn invoking Mephistopheles' (Barba 1968: 82).

Cornelius and Valdes taught Faustus a traditional Christian hymn probably from the eighth century sung at Lent. The first verses are taken from Micah, 'My people, what have I done to you?' (Micah 6:3). Sung in the context of the Catholic celebrations of Lent and Good Friday it was used and developed as a complaint of the dying Christ. In Poland this is one of the most respected and well-known religious hymns. It is usually sung during the Adoration of the Cross as a part of the Good Friday liturgy. Grotowski's use of the song as a means for summoning the Evil Spirit is truly risky. First, Faustus intoned this song timidly. Then Mephistopheles in female form echoes his song, and climbs up on the

---

7 It is possible that Barba made a mistake here—though it might seem presumptuous for someone who did not even see the show to correct the director's assistant. In the text it was Valdes who performed all the actions Barba assigns to Cornelius. A more experienced actor played Valdes, and so it seems probable that he played the lead character in this scene.

shorter table singing aloud 'You made the cross for the arms of mine'. Satan thus takes the words attributed to Christ as her own. Mirecka sings them with gusto, and at the same time sings as if parodying the pious voices of the faithful who—sinners themselves—enter into the role of the suffering Christ. Grotowski's *Doctor Faustus* displaces piety with sacrilege—for what else would you call Satan taking over the Saviour's prayer?

But this is just the beginning of the games the 13 Rows played with religious images and associated beliefs. As I have already mentioned, only the female Mephistopheles goes up on the table. In keeping with Marlowe's text, Satan first appears before Faustus as a woman, and Faustus' reaction is particularly odious and mean.

> I charge thee to return, and change thy shape;
> Thou art too ugly to attend on me:
> Go, and return an old Franciscan friar;
> That holy shape becomes a devil best.
> (Marlowe 1974[1604]: 19 [Scene 3, 25–29])

Faustus whispered these words to Mirecka. He casted doubt over her personal beauty, his denunciation smacking of misogyny. Furthermore, his insults may have cloaked a homoerotic longing, Faustus' desire to be tempted by a man.

His wish was granted. The female Mephistopheles left the stage-table, replaced by the male Mephistopheles who stood 'on one leg, a soaring angel' singing his lines 'accompanied by an angelic choir. Faustus tells him that he is ready to give his soul to the Devil in exchange for twenty-four years of life against God' (Barba 1968: 82). This scene is one of those that achieved legendary status over the years for showing Grotowski's company's acting skills.

> There is a moment in *The Tragical History of Dr Faustus* when Antek-Mephistopheles appears to Faust for the first time. He stands in the iconographic position of the Angel from the Annunciation scene. He stands on one leg, a bent knee—the other, also gently bent, pulled back, suspended in the air. One

of his arms is raised up, the other one rests on his chest. He
intones his powerful incantation with a voice that echoes with
distant worlds.

He stands still—an image, an impression, the very essence
of flight. An amazing, unearthly creature.

His joyless message, breathing power and triumph, lasts
for some time. I cannot recall a single moment when his arm
or leg moved. A masterpiece of technique.
(Flaszen 2010: 199–200)

This scene is another allusion to the iconography of the Catholic Counter-
Reformation baroque period. In Renaissance paintings of the
Annunciation—partly under the influence of Fra Angelico—the Angel
and Mother Mary are usually depicted indoors as figures standing on
the same level. The Angel is most often an unexpected guest entering
the Virgin's room. Grotowski rejected these 'earthly' depictions. He chose
a different, later variant of the composition, one featuring a descending
angel, and Mary sitting or kneeling below-most often scared-in a
dynamic, twisted pose, distracted from prayers, reading, or other tasks
by the heavenly messenger. Good examples of this later variant that may
have inspired Grotowski are images of the Annunciation painted by El
Greco (1660) and Peter Paul Rubens (*c.*1628). But it is also possible that
I am looking too far afield for Grotowski's inspirations. The arrangement
of the Annunciation adopted by Grotowski is Poland's most popular
church iconography. A good example can be seen on the curtain covering
a miraculous icon of the Holy Mother in the sanctuary at Kalwaria
Zebrzydowska, near Kraków. Grotowski probably saw it there.

This is perhaps the riskiest and most blasphemous substitution—
Faustus takes the place of Mother Mary in a scene meant to represent
the Immaculate Conception. This scene thus manifests a now-classic
representation of Satan displacing divine figures from canonical, sanctified positions, a representation popularized by works such as *Rosemary's
Baby* by Roman Polanski, connected to the conception and birth of the
Antichrist. Clearly, Grotowski is not Polanski, and does not trade in

obvious signals. Nevertheless, signs of an anti-Christ are so numerous in his *Doctor Faustus* that the performance evidently goes beyond the scope of the classic story about a Doctor surrendering his soul to the Devil. The performance thus pushed audiences to consider different possibilities, new ways of interpreting the fate of a 'saint against God'.

Perhaps a clarification would be helpful before we continue. I am not assigning any sort of satanic-occult tendencies to Grotowski or his production. Rather, I am looking for the elements Grotowski and his company used to construct Faustus' character and the entire *Doctor Faustus* performance. These elements gave the production a certain power. The creators set them at the very centre of the dramatic battle Jerzy Grotowski waged as a representative of a generation that treated the Second World War—with all its cruelties—not as a historical accident, but as a catastrophe that made belief in traditional visions of the world impossible. In the Polish culture that shaped Grotowski, Catholicism created the 'traditional vision' of the world against which he rebelled. Grotowski and other members of his generation—and even their elders such as Czesław Miłosz and Tadeusz Różewicz—could not honestly entertain catechistic generalizations and orthodoxies that were—and still are—unable to answer questions concerning God and Auschwitz, and how teaching God's providence and Christ's loving mercy could relate to gas chambers and crematoriums. And so, Grotowski and those of his generation often made risky attempts to find their own answers. They were either hot or cold, and they attacked God with all seriousness and acuteness, without compromise. They blasphemed against God because they felt that God deserved it. And they also did so out of a desire to be heard. And to hear God's answers.

The scene depicting Mephistopheles and Faustus in the 'Annunciation' was dynamic, and yet also paradoxically static. It masterfully represented Mephistopheles—who took the place of the Angel—not quite descending. Jahołkowski amplified the sense of peace and sanctity in the tableaux through his singing of the liturgical composition as used even today during Catholic Holy Mass, though in this case sung to convey that Lucifer was the 'Arch-regent and commander of all spirits' (Marlowe 1962[1604]:

21 [Scene 3, 66]). As I write these words, I can hear Jahołkowski sing them—which thankfully we can hear in Elster's film (1963: 23 min 34 sec–23 min 44 sec). A multi-voiced choir of actors accompany him. We cannot see them in Elster's film and yet they reach us—as can be guessed from the recording—from different parts of the auditorium.

In accordance with the 13 Rows' use of dialectic contrasts, this calm and gentle scene was followed by a brutal sequence, the first of several in which Cynkutis radically broke accepted social conventions, baring himself before the audience. Flaszen called the first of these scenes 'Mortification'. It was based on one of the last scenes from Marlowe's drama when Faustus is visited by the Evil and Good Angels just before his death, and battles the temptation—I use this word intentionally—to convert and to beg for God's mercy.

The 'Mortification' scene was the first of several scenes that together formed a chain in which Cynkutis performed 'organic' actions. In a way, this 'chain' resembled Ryszard Cieślak's famous performance as Don Fernando in *The Constant Prince*. What I mean is that Cynkutis' line of actions in *Doctor Faustus* did not have much in common with the narrative of Faustus' drama. Cynkutis and Grotowski created and developed this 'chain' as a process connected with Cynkutis' inner life and personal experiences. This inner action was presented as a series of masochistic self-abuses and self-rapes. In the context of Faustus' fate, Cynkutis' actions suggest that the 'holy rebel' was split in two, that his psychotic character forced him to punish himself, and that at the same time he derived sexual delight in the process.

In a manner characteristic of Grotowski's theatre, he inserted calmer scenes between two of Cynkutis' masochistic, 'wild' sequences. In accordance with the text, Grotowski's separation of these intense scenes effectively postponed the decisive moment in which Faustus signed his pact with the Devil. Flaszen titled the first of these intense scenes 'A walk and a spiritual conversation with Mephistopheles'. It was a simple scene in which Faustus and both Mephistopheleses circled the tables.

Faustus signed the pact in a scene titled 'Baptism'. The title underscores a clear example of a dramaturgy of opposites which Grotowski conspicuously applied in the performance. In Marlowe's drama, Mephistopheles brings fire to melt the blood from Faustus' arm because it congealed too quickly for him to sign the agreement. In his version, Grotowski replaces fire with water. 'Faustus is almost drowned in a river (the space between the tables). Thus, he is purified and ready for his new life' (Barba 1968: 82). In Elsner's film, we can pick out the moment when Mirecka delivers Mephistopheles' line, 'Here is fire' (1963: 23 min 55 sec–24 min 13 sec). She dunks Faustus' face in the 'river'—we can hear the sound of Cynkutis bubbling.

It is worth stopping a moment here to ask about the meaning behind such a blatant contradiction. One possible explanation is that Mirecka and Cynkutis engage in a kind of demonstration of how the Opole performance is different from the source text. However, this appears naive and redundant, given that the Laboratory Theatre is already known for its alternative stagings of source texts. Instead, it seems that Grotowski once again employed his dramaturgy of oppositions to achieve a kind of 'estrangement effect'—albeit one distinct from that found in Brecht. The conspicuously contradictory sequence brought the actors to the foreground—as if declaring their autonomy—thereby directing the spectators' attention to their actions. The text remains important as a medium for the basic myth, and as a vehicle for symbols and affects rooted in the classic tale, but at the same time the aim of the performance is not to stage the text but to use it as a compositional element. In this case, Grotowski deploys the text on the basis of opposites. The text talks about fire but in the performance it is water—and the relevant sacrament of baptism—that is important. And this importance is indicated by the contrast between the text and the situation. When Mephistopheles says 'Here is the fire' and then dunks Faustus into a space between the two tables representing for the moment a small river, her words heighten the estrangement effect, redirecting the audience's attention to the water and the baptism enacted within it. The sacraments used to stage the pact with the Devil are thus alienated by the unconventional manner of their use—not hidden but emphasized.

The next example of estrangement can be found at the end of the scene of 'Baptism' when the female Mephistopheles 'comforts Faustus by rocking him in her lap (the *Pietá*)' (Barba 1968: 82). Elster's film forces us to reject this description of the scene (1963: 24 min 16 sec–24 min 19 sec). In the footage, Mirecka does not comfort anyone. After Faustus uttered the words *Consummatum est* (it is finished), he briefly adopted the pose of a dead Christ and arranged himself in the female Mephistopheles' lap, resembling many artistic portrayals of the Lamentation (the *Pietá*). The logic of signs is firmly fixed and has nothing to do with 'consolation' or 'comforting'. Having signed his pact with the Devil, Faustus spoke the words uttered by the dying Christ, and then— quite logically—he takes Jesus' position. Faustus died as a Christian, the Lord's servant, and thus had the right to evoke the image of the dead Christ as a representation of such a death. Taking the position of the *Pietá* served to conflate the image of the dead Faustus with the image of a dead believer. Of course, this is also a blasphemy because baptism is a sacrament of life, and Faustus is baptized into eternal death.

Grotowski presents the consequences of this act in the next scene that Flaszen imprecisely titled 'Signing the pact with the devil: complete destitution' (2010[1964]: 98). I say Flaszen's title is imprecise because the signing of the contract as an action did not actually appear in the performance. Faustus had already verbally authorized his pact with the Devil in the previous scene. This next sequence, however, consisted of reading the pact—which had already been signed—as though announcing Faustus' bargain.

Faustus recited his contract aloud while both Mephistopheles lay still on their stomachs on the opposite side of his table, breathing evenly and audibly throughout. Faustus tore off his white robe, and at a certain point converted the rope with which it was tied into a noose. He then placed it around his neck, removed his shirt, shoes, and socks, and, half-naked, hung momentarily over the space between the tables, supported by his arms and legs. Then he arose and began reading again. Suddenly his body shook as if afflicted by an uncontrollable spasm. It is not clear in Elsner's film if Cynkutis was laughing or weeping—to me it sounds similar to the laughter of the dying Don Fernand in *The Constant Prince* (1963: 25 min 51 sec–26 min 00 sec). He dropped to his knees and laughed/sobbed with his forehead on the table. This entire sequence constituted Cynkutis' second chain of organic, interior actions—a series of self-divestments and self-abuses.

The last scene of the second part of the performance is one that Flaszen titled 'Getting dressed in sanctified robes' (2010[1964]: 98). The two Mephistopheleses presented Faustus with a white Dominican habit. This costume signals certain historical and cultural contexts. Dominicans are in fact an order dedicated to defeating heresy and blasphemy—they combat unauthorized sects, and Satanism in particular. They played a key role in the infamous work of the so-called 'Holy' Inquisition. The mere sight of Faustus—Hell's fresh prize—dressed in a Dominican habit, was a particularly pointed joke. His change in costume added to the fact that both Mephistopheleses wore Jesuit habits. Jesuits, another Catholic order dedicated to missionary work, are known for opposing deviations from the Church, especially the Protestant Reformation. Thus, the Devilish team was dressed in the uniforms of the guardians of Catholic orthodoxy. As such, this team of three was ready to conquer the world . . .

Mephistopheles' Lessons, Faustus' Miracles

The third part of the performance involved scenes with a more or less autonomous character that presented a series of 'stations'. On one hand, the structure of this series resembled and evoked medieval and Counter-Reformation miracle plays about saints. On the other hand, it resembles modernist dramas depicting 'the journey of life'—for example, *To Damascus* by August Strindberg. In his script, Grotowski retained most of the sequences Marlowe used to tell the story of Faustus. However, in accordance with the rules governing the whole performance, Grotowski assigned Marlowe's sequences different meanings by juxtaposing them with the actors' performances.

This was the case with the first sequence in this chain of 'stations'—which Flaszen titled 'Reading a Holy Book—a woman?' (2010[1964]: 98). In Marlowe's drama, the first thing Faustus requires of Mephistopheles is a wife to satisfy his desires. Mephistopheles summoned 'A Devil dressed like a woman'. Faustus expressed his displeasure bluntly: 'Here's a hot whore indeed!' (Marlowe 1962[1604]: 32 [Scene 5, 150]). Promising to bring Faustus 'the fairest courtesans,' Mephistopheles changed the subject by giving him a book of spells that also depicted all the mysteries of the universe. Grotowski linked the two sequences. In his version, Faustus treats the woman 'as if she were a book which held all the secrets of nature [. . .]'. The saint examines the slut as if he were carefully reading a book. He touches all the parts of her body and reads them as "planets," "plants," etc.' (Barba 1968: 83).

According to Agnieszka Wójtowicz who interviewed them, spectators found this scene 'very unpleasant, horrid' (2004: 104). This most likely means that it was overtly sexual, and that this 'touching of all parts of her body' meant an intimacy that breached accepted social boundaries. Did Faustus discover the secrets of nature by exploring the woman's body? This is a clearly sexist image of feminine passivity and surrender connecting this examination of the female body to the 'order' of the world as 'natural'. This image also represented an actualization of a patriarchal fantasy of a perfectly passive female lover. This sequence—along with the earlier reference to the '*Pietá*' and a later scene with the Beautiful Helen—proves that women and femininity were one of the main topics of the performance. Women and femininity appear as ambivalent constructs, marked by desire, fear, hate, and at times overt misogyny, hidden beneath or beside the main subject or topic being staged, yet continuously commented upon and therefore structurally central to those very scenes. In Grotowski's theatrical exploration of images and affects connected with sexuality—which were daring and risky considering the context—the topic was included in the performances but on the margins of the clearly visible, and therefore was somehow 'masked' with symbols and associations that were then considered more noble, mainly belonging to the realm of Catholicism (see Niziołek

2011; Adamiecka-Sitek 2012). Although creators and spectators tended to pass over these references in silence, actors and audiences' own psychological resources unleashed powerful, affective energies that were then transferred to other themes, whether acknowledged or not. Put slightly differently, Grotowski aroused affects thorough sexual scenes—which dealt with subjects neither he nor his actors could or would address—by attaching them to more acceptable, 'highbrow' philosophical and religious deliberations. In Faustus' case, these scenes strengthened the image of rebellion and martyrdom of the 'saint against God'. And yet, *Doctor Faustus* can be interpreted in a very different way from the point of view of the centrality of (in)visible scenes dealing with sex and sexuality as a process of struggle against the impulses of one's own taboo desires, and as a case study of a personality overwhelmed by repressed and banned misogynistic and homoerotic fantasies. In Grotowski's creation of a dual Mephistopheles, parental figures emerge, arousing desire and hate, attraction and fear in their charge. According to this interpretation, the 'Innocent' thus turns out to be Faustus—the one embroiled in a tangled web of desires, and the one whose drama constituted a game of heteronymous fantasies that in the end led to a complete collapse and disintegration of identity and consciousness.

Eugenio Barba groups the next three scenes under the title 'Mephistopheles' lessons'. These scenes depict Mephistopheles attempting to show Faustus the 'correct' path. Flaszen called the first of these scenes 'Temptation of the Saint', and Barba wrote that in this scene Mephistopheles functioned as a 'police informant' (Barba 1968: 83) who paradoxically tried to tempt Faustus to turn towards God as if Mephistopheles wanted to test, and confirm his providence over Faustus like a contemporary agent provocateur. Mephistopheles arranged the harmony of the spheres voiced by actors hidden behind wooden planks. According to one witness, 'voices in harmony rose softly right behind us, [...] the closeness wrapping us in the atmosphere in a way "background music" in a proscenium rarely does' (Seymour 1963: 34). And so, audiences' sensory experience instantly confirmed Mephistopheles' divinations—the harmony of the spheres was actually experienced as a harmony of voices. The microcosm of the theatre facilitated audiences' experience of actual cosmic harmony which exemplified the might and mastery of the Creator, the one Mephistopheles tempts Faustus to turn from. Mephistopheles' temptation was thus surprisingly reinforced by his apparently cosmic power inviting us to ask if Satan is a double agent who appears before the rebel only to take over and redirect his rebellion towards the 'correct' path stopping him from asking uncomfortable questions. The answer seems clear, as the whole of the performance begins to resemble George Orwell's *1984*[8] and similar tales of totalitarian regimes, where impostor rebels initiate revolutions only to betray and entrap would-be revolutionaries.

And yet, a sudden glitch in this theatrical microcosm ruined the charming quality of this scene.

> The conversation is interrupted by two guests who talk of beer and whores. These are the two actors who have been sitting for the whole performance among the spectators. [. . .] In their scenes they represent the banality that marks our everyday life. One of these comic scenes [. . .] is acted right after Faustus asks Mephistopheles, 'Now tell me who made the world?' Our daily platitudes are themselves arguments against God. Our saint demands to know who is responsible for the creation of such a world. Mephistopheles, servant of God's evil urge, falls into a real panic and refuses to answer: 'I will not.'
> (Barba 1968: 83–84)

Grotowski is once again very precise. He interrupts Faustus and Mephistopheles' conversation at the very point when in Marlowe's version the former asks about the Creator, and the latter—scared—refuses to answer, and thus clearly shows his limitations. In Marlowe's original, the explanation for this was rather simple—Mephistopheles is unable to say God's name because as the enemy he cannot confirm God's omnipotence. In Grotowski's performance, such reasoning would be illogical:

---

8 The Polish translation by Juliusz Mieroszewski was published 10 years before the Opole premiere of Faustus.

if Mephistopheles, as an agent of the Creator, uses the harmony of the spheres to temper Faustus' rebellion, he should have no difficulty naming the author of this remarkable composition. But at this very point the brutal reality intervenes, and Faustus' question then shifts to: 'Who is responsible for the poverty and ugliness of the human world?' This is precisely what Mephistopheles does not want—or is perhaps unable—to answer. Mephistopheles does not answer because this would lead Faustus to discover what Grotowski already tried to stage in *Cain*—that there is now difference between God and Satan.

I find it meaningful that Grotowski employs a grotesque farce akin to the one he developed during the period of *Mystery-Bouffe* as an argument against the Creator and as a way to reveal the multivalent nature of the world. In *Doctor Faustus* there is no trace of a world that 'dances from joy to pain', as Grotowski described it in the final words of the Opole *Cain*. Instead, Grotowski presents a powerful dualism and an opposition between flat, vulgar triviality and sublime harmonies. This pattern gradually emerged for Grotowski—first in the finale of *Forefathers' Eve* and later in *Kordian*—contrasting the elation felt by the protagonists with their indifferent surroundings, including the audience. In *Acropolis* it appeared as a complete lack of understanding between the stage and the witnesses surrounding it, and shortly after the Opole *Faustus* it almost became an organizational rule in the *Hamlet Study*, with its harsh opposition between vulgar peasants and an alienated Jewish intellectual. Grotowski would never reintegrate the unity of the human world that fell apart so clearly for the first time in *Doctor Faustus*—in which the triviality of the everyday became an argument against the Creator.

The series of 'Mephistopheles' lessons' concluded with a scene of the 'Seven Deadly Sins'. Wójtowicz provides us with a description of the scene based on the memories of the creators and spectators she interviewed. Mirecka and Jahołkowski performed each sin as Mephistopheles.

Each Sin spoke with a different voice and moved in a unique way particular to that Sin. Wrath (Jahołkowski) spoke with difficulty, his voice choking behind clenched teeth. His movements were sudden and quick. Envy (Mirecka) sung her lines [. . .]. Doctor [Faustus] (to Envy): 'Go from us, you envious rag!' speaking as if he were blessing her—the intonation contradicting the words and their meaning. Gluttony (Jahołkowski) spoke with its mouth full, constantly licking its fingers. Sloth (Mirecka) in turn moved lazily and softly like a cat, stretching, speaking in a muted tone, purring, charged with erotic undertones.

(Wójtowicz 2004: 105)

Grotowski clearly placed this sequence in a meaningful place in the script. Satan tried to turn Faustus' attention away from troubling questions about the Creator, and at the same time touched upon the matter of the fall of man. Mephistopheles clearly suggested that the destruction of the original harmony of creation was the fault of human desires that led towards sin. Faustus' response was equally resolute. He absolved the embodiments of Sins, and at the same time blessed them—meaning he felt they were justified and took their side. In this way he spoke out against the Creator of cosmic harmony on behalf of a lost and sinful humanity. Thus, Faustus partially echoed Konrad's gesture in *Forefathers' Eve*, though in a different context. He did not fight against God to save or to free a suffering nation. Rather, he did so to justify human desires and sins—along with the most trivial ones that—as it was performed in the previous scene—had destroyed the universal harmony praised by Mephistopheles.

The scene featuring the Seven Deadly Sins is the last sequence in 'Mephistopheles' Lessons', and the first of Faustus' miracles. Faustus absolved both Mephistopheleses of their sins, signifying his transformation from their student or protégé to an active agent. It is in this context and capacity that his character is presented in the next three sequences.

These next three sequences began with a 'Journey to Rome upon Dragons' wherein 'Faustus is transported to the Vatican by two dragons, the double Mephistopheles' (Barba 1968: 84). In this 'very heady scene' both Mephistopheleses carried Faustus on their shoulders, and together

'TO HEAVEN? YOU BLASPHEME IN VAIN' · **373**

they 'circl[ed] the table-stages three times' before 'becoming "invisible"' leaving Faustus to 'tak[e] up his place of honor at the Pope's feet, the Pope sitting in a dignified pose by a smaller table' (Wójtowicz 2004: 106).

This was the second time Grotowski depicted the figure of the Pope (Ryszard Cieślak) in his theatre. And just as in *Kordian*, Grotowski's Pope appeared as a figure connected to evil forces. Faustus was invited to be a guest at a feast that demonstrated Papal pride—and so, attributed one of the deadly sins to the Pope himself. In Marlowe's original this scene was evidently anti-Catholic; Grotowski retained this scene and expanded upon it. In Barba's description we see more blasphemous elements.

> Faustus, invisible at the feet of the Pope, is present at a banquet in St. Peter's [Cathedral]. The banquet table is made of the bodies of the double Mephistopheles, who recites the Ten Commandments. Faustus slaps the Pope, breaking him of his pride and vanity. He transforms the Pope into a humble man— this is Faustus' miracle.
> (Barba 1968: 84)

The Pope sat on a throne 'constructed' with the bodies of the 'disappeared' twin Mephistopheles. It was therefore Satan who formed the foundation of the Pope's power. While visibly serving as the basis of Papal power, Satan recited the Ten Commandments, the foundations of Judaeo-Christian ethics. A truly blasphemous image!

When Faustus slapped the Pope in the face he thereby cured him of vanity. Michael Kustow linked the act to Christ's washing of feet, evoking the Last Supper and the Maundy Thursday liturgy (1963: 14).[9] However, we do not know how exactly this scene was performed—including how the Pope acted out his being 'healed' or 'cured'. In Marlowe's original, after the Pope is slapped, monks enter the stage, parodying curses as they direct their spells at Faustus. In Grotowski's staging the group was

---

9 Traditionally in Catholic churches during the liturgy of the Maundy Thursday the priest washes the feet of elderly men. In earlier times these were other priests or monks, usually lower in rank. Today this custom is still observed but mainly by bishops. For information on the Polish traditions connected with this custom see Kosiński 2019: 53.

reduced to just one monk played by Andrzej Bielski who appeared from below the table to curse Faustus kneeling in front of him in a pose of praying penitent.

Faustus' next station is the court of the Roman Emperor Charles V (Andrzej Bielski). According to Flaszen, two scenes took place in the Emperor's court. In the first, Faustus summoned the ghosts of both Alexander the Great and his paramour, and then a scene featuring Benvolio followed. In his report on 'textual montage' in *Doctor Faustus*, Barba merged these scenes into a single sequence, consistent with Marlowe's version.

Barba considered Faustus summoning Alexander and his lover to be one of 'the miracles in the tradition of popular legends' (Barba 1968: 84). Faustus spat upon the 'earth'—the table top and then covered the eyes of the Emperor with the dust to allow him to see the ghost of Alexander the Great. The sequence resembled the Gospel description of healing of a man born blind (John 9: 1–7).

Probably directly this miracle one of the most effective and well-remembered scenes of the performance began: Faustus' consolation of Benvolio in his madness. In Marlowe's drama, Benvolio is a member of the emperor's court who conspires against Faustus. Faustus punished him by having horns grow from Benvolio's head. Ryszard Cieślak proposed giving Benvolio's character an entirely new context and Grotowski adopted it.

One of [Cieślak's] most important roles was Benvolio in Marlowe's *Faustus*, where he transformed himself into a sort of creature that became more and more destructive, because it didn't feel loved. This was a sort of eruption of hate against the world and the self, as a result of lack of love received. This character—minor in Marlowe's original—attained a specific importance in the Opole performance, and I think that from the point of view of the actor's craft it was Cieślak's first real achievement. (Grotowski 2012: 854)

According to Cieślak's own description, the scene began with a showcase of his acrobatic skills. When Benvolio saw Faustus he performed 'some kind of "tiger leaps"—a moment of stillness and then a somersault' (Cieślak 2015: 65). These 'tiger leaps' became Laboratory Theatre legends, as did the scene where Benvolio-Cieślak destroyed the world. Barba wrote 'Benvolio's rage is directed against the tables—he actually dismantles the table-tops, and turns sections of the tables over, all the while thinking he is dismembering Faustus' (Barba 1968: 84).

It is not surprising that this sudden action, occurring so close to the audience, left a powerful impression on them.

> There is one terrifying sequence in which the Emperor's servant goes berserk, and rushes around dismantling the rostrum-tops (inches away from us) and leaving only the skeletons of the tables. The world, for a moment, seems to be coming apart. (Kustow 1963: 14)

Andrzej Bielski recalled that he played the scene with Benvolio 'as a fan cheering him on to a great rebellion', and that he had to 'jump through that tall backrest onto a table, leaping over two rows of people' (Bielski 1995: 80). The fact that Benvolio had a supporting character from among the 13 Rows suggested that Grotowski incorporated chaotic, malevolent forces into Benvolio's apocalypse, forces that no one fully controlled—even if they occasionally obeyed Mephistopheles or Faustus. This was an element that problematized the bipolar structure observers often read into the performance, that of Faustus against God and his agents. There were yet other forces of disintegration operating alongside satanic perversity and human triviality—forces that were not fully subject to the semiotics or powers presented in the performance. These forces were therefore dangerous to all.

his is why Faustus' consolation of Benvolio, following the latter's destructive rampage, was the greatest miracle he performed. Wójtowicz provides the fullest available reconstruction of this scene.

Faustus turns the furious Benvolio into a small child, cradling him in his arms while the child wept, and whimpered ('oooooh'—one would have to know the sound of Cieślak's voice, so rough and sharp, to understand the effect of this). Faustus' second miracle. A counterpoint to this scene is presented in the second conversation between Bartek and Kuba:

> BARTEK: No more, sweet Kuba: let's go and clean our boots and the dirt from our hands,
>
> Bartek sang [a Polish folk song—DK] (meanwhile Faustus cradled the crying Benvolio) [...]
>
> Benvolio wept ever louder, once Kuba began to tell his tale of the horse trader. Bartek interrupted him: 'No more, sweet Kuba, etc'. And once again he began singing [...].
> (Wójtowicz 2004: 107)

Wójtowicz's description allows us to at least in part understand Kustow's comment that Faustus calmed Benvolio 'turning him into a child who shames us' (Kustow 1963: 14). I imagine that Cieślak's guttural weeping, and his big, strong frame being cradled in the arms of another man, could really be embarrassing to audiences—a pathetic return to infantile helplessness combined with intimate tenderness shown between two men, one of them perhaps even taking on a role conventionally attributed to a woman-mother.

Now Hast Thou but One Bare Hour to Live

The final image in the series of 'lessons', 'miracles' and retrospectives is an image of Benvolio weeping curled up in Faustus' arms. After this image, the action returned to the 'present': Faustus at his table informing the 'guests' at his 'last supper' that he wanted to reward them for their friendly attitude towards him. To do so, he proclaimed that he would summon the most renowned beauty of all time, Helen of Troy.

This was among the riskiest scenes of the entire performance. Flaszen labelled it with a remarkably long phrase compared to his titles for other scenes. 'Faustus summons Helen of Troy's spirit, alluding to the reproductive functions of love' (Flaszen 2010[1963]: 98). Barba used even more puzzling phrasing:

[Faustus] conjures up Helen of Troy, unmasking by comic allusions the female biological functions. Helen begins to make love to him—immediately she gives birth to a baby. Then, while in this erotic position, she becomes the wailing infant. Finally, she is transformed into a greedy baby at suck.
(Barba 1968: 84)

Unfortunately the English translation is incorrect here: it is not 'she'—Helen that is transformed into a baby, but he—Faustus. This is evident in the Italian version of the text published by Barba in his 1965 book *Alla ricerca del teatro perduto* (see below) and confirmed by one of the photos from the performance by Bogusław Opioła (inv. no. 276) showing Helen cradling Faustus in her arms. .

Agnieszka Wójtowicz, provides a detailed account following a certain interpretation.

The Beautiful Helen, summoned by the Doctor's gaze, crawled out from beneath the table and lay there motionless for some time. Not the ideal of beauty, but a woman alive and buzzing with excessive eroticisms (wearing a black tricot that emphasized her flawless curves). This scene was very much erotically charged, and it involved several attempts at a sex act. Helena, legs splayed, laid on her back on the table, and at the very moment when making love was about to happen—'and there were some three such times'—Faustus changed into a child and ran away from Helen-woman. He suddenly turned into an embryo, or a greedily suckling babe, only to then move away from her. This was a chase, while also conveying a fear of femininity. 'Decidedly fear of fulfilment, fear of sexual intercourse'. (Wójtowicz 2004: 108)

The informant Wójtowicz quotes here is Maciej Prus, at that time a young actor and a member of the company who played one of the folk spectators, Kuba. Prus was the first to openly address the sexual themes explored by Cynkutis and Grotowski in the Opole production of *Doctor*

Faustus (Wójtowicz 2004: 243). Prus claimed that the scene with Beautiful Helen was something he clearly recalled; it is really hard to doubt his honesty in this respect.

But this is not an end of ambiguities and riddles connected with the scene with Beautiful Helen. In the Italian version of his article, Eugenio Barba gave a completely different description that is absent from the English version:

> Helen provokes Faust erotically, to which he responds the first time like an obstetrician who frees her from an embryo; the second time he transforms himself into a living embryo, and the third time—into a suckling infant.
> (Barba 1965: 26)

This description suggest that the scene started not with love making but rather with a birth an act of abortion, followed by a birth and a scene of mother and child. The suggestion certainly changes the meaning of the whole sequence that is hard to interpret and provides us rather with questions and riddles not answers and solutions.

Tone Bull—the woman who played Helen—presents us with another riddle. In fact, very little is known about her aside from the fact that she was a young Norwegian actress and an intern at the company (see Barba 1999: 138). It was her first and last appearance on stage for the Laboratory Theatre. But one thing is sure: for Grotowski's company she was a stranger from another world, a young Swedish woman in a provincial town of Communist Poland. Prus clearly recalled that 'she was very finely shaped and had beautifully flowing hair'. He also added that 'it was thanks to her appearance that the scene had such a very erotic character. She was then replaced by Rena Mirecka, which turned it tasteless' (Wójtowicz 2004: 243).

A Freudian reading of the scene with Helen of Troy as the personification of femininity—both lover and mother who Faustus simultaneously desires and fears—appears obvious. What is not obvious is the meaning behind Faustus' actions. Prus wrote about Faustus' fear of and escape from sexual acts. Barba about the rebirth of Faustus as infant.

Instead of Faustus being driven back to childhood by fear of sexual fulfilment we would have a scene of rebirth, which may be associated with the archetypal figure of eternal mother and lover who constantly gives birth to her son-husband (see Kerenýi 1976). This in no way alters the ambivalence of the desire and fear Helen aroused in Faustus, but it significantly shifts the scene's meaning within the broader context of the performance.

Right before his condemnation, Helen symbolically birthed Faustus anew—which might be interpreted in such a way that turns the hero into an archetypical figure of a rebel, and implies that although his historical 'avatar' would soon die, his rebellion would live on. But this 'Dionysian' interpretation of Faustus as the personification of 'indestructible life' is complicated by his fascination with and fear of women—traits that are not 'Dionysian' at all. Quite the opposite. If Faustus enters the world of Dionysus, then he is more like the Theban King Pentheus. Pentheus feared women's ecstatic rituals, banned them and at the same time was driven by a desire to peep at them, for which his mother killed him. Rather than fuelling and strengthening him, Faustus' intricate blend of desire and fear renders him weak and pitiful. Perhaps it even questions the 'universal' meaning of the 'rebel saint' who acts in the name of 'humanity'. If Faustus' story is a male narrative, and women are consequently presented as strange, alien, dangerous figures of 'otherness', then it is impossible to accept that Faustus rebels against the powers who rule the world as 'a human being'. Rather, he rebels as man; and as such, he loses the fight.

The ambivalence of the scene between Faustus and Beautiful Helen is underscored by its culmination in representations of death.

> The double Mephistopheles shows Paradise to Faustus. This would have been his had he followed God's precepts: a good, calm, and pious death. Then they show him the hell that awaits him: a convulsive and violent death.
> (Barba 1968: 85)

380 · DARIUSZ KOSIŃSKI

This sequence was performed in a very simple way. Mirecka demonstrated a good death, dying calmly with her hands folded over her breast. Jahołkowski performed hell—meaning a convulsing death—by lying on his back on a table, and raising his body upwards so that it formed 'an arch that went as far as the human body allowed' (Wójtowicz 2004: 108). According to the creators' commentaries, these simple depictions of death were often interpreted as allegories of hell and heaven. I rather propose to interpret them more literally. There is no Heaven or Hell; only death exists, either peaceful or violent. Only death remains after life, though death also belongs to life. Grotowski deliberately eschewed any sort of signs of transcendence. He turned Marlowe's original images of eternal life and eternal death into performances of actual dying.

Barba described the inevitable finale that followed this scene of dying.

> The final scene. Faustus has but a few minutes to live. A long monologue which represents his last, and most outrageous, provocation of God.
>
>> Ah Faustus,
>> Now hast thou but one bare hour to live,
>> And then thou must be damned perpetually!
>> (Act 5, Scene 2, 130–31)
>
> In the original text, this monologue expresses Faustus' regret for having sold his soul to the Devil; he offers to return to God. In the production, this is an open struggle, the great encounter between the saint and God. Faustus, using gestures to argue with Heaven, and invoking the audience as his witness, makes suggestions that would save his soul, if God willed it, if He were truly merciful and all-powerful enough to rescue a soul at the instant of its damnation. First Faustus proposes that God stop the celestial spheres—time—but in vain.
>
>> Stand still, you ever-moving spheres of heaven,
>> That time may cease and midnight never come.
>> (Act 5, Scene 2, 133–34)

He addresses God, but answers himself, "O, I'll leap up to my God! Who pulls me down?" (Act 5, Scene 2, 142). Faustus observes an interesting phenomenon: the sky is covered with the blood of Christ, and just one-half drop would save him. He demands salvation:

> See, see, where Christ's blood streams in the firmament!
> One drop would save my soul, half a drop! . . .
> (Act 5, Scene 2, 143–44)

But Christ vanishes, even as Faustus implores him, and this prompts Faustus to say to his guests, "Where is it now? 'Tis gone" (Act 5, Scene 2, 147). Then God's angry face appears, and Faustus is frightened:

> . . . And see where God
> Stretcheth out his arm and bends his ireful brows!
> (Act 5, Scene 2, 147–48)

Faustus wants the earth to open and swallow him, and he throws himself to the ground.

> Mountains and hills, come, come, and fall on me,
> And hide me from the heavy wrath of God.
> (Act 5, Scene 2, 149–50)

But the earth is deaf to his prayers and he rises crying, "O no, it will not harbor me!" (Act 5, Scene 2, 153). The sky then resonates with the Word and in all the corners of the room the hidden actors, reciting like monks, chant prayers like the Ave Maria and the Pater Noster. Midnight sounds. Faustus' ecstasy is transformed into his Passion. The moment has come when the saint—after having shown his guests the guilty indifference, yes, even the sin of God—is ready for his martyrdom: eternal damnation. He is in rapture, his body shaken by spasms. The ecstatic failure of his voice becomes at the moment of his Passion a series of inarticulate cries—the piercing, pitiable shrieks of an animal

caught in a trap. His body shudders, and then all is silence. The
double Mephistopheles, dressed as two priests, enters and takes
Faustus to hell.
(Barba 1968: 85–86)

This description clearly shows that the creators of the Opole *Doctor
Faustus* connected scenes of Faustus' death to the Passion of Christ. This
was blasphemous because there was no doubt that this 'Passion' of
Faustus would save no one—it would not be followed by any sort of resurrection. In fact, the creators gave it an opposite meaning. It is no
coincidence that Barba described Faustus as resembling an animal,
devoid of the uniquely 'human' capacity for articulate speech. The tension
between these two images—the pathos of the Passion of Christ and the
howl of an animal 'led to slaughter'[10]—creates the scene's potency. But it
is important to notice that this time the way the Christian symbols were
used did not suggest any intended derision or apotheosis, quite the
opposite. The Passion of Faustus was stripped of all signs of salvation
and hope. Only cruel and undeserved suffering, and then death.

Antitheo-logian

More than ten years ago, I interpreted *The Tragical History of Doctor
Faustus* as Grotowski's first attempt to achieve the total act—which I
then described as a means for 'secular salvation', and an effective theatre
ritual. I understood it as a preliminary attempt—not yet successful, but
as a kind of 'rehearsal' for *The Constant Prince* (see Kosiński 2007: 429–
33). Now, however, I believe this interpretation is oversimplified—a subconscious projection shaped by our desire to see what we want to see. I
once argued that Grotowski's *Doctor Faustus* was an 'attempt, merely an
attempt' at the total act. But since then I have listened more carefully to
the numerous voices of Grotowski's closest collaborators who say that

---

10 In Polish post-war literature the image of animals 'led to slaughter' is strictly connected to
the horrors of concentration camps and the Shoah. This image was strengthened by the well-
known poem by Tadeusz Różewicz, *The Survivor* which starts with the verses: I am twenty-
four/led to slaughter/I survived.' (1977: 7).

Doctor Faustus was Grotowski's best theatre work, even more potent than *The Constant Prince*. After re-evaluating my earlier conclusions, I seek to revise my reading of *Doctor Faustus* and explore the source of the Opole production's power.

Many years after the premiere, Flaszen offered up a very inspiring answer.

> I'm not sure if Grotowski's struggle with *The Tragical History of Dr Faustus* [. . .] resulted in the complete exorcism of the unleashed powers. I am not sure if the performance brought purification, katharsis, a return to Order. It was the cry of a man facing a cold—and empty?—heaven. And a mocking, provocative laugh at the world's order.
>
> Few witnesses of Faust's Last Supper in a small theatrical room in the Main Square of Opole, sitting at high banquet tables, and being offered scenes from the life of their host, did not experience a final calm, the return—after the violent turbulences—of the Primordial Harmony of existence. Its dramaturgy had something unprecedented—something I would call the perception of hot coldness.
>
> (Flaszen 2010: 286–87; emphasis original)

Flaszen—who was passionately interested in mystery plays—considers this lack of purification and the failure of an eventual return to an old order to be a flaw, something the play got wrong. According to Flaszen, this 'failure', Grotowski's *Doctor Faustus*, also featured anti-theo-logicality.

> The performance progresses in a medieval atmosphere. Characters react ecstatically, hysterically, as if possessed. There is grotesque and horror, as in a dance of skeletons. To emphasize that the tragedy of Faustus is viewed in theological (or rather anti-theological) terms, all characters are dressed in clerical robes, cassocks, and monastic habits.
>
> (Flaszen 2010: 286–87)

384 · DARIUSZ KOSIŃSKI

The formula of 'anti-theological tragedy' can be interpreted to mean that the performance was aimed against orthodox Catholic theology—in other words, that the performance was 'heretical'. However, a closer reading of Flaszen's words reveals that the performance aimed to present a project of *logia*—Greek for 'knowledge' or 'wisdom'—that was anti-*theos*, Greek for 'against God'. In other words, it was a project of knowledge explicitly directed against God. I must stress that this is something other than an a-theology, an atheist anti-theology. Atheism is aimed against theism, against 'the belief in god'. An atheistic theology cannot be 'against god' because atheism is founded on the belief that there is no god. Antitheo-logy is a paradoxical 'theology'—a word derived from Greek meaning 'knowledge about god'. Antitheo-logy is thus paradoxical because it is a theology directed against God. This notion applies to Grotowski's work in the sense that his practical antitheo-logy was aimed against the religious concept of God, especially the one nourished by Catholic Christianity.

When discussing the main line and goals of Grotowski's research and rebellion it is very hard to avoid religious language. And introducing these topics—even in a 'secular sense', in ironic 'quotation marks', or by setting them in clear contrast to the religious elements against which Grotowski rebelled—instantly tempts us to enter the realm of micro or crypto-theology, or even to include Grotowski as among the leaders of New Age 'spirituality' (see Christof 2017). And yet the most important commentators on the Opole *Faustus* place Grotowski in the realm of practical anti-theology. As usual, Ludwik Flaszen takes the place of honour in this regard.

> Faustus is a saint, but one who is acting against God—because a saint who is fully consequential in his sanctity has to rebel against nature's creator. Blind nature is evil; it is governed by rules that contradict morality. God sets traps for man. 'The reward for sin is death', Faustus says in his monologue; 'If we say that we have no sin, we deceive ourselves, and there is no truth in us. Why, then, belike we must sin, and so as a consequence, die'. The director adds: Whatever we do, good or evil,

we will be condemned. Ethics based on supernatural sanctions lead to a vicious circle from which we cannot escape—except by a complete change of perspective, if such is possible.
(Flaszen 2010[1964]: 97)

In my opinion, one of Flaszen's points needs to be more precise. The extract from Marlowe's drama that Flaszen quotes—which is supposedly key in helping us understand the performance—speaks very clearly not about the inevitability of damnation but simply about the inevitability of death. With this qualification, Faustus' revelation seems clear. Human beings are condemned by the Creator—whoever this may be—to sin because nature contradicts morality (in the performance this topic is most vividly articulated in relation to sexual desire). And the 'punishment' for any sin is death. In this case, we can either accept a compromise by rejecting, suppressing, or transferring our desires and therefore accept illusory morality or we can enact a suicidal rebellion against the trap that is human life, and at the same time against the alleged creator of this trap, a creator some call God. And this is the rebellion Saint Faustus chooses.

Faustus is a saint and his saintliness shows itself as an absolute desire for pure truth. If the saint is to become one with his sainthood, he must rebel against God, Creator of the world, because the laws of the world are traps contradicting morality and truth.
[. . .]
Whatever we do—good or bad—we are damned. The saint is not able to accept as his model this God who ambushes man. God's laws are lies, He spies on the dishonour in our souls the better to damn us. Therefore, if one wants sainthood, one must be against God.

But what must the saint care for? His soul, of course. To use a modern expression, his own self-consciousness. Faustus, then, is not interested in philosophy or theology. He must reject this kind of knowledge and look for something else. His research begins precisely in his rebellion against God. But how does he rebel? By signing his pact with the Devil. In fact, Faustus is not only a saint but a martyr—even more so than the Christian saints and martyrs, because Faustus expects no reward. On the contrary, he knows that his due will be eternal damnation. (Barba 1968: 79–80)

Barba's interpretation is in line with Flaszen's commentary, developing it further. Antitheo-logy here means a search for a different knowledge connected with self-discovery. Faustus rejects theology, directly opposing God. He does so because God was the one who set the trap of life making it impossible for human beings to discover their true selves. Faustus' rejection also demands the freedom to transgress moral limitations, the imposition of which implies the inevitability of damnation. Faustus wants to discover his self outside of the frames of conventional morality and the suppression that it imposes—a suppression that in his case is mostly connected with sexual inhibitions. The sexual scenes in Doctor Faustus depict Faustus entangled in restrictions, rejections, and self-concealment, while also portraying his desperate struggle for freedom and self-discovery.

If this reading is accurate, then there can be no surprise that the performance features so many blasphemous attacks on the whole system of Catholic beliefs and symbols. For Catholicism, in particular, transformed sexuality and gender into domains of control and condemnation. Perhaps my thesis goes too far, but it seems that Grotowski's ideas and actions here closely align with Michel Foucault's *History of Sexuality* (1978), which argues that sexual taboos and relentless discussions of sexuality as forbidden serve as mechanisms for the Catholic Church's production and maintenance of power and knowledge. And like Foucault, Grotowski seems to see a chance for 'other knowledge' in the sphere of sexuality, a possibility for 'other knowledge' that just might allow an almost unthinkable, complete change of point of view.

But this antitheo-logical knowledge—which may by achieved *through* a break with a morality built on taboos and restrictions on sexuality—is not *about* sexuality. By attacking sexual taboos, Grotowski and his Faustus aimed at something deeper, connected to the questions explored in earlier performances. They were interested in confronting something that was and still is a burning question in the present day even if for pragmatic reasons we strive to forget it. Of all the reviewers and interpreters of the Opole *Doctor Faustus* that I have encountered, Alicja Zatrybówna was the only one who noticed this theme which perhaps finally is the most important.

> Zbigniew Cynkutis creates his Faustus not by pretending real human sufferings but by experiencing them. He amplifies sufferings, pushing himself to the limits of human endurance. [...] Overcome by madness, he howls. Stripped of illusions, he tears his clothes off. He is going as low as it is possible for a human being to go, bringing to mind experiences that still cannot be forgotten. The day after I saw *Faustus* I received a letter from someone who had lived during the occupation. He wrote:
>
> > We lived through shocks, breakdowns, bitterness, learning question marks—at a scale the citizens of the USA or distant France or Belgium could never understand ... We are still living in the tragic shadow cast over us by bombers displaying black cross insignia and by the crematoriums of Auschwitz.
>
> This letter provoked me to once again reconsider Faustus, as he was offered up by Grotowski. Faustus-Cynkutis appeals to the audience's creative faculties. Faustus' helpless nakedness is a synthesis of life during the occupation—the fight for bare life, plucked of all previous laws. A world stripped of illusions. The psychology of human collapse. The way 13 Rows staged their *Faustus* deals with contemporary problems thanks to its plethora of meanings. Each audience member is a hero. Every one finds a reflection of their own doubts and contradictions relating to their spiritual lives.
> (Zatrybówna 2006[1963]: 172)

388 · DARIUSZ KOSIŃSKI

Zatrybówna's notes are incredibly important.[11] Her observations allow us to link the Opole *Faustus* with *Acropolis*, the previous performance of the Theatre of 13 Rows, and point to something not thematized by Grotowski or Flaszen but that seems to be a key aspect of *Doctor Faustus*. I propose that the God who provoked and judged Faustus is, in fact, the God of the concentration camps. This cruel Lord is indifferent to human suffering, demanding hecatombs and the Holocaust in order to confirm that which to him is most important: his unquestionably total rule over all that is. Borrowing a phrase from Forefathers' Eve—which may seem archaic but is justified by Polish history—we might say that this God is not the Father of the world but rather its tyrannical Tsar.[12] Of course, in the second half of the twentieth century 'a Tsar' was no longer the embodiment of ruthless might as in the times of Mickiewicz. So, in order to find a more contemporary analogy to explain the Opole blasphemy, we must say that the God who sent the double agent to seduce and at the same time take over Faustus' rebellion was the Führer, Generalissimo, Party Secretary, the head and founder of a totalitarian apparatus in the shadow of which humans become a 'bare life', *homini sacri*. Seen from this perspective, Faustus' desperate rebellion is the act of a man who—in light of the experience of the camps, and after the Shoah—does not shy away from metaphysical questions, and instead

---

11 Zatrybówna is another example of a woman who sees important aspects of Grotowski's performances that are overlooked by men. Women reviewing the Theatre of 13 Rows' performances often read them in original ways—very differently than their male counterparts who were generally more keen to follow the points offered up by Flaszen and Grotowski, often repeating their comments. Meanwhile, it was women—e.g. Aleksandra Korewa reviewing *Orphée*, Zofia Jasińska reviewing *Cain*, Magda Leja reviewing *Shakuntala*—who gave voice to less 'formatted' audience experiences, representing 'a different point of view' and allowing us today to see anew these performances from years ago.

12 This is another item of proof that the Opole Faustus can be read as a kinsman of Konrad from *Forefathers' Eve*. Grotowski himself pointed to a connection between the Romantic tradition and his staging of Marlowe. 'We always worked on texts which retained for us their freshness, texts which were established in traditional ranks, alive not just for my friends and me, but also for the majority—if not for all—Poles; even when we played texts such as Marlowe, who had no established theatre tradition in Poland, there was a living connection through the literary raw materials, connected with a unique context of poetic thought, images, existentialist allusions, very close to Polish Romanticism' (Grotowski 2012: 364).

poses them in a way that is far more acute and radical than the existentialism of Sartre and Camus or the 'theatre of absurd'. Faustus' paradise is not empty; it is home to the cruelly rational Lord of Hosts. Any sort of rebellious acts against him are doomed to failure. In *Doctor Faustus* the analysis suggested in *Acropolis* goes all the way to the very end, and unmasks God's cruelty—a cruelty that does not save anyone, and yet represents a 'pure' form of 'truth'.

So, although there was no catharsis in the performance its title was apt. This really was the 'tragical history of Doctor Faustus 'whose absolute striving towards the truth, and his smashing of all manipulations and illusions led to his doom. In the moment of his martyrdom no angels descended from on high, no God gave him a wreath of victory, no choirs sang and no Merciful Lord smiled down upon him. The only ones who could see and were able (literally!) to survive—and maybe keep his rebellion from dying along with him—were the witnesses, the diners at Faustus' Last Supper.

Zatrybówna wrote that in the performance 'each audience member is a hero'. Her statement contains—among other things—the suggestion that the audience was drawn through theatrical devices into the actual action on stage. The sentence is also a record of the experience of a witness who did not delight in the acting, in the staging, or in the incredible interpretation, but who accepted Faustus' tragedy as her own. She really confronted the meaning of the tragedy—something we want to avoid most of our days.

This was in fact the same confrontation Grotowski aimed at in his earlier performances—this time pushed to the point at which profanation—retrieving sacral symbols and procedures for common use—became a blasphemy. At this 'point of blasphemy', the 13 Rows used sacral symbols and procedures to accuse the power at its source. In this sense, this was a theatre in which the creators accused God. Cynkutis-as-Faustus accused God in the name of his own generation, the generation of children whose fathers and mothers had been killed without mercy in order to establish a new order, and also the generation of human beings handed over to suffer an irresolvable conflict between desire and prohibition. This is what is so incredible in Grotowski's performances: he combined the most intimate with the most historical. In a scandalous and touching way, he combined suppressed sexual desires with memories of the Shoah, and desire and fear of femininity with the shadow cast by Auschwitz crematoriums. The final effect was that he aroused incredibly powerful, emotional reactions for which—and this is another important point to make—in the Opole *Faustus* there was no diffusion, no consolation, nothing audiences could accept as myths or models for correct behaviour. In *Doctor Faustus*, Christ did not return—not even to be dismissed by the lord of this world.

After Faustus was carried off like a slaughtered pig, the auditorium fell silent. Nobody told the witnesses what they were supposed to be thinking or doing. Nobody draped the red shroud of salvation over the naked body of the sacrificial victim[13]—nor was it offered up for silent adoration.. The radical dilemma of the Opole *Doctor Faustus* unfolded fully to its conclusion. 'Each audience member is a hero. Everyone finds a reflection of their own doubts and contradictions relating to their spiritual lives.' In the Opole *Faustus*, there was no manipulative use of the mythical script, and there was certainly no 'Good News'. Perhaps this is why many consider it Jerzy Grotowski's finest theatrical work.

Dariusz Kosiński

---

13 This refers to the closing image from *The Constant Prince*. I mention it here because it is an obvious allusion to the Resurrection. Red is the colour still used today in Catholic liturgy, and in traditional images it is the colour of the robe worn by the resurrected Christ.

CHAPTER NINE

Jerzy Grotowski's Hamlets

Hamlet Study Based on Texts
by William Shakespeare and Stanisław Wyspiański

The last production staged by the Laboratory Theatre of 13 Rows in Opole, which premiered on 17 March 1964 and closed on 30 May, was *Hamlet Study*, based on texts by William Shakespeare and Stanisław Wyspiański. The run was brief, with only 21 performances attended by a total of 643 spectators.[1] Grotowski cancelled the run and effectively erased the performance from the company's official record. He decided not to include *Hamlet Study* in a list of the most important performances of the Laboratory Theatre that the company published in the programme for *The Constant Prince* in April 1965. In later years, he rarely mentioned *Hamlet Study* and avoided discussing it when the subject arose. The reasons for 'hiding' *Hamlet Study* remain unclear and, therefore, intriguing. Did Grotowski consider the performance weakly constructed? Or was Ludwik Flaszen correct: the reason was political?

Answering these questions is far from easy. Few documents have survived to aid in reconstructing the performance. The Grotowski Institute Archive holds two copies of the script—one was prepared and submitted to state censors, and the other belonged to the actor Andrzej Bielski. The GIA also has a poster from the performance, four photographs taken by Ryszard Cieślak during rehearsals, and a thin booklet

---

1 To compare: *The Tragical History of Doctor Faustus* was performed in Opole 71 times to a total of 7556 spectators. *Cain*, 55 times to 4666 spectators. The numbers follow information in Mykita-Glensk 1976: 284–87.

featuring the cast list and a text by Flaszen (2010[1964]: 99–100). Along with these items Zbigniew Osiński discovered four additional photographs; a short, amateur-quality film from rehearsals also survived (*Rehearsal* 1964).[2] Due to a lack of funds, the company decided not to publish a separate booklet for the premiere of *Hamlet Study*, nor did they hire a photographer. The scarcity of reviews and reports in the press may also suggest that the company did not want the performance to be described and commented on. Indeed, the existing reports conceal more than they reveal. Furthermore, actors' recollections are fragmentary. The greatest amount of information at our disposal comes from Barba and Flaszen. In 1964, Barba penned a sketch of the performance titled 'Hamlet in the Laboratory Theatre of 13 Rows'. Barba wrote this text just after *Hamlet Study* premiered, but did not publish it until 1999 as a part of the chapter 'Hamlet Without Friends' in *The Land of Ashes and Diamonds*. Flaszen wrote '*Hamlet* in the Laboratory Theatre' in 1964 after the performance run ended, but did not publish it until 1992 (Flaszen 2010: 101–6). Flaszen also dealt with *Hamlet Study* in his essay, 'Grotowski Ludens' (2010: 212–80). In this essay, written more than 40 years after the fact, Flaszen recalls the circumstances of the premiere.

Study and Study

Waldemar Krygier's poster[3] for *Hamlet Study* reads 'adapted and directed by the ensemble under Jerzy Grotowski's supervision'.[4] The performance was a collective enterprise, the result of 13 Rows actors' improvisations. Grotowski prepared an initial script as a starting point, but during rehearsals the whole team influenced the development of the performance together. In his second text on *Hamlet Study*—published 28 years after the performance ended—Flaszen elaborates on the creative process.

---

2 The film is accessible online: https://rebrand.ly/u9dxpi4

3 The poster is accessible online: https://rebrand.ly/dkk7h2y

4 This is the way the Polish on the poster was translated in Flaszen's book (Flaszen 2010: 100).

The written script was not considered fixed and unable to be altered. The practice made it just a preliminary plan, a series of directional propositions. Its final shape emerged gradually. If a particular fragment did not stimulate the actors' and director's imagination, it was cut. Many scenes that are important from a literary perspective were left out if their power to stimulate proved to be weak in practice; some other fragments, albeit not so significant as literature, were kept. The reason for this procedure is that the project's objective was neither to stage Shakespeare's *Hamlet*, nor to test whether Wyspiański was right; it was to attempt spontaneous creativity in the theatre.
(Flaszen 2010[1964]: 101–2)

The final performance of *Hamlet Study* was created using an embodied process in which company participants collectively edited the script during rehearsals. Grotowski limited himself to giving 'basic suggestions' waiting to see what would emerge from the actors (2010[1964]: 101–2). They worked by improvising, testing various fragments of a script that 'was not considered fixed and unable to be altered' (2010[1964]: 101). Grotowski did not impose his will upon the actors, and instead left them the freedom to choose and follow narrative threads. It was a new way of working for the company—'a study of the acting method and of collective directing' (2010[1964]: 99). The performance emerged from the actors' search and improvisations.

The creative process is also one of the key themes of the book by Stanisław Wyspiański customarily titled as *Hamlet Study*. This 1905 book by the poet, painter, playwright and theatre artist is an original interpretation of *Hamlet*, a record of what Wyspiański was thinking about, how he was thinking with Shakespeare's drama. The full title of Wyspiański's book clearly shows the complexity of the text: '*The Tragical History of HAMLET Prince of Denmark* By William Shakespeare Reread and Thought Through by Stanisław Wyspiański. Following the Polish Text of Józef Paszkowski' (2019: 29). Wyspiański's text is an account of his thought and creative process as inspired by the work of another artist.

As a result, his 'commentary' becomes an autonomous work by the poet—a kind of theatre manifesto. At the same time, the text is a labyrinth to be explored and worked through in the course of reading. Thus, reading Wyspiański's text also becomes a creative act. The book is a hybrid text including elements of drama, prose and lyrics. It contains analyses of Shakespeare's tragedy, paraphrased monologues and scenes from the drama, and Wyspiański's poems, sketches for staging and reflections on theatre, set design, acting, dramaturgy and finally on Hamlet as a character and on the contemporary relevance of the Dane's attitude. Jan Kott characterized Wyspiański's text as 'a notebook of the director and set designer, who simultaneously arranges the play, creates the performance, and reforms theatre' (Kott 1965: 409).[5]

The first theme in Wyspiański's *Study*—which is key to the 13 Rows' work on the text—is his reading of Shakespeare's drama as a contemporary text efficacious for analysing the Polish reality, society and political situation. For Wyspiański, *Hamlet* is a form of commentary through which one can describe, interpret and understand contemporary experience. Wyspiański encapsulated this notion in his famous words: 'In Poland the Hamlet riddle is this: what is there to think about—in Poland?' (2019: 93). According to him, readings of *Hamlet* are always dependent on the time in which they are read, and the sociopolitical context and particular problems relevant to readers. In the case of performance, the key to reading the tragedy is in the hands of those staging it—writers, producers, actors and audiences—living in a specific historical moment. That is why, when *Hamlet* is performed in Poland, it reflects the souls of Poles and lays bare Polish insecurities for all the world to see. In Poland, Hamlet is always a contemporary figure (see Świątkowska 2019). For Grotowski, Hamlet was also a contemporary hero, and therefore his approach to *Hamlet* was an exploration of what there was 'to think about in Poland' in 1964.

Wyspiański—following the 'mouse trap' scene—treated theatre as if it were courtroom in which one could judge contemporaneity. He con-

---

5 Kott's essay on *Hamlet Study* was not included in the English edition of his *Shakespeare Our Contemporary*. The essay is titled 'Hamlet Wyspiańskiego' [Wyspiański's Hamlet] and can be found in Kott 1965: 407–28.

JERZY GROTOWSKI'S HAMLETS · 395

sidered theatre to have the power to reveal that which is false, to stir people's consciences, and to dish out justice. He also believed that theatre is a place where one can seek out truth, and that this truth can strip away that which is shameful by challenging consciences and passing down judgements. According to Wyspiański, Poles should see themselves in the mirror of *Hamlet* just as Claudius did while watching *The Murder of Gonzago*. Jacek Trznadel wrote that '*Hamlet* is for Wyspiański a play about roles and de-masking lies in society and history' (1988: 146). Staging Hamlet serves as a form of judgment of contemporaries, which is, in essence, what Grotowski and his company were doing.

Another theme the Laboratory Theatre took from Wyspiański's *Study* is embodying the creative process. Wyspiański writes *Hamlet* 'anew', takes up Shakespeare's mantle, and creates a 'Polish Hamlet'. This very process was intellectual creative work, thinking and living through Shakespeare. In this sense Wyspiański's *Study* is both a description and a completion of Shakespeare's creative act. It is the journey, not some destination. As Stanisław Lack observed, 'there is no difference at all' between the road and the destination: 'if [Wyspiański] manages to describe the road, the journey will be complete! [. . .] We do not want conclusions; we want as much road as possible. The aim therefore is not the result and conclusion in the end, but the whole journey' (Lack 1980: 175, 180). Similarly, for the Laboratory Theatre, a public performance was not the main goal. The working process of exploring acting methods and their collective creation was more important. Flaszen clearly articulated this at the time.

> It was intended not so much as a performance but as an etude. It is not addressed to the public. It is a form of training and, as is mentioned in the title, a study. It opens a certain phase in Jerzy Grotowski's work on his acting method. [. . .] It was presented to the public simply because at a certain phase in the work, [when] contact was needed between the actors and an audience.
>
> (Flaszen 2010[1964]: 101)

In the title of the performance, Grotowski both pointed to the text the company used as inspiration, and also indicated their method of creation. They analysed *Hamlet* through their personal experiences, and vice versa, they analysed themselves through the text. Their struggles and mistakes constituted the work all the way through to the end.

This begs the question of whether or not Grotowski desired to stage *Hamlet*, the most famous dramatic work in Western theatre? It seems that this was of secondary importance. The 'Polish *Hamlet*' the 13 Rows performed in Opole in 1964 radically departed from both Shakespeare's narrative structure and from Wyspiański's version. As I will shortly show, the company used both source texts in a very pragmatic, utilitarian way, as excuses and starting points for a series of group scene studies. They took both original texts out of context, gave passages different meanings, and transplanted the texts into modern circumstances. Already in his preliminary script, Grotowski remodelled Shakespeare's drama. He excluded key narrative threads, characters, and neither followed the original sequence of scenes nor the overall narrative structure of Shakespeare's *Hamlet*. Under the influence of the actors the performance evolved even further from the original drama. In his commentary on the premiere, Flaszen distilled their approach to—and departure from—the original texts. Flaszen:

> We do not 'play' *Hamlet*—either as a classic Shakespearean version, or in accordance with the staging suggestions included in Wyspiański's famous essay, *Hamlet Study*. By using fragments of Shakespeare's play and Wyspiański's commentary, we give our own version of the Danish prince's story: variations on selected Shakespearean motifs. A study of a motif.
> (Flaszen 2010[1964]: 99)

This description of their work as a 'study of a motif' indicated that the 13 Rows treated Shakespeare's drama as a mythical structure. The myth on which Shakespeare based his *Hamlet* is not the original story—a point that Wyspiański also emphasized. Shakespeare's drama did not encapsulate the entirety of the myth. Flaszen stressed that 'in Poland, as a result of the nation's spiritual situation, universal myths demand a particular way of being realized' (2010[1964]: 101). The 13 Rows had to deconstruct and dismantle the Shakespearean script in order to create a new, 'unique' work connected with their current time and place. They offered audiences 'variations on selected motifs' that they extracted from *Hamlet* and projected onto Polish reality. 'Shakespeare's text was undertaken as a spur to this' (2010[1964]: 101). By embracing this strategy— which was wholly justified by Wyspiański's practice—the Laboratory Theatre made it clear that their aim was not to replay the tragedy about the Prince of Denmark. Rather, they intended to work with the material 'taken from the classics' to actualize a myth and to tackle an archetype. Both Wyspiański and Grotowski wanted to use *Hamlet* to respond to their own realities, and to what they found most disturbing therein. According to Flaszen,

> *Hamlet* is a masterpiece with the capacity of a myth; set within a European cultural consciousness, it is able to draw out of us our truth about how we view the human condition. It could be said: show me how you see *Hamlet*, and I will tell you who you are.
>
> (Flaszen 2010[1964]: 101)

Flaszen wrote these words in 1964—around the same time that the English translations of Jan Kott's *Shakespeare Our Contemporary* were published.[6] Kott proposed a similar strategy for making Shakespeare's dramas more contemporary.

Two Scripts—Two Tales

The Grotowski Institute Archive preserved two scripts from the performance that reveal the company's method for working on their two source texts. The first script is the result of an earlier phase of work, and belonged to the actor Andrzej Bielski who played Guildenstern and the

---

6 The first English language edition of *Shakespeare Our Contemporary* was published in New York in 1964 with a foreword by Martin Esslin, and the book was published in London in 1965 with a foreword by Peter Brook.

Second Gravedigger. This 123-page typescript contains numerous hand-written additions, corrections and deletions to the play text as well as Bielski's own notes and marginalia (IG/R/318/4). Some of the pages are missing—the surviving 123 pages are numbered up to 132.

The second script is a later version the company prepared for the censorship office in Opole. On its cover is a hand-written note approving the proposed performance of *Hamlet Study* dated 24 March 1964, one week after the premiere (IG/R/318/1). The manuscript contains only 47 pages, roughly one-third the length of the earlier Bielski script. The difference in length between the two versions indicates the number of cuts the company made to the script during rehearsals. The shorter script likely reflects the outcome of the company's work, and served as the basis for the performance. So we have two radically different documents, one from the beginning of the process, and another from the final stages of work. A comparison allows us to reconstruct the course of the 13 Rows' creative process and the shape of their *Hamlet Study* performance.

Analysis of the first script indicates that Grotowski used both sources equally; 50% of his preliminary script came from Shakespeare, and 50% came from Wyspiański. And yet, Grotowski literally copied Wyspiański's title page and used it for the title page of his script. Grotowski used Wyspiański's book as the starting point and a model to structure his own version. Neither of the Opole scripts follows the narrative arc of Shakespeare's *Hamlet*. Grotowski used fragments from Shakespeare as illustrations and extensions of Wyspiański's thoughts. This helped him turn the Polish playwright's work into drama. Grotowski cut all of Shakespeare's side narratives and minor characters like Reynaldo, Voltemand, Cornelius, Osric, Fortinbras and the Captain. He used scenes from the play to bring key themes from Wyspiański's book to life. As a result, Grotowski treated what remained of Shakespeare's original—some 58 pages of script—with remarkable creative freedom. He used what was left of the original script to create a non-linear, non-chronological text that refused the original narrative arc's cause and effect.

Grotowski's original idea followed his penchant for building an entire performance around a single scene from his source drama. In his preliminary script for the Opole *Hamlet Study*, he used Shakespeare's graveyard scene (Act 5, Scene 1) as a frame for the whole performance, setting *Hamlet* in a cemetery and giving the First Gravedigger a main role, agency and power. For Wyspiański the cemetery scene was one of three main scenes.[7] In the cemetery, Hamlet achieves *anagnorisis*, realizing that the ensuing events are inevitable and that his death is necessary.

Grotowski's initial script begins with a conversation between two Gravediggers. When the prince arrives the First Gravedigger addresses him using the words Wyspiański's used to open his *Study*—'AROUND CHRISTMAS I was visited by Mr Kamiński, who said that he wanted to play Hamlet, and that he wanted to talk about *Hamlet*' (Wyspiański 2019: 33). Grotowski thus cast the Gravedigger as the author of *Hamlet Study*, and cast Hamlet as an actor who visits the cemetery in order to learn something about tragedy—and about himself. The ensuing dialogue concerns Shakespeare's writing style, the way he constructed the drama and formed its characters. Grotowski gave the Gravedigger an unusual function turning him into a guide for Hamlet to discover Shakespeare's world, a narrator of events and a commentator who mostly speaks using words from Wyspiański's *Study*. Grotowski used the Gravedigger's role as narrator and guide to inform characters of their fates and the roles they were to play. Hamlet is the Gravedigger's main conversation partner. In conversation with Hamlet, the Gravedigger reveals the rules involved in creating the tragedy and its form. He tells the prince about Shakespeare's writing methods, and warns him about the imminent development of the story. The Gravedigger already knows the result of the unfolding course of events; moreover, he provokes and directs them.

In the next scene, Hamlet asks the Gravedigger to play the flute (see *Hamlet*, Act 3, Scene 2). Grotowski gives the Gravedigger lines that originally belonged to Guildenstern. In Bielski's script it is the Gravedigger

---

7 The other two scenes Wyspiański singled out were "The Mousetrap" play-within-the-play, *The Murder of Gonzago* (Act 3, Scene 2) and the comparison of portraits in the closet scene between Hamlet and his mother Gertrude (Act 3, Scene 4).

who explains that he doesn't know how to play the flute, and this causes Hamlet to explode: 'You would play upon me! You would seem to know my stops, you would pluck out the heart of my mystery [. . .]. Do you think I am easier to be played on than a pipe? Call me what instrument you will, though you fret me you cannot play upon me' (Shakespeare 2007: Act 3, Scene 2, 356–63). This attack—aimed at a false friend in the original here sounds rather different. Hamlet protests the Gravedigger's absolute knowledge, and his 'know it all' attitude. He is angry that the Gravedigger knows his fate, and seems to know him better than he knows himself. In response, the Gravedigger begins to perorate using words from Wyspiański's *Hamlet Study* about setting the tragedy in the royal Wawel Castle in Kraków (Wyspiański 2019: 38). Here Grotowski makes perfect use of the dialogical character of Wyspiański's text, and distributes Wyspiański's deliberations between the Gravedigger and Hamlet. Hamlet asks questions that were rhetorical in Wyspiański's original—'Which is the castle in your mind? Where does that royal ghost wander around the towers in the night? [. . .] Which is the gallery "where sometimes he walked for hours", Prince Hamlet!' (Wyspiański 2019: 38). The all-knowing Gravedigger answers the prince's questions, and tells him that the Ghost wanders the terraces of Wawel Castle instantly drawing Hamlet into a conversation with his father's Ghost. In this fashion, the Gravedigger calls up the scene of the meeting between the prince and the Ghost (Act 1, Scene 5). Hamlet casts doubt upon the Ghost's provenance, 'The spirit that I have seen/ May be a de'il, and the de'il hath power/ T'assume a pleasing shape. Yea, and perhaps/ Out of my weakness and my melancholy/ As he is very potent with such spirits,/ Abuses me to damn me [. . .]' (Shakespeare 2007: Act 2, Scene 2, 533–38). The Gravedigger replies with Wyspiański's lines—'Hamlet's disbelief, or rather his search for "other grounds"—where does it come from?' (Wyspiański 2019: 39).

This short fragment clearly shows Grotowski's practice of intertwining both source texts. He introduces subsequent sequences with words from the *Study*, illustrating them by recalling relevant sections from Shakespeare's drama. The Gravedigger most frequently quotes paragraphs from the *Study*, reinforcing his role as the author and director of the unfolding Opole version. Grotowski follows Wyspiański's lead in diverging from Shakespeare, adapting fragments from various acts in the original drama to fit interpretations in Wyspiański's *Study*.

The Gravedigger persistently provokes Hamlet with questions. He butts into Hamlet's conversation with Rosencrantz and Guildenstern (Act 2, Scene 2), and repeatedly asks Hamlet about his identity. He continues asking questions throughout the script—including when Hamlet greets actors in Elsinore (Act 2, Scene 2), in his conversations with Ophelia (Act 3, Scene 1), when Hamlet delivers his monologues, and when he meets his mother (Act 3, Scene 4). As a 'director' the Gravedigger encourages Hamlet to take on the various roles suggested by Wyspiański. He explores different interpretations of Hamlet's role, speaking to him as a director would to an actor in rehearsals, guiding him in conceiving an approach to the character. The Gravedigger initiates select scenes from the original drama that throw Hamlet into different situations. The Gravedigger uses these situations to force Hamlet to go on a journey of self-discovery leading him through various stages of character development. He encourages the prince to deliver monologues that—according to Wyspiański—reflect different 'stages of Hamletian thinking' (2019: 141). He uses words taken from Wyspiański's *Study* to entreat Hamlet to perform the famous 'To be or not to be' monologue.

> And now the issue of the soliloquy that follows every actor around, nagging constantly: to be or not to be. Have you learned the lines? When will you play it? Will you ever play it? Will you say it well? Are you capable? Will you understand it? Will you cope?
> (Wyspiański 2019: 140)

Hamlet starts, 'To be or not to be: that is the question' (Act 3, Scene 1, 55). Once the prince is done, the Gravedigger comments on his words.

> [...] These soliloquies are: the stages of Hamletian thinking, the stations of the thinking of a man who has become accustomed to thinking aloud and who, by thinking aloud, is able to develop his thought and fly further, to ascend to a higher stage.
> (Wyspiański 2019: 141)

Encouraged by the Gravedigger's comments, Hamlet begins another monologue: 'How all occasions do inform against me/ And spur my dull revenge' (Shakespeare 2007: Act 4, Scene 4, 31–32). The Gravedigger sums up Hamlet's pronouncements: 'The intelligence of Hamlet was developing the intelligence of the audience, of the public' (Wyspiański 2019: 77; emphasis original). The Gravedigger is Hamlet's teacher, his companion and his shadow. He is present in almost all of Hamlet's scenes, helps him draw conclusions and leads him where he refuses to go—to the end. Wyspiański believed a person can only discover their true selves by visiting cemeteries and confronting death. The Gravedigger pushes Hamlet with his questions and commentaries to the one and only possible end.

But as death's accomplice the Gravedigger's power affects more than just Hamlet. He also summons other characters into the action and determines their fates. In one of the opening scenes, he summons Ophelia, who appears unaware of her role or the unfolding drama. She addresses the Gravedigger with words from Wyspiański's *Study*, 'Ophelia, who was she! Is she really Polonius' daughter?' The Gravedigger replies, 'Shakespeare's Ophelia is Polonius' daughter and a naive and noble girl' (Wyspiański 2019: 39, 40). Their dialogue involves Ophelia retelling the story of the prince's visit to her room (Act 2, Scene 1). Horatio asks a similar question: 'Horatio, who was he!' to which the Gravedigger replies, 'A faithful servant of the old king, Hamlet's father, and a sort of tutor (Orestes' *paidagogos*) to the young prince. Devoted to him heart and soul and ensuring that nothing rotten would happen in Denmark' (Wyspiański 2019: 40; emphasis original). In a similar way, the Gravedigger then enlightens Laertes and Fortinbras as to their identities.

Because the play takes place in a cemetery, and the Gravedigger sets other characters into motion—in a way breathing life into them— we are invited to interpret this as the Gravedigger dragging them out of their graves, summoning them from the land of the dead. In this he is reminiscent of the Sorcerer from Adam Mickiewicz's *Forefathers' Eve* which overlaps *Hamlet* to an extraordinary extent. Both summon the dead for a ritual performance where the undead re-enact their histories sharing knowledge with the living, knowledge that can only be attained once one dies. The characters summoned by the Gravedigger initially appear helpless, unaware of their identities or roles. The Gravedigger must enlighten them, give them their identities and assign them their roles in the tragedy. In the last sequence of Grotowski's initial script, it is the Gravedigger—not Horatio—who is with Hamlet as he dies. It is the Gravedigger who Hamlet asks to 'tell my story', and it is he who tells Hamlet's story in order to educate and warn the living (Act 5, Scene 2, 333). This confirms the Gravedigger's role as both sorcerer and director.

Grotowski's first version of the *Hamlet Study* is an example of the Tadeusz Kantor's Theatre of Death. As Leszek Kolankiewicz noted, the Polish theatre repeats at its origin the archetype of Dziady (Forefathers' Eve), the feast of the dead ritual celebrated twice annually, at the end of April and October. Mickiewicz claimed that the art itself emerged from the cult of the dead and that theatre was the feast of the dead, a moment for ghosts to return (Kolankiewicz 1999: 34).[8] The Sorcerer calls the dead up from their graves to play out their histories and pass lessons onto the living. We are not dealing with metaphysics here—this feast of the dead takes place in theatre and relates to theatre. *Hamlet* as a theatre of the feast of the dead is a unique concept in the tradition of 'Polish thinking about *Hamlet*'. Grotowski, too, saw in *Hamlet* a performance akin to *Forefathers' Eve*. And yet in subsequent stages of the Opole *Hamlet Study*, Grotowski radically departs from it.

The concept in the second surviving Opole script is completely different. First, Grotowski and the company gave up on Grotowski's initial idea to set the Opole *Hamlet* in a cemetery and to ascribe exceptional importance to this scene relative to others. There is no Gravedigger-director-Sorcerer, and no ghosts summoned in pursuit of self-awareness. Second, the company introduced major cuts to the comments from Wyspiański's *Study* as well as to scenes from Shakespeare's drama; only one-third of the text from Grotowski's original script remained. And

---

8 Kolankiewicz (1999) saw similarities between Forefathers' Eve and the origins of Greek tragedy.

third, the company arranged the remaining sequences as a series of confrontations between Hamlet and other characters with comments from Wyspiański interspersed throughout. Thus the 13 Rows' revision of Grotowski's script during rehearsals was not beholden to Wyspiański's *Study* or Shakespeare's drama. The company abandoned the original drama's narrative and avoided its cause-effect sequencing.

The main theme of the second Opole script was 'Hamlet and otherness'. The script presents Hamlet's otherness to the rest of the characters—the King, Rosencrantz, Guildenstern, his Mother, the Ghost and Ophelia. The Opole *Study* forces Hamlet into a confrontation with other characters where he has to defend himself. Here, Grotowski and his actors extracted notions of misunderstanding and alienation—in extreme cases even persecution and threat—from Hamlet's myth. Members of the court confront the protagonist within a series of tests and clashes. The 13 Rows arranged the text performatively not literally. They created it through improvisational acting, it was 'written on stage'. Flaszen noted that 'if a particular fragment did not stimulate the actors' and director's imagination, it was cut' (Flaszen 2010[1964]: 101).

Grotowski gave up on his original concept when he received strong signals from the actors. That which proved viable in performance—regardless of literary value—was all that remained. The company cut up their source material so as to extract emotions and tensions from it, and they used it to present various relationships. This is why the performance is so crucial to the company's creative journey. The text was used as material for the actors' études. They tested a new way of working as a collective, including collective directing. The actors' experience of the efficacy of a performance was far more important to their process than even the most brilliant dramaturgical or directorial concepts. What mattered in the final Opole version of *Hamlet Study* was neither the staging of a text nor the telling of the story of the Prince of Denmark. The 13 Rows confronted Hamlet's myth with the rules of the stage and with actors' imaginations, and subjected their source material to theatrical experimentation. The result of this experimental confrontation surprised both the audience and the company.

Theoretical Reason vs Practical Brawn

The Laboratory Theatre performed *Hamlet Study* in an almost empty space—with no raised stage and no set. They set up rows of audience chairs facing each other, and in between, they left a narrow strip for the actors to play on. Two bare spotlights lit the space from either end of the strip. The focus of the staging was the relationship between the public and the performers. Actors used very few elementary objects—chairs, clothes, scraps of fabric and a blanket. Their costumes consisted of trousers, shirts, belts and berets. Actors improvised their costumes from these basic elements according to the needs of the action they performed. They eliminated all non-essential elements, such as decoration, music and lighting effects. All production elements were created live by the actors. They sang, produced sound effects and redirected the flow of light and shapes in the performance space. In 1964, Flaszen commented that in the Opole *Hamlet Study* 'actors create everything: the setting and the mood, the time and the space. This is our idea of "poor theatre" taken to its extreme; the actor as the only instrument—and the spectator as the resonance box' (2010[1964]: 106).

This did not mean that the 13 Rows set Elsinore in a timeless space or that they stripped it of specific realities. Upon an empty stage, actors created the soundscape of a poor and powerless Polish village. Using their voices, they mimicked barking dogs, crowing rooster calls, cawing crows and ringing bells. Moans and calls came from various directions. Actors swayed like willow trees in the wind. They sounded like howling winds and uttered prayers. They also created an inner landscape steeped in melancholy, pointlessness and lack of willpower. Flaszen described it thus:

> From the court at Elsinore we move to a simple setting near the Vistula River bank, created by the actors without any set or props. Winds whistle plaintively, weeping willows sway, and crows caw. People meet in taverns and fairs, wandering across the fields and the wilderness. The landscape is not real, but archaic, immortalized in the national imagination by nineteenth-century poetry and paintings. Among the inhabitants of this—slightly imaginary—land, gloomy biological Brawn is

paired with a melancholic wailing, seeking Meaning and the Deed (capital letters are needed!) to the accompaniment of its lament; Inability, lurking everywhere, makes these human strivings discharge themselves in boorish and surrogate acts. Hamlet is also a child of this peculiar land.
(Flaszen 2010[1964]: 103)

Grotowski and company followed Wyspiański's proposal to update the events in Shakespeare's drama, and to set the action in a contemporary Polish context. However, the action did not take place in Wawel Castle as Wyspiański wished. Grotowski transformed the royal Danish-English tragedy into a Polish village drama taking place in decrepit, crude and impoverished rural Poland. Grotowski explained this concept in an interview for an Opole students' magazine in March 1964.

We incorporated into [the performance] elements of folk song, Christmas carols, patriotic songs. Our aim was to create an atmosphere as if the performance had a quintessentially Polish character, thereby becoming unfamiliar to those who know the Shakespearean original, and hard to grasp for those not familiar with the affairs of our nation. This will be performance about a Polish 'Hamletism', a crooked mirror of inter-human superstitions that could also take shape under our skies.
(Grotowski 2009[1964]: 99)

The Polish conflict par excellence at the root of the performance revolved around the yawning gap between the intelligentsia and common people. The Laboratory Theatre further nuanced this central conflict with issues related to ethnicity. Zygmunt Molik played Hamlet as a Jewish intellectual. He thus became a stereotypical 'other' set against a rural community that—for Grotowski—represented Claudius' court and its henchmen. Grotowski explained: 'Hamlet and the rest are two kinds of Hamletism hostile to one another and in fact filled with hate' (2009[1964]: 98). The performance made use of stereotypes and animosities, opposing intellectual reflection against power, 'Theoretical Reason and Practical Brawn look at each other, detached and hostile' (Flaszen 2010[1964]: 104).

These were two attitudes impossible to unite. The Laboratory Theatre showed both aspects through a 'crooked mirror of inter-human superstitions' as monstrous and engorged. In villagers' eyes Hamlet was 'an abstract reflection on life, a noble but impractical impulse towards justice and the world's reform. In the eyes of the community, he is a bookworm, a "zaddik" [leader of a Hasidic community] prattling on with smart slogans, a gesticulating little intellectual, a cowardly and cunning casuist, a squeaky voiced jumped up "yid"' (2010[1964]: 104). This difference was emphasized by the choice of costumes. Peasants were dressed carelessly, raggedy and barefoot, while Hamlet wore a white shirt, striped trousers and boots, carried a book and covered his head with a beret resembling a yarmulke. He was an alien, an outsider, an 'egghead', 'a scribbler living in a symbiosis with a library and avoids all shallow and banal joys for the masses' (Barba 2014[1965]). He was estranged from society, cut off from the community with which he continuously and unsuccessfully tried to bond.

In Bielski's notes on the first script, the opening scene appears under the name 'Étude of misery and poverty'. The scene was supposed to show the torpor and hopelessness of the world of the performance. The next scene's action took place in a rural inn that was the setting for the wedding of the King (Antoni Jahołkowski) and the Queen (Rena Mirecka), in effect a country party full of drunken revelry. Peasants drank vodka, sang coarse songs, and Hamlet did his best to join in though he did not succeed. His otherness aroused ire among the peasants leading them to provoke him, and to have fun at his expense. In this sorrowful Polish village, drunken peasants suddenly began speaking in Shakespearean style and decided to stage their own version of *Hamlet* as a joke. They took on Shakespearean roles, and dragged their 'local Jew' into a dangerous and duplicitous game. They chose him—as the weaker, other, alien—to be their Hamlet. They staged the appearance of the Ghost (Ryszard Cieślak) and provoked Hamlet to react. One of them crouched behind Hamlet's chair and goaded him with Shakespeare's words, 'It beckons you to go away with it' (Shakespeare 2007: Act 1, Scene 4, 58). Hamlet's conversation with the Ghost was interrupted with moans, groans, cries and a ringing bell. The étude concluded in a fiasco and a withdrawal. Flaszen commented that 'besides the Shakespearean motifs, the actual process of their staging becomes the étude's subject. This is a performance about the birth of a performance' (Flaszen 2010[1964]: 101). Wyspiański raised questions and doubts about *Hamlet*, facilitating a '"thinking aloud" about the staging that is in progress' (2010[1964]: 101). In this sense, the performance had a meta-theatrical character, dealing with the process of creating a performance. It was an authentic form of reflection upon *Hamlet* and various possibilities for staging the drama. Finally, the peasants were paralysed by their own powerlessness. Unable to complete their project, they stopped the performance and returned to drinking. Eugenio Barba described the scene:

> Now and then the peasants make an effort to play Shakespeare's text, do a rough outline of some scenes, and then withdraw declaring that it is an impossible task. They relapse into their basic vital attitude: drinking and fornicating. They are mean and brutal, always in a group, ready to tear each other into pieces.
> (Barba 1999: 78)

The peasants' aggression increased. They continued harassing Hamlet, ready to fight. Hamlet 'is the foolish victim of the gloomy village jesters. A stranger among his kinsmen, his helplessness incites others' brutality' (Flaszen 2010[1964]: 103). The peasants kept bursting out laughing, making fun of the outsider. And yet he believed in his new role. 'What was imagined played out and became the true reality in his mind' (Wójtowicz 2004: 124). This device of performing a play within a play not only allowed the presentation of the creative mechanisms of the theatre but also showed 'two Hamletisms' and two states of powerlessness: 'Peasants will never be able to perform *Hamlet*. Hamlet can never be fully realized in real action' (Wójtowicz 2004: 124).

Rena Mirecka was the only female actor in the company at the time, and she played both Gertrude and Ophelia. The peasants pushed Ophelia on Hamlet and listened with sensual glee to her talk with her 'lover'.

Mirecka threw her chequered blanket from her shoulders and she suddenly became a lithe, young girl in a white dress. In this moment, Grotowski addressed a problem that Wyspiański also tried to resolve in his *Study*. Is Ophelia a naive and innocent girl or a courtesan serving the King? In the performance Ophelia posed the question to Hamlet directly, 'in love is she a spring blossom or a courtesan?' (see Wyspiański 2019: 76). The Gravedigger (Ryszard Cieślak) answered for him, 'There was a Courtesan—planted by the king, feigning love'. Ophelia tried to defend herself, 'She might even have loved him but she was somebody enmeshed in a lie' (Wyspiański 2019: 40). Mirecka embodied this duality. At first, she turned to Hamlet 'sweetly, coquettishly' only to quickly switch to a coarse screech. Józef Kelera wrote about this duality in his review of the Opole performance.

> In which sort of theatre would an actress be bold enough, as is Rena Mirecka, to demonstrate in one action, in one sequence Ophelia's twin incarnations (a grand problem in Shakespeare-ology!): Ophelia-Virginal, soft, lyrical, spring-ling and in a sudden switch, in vocal acrobatics—Ophelia-Whore, charmer, spy and harlot, screeching with the voice of a tradeswoman from the market?
> (Kelera 2006[1964]: 176)

At the same time, her character was connected with Gertrude. Flaszen noted in his commentary on the premiere that 'the Queen takes off her scarf and transforms into Ophelia, a virgin in white; both characters share a bestial, wild female element' (2010[1964]: 100). It seems Mirecka smoothly switched between these types of character—wife and virgin/bawd, and between roles—Queen and Ophelia. Grotowski was rather interested in blurring these lines. After all, in the Opole perform-ance she was a peasant girl drawn from an inn into a play.

Hamlet greeting Rosencrantz and Guildenstern was staged as a bul-lying scene. The ringleaders of the village boys—Rosencrantz (Ryszard Cieślak) and Guildenstern (Andrzej Bielski)—took Hamlet's book from him and mocked him. Their jeering actions elicited laughter and giggles from the watching crowd. The key prop was an imaginary piece of bread—which Hamlet's 'friends' kept giving to him and then taking it. Upon proclaiming 'Denmark's a prison', Guildenstern stole the bread from Hamlet's lips and hid it in his trousers. During Hamlet's next lines—that Denmark is one of the worst prisons—Guildenstern once again took a slice of bread from Hamlet's lips, and this time hid it beneath his cap. Meanwhile, Rosencrantz stood behind Hamlet making his escape impossible. Finally, Hamlet's tormentors turned into dogs, Guildenstern fell on all fours, and began to growl. They literally attacked Hamlet, one of them 'biting' his leg. Then they stole Hamlet's bread again. Rosencrantz hid it in his shirt, and Guildenstern held up his open hands to show Hamlet he was not holding anything. They ambushed Hamlet from all sides, and watched from behind his back the rest of peasants react. Their sneering circling turned into premonitions of a fight. Guildenstern clenched his fists, and took up a pose suggesting his readiness to fight. Finally, they left Hamlet in peace. Hamlet recited the monologue 'What a piece of work is a man' (Act 2, Scene 2), which must have sounded coolly ironic in this scenario.

At this point in the script submitted to state censors, Hamlet and Ophelia had a conversation (Act 3, Scene 1). Andrzej Bielski's notes on the first script suggest that it was an erotic scene. Hamlet objectifies Ophelia to the extreme, and proceeds to rape her. A film shot during a rehearsal shows Molik approaching Mirecka (*Rehearsal* 1964). The scene emphasized naturalistic details and physiological precision. The rape was brutal and ended with Ophelia breaking down in tears. After he finished, Hamlet—exhausted—laid down beside her. The King (Antoni Jahołkowski) and Polonius (Andrzej 'Gaston' Kulig) stood by. They watched the whole thing with authentic horror, eyes peeled, hands covering their mouths and their figures shrinking. After the attack, Hamlet sent Ophelia to a nunnery which in Elizabethan slang meant brothel.

At the same time, the stage situation has changed. For the peasants the 'real' thing is to take part in a fight. Consequently, the rural court unexpectedly turned into an army. The script informs us that 'the King recruits in Denmark a horde of volunteers'(Grotowski 1964). This is a paraphrase of Horatio's phrase announcing that Fortinbras gathered 'a list of lawless resolutes' (Shakespeare 2007: Act 1, Scene 1, 97), a declaration that justified the militarization of the court in 13 Rows performance.

> The Elsinore court, whilst not losing its peasant character, becomes militarized. Hamlet's dream of a heroic deed takes military and insurgent forms; activities become brutal and violent, and the free choice of a heroic attitude degenerates into the humiliation of drafting and drill. The King has plenty of cannon-fodder at his disposal: he becomes either a corporal, delighting in the charms of the drill, or a gravedigger sending the troops to the battlefields. The liberating deed, embodied in a socially engaged action, gives primacy to tough and aggressive people who do not care for subtleties . . .
> (Flaszen 2010[1964]: 103–4)

Cunning peasants enlist 'their Jew' into the army, and yet everyone is against him. Being Jewish, he is disqualified from military service. His accent and his odd clothing do not help his case. He wanted to earn the respect of the peasant-soldiers, and become a member of their community. Thus, he wanted to take part in their military drill.

Zbigniew Raszewski provides an entry point to the militarization of the Opole *Hamlet Study* by describing the King in the scene.

> The King goes crazy for military action. He himself wears a uniform and is training his court, who are also dressed in military garb. He behaves like a corporal, inspecting his line ups, chastising disorderly soldiers, tearing at buttons and belts not properly secured. All of this takes place to the rhythm of words written by Wyspiański in his *Hamlet Study*.
> (Raszewski 2006[1964]: 234)

Hamlet is trained and toughened up. The King subjects all of the soldiers to a murderous training regime of running, falling, doing crunches, jumping and crawling on all fours. This form of training aimed to exhaust them. Hamlet's famous lines to the Players accompanied the action:

'Speak the speech, I pray you, as I pronounced it to you—trippingly on the tongue [. . .]' (Shakespeare 2007: Act 3, Scene 2, 1–2). Flaszen added that 'it can at the same time be treated as self-mockery by the director who wants to do away with accusations of being a "violator" of his actors' souls . . .' (2010[1964]: 104). This was not the first time, and it would not be the last.

The battle-tested soldiers of Opole's *Hamlet Study* village set off for war. Hamlet turns out to be a mediocre soldier, perhaps on account of his ideals, humanism and books. Eugenio Barba compared him to Isaac Babel in the cavalry brigade, 'the Jew from Odessa amongst the Cossacks, the experts in pogroms. The true warriors mock the intellectual' (Barba 1999: 79). Grzegorz Niziołek wrote that Grotowski used the stereotype of a Jew not being able to fight, deprived of a warrior spirit, a coward and deserter (2019: 147). When the fighting starts, Hamlet begins his 'To be or not to be' monologue. Barba described this powerful scene:

> The time of action arrives. Sadism, hate, threats fill the space. The soldier-peasants throw themselves at imaginary enemies. The acrid smell of sweat mixes with mingles with the frenzied shouts of murderers and the groans of the dying. Bodies roll on the ground, get to their feet again only to fall back, writhing. Rape and torture, cruelty and bestiality reveal the face of *homo miles*, military man. Hamlet takes refuge in an interminable monologue: to be or not to be? He is present as a distant witness, while the actors confront an imaginary adversary (lurking in the subconscious?) with a savage violence, which does not even spare their own bodies.
> (Barba 1999: 79)

When the moment of battle comes, Hamlet stares as soldiers turn into animals and torment their victims. He recites 'To be or not to be', and the subsequent fragments of the original text accompany successive scenes of torture and rape. Bielski precisely described these actions in his script: torture, slow murder, rape, the murder of rape victims with iron, the removal of corpses, searches for new victims, another attempt at rape and impotence in the midst of it. Each of the above actions listed in the script is accompanied by the actors' actions noted by each of the performers For example Andrzej Bielski noted in his script archived at the Grotowski Institute,

> 'Torturing': I take a terrified victim and with rising glee begin to sever through their gullet. Joy, laughter. A beast's delight. 'Slow killing': I take the second victim. Kicking the belly, I bring it down to ground level and begin to ever so slowly slaughter, entering into an ecstatic state (saliva dripping, eyes bulging). After the murder is done, I wipe the knife on a jacket.
> (Bielski 1964: 57–58)

The actions of rape and other forms of violence were repulsive in their realism and in the precision with which the actors carried out each act of causing pain and death. The scene was constructed on the basis of counterpoint—the actors set the bestiality of war in stark contrast with the most famous dramatic monologue of all time, and the pacifist attitude of Opole's Jewish Hamlet contrasted with the other soldiers' cruelty.

After a failed rape attempt on a victim, the Gravedigger (Cieślak) voiced Wyspiański's interpretation of various Hamlet monologues as representative of stages of Hamlet's thought, stages of his evolution. Following these words, Hamlet began another monologue, 'How all occasions do inform against me' (Shakespeare 2007: Act 4, Scene 4, 31), at which time the soldiers, after resting, returned to their butchering. They crushed victims' faces and abdomens with their heels. Hamlet opines 'What is a man/ If his chief good and market of his time/ Be but to sleep and feed? A beast—no more' (Shakespeare 2007: Act 4, Scene 4, 32–34), and the soldiers started getting drunk, sliding to the ground, then fell asleep and snored. Upon waking up they started another round of monstrous fury. Bielski described his actions in this scene: 'rabid I rise, smack my victim in the face, but fall powerless and observe that which Zygmunt [Hamlet] is doing' (Bielski in Grotowski 1964: 57 verso). Hamlet's reticence provoked aggression among the peasant-soldiers. Barba wrote that Hamlet 'wants to remain outside, not to surrender to the collective madness. The others grab him in, oblige him to torture, to "act", to participate in the brutality and contempt which unites the group' (Barba 1999: 79). Peasants brought Hamlet an imaginary victim and held the victim vulnerable for Hamlet to attack. In contrast to Hamlet's sublime oratory, he succumbed to the peasants' cajoling, and began to beat the invisible figure. In his script, Bielski wrote that Hamlet turned out to be even more violent than the rest of them. In this moment Hamlet underwent what Eugenio Barba calls a 'baptism of fire' (Barba 1999: 79). His attack ended with vomiting. Thanks to his actions he secured the peasants' respect, and for a moment even became one of them. Only aggression bonded this community.

Ludwik Flaszen wrote that:

Hamlet feels bad in the climate of an organized deed. He is weak and wise among the strong and cunning. Sometimes he recalls Kafka's Joseph K., dragged away for execution . . . Hamlet clearly aspires to single himself out from the mass. The Prince of Denmark becomes a liberal intelligent person with the noble and utopian programme of reforming the world—in a world of tough necessities.
(Flaszen 2010[1964]: 104)

Following his military action, Hamlet returned to the village, where a scene with his mother ensued. The war sequences gave way to the rural landscapes from earlier scenes. Actors signal the change of setting with their actions. Hamlet arrives at the village.

There he finds the peasants, identical to the soldiers he has just left, drinking, singing, and making love. Nobody recognizes him. Only a dog welcomes him back. The meeting with his mother ends with the murder of one the peasant, Polonius. Dragging the body behind him, Hamlet takes refuge in the public baths.
(Barba 1999: 79)

Hamlet found the peasants sitting down to a meal. The Queen was spinning yarn. The King arm-wrestled those recovering from their revelry. This scene took place in a gloomy silence. When Hamlet beat the King in arm-wrestling the peasants recognized him—like Odysseus upon his return to Ithaca. And then everyone froze. Hamlet approached the Queen, and a white sheet that had been a table-cloth became a bed sheet for a pallet in his mother's bedchamber. Juliusz Grodziński saw a rehearsal of this scene and described it thus:

> Hamlet and the Queen Mother on stage. Hamlet feels insecure and wants to return to his mother's womb, that same way he once entered the world. He lies on the floor, takes on the form of an embryo and makes motions so as to make me think for a moment that he might succeed, all the more that the Queen Mother is clearly horrified by his actions . . .
> (Grodziński 1964: 22)

After the rehearsal, Grotowski explained to Grodziński that 'Hamlet wants to crawl back into his mother's womb—this is a parody of the Freudian complex from which Hamlet suffers' (Grodziński 1964: 22). It was also a rape scene. The horrified Queen screamed 'Help!', and yet the peasants watching did not react. Once again, details were important here—physiological precision, exact gestures and movements. The extreme naturalism of acting in *Hamlet Study* was shocking—'the actor's body was the source of direct expression that worked upon the audience' (Wójtowicz 2004: 127). Throughout the performance, actors exposed the vulgarity, biological functions and the animalistic side of human nature. Barba described it:

> The actors' performance is a form of blackmail; it is not daily behaviour, but a physiology of an extraordinary state: sexual climax, agon, torture, rape. Inarticulate shouts and aberrant raucous voices [. . .]. Their performance does not convince: it terrorizes, disturbs, brutally shakes the defenceless spectator.
> (Barba 1999: 81)

The next scene was also based on physical actions and physiological means of expression. Unfortunately, the scarce information leaves us unable to report a precise order of actions. We know that the scene took place in a rural bathhouse where Hamlet had dragged Polonius' dead body after killing him. Peasants gathered in the bathhouse, undressed to their undergarments and 'washed'. They used their caps as sponges to scrub their bodies, soaked themselves with 'water' and washed each other's backs. They over-emphasized these actions by performing them slowly. The atmosphere became steamy, and filled the performance space with erotic tension. The peasants fondled one another. Their conduct became increasingly vulgar, and they uttered audible, sensual sighs.

> Gathered in the sauna, the peasants fight and squirm like a disgusting monster to which the nudity of the actors lends a bestial physiology. Their erotic games reflect the despiritualization of man, the animality. Hamlet alone, completely dressed, washes himself with a distinguished meticulousness.
> (Barba 1999: 79)

A photograph from the performance confirms that all the actors were nearly naked except for Hamlet (see Świątkowska 2016: 98). The photographer captured them in expressive poses—legs apart, hips thrust forward, touching themselves and other 'bathers'. Because most of the actors taking part are men the scene may be consider another example of a potent homoerotic subtext inserted by Grotowski within larger frameworks of disgusting, abject action.

Hamlet crouched on a chair, and turned away from them. He read a book, and seemed to ignore the actions of the others. The contrast of his otherness was provocative. He was completely dressed in trousers, a shirt and shoes. 'Hamlet, as the only character, maintains his difference in a solemn but inappropriate way, by staying dressed' (Flaszen 2010[1964]: 105). The peasants' suspicions were aroused when they splashed 'cold water' on Polonius—who lay between Hamlet and the peasants—and Polonius did not react. Eventually, the peasants discover he is dead. Rosencrantz and Guildenstern began to interrogate Hamlet, and started picking at his clothing. Soon Rosencrantz wanted to tear off Hamlet's shirt, and Guildenstern wanted to take off his boots. Rosencrantz bared himself before Hamlet—who remained silent and did not react to their vulgar taunts. The peasants-among them the King-became more and more aggressive towards him, and looked for a pretext to start a fight. In the end, the King threw the first punch at Hamlet, and the others joined in. Ophelia entered the bathhouse and distracted them. The peasants were immediately interested in her. They sat her down in their laps and touched her as she recited lines about her madness and sang her songs (Act 4, Scene 5, 16–73). In her madness she was easy prey for the debauched, aroused peasants. They passed her from hand to hand, from lap to lap. They grossly manhandled her in increasingly offensively ways, and their treatment of her kept escalating. The peasants' erotic, bathhouse games turned into mass rape.

> In the bathhouse episode, among the group bathing, the sensual panting and crude games [. . . and other] sinful goings-on, Ophelia dies. The carnality of perversion and the carnality of death show their ambiguous similarities. Excess turns into a church service, and ecstatic entertainment into a liturgy of mourning.
> (Flaszen 2010[1964]: 105–6)

Ophelia became a doll in the peasants' hands—'an atmosphere of simpletons' orgy' turned into a gang-rape that killed her (Flaszen 2014: 283). This was certainly a shocking and brutal scene. The actors' actions were tangible, physical and their physiological realism dominated the scene. Barba wrote about disgust and shame. Bielski noted that these actions were gross and overwrought (1964). The peasants erupted with animality and vulgarity—it was a huge dose of perversion. Barba characterized the scene as 'a terrifying and horrible vivisection that smells of sweat, blood and sperm—a merciless vision of the individual and the group swept along by instinct' (1999: 81). These drastic images exposed the depravity of human nature, and humans' penchant for untoward desire and aggression.

Ophelia's death aroused terror in the peasants. They laid her dead body next to Polonius, crossed both deceased's arms over their chests, and covered them both in a white sheet. The scene of Ophelia's madness, mass rape and death, turned into a funeral. The peasants surrendered to despair and performed a litany. 'Brawn, horrified by itself, transforms into culture, the creation of a guilty conscience' (Flaszen 2010[1964]: 100). Still naked, the peasants took part in a funeral liturgy. Barba's description:

> The peasants are astonished and terrified in the face of death's mystery and their nakedness becomes the very symbol of the human condition and anguish when pushed to extreme limits. Those same people who behaved like animals in heat rediscover a form of humanity made of up of prayers and laments, invocations and religious fervour. [...] Only a few moments before these creatures were prey to instincts that we observed with shame and disgust.
> (Barba 1999: 79–80)

As in earlier performances, the company joined the sacred and the profane—two extremes combined in a dialectic of derision and apotheosis.

After the argument with Laertes (Mieczysław Janowski) Hamlet is once and for all cast out from the village. He finds the army and joins the soldiers once again for the finale of the performance. The company built the *Hamlet Study* finale using text from the cemetery scene of Act 5 of Shakespeare's drama, beginning with the Gravedigger's song 'In youth when I did love, did love' (Shakespeare 2007: Act 5, Scene 1, 57). In the finale, the King (Jahołkowski)—having just served as Death's general sending troops off to die—became the Gravedigger. A military unit marched through the theatre space singing 'Bogurodzica' [The mother of God], a medieval religious hymn that Polish knights sang prior to battle. Half-naked peasants, hats askew, replicated various historic military formations becoming Slavic warriors, knights who fought at Grunwald, hussars, Polish cavalry called 'uhlans' and finally young soldiers of the Warsaw Uprising.[9] Barba described the finale:

---

9 Warsaw Uprising (1 August–2 October 1944) insurrection organized by the Polish Underground Resistance against the Nazi occupants. The Home Army tried unsuccessfully to seize control of

JERZY GROTOWSKI'S HAMLETS · **419**

We see the battalions advance, in formation, impassive, transfigured, towards the tomb of History:

Mother of God, blessed
Virgin Mary
Kyrie Eleison.

This religious litany, with which Polish warriors once invoked
divine protection when facing the Teutonic knights in Grunwald
and the Turks outside Vienna, accompanies the peasant-soldiers
on their march towards the battlefield.

The king is the Gravedigger. As the troops file past, he recognizes his soldiers but speaks of them in the past tense: they
are already corpses. Before the fate awaiting them, these men
do not hesitate, they do not object: reasoning makes man weak.
They take action and pay for it with their lives.
(Barba 1999: 80)

Flaszen described the scene as 'a sort of ballet interpretation of the military
history of Poland—with the tragic myth of fighting as the only solution
for the nation's society' (2010[1964]: 105). Grotowski synthesized the
history of Polish national uprisings and insurrections as a series of military
formations from different epochs that all similarly went into battle and
died. The *Study*'s peasants set off on a suicidal path to war as Poles have
done for centuries and as Polish tradition demands (see Kosiński 2019:
160–65). They were united by their readiness to give their lives in sacrifice.
In their unity, they were determined and crazed—almost in a trance. The
King led them as a servant of Death. As both the Gravedigger and the
King of cannon fodder, he sent more and more units to be slaughtered.
Hamlet tried to stop the march by leaping at the soldiers, shouting,
cursing, and crying. He finally lay down at their feet and barred their
way with his own body. In this scene Hamlet wore a yarmulke and a
long, black, shiny coat reminiscent of traditional Hasidic gaberdine.

---

the city. Approaching Soviet Army stopped on the eastern bank of Vistula River, and remained
idle enabling German Army to defeat the Polish resistance and destroy the city. It is estimated
that 16,000 insurgents and 200,000 civilians were killed. The Warsaw Uprising remains one of
the most tragic and controversial events of the Second World War, and the symbol of desperate
heroism and sacrifice.

Hamlet—a weakling and sissy when faced with the harsh soldiery—tries to stop the troops marching to war. He becomes a grotesque advocate of reason and humanitarianism. But does this humanitarianism count for anything when up against Necessity that pushes people to fight? The troops set off, spitting at the odd and alienated Job, trampling him underfoot—and they perish one by one.
(Flaszen 2010[1964]: 105)

Barba describes Hamlet's death:

[Hamlet] recites monologues: the brutality and the horror of war act as a stimulant on his brain. He wants to transmit his rational and humanistic message to the marching hordes. They spit in his face. He cries, throwing himself at their feet to stop them. They trample on him.
(Barba 1999: 80)

At the end of the battle, all the dead soldiers fall down, their bodies collapsing into awkward poses—their legs and arms askew, faces down. Among them Hamlet lies on his back—arms splayed in a crucifixion pose. The King stands in the background, his arms raised aloft and his face to the heavens. According to Flaszen and Barba, the King ended the performance by reciting the prayer *Kyrie Eleison*. Flaszen interpreted the finale as an act of regaining human solidarity in death. He wrote, 'Hamlet, trampled on the battlefield, expresses his yearning for solidarity and community, finally fraternizing with the people in this extreme situation. Is this the only way to overcome estrangement? Can opposing human elements be reconciled only through such a kind of shock?' (2010[1964]: 105). But Barba noticed that even though Hamlet wanted to stay by the peasants' side, and to join them, 'his form of impotence consists in the incapacity to feel, live and die with the others. Because he is unable to, and because the others do not want him to' (1999: 81). It is hard to believe there was any hope of achieving community, even a 'community of death,' after these acts of aggression revealed the deep-seated antagonisms between Hamlet and the peasants.

The finale scene became a moment of tragic recognition. With all force, it exposed Hamlet's final defeat: Hamlet not only did not preserve basic values, he did not change the course of History. The closing scene dismissed tragic reconciliation. It was too late for that.

(Wójtowicz 2004: 139).

According to Agnieszka Wójtowicz, Hamlet remained an alien until the very end. Hamlet and the peasants were divided by radically divergent value systems: the soldier-peasants were ready to make a pointless sacrifice which Hamlet did not believe made any sense. 'His reason wants to suffocate the myth that animates these people. He wants to strip them of their impulses, of their desire for submission, to give themselves and, in so doing, to act' (Barba 1999: 80). They represented action at all cost while he believed in humanism, and in the senselessness of war, a pointless sacrifice. They went into battle 'as if harvesting', in pursuit of greatness, while he had nothing but words. Until the very end there was no chance of reconciliation between them.

This Laboratory Theatre performance diverged sharply from the first script, and even more so from its sources, Shakespeare's *Hamlet* and Wyspiański's *Hamlet Study*. Audiences expecting to see a staging of the story of 'the Prince of Denmark' would have been shocked. The performance they witnessed featured mere scraps of the original Shakespearean drama. The company chose not to follow any conventional continuity, and they dropped many key narrative threads and characters. The 13 Rows used Shakespeare's tragedy and Wyspiański's commentary to create situations with new meanings, and placed them in new contexts and realities. The company overlaid the text not with prepared actions that illustrated it but with a completely different, contrasting conception of theatrical composition. Zbigniew Raszewski stressed that the company played the performance in some instances counter to the text, and sometimes in spite of it. 'Actors saying one thing and acting out another' (2006: 234). For example, drastic images of war accompanied Hamlet's 'To be or not to be' monologue.

422 · WANDA ŚWIĄTKOWSKA

Reviewers accused the director of creating a performance that was made up of a sequence of études that did not form a coherent whole. Raszewski:

> We cannot see any sort of construction in this staging of *Hamlet*, various scenes chasing one after the other and often without effect. Each taken separately is evidence of the director's unique imagination. Arranged together they refuse to join up. They lack the sort of causality which would give the impression of necessity.
> (Raszewski 2006: 236)

Many years later Andrzej Żurowski entered into a polemic with Raszewski's review, coming to Grotowski's defence.

> But a certain defined construction was in place. It was based on counterpoint—the contrasting moods and intellectual content of individual sequences that at the same time featured contrasts between the lofty and the trivial. This overt form of expression is highly characteristic of Grotowski's stylistics, [...] seen as early as *Kordian*, when the gurgling of rinsed throats accompanied the moment when the hero has to make an existential decision. In *Hamlet* this technique of juxtaposed extremes governed the whole performance, and created associative sequences that gave the performance rhythm and shaped its structural integrity.
> (Żurowski 2001: 97)

Action on the stage altered the meanings of words—the former being provocative and blasphemous towards the latter. Grotowski was not interested in staging the drama. Rather, he was interested in crashing his source texts into the mechanisms of the stage and actors' imaginations. The text was subjected to experimentation, in which performers' actions had decisive impact on the final shape of each scene. The performance emerged from improvisations conducted using an associative method. Words merely served as raw material for the actors to work with, and

Grotowski radically departed from a theatre that 'staged plays'—thus entering into a new phase of his research.

Many of the scenes from the performance can no longer be reconstructed, and yet if we were to attempt to summarize the main action of the Opole *Hamlet Study* these scenes would fit into the performance's repeated chain of ridicule, humiliation, sexual dominance, aggression and violence. Generally speaking, we can divide the performance into two analogical parts that take place in two spaces: a rural environment including the inn and the bath-house and on a battlefield with scenes of marching and fighting. Thus, the performance took place both at 'home' and in 'history'. In both of these symbolic places the same process of marking, excluding and killing victims appears again and again, as in the cases of the Jewish Hamlet and Ophelia. These processes end in scenes wherein the community kills those they had already stigmatized with irrevocable otherness. And the result of their deaths is a unification of the community with a solidarity wrought from crime and guilt. According to René Girard—who developed and described this model anthropologically—this is the process of a sacral, ritual relation to the world that gave rise to all religions and cultures (1977). Grotowski explored this model many times in his performances. We can see it at work in *Forefathers' Eve*, and it found its fullest development soon thereafter in *The Constant Prince*. The 13 Rows showed it clearly in *Hamlet Study* by displaying a mechanism of Polish culture, the reoccurring history of victimizing Jews.

The Jewish Hamlet in Relation to the Events of 1968

The fact that the performance underscored Poland's violent history of victimizing Jews was the main reason why the Opole performance was presented only for a short time. It was not cancelled because a handful of critics considered it an artistic fiasco. Instead, it was likely cancelled because it addressed themes that were controversial in Poland at the time—and remain so today. These themes were so controversial that the performance was dangerous for the company.

In the 1960s, a wave of nationalist rhetoric rose up in Poland. Anti-Semitism became an official ideology of the Communist Party. This process culminated with events in March 1968 which sparked widespread anti-intelligentsia and anti-Semitic persecution. When the authorities cancelled a production of *Forefathers' Eve* staged by Kazimierz Dejmek at the National Theatre, students of Warsaw University organized demonstrations in defence of the production on 8 March 1968. The authorities forcefully repressed the demonstrations using police and paramilitary violence, arrests and expulsion from the university.

On 19 March Władysław Gomułka—the First Secretary of the Polish Communist Party—gave a public speech in which he stressed the Jewish origins of those who had organized the demonstrations. The following day, Communist Party activists organized rallies in workplaces around Poland in support of Gomułka. State-owned media followed up with a campaign that fanned anti-Semitic rhetoric and feelings. Communist propaganda characterized the student speeches and demonstrations organized by the intelligentsia in defence of free speech as provocations and 'Zionist' conspiracies. This was quickly followed by purges and anti-Semitic campaigns forcing thousands of Polish Jews to abandon their homes (see Eisler 1998).

'Of course, as usual the Jews were blamed,' Flaszen lamented many years later. 'This time called "Zionists"—a label tested in Soviet propaganda laboratories. After all, Polish national-Communists used this official term—with a wink—barely covering the evident anti-Semitism and racism similar to the ideology of Polish ultra-nationalists before World War Two' (Flaszen 2010: 251). The propaganda tried to convince people that 'Zionists' functioned as secret enemies of the Polish nation, bourgeois urbanites, servants of American imperialism and agents of an international conspiracy directed against socialism. In the final days of July 1967, Moscow began an unprecedented propaganda campaign against Zionism accused of being a global danger. This characterization of Zionism soon became an excuse for all sorts of anti-Semitic purges that intensified after Israel won the Six-Day War in 1967.

The anti-Semitic campaign unleashed in Poland in 1968 led to some 13,000 Jews being stripped of their Polish nationality and deported. First, they were fired and rendered unemployable. They were removed from places of learning, terrorized, blackmailed and forced to emigrate. They were given travel documents that barred them from ever returning—in effect 'one-way tickets.' The political muscle in this programme were the so-called 'Partisans'—an extremely nationalistic branch of the Polish Communist Party that gathered around the deputy minister of internal affairs, General Mieczysław Moczar. The Partisans received support from groups of lower socio-economic status in Poland—peasants and laborers—and the ruling party used them to purge the intelligentsia under the auspices of a struggle against Zionism. Flaszen remembered the television reports from rallies organized by workers carrying banners with statements like 'Hands off Poland!', 'Down with the lackeys of global Zionism!' and 'Zionism Shall Not Pass!' (2010: 252). Authorities used this anti-Jewish campaign to channel social disappointments, distracting people from the economic crisis Poland was experiencing and to direct animosity against Jews. Flaszen wrote in a small brochure prepared for the premiere of *Hamlet Study* that 'there is always a need for the Jew to be beaten—and a need for the "pogromer", who absolves us from the abstract' (2010: 99).

Flaszen frequently faced attacks due to his Jewish heritage, which he later recounted. He supposed that he had also been added to the list of those to be eliminated from public life, and even to be deported. He stressed that 'Grotowski observed carefully the gradual increase in this wave for several years' (2010: 253). Flaszen also mentions that the scale of events that took place in 1968 were a shock for them both.

> Jews and Poles of Jewish descent of high standing, writers, intellectuals, and artists were hounded in the press and media; also ordinary people of 'improper' ancestry were willingly dismissed. In addition, intellectuals and artists without an 'ancestral burden' yet undesirable to the regime or involved in opposition activities were labelled 'Zionists'.
>
> (Flaszen 2010: 254)

Flaszen considered leaving the theatre. In 1968, Grotowski was afraid of being arrested, and considered committing suicide—he even asked Eugenio Barba to bring him cyanide from the West (see Flaszen 2010: 255). 1968 was also a difficult time in his private life. Grotowski's father Marian died in Paraguay. Grotowski last saw his father when he was just six years old in September 1939. In 1968, Grotowski's kidney dysfunction intensified and he underwent dialysis treatments abroad.

Flaszen convincingly argues that four years earlier Grotowski had predicted the things happening right before their eyes in 1968, and had put these predictions on stage in *Hamlet Study*.

> Our production, after long weaving and searching, became a sort of vision of the phenomenon of Communist populism and its deep (not to say native, indigenous) sources—a vision of some archaic country of peasants and soldiers, with the lonely intellectual, Hamlet-Jew, excluded from the community of vigorous people: an image (taken to an absurd dimension) of the Polish intellectual as seen by the 'people'—the eternal problems of the Polish elite, alienated from the 'deep' country. I remember that in the Soviet Union, anybody who wore glasses was thought to be a Jew.
> (Flaszen 2010: 253)

In 1964 Grotowski accurately diagnosed the forthcoming events. *Hamlet Study* reflected these enduring antagonisms and societal attitudes in Poland. Flaszen stressed that '*Hamlet Study*, created in 1964, unfinished, performed just a few times for a small group of spectators, was an indicator of the process that revealed itself fully in March 1968 (2010: 254). Years later, theatre historians also admitted that Grotowski wisely forecasted the mood of those times. Some found his performance a unique warning of what was to come. Elżbieta Morawiec argued that *Hamlet Study* contained a 'precise prefiguration of March 1968' (1991: 210). She wrote that *Hamlet Study* was 'a performance about a contemporary nation hidden beneath the respectful costume of a great classic work. It was dangerously transparent, and hence this road was quickly abandoned' (210). The protagonist of the performance was a 'simple populace who surrendered to the will of their king, ready to die and to exterminate Hamlets' (211).

However, the potential scandal that *Hamlet Study* might have caused was not only related to Grotowski diagnosing the anti-Semitic currents running through Polish society. He also showed Poles in a way in which no one in Poland wanted to see themselves—as backwards peasants who spit in the faces of Jews, and who not only mock but also cheat, rob and finally kill them. In other words, it was the way that he touched upon the taboo subject of Polish anti-Semitism. After the end of the Second World War and the Shoah this topic was not widely discussed in Poland. Grzegorz Niziołek wrote that Grotowski presented an

> exceptionally obscene image of violence, whose target was the Jew, [. . .] and the fact that his persecutors were the Polish 'populace', peasants, 'boors', endowed with male vigour and brawn—and thus an image that in Polish post-war reality, following the experience of the Holocaust, was absolutely censored (morally, politically, ideologically, linguistically) and devoid of the ethnographic 'innocence' (or 'sinlessness') of anti-Judaic popular prejudices.
> (Niziołek 2019: 146)

The 13 Rows' performance unmasked Polish anti-Semitism, and thus transgressed a social taboo. Their efforts adjust Wyspiański's famous formula: 'what is there—NOT to think about in Poland?' The 13 Rows constructed their performance around scenes of violence, aggression and hatred towards Jews. Their *Hamlet Study* brought to mind the pogroms following the end of the Second World War, as well as antagonisms deeply ingrained in the Polish subconscious. Grotowski and his company touched upon a national trauma, and opened still-healing wounds. They recalled pogroms against Jews, and most shameful of all, the acts of some Poles who helped Nazis catch Jews, Poles who blackmailed Jews, stole their property, those who actively and tacitly participated in genocide and generally caused Polish society to be passive in the face of unthinkable atrocities (see Niziołek 2019: 17–50).

After the Second World War, this history was shamefully concealed and resolutely falsified. To some extent, it still is today. According to Niziołek 'After the war, Polish antisemitism was deprived of a language. The more it kept silent, and the more people kept silent about it, the more it became a powerful reservoir of social energy, awaiting political investment' (2019: 249). Niziołek stresses that anti-Semitic attitudes among Poles were used in political games. 'There were two warring factions within the Communist Party, whose conflict shaped Polish political life in the years 1956 to 1968, known in popular parlance as the "Jews" and the "Boors" ' (2019: 249). The company in *Hamlet Study* made direct reference to this antagonism when they defined the two sides of the conflict.

The finale of the performance—in which Polish soldiers trample the Jewish Hamlet—was in this context particularly shocking. Raszewski protested against this theatrical choice.

> Let us take a closer look at Hamlet. In the Opole staging, he is a passionate, but insightful Jew. His partners have taken on the shape of Warsaw Insurgents. Hamlet tries to explain to them that their struggles border on madness. He leaps towards each soldier, holding a copy of the Talmud, and then each soldier spits in his face. The soldiers, singing insurgent songs, clearly resemble uprising military units such as 'Zośka' Battalion. Who cannot recall the photo in which the laughing 'Zośka' soldiers embrace the Jews from Gęsiówka concentration camp they had just liberated. We can all remember it, and perhaps all appreciate it.
> (Raszewski 2006: 235)

In this passage, Raszewski makes reference to a concentration camp functioning during the occupation in the ruins of what was once a ghetto at Gęsia Street in Warsaw—known otherwise as 'Gęsiówka'. On 5 August 1944—the fifth day of the Warsaw Uprising—soldiers from the 'Zośka' Battalion liberated the camp and freed 348 Jewish prisoners.[10] Raszewski

---

10 Earlier the Nazis, afraid of approaching Soviet Army, evacuated most of the prisoners forcing them on a 'death march'.

uses this example of Poles helping Jews—as is often done even today by defenders of Poland's 'good name'—to challenge the way the 13 Rows depicted Polish troops in *Hamlet Study*. The famous theatre historian presented himself as a defender of national dignity, and in order to do so he cited an honourable act—the liberation of Gęsiówka—to undermine the Laboratory Theatre's shocking image of the Polish national army's anti-Semitism. Barba wondered how it might have impacted members of the audience who remembered times of war.

> I wonder what they must have thought on seeing *Hamlet Study* in which the protagonist is an intellectual who speaks Polish with a Jewish inflection, among peasants who spit on him while singing patriotic songs from the Armia Krajowa [the Home Army].[11] Raszewski, who served in the Armia Krajowa, must certainly have been disconcerted.
> (Barba 1999: 83)

When the Theatre of 13 Rows showed the animosity between Polish peasant-soldiers and the Jewish Hamlet, the production initially exposed deeply hidden superstitions, resentments, and anti-Semitism that would erupt four years later, releasing long-suppressed hatred. Secondly, Grotowski challenged one of the most sacred values in Polish history and culture: the insurgent ethos and the myths of romantic uprisings and heroic deaths. He negated Polish myths of fighting for national freedom revealing their dark side, and the de-poeticised, un-heroic motives behind them. Sadly, four years later the events of 1968 proved that the artists were right.

Niziołek argues against Flaszen's interpretation of the *Hamlet Study* finale—that it presented the 'brotherhood' of the Jew and the peasants 'in extreme situations', a union brought about by death. Niziołek stresses that it was 'precisely their manner of dying that ultimately separated Polish and Jewish fates, paralyzing mutual relations. Death in this case

---

11 Armia Krajowa (Home Army) was the major military resistance force in German-occupied Poland during the Second World War. The Home Army was formed in February 1942 and ruled by the Polish government in exile residing in London.

did not unite but separated irrevocably' (2019: 156). When 'Polish heroes' fell fighting in the Warsaw Uprising, Jewish victims were dying in gas chambers and ghettos. And the crucial difference was clearly performed in the finale of the Opole *Study*.

In a well-known 1964 interview with Barba that was published later in *Towards a Poor Theatre* as 'The Theatre's New Testament' Grotowski explained that:

> even though we often use classical texts, ours is a contemporary theatre in that it confronts our very roots with our current behaviour and stereotypes, and in this way shows us our 'today' in perspective with 'yesterday', and our 'yesterday' with 'today'.
> (Grotowski 1968a: 51–52)

Grotowski made use of classical texts in order to confront them with contemporary experience. The performance had to emerge out of and refer to that which was all around.

> To spark off this particular process of provocation in the audience, one must break away from the trampoline represented by the text and which is already overloaded with a number of general associations. For this we need either a classical text to which, through a sort of profanation, we simultaneously restore its truth, or a modern text which might well be banal and stereotyped in its content, but nevertheless rooted in the psyche of society.
> (Grotowski 1968a: 43)

Pushing the text-myth to excess and profanation would not be possible without actual context, realistic resonance and being 'rooted in the psyche of society'.

Grotowski and his company made use of this very strategy when he told the story of Hamlet as a Jew among a community of peasants. He reached for collective perceptions on the subject of Jewish-Polish relations, a taboo topic, 'the true Gorgon of Polish post-war reality' (Niziołek 2019: 153). He unmasked Polish anti-Semitism, and aroused a sense of shock through his provocation. He exposed a collective secret, evoked a sense of guilt and fear in the audience, and confronted them directly through his performance. He unearthed suppressed truths and subjected them to a harsh examination to foster self-awareness. Grotowski orchestrated a painful confrontation for the audience, compelling them to critically examine their national history, which was often neither noble nor heroic. He violated audience expectations, and wrecked national myths relating to Poland and Poles. He revealed hidden social antagonisms—including anti-Semitism—to provoke each viewer to an act of cleansing. In effect, the performance functioned as shock therapy that the company used to reveal the falsity of myths in hopes of freeing audiences from automatism and latent stereotypes. Flaszen wrote that 'by violating the spectators' imaginations, the actors mean to force them— by way of excess—to make similar purifying acts in their thoughts and their imaginations' (Flaszen 2010[1964]: 102). The company articulated this aim in a provocative call to audiences formulated in the brochure the 13 Rows prepared for the premiere. 'We would be glad, sweetie, if you would make a study of your own soul after seeing our *Hamlet Study*' (2010[1964]: 100).

In this sense, Grotowski's company fulfilled Wyspiański's vision: reading Shakespeare's drama as a contemporary text to pose a critical question: 'what is there—to think about in Poland?' and clearly showing what was NOT to think about in Poland. Talking openly about Polish anti-Semitism in 1964 was scandalous, and perhaps is the reason this performance was cancelled and later passed over in the annals of the Laboratory Theatre.

In 1964 such a performance was clearly provocative and politically subversive. The artists themselves were well aware that they were walking on thin ice. The performance represented too much of a risk, and the company likely pulled out of it for their own safety. Barba wrote that it clearly was a 'slap in the face for everyone, friends and enemies alike; it [. . .] shook the criteria and the norms of Polish socialism. [. . .] It is understandable that the Polish authorities were irritated' (Barba 1999: 81–82). It was a blatantly political performance that involved discussions that were beginning at that time—about 'Polishness' and 'Jewishness'. It was so controversial that its staging endangered the existence of the company. The fusion of revered classics, national myths, concealed Polish antisemitism, and latent resentments created an explosive mix that unsettled authorities, audiences, and the company itself. Barba described it in the following picturesque fashion:

> Let us imagine a festering and fetid wound, covered by a white bandage. Suddenly the bandage is stripped off and the scab gets torn away. Pain mingles with disgust at the puss and the blood. That is Grotowski's *Study on Hamlet*.
> (Barba 1999: 81)

Years later, Flaszen summarized the potency of their production—'This went against everything' (Osiński 2013: 99). Flaszen himself—a Polish intellectual of Jewish origin—was afraid to publish the text he wrote at the time of the premiere. *Hamlet in the Laboratory Theatre* was not printed until 28 years later. During a meeting at the Grotowski Institute in January 2013 that I also attended Flaszen admitted that he had been afraid of reactions related to this performance, and that he was the one who convinced Grotowski to cease staging it.

Could it be that the decision to withdraw such a vivid political performance came not from external pressure, but from within the company itself? Perhaps this time censors were not to blame. Wójtowicz combed through Opole archives of documents related to state censorship at the time, and found a note censors wrote about *Hamlet Study*. The note stated, 'Overall, this performance, though undoubtedly interesting for connoisseurs, reaches such a level of non-communicativeness that it surpasses anything before it' (Wójtowicz 2004: 159). Hence the censors, who had seen the performance and accepted the script, did not see in it any sort of political potential. Were they being overly friendly towards the company or simply short sighted? Judging from their report, it seems that they misread the essence of this performance, and limited their interpretation to *Hamlet Study*'s 'non-communicativeness' which led them to treat it as just another incomprehensible theatre experiment.

The few surviving reviews and press reports from the performance pass over the 'Jewish question' in a telling silence. In fact, only Raszewski—already quoted above—refers to it directly. Other critics appealed to readers' ability to read between the lines. For example, Wilhelm Mach wrote 'We watched [. . .] *Hamlet Study*—uneasy and worrying, controversial, though rich in intellectual ideas, formally innovative as a philosophical and moral dissection based on Shakespearean elements. An incredible work, very contemporary and very Polish' (Mach 1964: 3). In line with a well-known secret code, the closing words hinted at the critic's awareness of the piece's tone without explicitly stating it. On the other hand, Józef Kelera did not conceal his surprise. 'Hamlet in Opole speaks with a Jewish accent!!! It is no "trick" without meaning, though meaning should not have been transposed literally: there is in it both logic and expression—severity, rapacity' (Kelera 2006[1964]: 175). The three exclamation marks stress how unbelievable it was to him that the company staged a Jewish Hamlet. The critic did not interpret this choice, and instead limited himself to speak with subtext—'severity, rapacity'. These are examples of Aesopian language that might have been used to protect the artists themselves from attacks. Reviewers seemed to consciously avoid describing the scandalous and provocative thesis of the performance. Instead, they signalled its contemporary meanings. In the end, the artists themselves decided against outright provocation and stopped performing the piece. Dariusz Kosiński commented, 'Having touched upon something so painful and difficult, he [Grotowski] quickly retreated' (2012).

A Step Towards . . .

Hamlet Study marked a key step in the Laboratory Theatre's creative journey—redefining how they approached texts, developed acting techniques, staged performances, and engaged actors in the creative process. The performance also influenced the themes explored in their subsequent works, *The Constant Prince* (1965) and *Apocalypsis cum figuris* (1968).

In a letter to Osiński from May 1964 Grotowski wrote about *Hamlet Study*.

For me it is not a performance, but a key étude (a stream of études) in terms of acting beyond the limits of shame. An essential and logical stage of work. Also an étude on poverty. I stand before a stage which is 'richer' (in terms of 'poor theatre' of course) and this completion of poverty is terribly necessary (costumes, space, etc.).
(Osiński 2013: 206)

Above all, Grotowski pointed to the crafting of a new style of acting, training and an extremely limited use of theatrical effects. After more than 25 years he stressed that *Hamlet Study* was an essential step towards further artistic endeavours both individual and within his company:

In 1964 at my Teatr Laboratorium in Poland, we made a performance based on *Hamlet*, then considered a disaster by the critics. For me it wasn't a disaster. For me it was a preparation for a very special work, and, in effect, several years later I did *Apocalypsis cum figuris*. To draw nearer in this special approach, it was necessary to work with the same persons, the same company. The first step (*Hamlet*) proved incomplete. It didn't miss the mark, but it wasn't fulfilled right to the end. Yet it was close to discovery of some essential possibilities. Then, with the other performance, it was possible to take the next step.
(Grotowski 1995: 118)

This double-sided evaluation of the performance is also very much present in the actors' testimonies—on the one hand the sketchiness of the performance, its form of 'a stream of études' and its presentation of an 'unfinished experience' (Flaszen 2010: 106) and on the other hand its value as 'a step towards'.

Ryszard Cieślak acknowledged the low number of performances and small audiences. He recalled that they played the performance rarely, to a nearly empty house, unappreciated and not understood. He also referred to it as 'great', and as a key step for the whole company as well as for him personally.

And now there is this key passage for me. The next performance was *Hamlet Study* by Wyspiański. I say 'passage', because we probably played it a total of 10 times. Even though it really was a great performance, but people couldn't understand it back then. At times we only had four people in the audience. Five was a lot. Sometimes, only two showed up, but we played for them too. And yet there were nights when no one showed, and then we didn't play. This is that 'passage' which was essential for me. Grotowski found in me something which was not just power in a physical sense, but the start of a search within something delicate, more delicate than before.
(Cieślak 2010: 78).

For Cieślak the performance was transformative in spite of it being a disaster in terms of attendance. It was the start of a new way of working with Grotowski for him, a change in his relationship with the director. Andrzej Bielski seemed to remember that 'Rysiek became very close to Grotowski then. He was his assistant, co-director' (1995: 80). Zygmunt Molik recalled in an interview with Giuliano Campo that Cieślak 'did a fantastic role in *Hamlet*. In the bathroom, taking an imaginary shower, he did it in a genius manner, acted amazingly (Molik and Campo 2010: 129). Grotowski cultivated Cieślak's openness to another way of working, a more intimate way based on personal experience; and also Cieślak's readiness to take risks, to unconditionally surrender. He found in him a readiness for 'acting beyond the borders of embarrassment'. The next role that Grotowski offered Cieślak was Don Fernand in *The Constant Prince* based on work by Calderon and Słowacki.

The other actors also stressed a breakthrough that took place in them and in their work thanks to *Hamlet Study*. In their recollections, one can sense a bitterness and a sadness that the performance was not appreciated, though at the same time there was also a sense of satisfaction that they had taken something from working on it that was theirs alone, and that had an inner value—hidden and not meant for audiences. This work enriched their personal development, acting techniques, and collaboration with Grotowski, even if its effects remained invisible to outsiders. Each actor discovered new capabilities to be developed later. *Hamlet Study* was a key breakthrough in their artistic evolution, a start of a new journey, a new sense of the self up on stage and a new way of working.

Andrzej Bielski claimed that 'this was a search for a way into *The Prince*. Grotowski was in some way testing his company's abilities, their improvisational skills, abilities to create on a theme, an association' (Bielski 1995: 80). Bielski also felt that it was a work 'slow[ly] moving away from theatre', a work focused on personal searches, on self-discovery and exposure and not a theatrical work. He admitted he preferred traditional theatre and was unprepared for the openness, autonomy, and rejection of privacy demanded—all things that characterized Cieślak. In April 1965, Bielski left the company and went to work with a theatre company in Wrocław now known as the Contemporary Theatre. He stayed there until his final years.

For Antoni Jahołkowski, *Hamlet Study* was a stage on the way towards *Apocalypsis cum figuris* and the beginning of a new way of working on roles. In conversations with Tadeusz Burzyński he explained.

> It was a sort of rediscovery of mine, an appreciation of the possibility of a different, previously unknown quality of presence in the space—a kind of new 'body language'. It was physical— and very concrete. It didn't result from 'formal' research, but rather from searching for a relationship between the body and the space, objects, partners. [. . .] Practically, this experience opened possibilities that allowed me to find my place in *Apocalypsis cum figuris*. [. . .] I went through a period of longings for what I might call 'a great role'. This disappeared completely after the work on *Hamlet*. After that experience, those desires faded. After all, the essence of work is in how I fulfil myself, not in the prestige attached to it (which in any case is relative). What is important doesn't depend on the amount of text, but on the intensity of being. This is, I imagine, easy to

sense in the performances of *Apocalypsis*, where this is the most essential aspect from our point of view.
(Jahołkowski 2015[1979]: 97, 98; emphasis original)

Flaszen wrote about Jahołkowski's final roles. 'In Grotowski's productions, Antek is usually the leader of a bunch of people, a group, a society, a community. As leader he provokes, catalyses, evokes events and actions that become a ritual of initiation, a celebration of mystery' (Flaszen 2010: 198). However, that which he heads up and wants to govern evades his grasp, and his ability to understand, and as the one leading the ritual he fails. As the King in *Hamlet Study* he was very much this sort of character, where he also suffered a defeat.

Zygmunt Molik—who played the main protagonist—was more cautious than Jahołkowski in expressing his feelings about the performance, and more laconic in his evaluation. In conversation with Teresa Wilniewczyc, Molik confirmed that *Hamlet Study* 'was a turning point in our work'—but he was also quick to add that '*Hamlet* was for me a very difficult performance, incredibly perverse, thought up by Grotowski and Flaszen to be confrontational' (2001: 115). For Molik it was a breakthrough. In his own words, he reached the limits of his capabilities in this role. He felt he had to leave the company temporarily. He recalled, 'I was so exploited and exhausted that physically I was unable to carry on working. [. . .] Grot and Flaszen went wild when I left, did everything to keep me, but I was unable to. I had just completed several years of heavy, physical hardship. [. . .] I had to rest' (2001: 115). In September of 1965, Molik took a sabbatical from working with Grotowski and went to work with a popular theatre in Kraków (he returned to the company in March 1967).

Years later, Eugenio Barba confirmed that Grotowski and his actors had mixed feelings about the performance.

This production must also have aroused conflicting reactions in Grotowski. Today he maintains that it was a fundamental stage in his method in order for the actor to attain the 'total act' as incarnated by Ryszard Cieślak in the role of the Constant

> Prince. But I believe that, at the time and over the next few years, Grotowski did not consider *Hamlet Study* to be a successful production.
> (Barba 1999: 82)

In *Hamlet Study* Grotowski tested a new method of working as a collective that was based on improvisational and complex ways of treating the script. He gave the actors a lot of autonomy and used their ideas and suggestions. As co-authors of the adaptation and co-directors of the performance everyone signed the finished product as 'the ensemble under Jerzy Grotowski's supervision'. The effect of this style of working was a certain sort of chaos and in the words of Raszewski a 'lack of construction'. But Grotowski went on to develop this mode of work in *Apocalypsis cum figuris* combining improvisation and clear structure. During preparations for *Hamlet Study*, he gained the experience necessary to achieve this. Hence, even if in hindsight he considered *Hamlet Study* to be incomplete he also thought it was essential.

Certain themes from *Hamlet Study* returned in *The Constant Prince* and in *Apocalypsis cum figuris*. In all three performances the key theme was the confrontation of the collective against the individual outsider. In *Apocalypsis* the collective marked the individual as it did in *Hamlet Study* by using a meta-theatrical device. In the Opole performance drunken peasants staged *Hamlet* for laughs, and in the company's Wrocław *Apocalypsis* a drunken 'gang' staged the life and times of Jesus Christ as a joke. One can also find many similarities between the protagonists of all three performances: the Jewish Hamlet, Don Fernand and the Simpleton are all 'others'—excluded, ridiculed and persecuted. These three final performances of the Laboratory Theatre show 'masochistic images of persecuted and helpless human beings' (Niziołek 2013: 342). In these performances the collective was looking for a scapegoat. And although in *The Constant Prince* this sacrifice brought about purification, it was rejected in *Apocalypsis* and in *Hamlet Study* it proved to be impossible. In 1964, Grotowski rejected the myth of salvific sacrifice as an act that brings about order. Hamlet died for nothing.

By this point, it should be obvious why the title of this chapter is plural, 'Jerzy Grotowski's Hamlets'. If we think of Shakespeare's *Hamlet* as a source then we have to admit that Grotowski travelled a long way from his source, meeting and creating other 'avatars' of the Prince of Denmark along the way. But still, Shakespeare's *Hamlet* was at the root of his concept. *Hamlet* by William Shakespeare appears in the 13 Rows repertoire plan for the 1959/1960 season (see Osiński 1998: 25, 28, 33).

In December 1958 Grotowski told Jerzy Falkowski in an interview that he was

> thinking of a contemporary version of *Hamlet*, a *Hamlet* 'from provincial Poland' (based on Shakespeare's text, using contemporary journalism and other texts as a resource). The performance played by a company of a handful of actors, based on the rule of a self-aware dialogue between the actors and the audience, a dialogue which allowed each actor to present a number of characters.
> (Grotowski 2012 100)

This shows that from the very start Grotowski was thinking about a contemporary *Hamlet*, relevant to the debates of that time. Furthermore, his announcement reveals his goals for *Hamlet Study*: a small-scale performance for a small group of actors who would perform several roles. And above all, it was to be a '*Hamlet* from provincial Poland', set in a small Polish town or village.

In his conversation with Falkowski, Grotowski outlines his first *Hamlet*, Shakespeare reinterpreted in a Polish context. And he comes close to his second *Hamlet*, a Wyspiański-inspired *Hamlet* read through the prism of contemporary realities. Wyspiański showed Grotowski not only how to read Shakespeare's original—'overcome with thought'—but also how to tell the story of one's own people using the works of others, and how to put a mirror up to his present times and put it on trial using theatre.

Grotowski's next two Hamlets emerged from two scripts. The Hamlet from Grotowski's initial script was a Hamlet of the cemetery, a spirit summoned by the Sorcerer in this unique and incredible adaptation of the theatre of the dead. In the second script, Hamlet was alienated, his story restricted to scenes of confrontation, clashes and tests of strength. Another Hamlet appeared in the performance itself, emerging from the company's creative process. This Hamlet was a Jewish intellectual persecuted by peasant-soldiers in a grim and depraved Polish setting—a scandalous and brutal performance that remains hard to imagine today.

Wanda Świątkowska

Conclusion

Together with Wanda Świątkowska, I have now presented and interpreted the performances created by Jerzy Grotowski and his Theatre of 13 Rows in the order in which they appeared between 1959 and 1964 at their theatre in Opole, Poland. In turn, I frequently pointed to elements that occur, and reoccur, in these performances—including those performances that would later become Grotowski's best-known works. These elements were decisive in determining the singularity of Grotowski's theatre. In concluding this book, I gather these observations to draw attention to elements too often overshadowed by categories like 'poor theatre' and 'total act', terms later used to retrospectively analyse Grotowski's work from this period.

First of all, I underline the decisive shift towards the liveness of performance, and the ways it impacted audiences who were in effect transformed into witnesses and even participants. As I have stressed, Grotowski maintained an essential direction in all his research. He did not create an 'idea' or a 'concept' for 'production', instead he crafted an inimitable theatrical micro-universe that could neither be replicated under different circumstances nor be transposed to a performance of another kind. In creating his performances—especially after he began his collaboration with designer Jerzy Gurawski—Grotowski invented a specific setting and established certain rules and procedures for each new performance. In so doing, he paid particular attention to the relationship between actors and audiences. He did not seek to create a complete theatre work, a 'show' to be watched and admired. Rather, he aimed to create prepared experiences, performance events. Their meaning was only partly pre-established by the creators because they were not based on any 'message' or 'idea' that could have been 'read' into the performances. Instead, their meaning aligned with the potential for collective changes in thought and action beyond the theatre. Grotowski was not interested in presenting original theatre works, and certainly not in staging his own versions of famous dramas. Through the theatre, Grotowski tried to change the world around him in line with his philosophical project. This project involved a reaction to the social, cultural and existential catastrophe caused by the Second World War and its horrors.

It is important to remember that Grotowski's work was experimental; that during his research, he modified his diagnoses and repeatedly tested new solutions. These experiments included not only the rehearsals but also each individual performance which, as far as we know, he always attended. Grotowski drew conclusions from these experiences combining them with new questions and problems. These amalgamations became starting points for further experiments. Grotowski's theatre was not a series of productions but a continuous process of research and discovery. He developed his research in line with an overarching logic according to which the outcomes of one staging became the assumptions tested in subsequent stagings.

Another key element in Grotowski's theatre that we underscored was his resolute resistance against all that seemed easy and expected, and his persistent drive to surprise audiences, strip away their self-assurance and force them to constantly deepen their awareness. One of the most important strategies Grotowski deployed was his interruption, and even outright refusal, of established conventional theatrical mechanisms of identification and empathy. This strategy gave rise to his frequent change of emotional registers and moods, and to his performances' stylistics and aesthetics. Grotowski's permanent use of dissonance and apparent disharmony grew out of this strategy—it was not the result of his aesthetic tendencies or his personal taste. He almost intuitively avoided all overly obvious solutions, and gradually learned to create compositions comprised of many overlapping layers, condensed, and arousing numerous associations, emotions and affects.

This diversity and ambivalence of meaning in Grotowski's theatre was after all created by something characteristic of his style—his strategy of clashing and overlapping cultural tropes and allusions. He took recognizable symbols, signs, sounds, words and images and used them in radically different ways. He deployed them in mutually contrasting juxtapositions, radical shifts in context and inversions or modifications of meaning. Grotowski was particularly keen on doing this with Catholic iconography, symbols and sounds, and especially those connected with liturgy, which is one of the basic dramaturgical models of his performances.

The dramaturgical mechanisms of Grotowski's theatre involved a process of establishing numerous, interrelated layers of its reality and fiction. The basic foundation was always a theatrical event in which both actors and audiences participated. On top of this most obvious level, Grotowski overlaid an often grotesque reimagination—akin to a funhouse mirror reflection, a meta-theatrical frame. From within this meta-theatrical frame, Grotowski played out and presented actions belonging to the central threads of each performance. He forged different links and connections and constantly built and shifted between them, utterly destroying any certainty regarding which layer was 'fictional' and which one was 'real'. In the end, his performances negated all the layers built within them by revealing their shared foundations. This was an act of existential and metaphysical provocation, and sometimes scandalous, a shock to spectators. Grotowski discovered this connection to audiences as an 'inner' performance that cut through the meta-theatrical framework working on the level of the fundamental situation of the theatre event. Experiencing this event in all its complexity, the audience thus became participants and at the same time witnesses of something 'real'. Grotowski and his company required this revelation and transformation achieved through theatre as a necessary condition of the effectiveness of the procedures they chose and applied in performance. Seen in this way, one can understand the essential importance of performativity in their work.

According to this reconstruction of the 13 Rows' dramaturgical model, meta-theatricality was a fundamental quality of each performance. They accomplished this meta-theatricality by creating and presenting overall situations shared by actors and audiences. Those meta-theatrical situations had strong themes related to performance—for example the 'party' in *Forefathers' Eve*, the hospital examination in *Kordian* and Faust's autobiographical, 'last supper' story-telling. All Opole performances up to and including *Shakuntala*, as well as *Acropolis* and *Hamlet Study*, presented theatrical performances within the performance. Each declared the performative situation clearly and openly in a prologue. Sometimes—as in *Mystery-Bouffe*, *Shakuntala* and *Acropolis*—the 13 Rows directly referenced old theatrical conventions. In so doing, they presented a main character who both played an important role in the performance while at the same time being able to step outside of it as its creator. Grotowski used this director figure as an ironic, even self-critical, presentation of himself.

In earlier performances, one could consider a 'drama of stations' to be the dominant model of composition and dramaturgy: a relatively autonomous sequence of events and accidents arranged to present the protagonist's biography—a collective biography in the case of *Mystery-Bouffe*. This sequencing produced a dramaturgical reflection on the essential theme of journeys played out in *Cain*, *Mystery-Bouffe* and in some ways *Shakuntala*. In later performances this journey through stations was internalized and became a meta-play. Instead of setting off on a geographical journey as in Cain, individuals such as Konrad, Kordian and Faust—and even the community of prisoners in *Acropolis*—play out their respective meta-plays. In this way, the 13 Rows subjected audiences' own experience of performances to self-analysis, and thus, spectators became witnesses to the journey while reflecting on their own paths within and beyond theatre.

The company's implementation of this framework evolved. In subsequent productions they transformed it into a clearly demonstrated process of embodiment as an actor slowly transformed into a defined, model character. At first, the 'model' appeared to be external to the protagonist. The collective forced it upon him, most often violently. But finally, the model became a tool for discovery, for revealing human truths embodied in the performative act, a deep, personal experience of the actor. Even as this experience affects the performer, it is offered to audiences in the hope that it will be recognized and experienced as a journey. By this experience the spectators are called to transform into witnesses ready to testify and relate their own lives to the theatre event. This process of active testimony was to be an ultimate confirmation of the reality of that which all the participants experienced in the theatre.

It is at this point necessary to stress once again that the 13 Rows' use of ridicule and derision of the character and the actor complicated this process making it difficult. This approach undermined and negated its very own process. In this sense we can talk about a dramaturgy of the 'derided Messiah' as fundamental to Grotowski's theatre in a way that changes sneers into challenges and metaphysical provocations. The key element of the drama is in the community's rejection of this 'saviour'— always male—who acts and sacrifices himself for the community. The community not only ridicules, debases and rejects this 'Messiah', but also within the realm of the performance, he fails to achieve his goal; he dies or in some other way loses in the end. The only way for him to be saved was by the witnesses accepting him, responding to him from 'the ground of one's own life' (Grotowski 2012: 386). This model held true for all the performances created after *Forefathers' Eve*, performances which constitute an ambivalent continuation of, and polemics with, the great tradition of Romantic drama. However, this model also appears earlier, most directly in *Cain*, most veiled in *Orphée* and most interestingly in *Mystery-Bouffe* and *Shakuntala*. In these productions, the 'saviour' function is embodied in the allegory of historical process (Promotor) or by a pair of leading actors embodying a power that is both life giving and is death itself at the gates of life ('Shiva').

At the risk of generalizing, I propose the thesis that each of Grotowski's performances was an attempt at embodiment—understood as an act of theatrical, and hence 'artificial' yet visible and tangible transformation, even transubstantiation. This transubstantiation is the most important dimension in the anti-theological liturgy of Grotowski's theatre, the key reason why Grotowski devoted his creative life to research in the realm of 'performative arts'. What he was looking for was a materialist, non-religious transubstantiation. This idea warrants further development through a deep study of religious experience. I am putting it here as a proposition for research in the future

In line with Grotowski's tendency to make things more difficult, he tried to evoke this experience from a vantage point situated and animated by forces traditionally associated with low, 'heavy', taboo themes—some so taboo as to be excluded outright as pathologically 'perverse'. These forces were often related to sexual desires—especially desires involving excess and transgressing cultural norms (for Grotowski's time and place). Above all, homosexuality, autoeroticism and sadomasochistic acts were Grotowski's starting points for awakening a force that evaded rational thought and discourse, and that the mainstream culture of 1950s Poland often condemned or excluded. This affective force drove the process of the 13 Rows' materialistic transubstantiation. Non-normative desires were both the object of transformation and the source of energy that made transformation possible.

Grotowski more fully realized this transformative process in later performances. He would continue working to perfect it during his paratheatrical and art-as-vehicle[1] research until the end of his life. These subjects and Grotowski's later work are not part of this book. I mention it as I conclude this volume because it is a process that gradually emerged

---

1 In December 1970, in New York Grotowski announced that he would not create any other theatre production. In the first half of 1970s together with a new team composed of mostly of young collaborators (with only a few experienced actors of the Laboratory Theatre) he was working on so called 'para-theatre'—different performative structures demanding active participation of all involved. From 1976 until the end of his life Grotowski developed precise work on transcultural performance finally called Action. Subsequent stages of this work bore separate names connected with different projects and programs (Theatre of Sources, Objective Drama, Ritual Arts) and are sometimes described as different stages of Grotowski's research. But form today's perspective it seems just to treat the whole period 1979–99 as one and call it by the name Grotowski used—art as vehicle (see Grotowski 1995).

from the performances covered here. Perhaps we should see the flashes of non-normative desires and unconventional sexual behaviours that so often appear in Grotowski's work from a completely different perspective. We might negate the need to 'cure' them through 'transformation' if we refuse to relegate them to a 'low' position in a vertical model of 'transubstantiation'. We must not negate needs Grotowski clearly accepted as a given. Deconstructing or queering Grotowski's dramaturgical and anthropological model is still mostly ahead of us, though initial attempts have already been made.[2] Many people—especially those who were once Grotowski's allies—consider such attempts to be scandalous and unacceptable. However, if we do not confront this stage of profanation and blasphemy directed against 'Gurutowski' himself we will not be able to liberate him from a glorious past that is always retold in the same way. In Poland, a certain 'cult' of Grotowski—his almost 'sacred' elevation—has become a wall that separates him from contemporaneity. The problem is not that we reject what Grotowski has to offer us today; the problem is that we do not listen to what he still has to say. His offering to help us overcome depression and despair is simply not heard.

By returning to performances created before Grotowski's discovery of the total act—and even before the 13 Rows embarked on a path of blasphemous desecration—we offer up our own act of profanation, and negate the elevated place of the highest prizes, those 'states of grace', 'transilluminations' and 'transformations'. We must cross over, and invade the inaccessible sphere of sacred essence and the holy performer with profanations. We need to recognize a human being who 'precedes the differences' not as our anthropological ancestor but as a being as such.

Maybe this is a good place to remind that being as such (in Latin *quodlibet ens*) is the formula recalled by Giorgio Agamben who sees hope for a future and chance for salvation in 'the absolutely non-thing experience of a pure exteriority' (Agamben 2007b: 67).

---

2 See for example the reinterpretations by Ben Spatz (2020: 180–83) and *Książę* [The prince], a film (or rather—as the creators call it—a 'performance for camera') by Karol Radziszewski and Dorota Sajewska, 2014.

I would dare to say that what the Italian philosopher develops theoretically in his writings, Polish director researched in his practises leading to experiencing what Agamben describes as a crucial possibility:

> A being that is never itself, but is only the existent. It is never existent, but it is the existent, completely and without refuge. It neither founds nor directs nor nullifies the existent; it is only its being exposed, its nimbus, its limit. The existent no longer refers back to being; it is in the midst of being, and being is entirely abandoned in the existent. Without refuge and nonetheless safe—safe in its being irreparable.
> (Agamben 2007b: 99)

I am using Agamben's word to describe with different language what Grotowski was looking for: a secular salvation. This salvation is not going to be achieved through following a religious path—or transforming into someone else.. Rather, this salvation is achieved by presenting one's own being-as-such.

Agamben points to this sort of presentation as a 'limit of existence', and in doing so he escapes the trap of the all-encompassing spectacle—clearly arguing both for the impossibility of 'not playing', and the impossibility of 'being yourself'. For Agamben, living life is a performance of something—not a manifestation or an embodiment but an exposure and externalisation of pure existence.

If performance is thought of as a theatrical term, and we search for theatrical language that can help describe being-as-such (as Agamben defines it), then it is hard to imagine a richer source than the original vocabulary that Grotowski created. Exposure, *via negativa*, organicity, *hic et nunc* and finally, energy.[3] These Grotowskian words and concepts give us the chance to build a living connection between Grotowski's achievements and contemporaneity—related not to a single performer

---

3 I am aware that these key words were not explained in the book. But I do hope that at least some readers interested in Grotowski are familiar with them. If not—please take this sentence as an invitation to read his texts. I hope that the English-speaking community will soon have the opportunity that Polish and Italian readers already enjoy—to read the entire corpus of Grotowski's texts.

working close to essence but related to human beings exposed in the utter externalization of their being-as-such.

The shift I believe necessary to utilize Grotowski's practice and thought today requires us to be completely unprofessional theatrically speaking. With a brevity appropriate to profanation, neither heavy nor slow, and never arriving at a finally learned 'method', but rather toying with it, radically opening it up, popularizing it. Not lengthy rehearsals and isolation from the world but rather 'playing Grotowski'. In the circle of his 'tradition' this might be the biggest sort of scandal and sacrilege. Separated in the laboratory and hermitage, smothered in restrictions connected with copyrights and clauses in last wills, hidden and destined for the chosen few, the tradition avoids as much as it can a popular usage, a lack of gravity and being the object of games and jokes. There is a bitter paradox in having the works of a man who enjoyed toying dangerously with others turned into a tomb that the faithful enter in silence to kiss the sacred ground. In order to free it from this sarcophagus, we need a revolution of anarchic profanation.

Dariusz Kosiński

WORKS CITED

ADAMIECKA-SITEK, Agata. 2012. 'Grotowski, kobiety i homoseksualiści. Na margine-sach "człowieczego dramatu" ' [Grotowski, women and homosexuals: On the margins of the 'Human Drama']. *Didaskalia: Gazeta Teatralna* 112: 94–105.

AGAMBEN, Giorgio. 2007a. *Profanations* (Jeff Fort trans.). New York: Zone Books.

AGAMBEN, Giorgio. 2007b. *The Coming Community* (Michael Hardt trans.). Minneapolis: University of Minnesota Press.

AUSLANDER, Philip (ed.). 2003. *Performance: Critical Concepts in Literary and Culture Studies*, VOL. 1. London: Routledge.

BADIOU, Alain. 2003. *Saint Paul: The Foundation of Universalism* (Ray Brassler trans.). Stanford, CA: Stanford University Press.

BADIOU, Alain. 2005. *Being and Event* (Oliver Feltham trans.). New York: Continuum.

BADIOU, Alain. 2013. *Ethics: An Essay on the Understanding of Evil* (Peter Hallward trans. and introd.). London and New York: Verso.

BĄK, Bogdan. 1960. 'Misteryjne "Misterium" ' [Mysterious 'Mystery-play']. *Odra* 34: 6. Accessed online: https://bit.ly/3nOuA4L.

BARBA, Eugenio. 1965. *Alla ricerca del teatro perduto: Una proposta dell'avan-guardia polaca* [In the search of a lost theatre: A proposition of Polish avant-garde theatre]. Padova: Marsilio Editori.

BARBA, Eugenio. 1968. 'Dr Faustus: Textual Montage' (Richard Schechner trans.) in Jerzy Grotowski, *Towards a Poor Theatre* (Peter Brook pref.). Holstebro: Odin Teaters Verlag, pp. 79–87.

BARBA, Eugenio. 1999. *Land of Ashes and Diamonds: My Apprenticeship in Poland*. Abersytwyth: Black Mountain Press.

BARBA, Eugenio. 2010. *On Directing and Dramaturgy: Burning the House*. London and New York: Routledge.

BARBA, Eugenio. 2014[1965]. 'Technika gry aktorskiej jako samopenetracja i sztuczność' [Actor's technique as self-penetration and artificiality] (Katarzyna Woźniak ed.). *Performer* 8. Available online: http://bit.ly/3ln3K2d.

BARSKA, Barbara. n.d. Unpublished interview by Agnieszka Wójtowicz. Recording copy stored at the Grotowski Institute Archive, Wrocław.

BARTKOWIAK, Tadeusz. 2001. 'Pierwszy sezon w Teatrze 13 Rzędów w Opolu' [The first season in Theatre of 13 Rows] (Krzysztof Bogdanko ed.). *Odra* 11: 65–66.

BIELSKI, Andrzej. 1964. 'Notes to *Studium o Hamlecie*' [Hamlet's study]. Manuscript. Grotowski Institute Archive, Wrocław. IG/R/324/1.

BIELSKI, Andrzej. 1995. 'Grotowski dał nam szansę' [Grotowski gave us a chance], Interview by Teresa Błajet-Wilnewczyc, *Notatnik Teatralny* 10: 70–83.

BŁOŃSKI, Jan. 2007. *Wyspiański wielokrotnie* [Many times Wyspiański]. Kraków: Universitas.

BRATKOWSKI, Stefan. 1965. *Podróż na peryferie* [A journey through peripheries]. Warsaw: Książka i Wiedza.

BYRON, George Gordon. 1821. *Cain*. Available online: http://bit.ly/4Oofv7v.

BYRSKI, Maria Krzysztof. 1979. *Methodology of the Analysis of Sanskrit Drama*. Warsaw: Wydawnictwo Uniwersytetu Warszawskiego.

CHODZIESKI, Jan. 1962. '13 Rzędów' [13 Rows]. *Widnokrąg* 46: 4.

CHOJAK, Bruno (ed.). 1968. *Tekst inscenizacji 'Akropolis' Jerzego Grotowskiego i Józefa Szajny 'Acropolis' do słów Stanisława Wyspiańskiego, skorelowany z amerykańską rejestracją telewizyjną z 1968 roku* [The script of *Acropolis* by Jerzy Grotowski and Józef Szajna with the words of Stanisław Wyspiański correlated with the American TV version from 1968]. Typescript. Grotowski Institute Archive, Wrocław.

CHRISTOF, Catharine. 2017. *Rethinking Religion in the Theatre of Grotowski*. London and New York: Routledge.

CIEŚLAK, Ryszard. 2010. 'Rozmowa Konstantinosa Themelisa z Ryszardem Cieślakiem' [A conversation between Konstantinos Themelis and Ryszard Cieślak] (Bruno Chojak and Włodzimierz Garsztka eds) in *Grotowski–Cieślak: Spojrzenia* [Grotowski–Cieślak: Perspectives] (Małgorzata Leyko and Maciej Michalski eds). Kalisz: Miejska Biblioteka Publiczna im. Adama Asnyka, pp. 89–94.

CIEŚLAK, Ryszard. 2015. 'The Madness of Benvolio' (Justyna Drobnik-Rogers trans.) in *Voices from Within: Grotowski's Polish Collaborators* (Paul Allain and Grzegorz Ziółkowski eds). London: Polish Theatre Perspectives, pp. 61–71.

COCTEAU, Jean. 1961[1926]. *Orphée* (Carl Wildman trans.) in *Five plays*. New York: Hill and Wang, pp. 1–46.

452 · WORKS CITED

Cʏɴᴋᴜᴛɪs, Zbigniew. 2000. 'Notebook-diary' (Zbigniew Jędrychowski ed., Duncan Jamieson and Adela Karsznia trans) in *Voices From Within: Grotowski's Polish Collaborators* (Paul Allain and Grzegorz Ziółkowski eds). London: Polish Theatre Perspectives, pp. 75–78.

Dᴀɴowɪcz, Bogdan. 1959. ' "Orfeusz" Cocteau i problemy egzystencjalne' ['Orphée' by Cocteau and the existential problems]. *Od Nowa* 6: 7. Available online: http://bit.ly/3OtztZR.

Dᴇʟᴇᴜᴢᴇ, Gilles, and Felix Guattari. 1987. *A Thousand Plateaus* (Brian Massumi trans.). Minneapolis: University of Minnesota Press.

Dᴏᴍᴀɢᴀʟɪᴋ, Krzysztof (dir.). 1979. 'Pełen guślarstwa obrzęd świętokradzki . . . ': O Teatrze Laboratorium Jerzego Grotowskiego ['A blasphemous rite full of sorcery': On the Laboratory Theatre of Jerzy Grotowski]. Telewizja Polska.

Eʙᴇʀʜᴀʀᴅᴛ, Konrad. 1960. 'Rzecz o niemocy teatru' [On the powerlessness of a theatre]. *Ekran* 19: 6, 11.

Eɪsʟᴇʀ, Jerzy. 1998. 'March 1968 in Poland' in *1968: The World Transformed* (Daniel Mattern, Carol Fink, Phillip Gassert and Daniel Junker eds). Cambridge: Cambridge University Press, pp. 237–52.

Eʟsᴛᴇʀ, Michael (dir.). 1963. *Letter from Opole*. Państwowa Wyższa Szkoła Teatralna i Filmowa in Łódź. Fragments available online: https://bit.ly/44EDEZd.

Fᴀʟᴋᴏᴡsᴋɪ, Jerzy. (dir.). 1962a. *Jaki dziś Kordian smutny . . .* [How sad Kordian is today . . .]. Radio Opole. Copy of the recording from the Grotowski Institute Archive, Wrocław.

Fᴀʟᴋᴏᴡsᴋɪ, Jerzy. (dir.). 1962b. *Akropolis naszych czasów* [Acropolis of our times]. Polskie Radio Opole. Copy of the recording from the Grotowski Institute Archive, Wrocław.

Fᴀʟᴋᴏᴡsᴋɪ, Jerzy. 2016[1960]. 'Majakowski na głowie i w cynowej balii' [Mayakovsky upside down and in the tin tub] in *Misterium zgrozy i urzeczenia*: *Przedstawienia Jerzego Grotowskiego i Teatru Laboratorium* [Mysterium tremendum et fascinosum: Performances of Jerzy Grotowski and Laboratory Theatre] (Janusz Degler and Grzegorz Ziółkowski eds). Wrocław: Instytut im. J. Grotowskiego, pp. 113–17.

Fɪsᴄʜᴇʀ-Lɪᴄʜᴛᴇ, Erika. 2008. *The Transformative Power of Performance: A New Aesthetics* (Saskya Iris Jain trans.). London and New York: Routledge.

Fʟᴀsᴢᴇɴ, Ludwik. 2006. 'Filolog w teatrze i inni' [Philologist in theatre and others]. *Odra* 11: 79–81. Also in *Misterium zgrozy i urzeczenia. Przedstawienia Jerzego Grotowskiego i Teatru Laboratorium* [Mysterium Tremendum et Fascinosum: Performances of Jerzy Grotowski and Laboratory Theatre] (Janusz Degler and Grzegorz Ziółkowski eds). Wrocław: Instytut im. J. Grotowskiego, pp. 162–65.

WORKS CITED · **453**

FLASZEN, Ludwik. 2010. *Grotowski & Company* (Andrzej Wojtasiuk and Paul Allain trans, Paul Allain ed. and introd., with editorial assistance by Monika Blige and a tribute by Eugenio Barba). Holstebro, Wrocław and Malta: Icarus.

FLASZEN, Ludwik. 2014. *Grotowski et Company: Sources et Variations* (Monika Blige ed.). Wrocław: Grotowski Institute.

FOUCAULT, Michael. 1978. *History of Sexuality, Volume I: An Introduction* (Robert Hurley trans.). New York: Pantheon Books.

GAWLIK, Jan Paweł. 1960. 'Uniwersalizacja mitu czy mit uniwersalizacji' [A universalisation of the myth or a myth of universalisation]. *Życie Literackie* 427: 9.

GAWLIK, Jan Paweł. 2006. 'Akropolis 1962' [Acropolis 1962] in *Misterium zgrozy i urzeczenia: Przedstawienia Jerzego Grotowskiego i Teatru Laboratorium* [Mysterium Tremendum et Fascinosum: Performances of Jerzy Grotowski and Laboratory Theatre] (Janusz Degler and Grzegorz Ziółkowski eds). Wrocław: Instytut im. J. Grotowskiego, pp. 167–70.

GIRARD, René. 1977. *Violence and the Sacred* (Patrick Gregory trans.). Baltimore, MD: Johns Hopkins University Press.

GIRARD, René. 1986. *The Scapegoat* (Yvonne Freccero trans.). Baltimore, MD: Johns Hopkins University Press.

GRODZIŃSKI, Juliusz. 1964. 'Hamlet—w rękach szamanów' [Hamlet—in the hands of shamans]. *Panorama Północy* 12–13: 22.

GROTOWSKI, Jerzy. 1956. *Orfeusz* [Orpheus]. Manuscript. Grotowski Institute Archive, Wrocław. Inventory no. 28/08/01.

GROTOWSKI, Jerzy. 1960a. *Kain: Groteska czyli misterium* [Cain: A grotesque or mystery play] (Józef Paszkowski trans.), stage script based on *Cain* by George Gordon Byron. Typescript. Grotowski Institute Archive, Wrocław.

GROTOWSKI, Jerzy. 1960b. *Misterium-Buffo* [Mystery-Bouffe], stage script based on texts by Vladimir Mayakovsky. Typescript. Grotowski Institute Archive, Wrocław. Inventory no. IG/R/82.

GROTOWSKI, Jerzy. 1960c. *Siakuntala* [Shakuntala], stage script based on drama by Kalidasa. Typescript. Grotowski Institute Archive, Wrocław. Inventory no. IG/R/73.

GROTOWSKI, Jerzy. 1963. *Tragiczne dzieje doktora Fausta* [The tragical story of Doctor Faustus], after Christopher Marlowe, a script for the performance. Typescript. Grotowski Institute Archive, Wrocław. Inventory no. IG/R/85.

GROTOWSKI, Jerzy. 1964. *Hamlet Study*, performance script (copy owned by Andrzej Bielski). Typescript. Grotowski Institute Archive, inv.no. IG/R/318/4.

GROTOWSKI, Jerzy. 1968a. *Towards a Poor Theatre* (Peter Brook pref.). Holstebro: Odin Teaters Verlag.

GROTOWSKI, Jerzy. 1968b. 'Interview with Jerzy Grotowski', Interview by Richard Schechner and Theodore Hoffman (Richard Schechner and Jaques Chwat eds). *The Drama Review* 13(1): 29–45.

GROTOWSKI, Jerzy. 1969a. Untitled letter to the public in the leaflet for the New York presentations of *Apocalypsis cum figuris*, New York.

GROTOWSKI, Jerzy. 1969b. 'I Said Yes to the Past', Interview by Margaret Croyden (Helen Klibbe trans. from French). *Village Voice* (23 January 1969), pp. 41–42.

GROTOWSKI, Jerzy. 1995. 'From the Theatre Company to Art As Vehicle' in Thomas Richards, *Working with Grotowski on Physical Actions*. London and New York: Routledge, pp. 115–35.

GROTOWSKI, Jerzy. 2008[1969]. 'On the Genesis of *Apocalypsis*' (Kris Salata trans.). *The Drama Review* 52(2): 40–51.

GROTOWSKI, Jerzy. 2009[1964]. 'Nowe "Być albo nie być" w Teatrze Laboratorium' [New "To be or not to be" in the laboratory theatre], Interview with Stanisław Nyczaj and Jerzy Wróblewki in Stanisław Nyczaj, *Przedążyć pęd ziemi*. Kielce: Ston 2.

GROTOWSKI, Jerzy. 2012. *Teksty zebrane* [Collected texts] (Agata Adamiecka-Sitek, Mario Biagini, Dariusz Kosiński, Carla Polastrelli, Thomas Richards, and Igor Stokfiszewski eds). Wrocław / Warsaw: Instytut im. Jerzego Grotowskiego / Instytut Teatralny im. Zbigniewa Raszewskiego / Wydawnictwo Krytyki Politycznej.

GURAWSKI, Jerzy 2015[1984]. 'An Architect at the Teatr Laboratorium' (Justyna Drobnik-Rogers trans.) in *Voices from Within: Grotowski's Polish Collaborators* (Paul Allain and Grzegorz Ziółkowski eds). London: Polish Theatre Perspectives, pp. 85–90.

GURAWSKI, Jerzy. 1992. 'Grotowski miał sześć palców' [Grotowski had six fingers]. *Notatnik Teatralny* 4: 51–57.

JAHOŁKOWSKI, Antoni. 2015[1979]. 'Curiosity and the Readiness to Search for the New' in *Voices From Within: Grotowski's Polish Collaborators* (Paul Allain and Grzegorz Ziółkowski eds). London: Polish Theatre Perspectives, pp. 95–99.

JASIŃSKA, Zofia. 1960. 'Młodzi szukają' [The young ones are searching]. *Więź* 5: 149–53. Available online: http://rb.gy/f1oj68.

JĘDRZEJCZYK, Olgierd. 1960. 'Opolska Shakuntala' [Shakuntala in Opole]. *Gazeta Krakowska* 307: 6. Available online: http://rb.gy/9539k1.

JONAS, Hans. 2001. *The Gnostic Religion: The Message of the Alien God and the Beginnings of Christianity*. Boston, MA: Beacon Press.

KĀLIDĀSA. 1999. *Shakuntala* (Arthur W. Ryder trans.). Cambridge, Ontario: In Parentheses Publications.

KELERA, Józef. 2006[1964]. 'Hamlet i inni' [Hamlet and others] in *Misterium zgrozy i urzeczenia. Przedstawienia Jerzego Grotowskiego i Teatru Laboratorium* [Mysterium tremendum et fascinosum: Performances of Jerzy Grotowski and Laboratory Theatre] (Janusz Degler and Grzegorz Ziółkowski eds). Wrocław: Instytut im. J. Grotowskiego, pp. 174–77.

KERENÝI, Carl. 1976. *Dionysos: Archetypal Image of Indestructible Life* (Ralph Manheim trans. from German). Princeton, NJ: Princeton University Press.

KŁOSSOWICZ, Jan. 1964. 'Podróż do źródeł teatru' [A journey to the sources of a theatre]. *Polityka* 51–2: 7.

KOLANKIEWICZ, Leszek. 1999. *Dziady: Teatr święta zmarłych* [Dziady: The theatre of the fieste of the dead]. Gdańsk: słowo/obraz terytoria.

KOŁDRZAK, Elżbieta. 2014. *Śakuntala* [*Abhidźñanaśakuntalam*]: *Dramat staroindyjski Kalidasy*. Łódź: Wydawnictwo Uniwersytetu Łódzkiego.

KOREWA, Aleksandra. 1959. 'Polemika z Jean Cocteau' [A polemics with Jean Cocteau]. *Współczesność* 22–23: 5. Available online: http://bit.ly/3UZmlse.

KOSIŃSKI, Dariusz. 2004. *Sceny z życia dramatu* [The scenes from the life of the drama]. Kraków: Księgarnia Akademicka.

KOSIŃSKI, Dariusz. 2007. *Polski teatr przemiany* [Polish theatre of transformation]. Wrocław: Instytut im. Jerzego Grotowskiego.

KOSIŃSKI, Dariusz. 2012. '*Hamlet*'s Study', *Grotowski.net*. Available online: https://bit.ly/3ErovQf.

KOSIŃSKI, Dariusz. 2015. *Grotowski: Profanacje* [Grotowski: Profanations]. Wrocław: Instytut im. Jerzego Grotowskiego.

KOSIŃSKI, Dariusz. 2016. *Do nieba? Bluźnisz daremnie* [To heaven? You blaspheme in vain]. *Pamiętnik Teatralny* 1–2: 5–49.

KOSIŃSKI, Dariusz. 2018. *Farsy-misteria: Przedstawienia Jerzego Grotowskiego w Teatrze 13 Rzędów w latach 1959–1960* [Farces-mysteries: Jerzy Grotowski's performances at the Theatre of 13 Rows, 1959–1960]. Wrocław: Instytut im. Jerzego Grotowskiego.

KOSIŃSKI, Dariusz. 2019. *Performing Poland: Rethinking Histories and Theatres* (Paul Vickers trans.). Cardiff: Performance Research Books.

WORKS CITED

Kott, Jan. 1965. *Szekspir współczesny* [Shakespeare our contemporary]. Warsaw: Państwowy Instytut Wydawniczy.

Kreczmar, Jerzy. 1961. 'Szkice i projekty' [Sketches and projects]. *Teatr* 17: 23.

Krygier, Waldemar. 2001. 'Uwagi o współpracy z Grotem' [Some notes about the collaboration with Grot]. *Notatnik Teatralny* 22–23: 76–78.

Kubacki, Wacław. 2006[1962]. ' "Kordian" na wariackich papierach' ['Kordian' with the documents of the mad person] in *Misterium zgrozy i urzeczenia: Przedstawienia Jerzego Grotowskiego i Teatru Laboratorium* [Mysterium Tremendum et Fascinosum: Performances of Jerzy Grotowski and Laboratory Theatre] (Janusz Degler and Grzegorz Ziółkowski eds). Wrocław Instytut im. J. Grotowskiego, pp. 152–61.

Kudliński, Tadeusz. 1960. 'Świat se tańcuje' [The world is dancing]. *Dziennik Polski* 61: 4.

Kudliński, Tadeusz. 2006a[1961]. 'Siakuntala—biomechaniczna' [Shakuntala—bio-mechanical] in *Misterium zgrozy i urzeczenia. Przedstawienia Jerzego Grotowskiego i Teatru Laboratorium* [Mysterium Tremendum et Fascinosum: Performances of Jerzy Grotowski and Laboratory Theatre] (Janusz Degler and Grzegorz Ziółkowski eds). Wrocław: Instytut im. J. Grotowskiego, pp. 136–38.

Kudliński, Tadeusz. 2006b[1961]. ' "Dziady" w 13 Rzędach, czyli krakowiacy w Opolu' ['Forefathers Eve' at 13 Rows, or the Cracovians in Opole] in *Misterium zgrozy i urzeczenia. Przedstawienia Jerzego Grotowskiego i Teatru Laboratorium* [Mysterium Tremendum et Fascinosum: Performances of Jerzy Grotowski and Laboratory Theatre] (Janusz Degler and Grzegorz Ziółkowski eds). Wrocław: Instytut im. J. Grotowskiego, pp. 139–40.

Kumiega, Jennifer. 1985. *The Theatre of Grotowski*. London: Methuen.

Kustow, Michael. 1963. 'Ludens Mysterium Tremendum et Fascinosum'. *Encore* (October), pp. 9–14.

Kwiatkowski, Jerzy. 1962. 'Wewnątrz "Kordiana" ' [Inside 'Kordian']. *Współczesność* 13: 4. Available online: https://rebrand.ly/8bveyqi.

Lack, Stanisław. 1980. *Wybór pism krytycznych* [Selected critical essays]. Kraków: Wydawnictwo Literackie.

Mach, Wilhelm. 1964. 'Wiosna Opolska' [Spring in Opole]. *Życie Warszawy* 155: 3.

Magnat, Virginie. 2015. *Grotowski, Women, and Contemporary Performance*. London and New York: Routledge.

Manusmriti: The Laws of Manu (Gerard Buhler trans.). 2019. Available online: https://bit.ly/3r6cOLR.

MARLOWE, Christopher. 1962[1604]. *The Tragical History of Dr Faustus* (John D. Jump ed). Manchester: Manchester University Press.

MASTERNAK, Agnieszka. 2013. 'Troja–Wawel–Auschwitz: Stosunek scenariusza Jerzego Grotowskiego do "Akropolis" Stanisława Wyspiańskiego na przykładzie aktu trojańskiego' [Troy–Wawel–Auschwitz: The relation between Jerzy Grotowski's script and Stanisław Wyspiański'a 'Acropolis' on the example of the Troyan Act]. *Performer* 6. Available online: https://rebrand.ly/txugs60.

Materiały i dyskusje [Materials and discussions]. 1959–1963. Opole: Theatre of 13 Rows.

MAYAKOVSKY, Vladimir. 2014. *Plays* (Guy Daniels trans.). Evanston, IL: Northwestern University Press.

MEYERHOLD, Vsevolod. 2016[1912]. 'The Fairground Booth' in *Meyerhold on Theatre* (Edward Braun ed. and trans.). London and New York: Bloomsbury, pp. 145–70.

MICKIEWICZ, Adam. 2016[1823]. *Forefathers Eve* (Charles Kraszewski trans.). London: Glagoslav Publications.

MIODOŃSKA-BROOKES, Ewa. 1980. *Wawel-Akropolis*: *Studium o dramacie Stanisława Wyspiańskiego* [Wawel-Acropolis: A study on the drama by Stanisław Wyspiański]. Kraków: Wydawnictwo Literackie.

MIODOŃSKA-BROOKES, Ewa. 1985. Introduction to Stanisław Wyspiański, *Acropolis* (Ewa Miodońska-Brookes ed.). Wrocław: Wydawnictwo Zakładu Narodowego im. Ossolińskich, pp. *iii–xcviii*.

MODZELEWSKI, Karol. 2010. 'Grotowski polityczny' [Political Grotowski]. *Konteksty*: *Polska Sztuka Ludowa* 4: 69–71.

MOLIK, Zygmunt, and Giuliano Campo. 2010. *Zygmunt Molik's Voice and Body Work*: *The Legacy of Jerzy Grotowski*. London and New York: Routledge.

MOLIK, Zygmunt. 2001. 'Całe moje życie' [My whole life], Conversation with Teresa Wilniewczyc. *Notatnik Teatralny* 22–23: 111–23.

MORAWIEC, Elżbieta. 1991. *Powidoki teatru*: *Świadomość teatralna w polskim teatrze powojennym* [Afterimages of theatre: Theatrical conscience in Polish post-war theatre]. Kraków: Wydawnictwo Literackie.

MOŚCICKI, Paweł. 2015. 'Engagement and Autonomy of Theatre', *Polish Theatre Journal* 1. Available online: https://bit.ly/3nTpBQe.

MYKITA-GLENSK, Czesława. 1976. *Życie teatralne Opola*: *Od czasów najdawniejszych do współczesności* [Theatre life in Opole: From ancient times to contemporary ones]. Opole: Instytut Śląski.

NIZIOŁEK, Grzegorz. 2011. 'Demontaż widzenia' [Dismantling the seeing]. *Performer* 2. Available online: http://bit.ly/3i55wTN.

NIZIOŁEK, Grzegorz. 2012. 'Efekt kiczu. Dziedzictwo Grotowskiego i Swinarskiego w polskim teatrze' [A kitsch effect: The heritage of Grotowski and Swinarski in Polish theatre] in *Zła pamięć: Przeciw-historia w polskim teatrze i dramacie* [Bad memory: Counter-history in Polish theatre] (Monika Kwaśniewska and Grzegorz Niziołek eds). Wrocław: Instytut im. Jerzego Grotowskiego.

NIZIOŁEK, Grzegorz. 2013. *Polski teatr Zagłady.* [Polish theatre of Holocaust]. Warsaw: Instytut Teatralny im. Z. Raszewskiego, Wydawnictwo 'Krytyki Politycznej'.

NIZIOŁEK, Grzegorz. 2019. *Polish Theatre of the Holocaust* (Ursula Phillips trans.). London and New York: Methuen.

OSIŃSKA, Katarzyna. 2009. *Teatr rosyjski XX wieku wobec tradycji (Kontynuacje, zerwania, transformacje)* [Russian theatre of the 20th century in relation to tradition (Continuations, breaks, transformations)]. Gdańsk: słowo/obraz terytoria.

OSIŃSKI, Zbigniew. 1972. *Teatr Dionizosa. Romantyzm w polskim teatrze współczesnym* [The theatre of Dionysus: Romanticism in Polish contemporary theatre]. Kraków: Wydawnictwo Literackie.

OSIŃSKI, Zbigniew. 1986. *Grotowski and His Laboratory* (Lillian Valee and Robert Findlay trans and abbrev.). New York: PAJ Publications.

OSIŃSKI, Zbigniew. 1998. *Teatr '13 Rzędów' i Teatr Laboratorium '13 Rzędów', Opole 1959–1964: Kronika—bibliografia* [Theatre of 13 Rows and Theatre-Laboratory of 13 Rows, Opole, 1959–1964: Chronicle—Bibliography]. Opole: Wydawnictwo Uniwersytetu Opolskiego.

OSIŃSKI, Zbigniew. 2009. *Grotowski: Żródła, inspiracje, konteksty. Prace z lat 1999–2009* [Grotowski: Sources, inspirations, contexts. Works from 1999–2009]. Gdańsk: słowo / obraz terytoria.

OSIŃSKI, Zbigniew. 2013. *Spotkania z Jerzym Grotowskim: Notatki, listy, studium* [Meetings with Jerzy Grotowski: Notes, letters, study]. Gdańsk: słowo / obraz terytoria.

OVADIAH, Asher. 2014. 'The Symbolic Significance of the Menorah', *Liber Annuus* (January). Available online: https://bit.ly/3PstqH2.

PAAVOLAINEN, TEEMU. 2012. *Theatre / Ecology / Cognition: Theorising Performer-Object Interaction in Grotowski, Kantor and Meyerhold*. London and New York: Palgrave Macmillan.

PIWIŃSKA, Marta. 2006[1962]. ' "Kordian" w Teatrze 13 Rzędów' ['Kordian' at The Theatre of 13 Rows] in *Misterium zgrozy i urzeczenia: Przedstawienia Jerzego Grotowskiego i Teatru Laboratorium* [Mysterium Tremendum et Fascinosum: Performances of Jerzy Grotowski and Laboratory Theatre] (Janusz Degler and Grzegorz Ziółkowski eds). Wrocław: Instytut im. J. Grotowskiego, pp. 148–52.

PŁOSZEWSKI, Leon. 1959. 'Dodatek krytyczny' [A critical appendix] to Stanisław Wyspiański, *Dzieła zebrane* [Collected works], VOL. 7. Kraków: Wydawnictwo Literackie, pp. 388–92.

POLISH FILM CHRONICLES. 1960. Theme 12A/60, produced by Wytwórnia Filmów Dokumentalnych, shot by Antoni Staśkiewicz. Available online: https://bit.ly/45UiuXW.

RASZEWSKI, Zbigniew. 1997. *Raptularz 1968–1969* [A diary 1968–1969]. Kraków: Znak.

RASZEWSKI, Zbigniew. 2006[1964]. 'Teatr 13 Rzędów' [Theatre of 13 Rows] in *Misterium zgrozy i urzeczenia: Przedstawienia Jerzego Grotowskiego i Teatru Laboratorium* [Mysterium Tremendum et Fascinosum: Performances of Jerzy Grotowski and Laboratory Theatre] (Janusz Degler and Grzegorz Ziółkowski eds). Wrocław: Instytut im. J. Grotowskiego, pp. 229–37.

Rehearsal. 1964. Documentary footage. Akademicki Klub Filmowy 'Kręciołek'. Available online: https://rebrand.ly/27r5mgf.

ROMANSKA, Magda. 2012. *The Post-Traumatic Theatre of Grotowski and Kantor: History and Holocaust in 'Acropolis' and 'Dead Class'*. London, New York and Delhi: Anthem Press.

RÓŻEWICZ, Tadeusz. 1977. *'The Survivor' and Other Poems* (Magnus J. Krynski and Robert A. Maguire trans and eds). Princeton, NJ: Princeton University Press.

SCHECHNER, Richard and Lisa Wolford (eds). 1997. *The Grotowski Sourcebook*. London and New York: Routledge.

SCHECHNER, Richard. 1968. '6 Axioms for Environmental Theatre'. *The Drama Review* 12(3): 41–64.

SCHECHNER, Richard. 1973. *Environmental Theatre*. New York: Hawthorn Books.

SCHECHNER, Richard. 1981. 'Performers and Spectators Transported and Transformed'. *The Kenyon Review: New Series* 3(4) (Autumn): 83–113.

SENWTOWA, Zofia (aka Aunt Agnes). 1962. 'Deficytowy artykuł' [Lacking goods]. *Trybuna Opolska* 244: 6.

SEYMOUR, Allan. 1963. 'Revelation in Poland'. *Plays and Players* (October), pp. 33–34.

460 · WORKS CITED

SHAKESPEARE, William. 2007. *Hamlet* (Ann Thompson and Neil Taylor eds). London: Arden Shakespeare.

SINKO, Grzegorz. 2006a[1959]. 'Cocteau nadal zabawny' [Cocteau still amusing] in Janusz Degler and Grzegorz Ziółkowski (eds), *Misterium zgrozy i urzeczenia: Przedstawienia Jerzego Grotowskiego i Teatru Laboratorium* [Mysterium tremendum et fascinosum: Performances of Jerzy Grotowski and Laboratory Theatre]. Wrocław: Instytut im. J. Grotowskiego, pp. 110–12.

SINKO, Grzegorz. 2006b[1959]. 'Martwy Byron i żywy Grotowski' [Dead Byron and Grotowski alive] in Janusz Degler and Grzegorz Ziółkowski (eds), *Misterium zgrozy i urzeczenia: Przedstawienia Jerzego Grotowskiego i Teatru Laboratorium* [Mysterium tremendum et fascinosum: Performances of Jerzy Grotowski and Laboratory Theatre]. Wrocław: Instytut im. J. Grotowskiego, pp. 113–20.

SŁAWIŃSKA, Irena T. 1963. 'Wyspiański w krematorium' [Wyspiański in crematory]. *Trybuna Robotnicza* 13: 3.

SPATZ, Ben. 2020. *Blue Sky Body: Thresholds for Embodied Research*. London and New York: Routledge.

STANKOWSKA, Halina. 1962. 'Kordian w kaftanie bezpieczeństwa' [Kordian in a strait-jacket]. *Trybuna Opolska* 63: 3.

Starzec z Śmiercią [The old man with death]. 1959. In Julian Lewański (ed.), *Dramaty staropolskie. Antologia* [Old Polish drama: An anthology], VOL. 1. Warsaw: Państwowy Instytut Wydawniczy, pp. 639–46.

ŚWIĄTKOWSKA, Wanda. 2016. *Hamleci Jerzego Grotowskiego* [Hamlets of Jerzy Grotowski]. Wrocław: Instytut im. Jerzego Grotowskiego.

ŚWIĄTKOWSKA, Wanda. 2019. *Hamlet.pl: Myślenie 'Hamletem' w powojennej kulturze polskiej* [Hamlet.pl: Thinking with *Hamlet* in the post-war Polish culture]. Kraków: Wydawnictwo Uniwersytetu Jagiellońskiego.

SZCZAWIŃSKI, Józef. 1962. 'Szaleństwo z metodą' [A madness with a method]. *Kierunki* 15: 2–10.

TOMASZEWSKI, Irene. 2013. 'Wanda Dynowska / Umadevi: A Polish Guide to Indian Culture'. *Cosmopolitan Review* 5(2). Available online: http://cosmopolitanreview.com/wanda-dynowska-umadevi/.

Trybuna Opolska. 1960. 'Biblijna Tragigroteska w Teatrze 13 Rzędów' [Biblical tragi-grotesque in the Theatre of 13 Rows]. 24: 4.

TRZNADEL, Jacek. 1988. *Polski Hamlet: Kłopoty z działaniem* [Polish *Hamlet*: The troubles with acting]. Paris: Libella.

VATSAYANA. 1883. *Kamasutra* (Richard Burton trans.). Available online: https://rebrand.ly/ey6gqbx.

VOGLER, Henryk. 1959. 'Orfeusz zgwałcony, ale niedopieszczony' [Orpheus raped but not fully caressed]. *Życie Literackie* 49: 5–10. Available online: http://bit.ly/3gvkjXh.

VYASA. 2019. *The Mahabharata of Krishna-Dwaipayana Vyasa* (Kisari Mohan Ganguli trans.). Available online: https://rebrand.ly/eox5cng.

WÓJTOWICZ, Agnieszka. 2004. *Od Orfeusza do Studium o Hamlecie. Teatr 13 Rzędów w Opolu* [From *Orpheus* to *Hamlet Study*: Theatre of 13 Rows in Opole, 1959–1964]. Wrocław: Wydawnictwo Uniwersytetu Wrocławskiego.

WRÓBLEWSKI, Andrzej. 1959. '13 Rzędów' [13 Rows]. *Teatr* 24: 23.

WRÓBLEWSKI, Andrzej. 1960. 'Udana próba zbliżenia' [A fortunate attempt at coming closer]. *Teatr* 6: 23.

WYSPIAŃSKI, Stanisław. 2019. *The Hamlet Study and the Death of Ophelia* (Barbara Bogoczek and Tony Howard trans, Tony Howard intro.). London: Shakespeare's Globe.

ZAGÓRSKA, Bożena. 1959. 'Orfeusz w Opolu' [Orphée in Opole]. *Echo Krakowa* 247: 3.

ZAGÓRSKI, Jerzy. 1960. 'Między heroizmem a zuchwałością' [Between a heroism and an audacity]. *Kurier Polski* 84: 4. Available online: https://grotowski.net/performer/performer-11-12/miedzy-heroizmem-zuch-waloscia

ZAGÓRSKI, Jerzy. 1961. 'Zasypane źródło' [A buried source]. *Kurier Polski* 276: 4. Available online: https://rebrand.ly/rd6dkp2.

ZATRYBÓWNA, Alicja. 2006[1963]. '13 Rzędów. Antyteatr czy teatr nowoczesny?' [13 Rows: Anti-theatre or a Modern Theatre] in *Misterium zgrozy i urzeczenia*: *Przedstawienia Jerzego Grotowskiego i Teatru Laboratorium* [Mysterium Tremendum et Fascinosum: Performances of Jerzy Grotowski and Laboratory Theatre] (Janusz Degler and Grzegorz Ziółkowski eds). Wrocław: Instytut im. J. Grotowskiego, pp. 171–73.

ZDANOWICZ, Janina. 1960. 'Uwspółcześniony Majakowski' [Mayakovsky modernized]. *Ekran* 35: 10. Available online: https://rebrand.ly/mo6420n.

ŻUROWSKI, Andrzej. 2001. *Myślenie Szekspirem* [Thinking with Shakespeare]. Gdańsk: Tower Press.

INDEX

Adamiecka-Sitek, Agata, 18, 170, 369
Agamben, Giorgio, 6, 216, 217, 447, 448
Angelico, Fra, 362
Arp, Jean, 176
Artaud, Antonin, 4

Babel, Isaac, 412
Badiou, Alain, 6, 249, 284, 342, 343
Bąk, Bogdan, 99
Barba, Eugenio, 27, 54, 243, 271, 274–76, 296, 345, 348, 349, 353, 354, 356, 358–61, 365, 366, 368–70, 372–80, 382, 386, 392, 407, 408, 412–21, 426, 429–32, 437, 438
Barska, Barbara, 16, 18, 24–26, 58, 128, 146, 154, 294
Bartkowiak, Tadeusz, 21, 24, 60, 63, 93, 94, 98
Benveniste, Émile, 216
Bielski, Andrzej, 97, 98, 129, 145, 172, 182, 189, 190, 194, 198, 235, 236, 240, 254, 255, 360, 374, 375, 391, 397–99, 409–14, 417, 435, 436
Bosch, Hieronymus, 87, 88
Brant, Sebastian, 87
Bratkowski, Stefan, 289, 293, 323
Broniewski, Władysław, 168, 169
Burzyński, Tadeusz, 436

Byron, George Gordon, 39, 40, 43, 44, 46, 49, 63, 65, 67, 70, 75, 77, 79, 81
Byrski, Krzysztof Maria, 115, 133, 134, 138

Campo, Giuliano, 435
Chagall, Marc, 16
Chmiel, Adam, 316, 317
Cieślak, Ryszard, 170, 196, 236, 240, 254, 255, 288, 289, 297, 328, 360, 364, 373–76, 391, 407, 409, 413, 434–37
Cocteau, Jean, 1, 9, 11, 12–19, 20, 24–29, 33–35, 38, 53
Croyden, Margaret, 300, 332
Cynkutis, Zbigniew, 170, 189, 239, 242, 244, 246, 253, 255, 271, 274, 295, 297, 345, 353–55, 359, 360, 364, 365, 367, 377, 387

Danowicz, Bogdan, 14, 16, 21, 24, 27, 30, 36
Dejmek, Kazimierz, 424
Deleuze, Gilles, 112
Dynowska, Wanda, 131, 133

Ellis, Aaron, 7
Elster, Michael, 347, 354, 358–60, 364, 366

Falkowski, Jerzy, 89, 90, 92, 93, 96, 98, 100–102, 162, 163, 165, 168, 187, 201, 203, 221, 233, 236, 239, 244, 251–53, 298, 334, 439

Fischer-Lichte, Erika, 35

Flaszen, Ludwik, 6, 9, 16, 19, 20, 22, 36, 58, 61, 65, 66, 75, 79, 88, 89, 102, 127, 156–60, 162, 164, 167, 168, 172, 176–80, 182, 184, 186–88, 190, 192–95, 198, 199, 201, 203, 205–7, 213, 219, 220, 232–37, 240–42, 245, 247, 248, 250–55, 257–59, 262–64, 266–69, 294, 296, 299, 308, 313, 315, 316, 318, 322, 325–29, 332, 335, 336, 346, 347, 351–53, 356–58, 360, 362, 364, 366–69, 374, 376, 383–85, 388, 391–93, 395–97, 404–6, 408, 409, 411, 412, 414, 416–20, 424–26, 429, 431, 432, 434, 437

Flavius, Joseph, 186

Gawlik, Jan Paweł, 27, 67, 69, 76–79, 312

Girard, René, 207, 423

Gombrowicz, Witold, 4

Gomułka, Władysław, 424

Grodziński, Juliusz, 415

Guattari, Felix, 112

Gurawski, Jerzy, 60, 124–27, 132, 143, 151, 175–78, 186, 190, 227–30, 233–35, 237, 303, 313, 346, 347, 441

Hoffman, Theodore, 277

Jahołkowski, Antoni, 21, 27, 56, 62, 66, 94, 96, 97, 99–102, 144, 145, 187, 189–91, 198–200, 235, 240, 297, 355, 359, 363, 364, 371, 372, 380, 407, 410, 418, 436, 437

Janowski, Mieczysław, 295, 351, 418

Jasińska, Zofia, 75, 76, 388

Jędrzejczyk, Olgierd, 158

Jeleński, Jerzy, 12, 13

Kālidāsa, , 114, 115, 124, 125, 128, 130–37, 139–41, 147–49, 152, 159

Kantor, Tadeusz, 37, 324, 330, 334, 403

Kaszycki, Jerzy, 21

Kelera, Józef, 20, 409, 433

Kępiński, Antoni, 341

Kolankiewicz, Leszek, 403

Komorowska, Maja, 170, 238, 241, 242, 289, 290, 292–94, 323, 324

Kopczewski, Aleksander, 240

Korewa, Aleksandra, 21, 22, 31–33, 388

Kosiński, Dariusz, 6, 38, 80, 113, 160, 162, 207, 212, 226, 263, 285, 288, 309, 333, 344, 373, 382, 390, 419, 433, 449

Kott, Jan, 210, 394, 397

Kreczmar, Jerzy, 191

Krygier, Waldemar, 171, 180, 182, 189, 201, 392

Krzysztoń, Jerzy, 16

Kubacki, Wacław, 237, 258

Kudliński, Tadeusz, 72, 73, 158–60, 175, 176, 182, 184, 204, 205, 274

Kulig, Andrzej, 295, 410

464 · INDEX

Kumiega, Jennifer, 2
Kurczyna, Adam, 14, 15, 23, 24, 26,
    59, 61, 69, 90, 94–96, 129
Kuroń, Jacek, 222, 262
Kustow, Michael, 352, 359, 373, 375,
    376
Kwiatkowski, Jerzy, 264, 270, 272–
    74, 276, 280, 281

Lack, Stanisław, 395
Lewański, Julian, 83
Lubowiecka, Ewa, 129, 144–46, 148,
    149, 154, 183, 189, 190, 195,
    290–94

Mach, Wilhelm, 433
Marlowe, Christopher, 1, 193, 288,
    345, 347, 349, 351, 353, 356,
    359, 361, 364, 365, 367, 368,
    370, 373, 374, 380, 385, 388
Masternak, Agnieszka, 309–11
Maszkowski, Wincenty, 87, 88, 127–
    29
Mayakovsky, Vladimir, 81, 82, 84–88,
    92, 94, 100, 103, 108, 111
Meyerhold, Vsevolod, 4, 37, 38, 91
Mickiewicz, Adam, 161–65, 168,
    171–75, 180, 183, 185–92,
    198–202, 206–11, 218, 219,
    224, 244, 264, 271, 308, 349,
    388, 402, 403
Miłosz, Czesław, 363
Minticz, Lidia, 53, 55
Miodońska-Brookes, Ewa, 304, 305,
    311
Mirecka, Rena, 21, 22, 39, 56, 57, 62,
    66, 90, 94, 95, 98, 100, 101,
    142, 143, 145, 146, 149, 170,
    183, 189, 191, 195, 240, 289,
    290, 292–94, 297, 321, 325–

27, 355, 359, 361, 365, 366,
    371, 372, 378, 380, 407–10
Moczar, Mieczysław, 425
Modzelewski, Karol, 222–24, 262
Molik, Zygmunt, 20, 24, 59, 64, 90,
    94, 95, 142, 143, 145, 170, 188,
    192, 194, 196, 199–202, 235,
    237, 240, 246, 255, 297, 315,
    316, 318, 319, 324, 351, 352,
    358, 406, 410, 435, 437
Moskwiak, Andrzej, 240, 245
Mozer, Zdzisław, 189, 199
Munk, Andrzej, 162

Niziołek, Grzegorz, 18, 283, 310, 341,
    344, 368, 412, 427–30, 438

Okoński, Ryszard, 197, 201
Olejnik, Leonard, 17, 93
Opioła, Bogusław, 377
Osiński, Zbigniew, 1, 2, 9, 89, 188,
    290, 292, 294–96, 339, 392,
    432–34, 439

Paavolainen, Teemu, 336
Paluchiewicz, Andrzej, 297, 328
Parvi, Zenon, 316, 317
Paszkowski, Józef, 39, 393
Piwińska, Marta, 246, 270, 276
Płoszewski, Leon, 316
Porazińska, Janina, 329
Prus, Maciej, 241, 291, 292, 295,
    351, 358, 377, 378

Raszewski, Zbigniew, 305, 308, 319,
    340, 411, 421, 422, 428, 429,
    433, 438
Romanska, Magda, 307
Rubens, Pieter Paul, 362

Schechner, Richard, 2, 7, 176, 260, 277, 279, 282, 301, 305, 306, 324, 332, 334, 350

Scierski, Stanisław, 297

Senwtowa, Zofia, 337

Shakespeare, William, 1, 10, 283, 307, 391, 393–402, 406–8, 411–13, 418, 421, 431, 439

Shalamov, Varlam, 343

Shankara, Adi, 131, 132

Sinko, Grzegorz, 26, 69

Słowacki, Juliusz, 161, 211, 213, 218, 219, 224–27, 235–39, 241, 243, 247, 253, 259, 260, 270, 271, 276, 277, 303, 307, 435

Sobolewski, Jan, 172

Stanislavsky, Konstantin, 4

Stankowska, Halina, 245, 246

Strindberg, August, 367

Świątkowska, Wanda, 1, 6, 138, 295, 394, 416, 440, 441

Swinarski, Konrad, 283

Szajna, Józef, 290, 313, 333, 334, 336

Szczawiński, Józef, 202, 203, 250, 280

Szreniawski, Stanisław, 16, 27, 58, 61

Thibaudat, Paul, 335

Trznadel, Jacek, 395

Vogler, Henryk, 13, 16, 18

Wajda, Andrzej, 162, 220, 275

Wanat, Andrzej, 220, 221, 225

Węglowski, Edward, 235, 238–40, 242

Wilniewczyc, Teresa, 437

Witkiewicz, Stanisław Ignacy, 4, 74

Wójtowicz, Agnieszka, 1, 24, 59, 61, 66–70, 126–29, 182, 184, 188, 195, 199, 200, 220, 225, 229–31, 233, 234, 236–39, 241–43, 255, 292, 345, 358, 368, 371–73, 375–78, 380, 408, 415, 421, 432

Wróblewski, Andrzej, 29, 54, 60, 64

Wylam, Lisa Wolford, 2

Wyspiański, Stanisław, 1, 2, 161, 286, 296, 298, 299, 303–12, 316, 318, 320–22, 326–30, 334, 336, 338, 349, 391, 393–404, 406, 408, 409, 411, 413, 421, 427, 431, 435, 439

Zagórski, Jerzy, 28, 37, 181

Zatrybówna, Alicja, 387–89

Zdanowicz, Janina, 90, 91, 105